In Praise of *Risky Business*

"Lawrence Powell has brought together a wonderful group of leading insurance and risk scholars to produce the most insightful book on property and casualty insurance industry in many years. ***Risky Business*** explains why market-based insurance should be celebrated for its innovation and competitiveness. Instead it is a constant target for politically motivated critics and politicians who excoriate the industry. The book critically examines the continual call for ever-more regulation that harms the public by driving up the cost of insurance and limiting competition and innovation."

> —**Roger E. Meiners**, Goolsby Distinguished Professor of Economics and Law, University of Texas at Arlington

"Did you ever wonder why public officials representing the Gulf Coast states pressured some of the nation's leading property and casualty insurers into paying claims for damage caused by Hurricane Katrina, even though some hazards clearly were not covered? Or why Congress authorized grants up to $150,000 to homeowners on floodplains that were not covered by federal flood insurance even though such insurance is mandatory? Or why the nearly bankrupt National Flood Insurance Program does not cover the cost of replacing real property, but only the borrower's remaining mortgage balance? Many such important questions about property and casualty insurance in the U.S. are asked and answered by the scholars assembled by Lawrence Powell in ***Risky Business***. This superb book traces the serious problems facing consumers in insuring properties against fire, flood, earthquakes and other hazards under the Byzantine and politicized regulatory regimes in which insurance companies operate. ***Risky Business*** documents the many problems created by today's regulations, offers and evaluates market-based alternatives, and points the way to reform. It is must reading for anyone interested in the economics and politics of government regulation."

> —**William F. Shughart II**, J. Fish Smith Professor in Public Choice, Utah State University

"*Risky Business* is a very timely and important book. Each of its well-crafted chapters examines a distinct aspect of the insurance regulatory debate currently taking place, but all lead to the same conclusion: insurance regulation should not be used to distort a well-functioning private insurance market. As the authors point out, insurance regulation can distort insurance markets in ways that hurt consumers, the very people intended to be benefitted. This book should be read by anyone seriously looking at how to effectively benefit and protect insurance consumers."

— **Lawrence Mirel**, former Commissioner of Insurance,
Securities and Banking, District of Columbia; Partner, Wiley Rein LLP

"Everyone knows that health insurance is a mess, and many understand that this is the result of government intervention. The insightful book *Risky Business* shows that health insurance is hardly unique—government intervention imposes costs and inefficiencies on property and casualty insurance (particularly important in areas of storm, flood, fire and other risks). Insurance can seem complex and confusing, leading to misguided calls for regulation, and politicians have been all too eager to respond. *Risky Business* now charts an essential new course for market-based reform."

— **Paul H. Rubin**, Samuel Candler Dobbs Professor of Economics,
Emory University

"Insurance is one of the most pervasive and yet least understood industries. The very fine and careful book *Risky Business* offers in one convenient place clear and compelling explanations of both its economic foundations and its regulatory strengths and weaknesses, with a prudent eye toward sensible and incremental market-based reforms, which should prove of great value to the industry specialist and the concerned citizen alike."

— **Richard A. Epstein**, Laurence A. Tisch Professor of Law,
New York University

"*Risky Business* will open your mind to the world of insurance and how interest groups have manipulated the government's regulatory power to pervert market forces. There are many legitimate insurance products, but sometimes when special-interest politics weigh in, risks shift to taxpayers. Protect yourself and read *Risky Business*."

— **John O. Norquist**, President and Chief Executive Officer,
Congress for the New Urbanism; former Mayor of Milwaukee

RISKY BUSINESS

THE INDEPENDENT INSTITUTE is a non-profit, non-partisan, scholarly research and educational organization that sponsors comprehensive studies in political economy. Our mission is to boldly advance peaceful, prosperous, and free societies, grounded in a commitment to human worth and dignity.

Politicized decision-making in society has confined public debate to a narrow reconsideration of existing policies. Given the prevailing influence of partisan interests, little social innovation has occurred. In order to understand both the nature of and possible solutions to major public issues, the Independent Institute adheres to the highest standards of independent inquiry, regardless of political or social biases and conventions. The resulting studies are widely distributed as books and other publications, and are debated in numerous conference and media programs. Through this uncommon depth and clarity, the Independent Institute is redefining public debate and fostering new and effective directions for government reform.

100 Swan Way, Oakland, California 94621-1428, U.S.A.
Telephone: 510-632-1366 • Facsimile: 510-568-6040 • Email: info@independent.org • www.independent.org

RISKY BUSINESS

INSURANCE
MARKETS and REGULATION

EDITED BY
LAWRENCE S. POWELL

The INDEPENDENT INSTITUTE

Oakland, California

The Independent Institute
100 Swan Way, Oakland, CA 94621-1428
Telephone: 510-632-1366
Fax: 510-568-6040
Email: info@independent.org
Website: www.independent.org

Library of Congress Cataloging-in-Publication Data

Powell, Lawrence S.
  Risky business : insurance markets and regulation / Lawrence S. Powell.
      pages cm
  Includes bibliographical references and index.
  ISBN 978-1-59813-116-1 (hbk. : alk. paper) — ISBN 978-1-59813-117-8 (pbk. : alk. paper)
  1. Insurance—United States. 2. Insurance—State supervision—United States.
  3. Insurance law—United States. I. Title.
  HG8535.P734 2012
  368.00973—dc23   2012038725

Cover Design: Keith Criss
Cover Image: © Robert Churchill / Getty Vetta Collection
Interior Design and Composition by Leigh McLellan Design

Contents

1 Introduction   1
   Lawrence S. Powell

2 The Economics and Politics of Insurance   9
   Arnold Kling

3 Insurance Markets and Regulation:
   Case Studies in Failure   29
   Martin F. Grace

4 The Effects of Credit-Based Insurance
   Scoring on Insurance Markets   67
   Lawrence S. Powell

5 Catastrophes and Performance in Property
   Insurance Markets: A Comparison of Personal
   and Commercial Lines   81
   Patricia H. Born
   Barbara Klimaszewski-Blettner

6 "Watery Marauders": How the Federal Government
   Retarded the Development of Private Flood Insurance   115
   Eli Lehrer

7 Alternative Frameworks for Insurance Regulation
   in the United States   145
   Martin F. Grace
   Robert W. Klein

8 A Comparison of Insurance Regulation in
the United States and the European Union 183
Martin Eling
Robert W. Klein
Joan T. Schmit

9 Estimating Efficiency Effects of Uniform
Regulation in Property and Casualty Insurance 227
David L. Eckles
Lawrence S. Powell

10 Performance of Risk Retention Groups:
Drawing Inferences from a Prototype of
Competitive Federalism 245
J. Tyler Leverty

Notes 266

Index 295

About the Contributors 308

1

Introduction

Lawrence S. Powell

DOES YOUR INSURANCE cost too much? To many, this seems like a simple question with an obvious answer. A common response might be, "Of course it costs too much." In addition, very few people are capable of calculating the value of insurance. Politicians' awareness of these two widespread truths has led insurance regulation down a troubling path. The political arena pits policymakers against insurance companies in an "us" versus "them" scenario founded mostly in fiction. As a result, we find broad public support for bizarre applications of legislation and regulation to insurance that do not serve consumers' interests.

For their part, policymakers face moving and sometimes conflicting objectives of serving and satisfying constituents, most of whom know little about the forces at work within an insurance market. Insurance is too important to society and to commerce to be left as a political pawn. The obvious positive action is to inform politicians and their constituents about the mixed bag of modern insurance regulation. Thus, the primary purpose of this publication is to provide clear information and supporting evidence about choices in insurance regulation in a format that is accessible and meaningful to policymakers and consumers.

To this end, the collection of essays in *Risky Business* pursues two related objectives. In the first six chapters, we explain the case for market-based regulatory reform. In chapters seven through ten, we consider potential changes to the current system of insurance regulation in the United States.

As a preview of our conclusions, we find that heavy-handed regulation of pricing and underwriting is a poor strategy for serving consumers. When regulation forces prices below the competitive market level, private insurers must either implement unfair cross subsidies or withdraw from the market. In the former case, good drivers, to give just one example, are penalized to benefit bad drivers. In the latter case, reductions in the supply of insurance lead to sharp increases in price.

The economic and political considerations that often drive public policy decisions concerning insurance would improve if consumers and policymakers sought and applied available information. Policymakers have enacted many laws that do not benefit their constituents. One explanation for subpar regulation is that policymakers might not understand the economics of insurance markets and regulation. Another possible explanation is that policymakers are well informed, but they take advantage of the ignorance of their constituents; using insurance regulation to gain favor with certain influential groups. Florida Governor Charlie Crist's political attack against homeowners insurance companies is clearly an example of the latter behavior. In both cases, educating the appropriate party would improve regulatory outcomes.

Finally, we show that the current regulatory system includes unnecessary costs and that it could be improved by increasing uniformity across states and by including select elements of alternative systems. We find the current system of fifty-six separate jurisdictions in the United States adds billions of dollars in duplicative regulation costs. By creating a more uniform system, lower costs will be passed on to consumers. Furthermore, by modeling some regulatory changes after the new system being implemented in Europe, such as a principles-based regulatory approach, we can improve the current system.

The Case for Market-Based Regulatory Reform

Optimal insurance regulation seeks a delicate balance between enhancing industry competition and maintaining appropriate oversight. Competition among firms is the cornerstone of effective consumer protection. When suppliers compete for consumers' business, the prevailing price shifts from the highest price consumers will pay to lowest price at which providers will participate in the market. Some level of regulation is also desirable to monitor insurer solvency and some types of antimarket behavior.

All too often, crises draw extreme reactions from policymakers. Such reactions almost uniformly involve increasing regulatory stringency, stifling competition, and exacerbating problems they intended to solve.

In Chapter 3, Martin Grace examines the difference in timing consider-ations between insurance companies and politicians. Politicians are concerned with winning the next election—a relatively near-term event. Insurers are concerned about paying for large catastrophic losses that might happen once in a decade, or even once in a century. Therefore, if a politician can engineer a reduction in rates, even if it leads to a smaller asset pool on which to draw in an emergency, that's a friendly gamble. Insurance companies must profit in years without catastrophic losses in order to fund large losses when they do happen. Elected officials, however, can gain political support by reducing insurance profits in the good years, even at the price of making bad years worse.

As supporting evidence, Grace describes a host of colossal regulatory fail-ures including Florida's market for windstorm coverage; automobile insurance markets in Massachusetts, New Jersey, and South Carolina; and the workers compensation insurance market in Maine. For example, following large losses from hurricane Andrew, regulators in Florida restricted premium increases. As a result, many companies chose not to sell insurance in Florida and the state-owned Citizens Insurance Company found itself underwriting more than 50 percent of houses in the state.

In each case, policymakers responded to increasing prices with suppressive rate regulation. As a result, market problems were exacerbated, prices rose, and the security of these insurance markets was threatened.

Chapter 4 examines a related problem of restricting information used in underwriting and pricing insurance. Insurance regulation can be used to favor groups with strong political influence. Any time regulators restrict the use of accurate rating variables, it creates an explicit subsidy. In automobile insur-ance, for example, the subsidy takes money from the average good driver for the expressed purpose of paying part of the cost of the average bad driver's insurance premium. One likely example of this behavior is the explicit subsidy Massachusetts regulators afford to Boston residents. Drivers outside of Boston pay substantially more for automobile insurance relative to expected loss than do Boston drivers.[1]

In Chapter 4, I tackle the subject of credit-based insurance scores (CBIS) in pricing and underwriting automobile insurance. CBIS has been one of the most controversial rating variables for the last two decades. I describe how CBIS is used and review the existing research demonstrating it is among the most accurate rating variables. The innovation of this research is to measure the effects of CBIS on insurance markets. Using a novel measure of CBIS activity, I show that increases in scoring coincided with decreases in the number of drivers who were considered too risky to buy insurance from private companies and decreases in the cost and price of automobile insurance. In other words, Chapter 4 demonstrates the benefits to consumers from using the most accurate rating information.

In Chapter 5, Professors Patricia Born and Barbara Klimaszewski-Blettner provide empirical evidence of the benefits to consumers from limiting rate regulation. They compare responses in insurer performance measures between personal lines and commercial lines of insurance following unexpected catastrophic losses. This comparison is meaningful because personal lines of insurance (e.g., homeowners and automobile) face many more regulatory restrictions than do commercial lines. An insurer must hold capital in excess of expected losses to ensure claim payment when losses are greater than anticipated. The more capital an insurance company has, the more insurance it can safely sell. After a catastrophic loss, insurers must raise new capital to replenish underwriting capacity, or they must decrease the amount of insurance they sell.

The authors find commercial insurance markets much more resilient to catastrophic losses than are personal lines markets. Because regulation restricts insurers' ability to charge adequate prices, personal lines markets often face severe shortages of capacity, leading to drastic price increases following unexpected catastrophic losses. In comparison, politicians interfere less with commercial lines, and disruption in those markets is less pronounced.

In Chapter 6, Eli Lehrer provides a political-economic analysis of the National Flood Insurance Program (NFIP). While many scholars and practitioners have historically assumed that NFIP was created to address a market failure, Lehrer shows that NFIP did not emerge because of market failure alone. Lehrer argues convincingly that private markets would have developed flood insurance products but for the government's strong signal that it would offer this coverage at a subsidized rate.

The overarching theme of Chapters 3 through 6 is that consumers pay the price of heavy-handed insurance regulation. While policymakers are sometimes urged by their constituents to interfere in insurance markets, the informed response is to let markets protect consumers.

Assessing Potential Alternatives to Current Regulation

Insurance regulation in the United States is at a crossroads. Various stakeholders in the regulatory system have been clamoring for change relentlessly. Chapters 7 through 10 discuss the current regulatory system and compare it to alternative systems. We also measure the cost of the current system and potential costs and benefits to expect if policymakers implement substantial changes.

U.S. insurance companies are currently regulated at the state level, subjecting multistate insurers to different regulatory requirements from each state in which they are licensed. Should the United States abandon the fifty-state regulatory approach and move to a unified federal regulatory system? Or should insurance be regulated by a competitive federalist system in which insurers may choose one state to regulate them throughout all fifty states, as occurs in corporate law today? Results and conclusions from this project inform policymakers on this important issue and serve as a roadmap to regulatory reform.

Motivated by an array of interests ranging from an economic downturn to the aftermath of gulf coast hurricanes to modernization of global financial services markets, critics of the state-level regulatory system include an uncommon alliance of political actors and financial industry interests, substantially blurring party lines on the ultimate outcome of this national debate. The common thread in their goals is to effect some form of federal insurance regulation; however, there are wide differences in their motives. Politicians and self-titled "consumer advocates" from states with substantial hurricane exposure wish to repeal the McCarran-Ferguson Act of 1945 to subject insurers to federal antitrust laws so that federal officials can regulate insurance prices.[2] Financial services firms, including most life insurers and some larger property and liability insurers, reinsurers, and intermediaries, desire the option of a federal charter or some other vehicle to facilitate streamlining of the current fragmented system for efficiency gains. For example, multistate carriers currently are required to seek approval of new products in each state where they will be sold. Many believe this redundancy of approval creates deadweight costs that must be passed on to consumers. Some also suggest this system hampersU.S. firms' ability to compete in the global market.

Opposition to this move toward federal regulation comes primarily from smaller property and liability insurance carriers and intermediaries.[3] These groups are concerned about potential litigation and information costs expected to follow any change in the McCarran-Ferguson Act of 1945, the current law of the land, which gives states the responsibility of regulating the business of insurance and provides a limited antitrust exemption that allows insurers—especially smaller insurers—to participate and compete in domestic insurance markets. Because McCarran has been in effect for more than six decades, many of the potential uncertainties regarding antitrust issues have been litigated and resolved under the current regime.

Last, but certainly not least, state-level policymakers are concerned about their ability to maintain claims on insurance-premium tax revenues. In most states, insurance-premium taxes are among the largest sources of revenue. These revenues are not earmarked specifically to support costs of insurance regulation. They are often directed to the general state budget, creating a pseudo-hidden tax on all consumers of insurance. Premium tax rates are applied to total written premiums and range from 0.25 percent in Illinois up to 6.5 percent for some lines of insurance in Arkansas and Hawaii. This concern is voiced often by state-level political interest groups, including the National Conference of Insurance Legislators (NCOIL).

As insurance interests tire of waiting for meaningful reform at the state level, many of the current proposals to effect change have begun to involve some form of federal insurance charter, or a competitive regulatory environment that would create choices for insurers facing relatively onerous, innovation-stifling state regulation. However, these proposals carry the potential for both cost and benefit. Chapter 7 through 10 seek to describe these alternatives and estimate the costs and benefits of changes to the insurance regulation system.

In Chapter 7, Martin Grace and Robert Klein provide a thorough description of the history and current structure of the U.S. insurance regulatory system. Building from this foundation, they go on to describe several alternative systems being considered by Congress. The authors compare and contrast the status quo with a federal regulatory system, an optional federal charter, and a system of competitive federalism. While each system has certain benefits, Grace and Klein predict that both practical considerations and politics will encumber efforts to rationalize insurance regulation. Hence, a major revamping of the current system is unlikely to occur in the near future. What we are likely to see are smaller incremental changes at both the state and federal level that have been the industry's historical legacy. These changes will not achieve the objectives of reformists, but they may help set the stage for more substantive reforms under more favorable political conditions.

In Chapter 8, Martin Eling, Robert Klein, and Joan Schmit compare insurance regulation in the United States to that in the European Union (EU). The authors describe solvency regulation in the U.S. system as a static accounting system. In comparison, the EU system is dynamic and holistic. They also note the strong case for avoiding price regulation in any new regulatory structure. They encourage U.S. regulators to keep in mind a variety of ideas that emerge from the EU's Solvency II process when revising the U.S. system. Among the most important of these is the notion of a principles-based approach.

The last two chapters in this book attempt to measure the costs of the current system compared to alternative systems. In Chapter 9, David Eckles and I measure the cost of multiple regulatory systems compared to one uniform system. We estimate the effects on efficiency and expenses of increasing the number of states in which an insurer operates. We find the cost of multistate regulation to be significant and positive. By creating a uniform regulatory system, regulatory cost would decrease by approximately $1.6 billion per year.

In Chapter 10, Ty Leverty compares the operating expenses of risk retention groups (RRGs) to those of similar insurers operating under a traditional charter. Because an RRG is only regulated by its home state, the difference serves as an estimate of potential cost savings from implementing a competitive federalism system. Using an efficiency methodology, Leverty demonstrates that a system of competitive federalism could save as much as $1.2 billion annually compared to the status quo.

In summary, this book offers a wealth of information to policymakers currently considering changes to the U.S. insurance regulation system. Specific suggestions include:

1. Embrace market-based reforms of insurance pricing and underwriting
2. Resist the populist cry to respond to disasters with heavy-handed regulation
3. Follow a cautious path toward principles-based regulation, learning from mistakes made abroad
4. Streamline insurance regulation by implementing uniform regulations across jurisdictions.

2

The Economics and Politics of Insurance

Arnold Kling

CAPITALISM IS ABOUT RISK. It's also about insurance. Thirty-eight companies in the Fortune 500 are in the insurance business. Insurance companies are also second only to banks in getting their name placed on major sports stadiums. The latter is an interesting sign of the importance that insurance companies place on signaling solidity and permanence, as well as perhaps a subtle recognition of the role of the state in regulating insurance.[1,2] Overall, the insurance industry adds about 3.2 percent to U.S. GDP.[3] The raw contribution of the insurance industry to GDP, however, is a significant underestimate of the importance of insurance. Without insurance—that is, without the proper allocation of risk across industries and people—much economic activity would not take place.

The essence of insurance is the transfer, pooling, and subdividing of risk. Transfer reallocates risk to those most able to bear it; pooling reduces uncertainty, and subdividing makes the risk more tolerable for the risk bearers. An Athenian entrepreneur wants to trade Greek olive oil for Chinese silk. He needs to hire a ship to carry the goods across the sea. In the simplest case, there is a "good" state (the ship returns safely) and a "bad" state (the ship sinks and the entrepreneur loses everything). Without insurance the entrepreneur may forgo the trade and invest in a less profitable but less risky business. With insurance, the shipping entrepreneur gives up a small amount (the insurance premium) in the good state in return for receiving large compensation (an insurance claim) in the bad state. The entrepreneur transfers the risk to others and in so doing is able to pursue the more profitable strategy. But if the entrepreneur is not willing to take the risk of a sinking ship, why would an insurance firm? An insurance firm will willingly take on risks that a single entrepreneur would not because of pooling and subdivision. An insurance firm can insure many ships (pooling), which reduces uncertainty about the average payout, and it can subdivide any losses among all the owners of the insurance firm, so even a large loss doesn't break any individual. As a result, there is an opportunity for a mutually profitable trade between entrepreneur and insurance firm.

If insuring 1,000 ships is expected to result in $10 million in claims, then the actuarially fair premium is $10 million/1,000, or $10,000 per ship. By charging this premium, the insurance company would on average just break even. For a private insurance market to develop, however, sellers must be able to charge more than this actuarially fair premium. This, in turn, means that buyers must be willing to pay more than the actuarially fair premium. Economists say that consumers who are willing to pay more than the actuarially fair premium for insurance are displaying risk aversion. They are behaving as if they value an additional increment of wealth less highly than an equivalent decrement of wealth. If the marginal utility of wealth declines in this fashion, then the consumer should be willing to forgo some amount of expected wealth in order to avoid a large loss of wealth in the bad state.

For the supply of insurance, accurate information about probabilities is important. Life insurance took off after the development of the first usable actuarial tables, for example. With modern computers and databases, the accuracy of statistical computation presumably has risen, which should tend to increase the ability of companies to supply insurance. Because the cost of assessing risk probabilities is falling, consumers may find that the cost of obtaining various types of insurance will fall. This may lead to an increase in the use of insurance in the economy.

One challenge with measuring the importance of the insurance industry is the problem of defining insurance. Many economic activities that involve trading and pooling of risk are not classified as insurance. On the other hand, many activities of insurance companies, particularly in the area of health care, involve more administration than risk sharing. For example, many financial derivatives, including options on commodities or financial instruments, can be thought of as insurance. However, these would not be included in typical measures of the insurance industry. Even if financial derivatives were to be included, it is not clear how to measure the value of what is being exchanged in the market. The notional value of an interest rate swap might be hundreds of millions of dollars, but the true economic value is presumably much smaller.

Note that two of the largest firms to fail during the financial crisis of 2008, Fannie Mae and Freddie Mac, were in the mortgage insurance business, protecting investors against individual mortgage defaults. In fact, it was losses on this mortgage insurance business that required the firms to be taken over by the Treasury. Yet neither Freddie nor Fannie were classified as insurance companies in either government or private compilations. In fact, many of the financial products that became notorious during the 2008 financial crisis, including private mortgage-backed securities (issued by institutions other than Freddie Mac or Fannie Mae), collateralized debt obligations (CDOs), and credit default swaps (CDSs), can be thought of as insurance products. All of these instruments involved the pooling of risk in order to spread the losses from mortgage defaults. Note that, *ex post*, it appears that many institutional investors incurred losses that they had thought were highly unlikely to occur. It can be argued that *ex ante*, risk was often underpriced.

Other noninsurance companies that offer insurance include manufacturers of products that come with warranties. Whether a warranty is bundled with the price of the product or sold separately, the warranty is a form of insurance. Banks and mutual funds engage in risk pooling. However, their activities are not counted as insurance by Commerce Department statisticians. On the other hand, an argument can be made that health insurance companies are not really in the insurance business. In particular, when a large firm contracts with a health insurance company, what the firm receives is mostly administrative services, with little or no actual insurance. The health insurance company will design and administer the employee health plan, but the benefits paid under the plan come out of the corporate treasury. It is true, however, that in many cases, the health insurance company will insure the firm against exceptionally large total health care payouts. In those cases, the firm is the primary provider of health insurance to its employees, and the insurance company is the re-insurer of the firm.

At a deeper level, some economists question whether health insurance as it exists today is really insurance at all. That is because health insurance reimburses for services, even when the amounts are relatively small. Health insurance acts like a prepaid medical plan, rather than an insurance policy for catastrophic risk.[4] John Cochrane has argued that what he calls *health-status insurance* would act more like genuine insurance for health risk.[5] To the extent that health risk turns out to be predictable based on genetic testing, Alex Tabarrok has suggested that the insurable event is the bad draw in a genetic test.[6] Much of what health insurance companies do involves negotiating with providers over fees and administering claims. Actuarial analysis and risk measurement are relatively less important.

In summary, we do not have a satisfactory measure of the importance of insurance in the economy. Many activities that pool or redistribute risk take place outside the insurance industry. On the other hand, health insurance companies provide much of their value added through design and administration of health plans, rather than through risk assessment and pooling.

The rest of this chapter proceeds as follows. First, I review the basic economics of insurance. Next, I look at a number of insurance phenomena that are puzzling to economists. These include anomalies in consumer choices with respect to insurance, which perhaps require explanations based on behavioral economics. They also include the use of insurance by firms, the nonexistence of some insurance markets that seemingly would be useful, and sociological explanations for patterns of insurance purchase. Finally, I discuss government's role in insurance markets, including government provision of insurance and the role of regulation.

Basic Economics of Insurance

As noted earlier, the economic explanation for the demand for insurance is risk aversion. If an individual has diminishing marginal utility of wealth, then it is rational for the individual to pay in order to reduce the potential for a large loss.

Suppose that we are trying to predict whether an individual will seek insurance about a particular random variable, such as an automobile accident or a house fire. The theory of risk aversion tells us that people will pay more than an actuarially fair premium if and only if it is worth it for them to avoid a large loss. What matters is the difference between what the individual's wealth would be under an average realization of the random variable and what it would be under an adverse realization of the random variable. If the worst outcome for a random variable will not lower an individual's wealth very much relative to what the individual expects on average, then there is no motivation to purchase insurance.

The theory of risk aversion offers predictions about the demand side of insurance markets. To be insurable, an event must be rare. If it is a common event, then it already affects the individual's expected wealth. At age 90, the event "needing expensive medical care some time in the next five years" is so likely that it already dominates one's expected wealth. At age 20, the event "needing expensive medical care some time in the next five years" is sufficiently rare that, should it occur, it would reduce one's wealth substantially below its expected value. Therefore, even though intuition suggests a greater "need" for long-term care insurance at age 90, long-term care is a more insurable event at age 20. In addition, the event must be very costly, so that it would have a major adverse effect on the individual's wealth. I should not be willing to pay a premium to insure against an event that has only a minimal effect on my wealth.

The supply of insurance can be constrained by several factors. First, some risks may not be spread through pooling, in which case an insurance company may not be able to demonstrate the ability to remain solvent in the case of catastrophic events. Second, there may be insufficient control over moral hazard. Finally, there may be insufficient control over adverse selection.

An individual farmer would like to buy insurance against a devastating drought or disease. However, if the crop is a major part of the economy, a major drought or disease would bankrupt any insurance company. In that case, no firm can credibly offer insurance because if the bad event occurs, the insurance company itself would be bankrupt. Other events for which insurance might not be credible include property insurance in the event of nuclear war or health insurance in the event of a pandemic.

Moral hazard exists when the insured party has some control over the likelihood of an adverse event. Someone with health insurance has less incentive to prevent illness. Someone with auto insurance has less incentive to prevent minor accidents. However, because most of the incentive for prudent behavior remains, moral hazard does not preclude insurance in these instances. On the other hand, an entrepreneur might want to take out insurance against the possibility of starting a business that subsequently fails. In that case, the entrepreneur would lose a lot of the incentive to select a business strategy that is likely to succeed or to work as hard as possible to execute that strategy. This moral hazard may preclude the possibility of business failure insurance for entrepreneurs.

In the years leading up to the financial crisis, the mortgage finance system developed many layers of moral hazard. Because down payments on many houses were little or nothing, borrowers had little incentive to continue making mortgage payments after their homes lost value. In effect, borrowers were insured against a decline in house prices. The mortgage originators did not have an incentive to make good loans because they sold the loans to investors. The originators were insured against incurring losses from underwriting mistakes. Executives at the companies that purchased mortgage securities did not have an incentive to look into loan quality because the securities were rated AAA by rating agencies. The AAA ratings insured the executives against facing punishment for their judgment. The rating agencies, in turn, did not have a strong enough incentive to rate the securities correctly. They were insured against bearing costs from overrating securities, while underrating securities would have caused them to lose business. Finally, because of deposit insurance, the average bank depositor did not have an incentive to investigate how the entire system operated. The depositor was insured against adverse financial performance by the bank.

Insurance companies have a number of tools available for addressing moral hazard. They can set terms in the insurance contract that specify conditions under which claims can be made or under which policies can be canceled. Or they can vary the premiums based on behavior. For example, when insurance companies provide insurance for directors and officers of corporations that protect against shareholder lawsuits, the insurance contract will specify that deliberate violations of law or fiduciary responsibility are not covered. In the case of deposit insurance, the insurance agency sets capital standards and other regulatory requirements for banks. If deposit insurance were private, this sort of regulation and monitoring would be undertaken contractually.

Health insurance companies can reduce moral hazard by offering lower premiums to customers who do not smoke. Automobile insurance companies can reduce moral hazard by offering lower premiums to drivers with good driving records. They also can offer lower premiums to drivers who install antitheft devices in their cars in order to give drivers the incentive to take precautions against theft.

Where moral hazard presents a potentially significant problem, insurance companies may audit the entities that they insure. For example, a property and casualty insurance company could choose to periodically inspect a factory or office building in order to confirm that the owner is taking reasonable precautions against fire and other hazards. Deductibles and co-payments also can serve to reduce moral hazard. When the insurance company compensates the individual for only part of a loss, the individual retains an incentive to avoid the loss.

Adverse selection can pose a problem when consumers have valuable information about individual risk that the insurance company lacks. For example, if people who know that they are fatally ill are able to take out life insurance, they can cause life insurance companies to incur large losses. Insurance companies will try to mitigate against adverse selection by undertaking due diligence in screening potential customers. For example, a life insurance company may require a medical examination before writing a policy.

However, as Michael Rothschild and Joseph Stiglitz famously pointed out, it is possible for adverse selection to be so severe that it precludes a viable insurance market.[7] If the insurance company lacks information that would enable it to price individual risk, it has to offer a generic premium. At an insurance premium that would be fair on average, lowest-risk customers exit the market. This forces insurance companies to raise their generic premium. However, at a higher insurance premium, the next tier of customers exits the market. At a still higher premium, all but the most risky customers exit the market. At this point, there is no longer an insurance market.

Whether adverse selection is sufficient to destroy an insurance market depends on the risk aversion of the individuals and the amount of private information they have on their riskiness. If individuals have a lot of risk aversion and very little private information, then enough people will remain in the insurance market to allow for risk pooling. On the other hand, if people have a lot of private information relative to their degree of risk aversion, then the insurance market can break down.

The critical issue is whether customers who know that they are low risk are willing to remain in the risk pool at the generic premium. If they are sufficiently risk averse, they will remain in the pool, even though the premium will be well above what would be actuarially fair, given full knowledge of their situation. In the case of health insurance, Mark Pauly and Bradley Herring argue that risk pooling does not break down.[8] Apparently, healthier individuals also tend to be risk averse.

If adverse selection is a severe problem, one solution is to change the nature of the insurance contract. The key is to be able to offer an insurance contract to individuals before they learn important information about their risk characteristics. The proposals by Cochrane and Tabarrok, mentioned above, might serve that purpose.

Insurance Anomalies and Behavioral Economics

The basic economic theory of insurance does not seem to account for many forms of insurance that are popular. By the same token, the basic economic theory would predict that some insurance markets would be better developed than is the case in practice. An example of an insurance market that is not well developed is the market for long-term care. If a family member suffers a stroke or other debilitating illness at age 60, that person could require individual care for decades. Given the expense involved in providing this sort of care, it would seem rational to insure against this risk. However, most people do not have long-term care insurance. Some economists have argued that the availability of Medicaid for nursing home care reduces the incentive to obtain long-term care insurance. Other possible explanations will be discussed below.

On the other hand, people will purchase extended warranties on small appliances, such as televisions or even toaster ovens. The cost of replacing a broken appliance is far from devastating, so that the amount of risk aversion that would be required to justify purchasing such an extended warranty is implausibly high. Someone with sufficient risk aversion to motivate purchase of an extended warranty on a television would presumably have just about every form of insurance available on the market as well as many forms that are not.

Behavioral economists attempt to explain insurance market anomalies on the basis of various heuristic biases of consumers. For example, there is *loss aversion,* which says that the possibility of a small loss can cause unhappiness. When someone contemplates the prospect of a television or toaster oven breaking and having to be replaced, that is upsetting. Having an extended warranty provides comfort.

Another behavioral factor is *availability bias,* which is the tendency to make purchases based on recent experience. Recent experience is more available to your brain than forgotten experience or statistical evidence. According to the theory of availability bias, the more heightened your awareness of a particular risk, the more likely you are to insure against it. For example, consider flight insurance, which is a life insurance policy that pays a beneficiary in case someone dies in a plane crash. Hardly anyone purchases flight insurance when they are at home getting ready for a trip. But when flight insurance is sold at the airport, some people will obtain it. Presumably, when people are in an airport, their fears of flying are triggered, and they are much more aware of the possibility of a plane crash. This makes flight insurance more desirable. The theory of availability bias also may help explain the purchase of extended warranties. Suppose that the last time you bought a toaster oven, it broke down shortly after the manufacturer's warranty expired. In that case, you will be highly aware of the risk that a new toaster oven will break, and you will be more inclined to purchase an extended warranty.

Another bias is known as *hyperbolic discounting* or being *present-biased.* The theory is that the trade-offs people make in the present are different than the trade-offs they make concerning future possibilities. Today, you might prefer receiving $10 to receiving $11 in one year, but you might prefer receiving $11 in six years to receiving $10 in five years. One could argue that people underestimate their future discount rates. Suppose that people underestimate their future risk aversion. This could explain their lack of interest in purchasing long-term care insurance. Long-term care insurance is more likely to pay off in, say, five years, than it is to pay off within the next few months. If people underestimate their future risk aversion, they may underinvest in long-term care insurance.[9]

Note, however, that David Cutler has offered an alternative explanation for the failure to insure long-term risks.[10] It may be that structural changes over time constitute a large risk that is not diversifiable. For example, suppose that it is possible that in ten years people in a highly debilitated state will have much longer life expectancies than is the case today because of progress in life-extending medical treatment. If this risk exists for one person, then it exists for everyone, which makes it nondiversifiable and hence not really insurable.

Cutler is suggesting that for health insurance that will pay off well into the future, systematic risk may dominate idiosyncratic risk. Even though as individuals we would like to be insured against these systemic risks, the cost of providing insurance is prohibitive. Because diversification does not protect that insurance company against risk, its only viable approach would be to charge high premiums and maintain a large capital base.

Business Purchase of Insurance

Another anomaly in insurance markets is the purchase of insurance by firms. If anything, businesses seem to demand more kinds of insurance than individuals. For example, companies that hire celebrities to promote their brands will obtain insurance against the risk that the celebrity will engage in behavior that leads to disgrace.[11]

While individual risk aversion is reasonable, modern finance theory suggests that capital markets provide diversification, so that large companies would not be expected to purchase insurance. The argument is that individual investors can diversify risk by holding a broad market portfolio of stocks. They do not need risk to be diversified within an individual firm. For example, suppose that I own a fraction of a company that could lose value in a fire, and I own an equal fraction of a fire insurance company. If the at-risk company buys fire insurance, that has no effect on my wealth. In the case of a fire, the value of what I gain from my holdings in the at-risk company offsets the value that I lose from my holdings in the fire insurance company. As one corporate risk management text puts it, "firm-specific risks can be diversified by shareholders and so loss control activities usually will not decrease a firm's opportunity cost of capital."[12]

Nonetheless, there are a number of reasons for firms to purchase insurance. As Harrington and Niehaus point out, firms can profit from specialized advice on loss prevention, such as recommendations for fire and workplace accident safety. Insurance companies, with "skin in the game," have an incentive to provide advice that balances costs and benefits. Hence, the best loss-prevention advice may come bundled with insurance. Another factor is that capital markets are not perfect, so that cost of raising external funds is higher than the cost of using internal funds, and insurance reduces the likelihood of needing external funds. Another friction in capital markets is the cost of bankruptcy, which can be made less likely by purchasing insurance. Finally, there are a number of ways in which an insured firm might pay lower taxes on average than an uninsured firm.[13]

Even if owners of a firm do not require insurance against diversifiable risk, executives have a large share of their wealth, in the form of human capital, tied up in the firm. If their firms did not purchase insurance, the executives might require higher salaries to compensate for taking additional risk.

In the early history of business insurance, capital markets were not so well developed. Marine insurance is one of the first forms of insurance to be widely offered. The Royal Exchange Assurance, which was chartered in Britain in 1720, was perhaps the first modern insurance company. Individuals and small firms would finance shipping voyages in which the collateral for the loans would be lost if the ships sank. Marine insurance guaranteed the value of the collateral, which left investors facing a smaller set of risks. They could still lose money if the goods shipped failed to realize their anticipated value, but they were insured against the risk of the ship sinking.

This function of risk specialization may explain the widespread use of insurance by businesses. The owners of a firm, particularly if it is privately held, would like to understand and limit the nature of the risks that they are undertaking. When the firm purchases insurance, the owners can be more confident that they are not absorbing risks that they have not investigated and understood.

Sociology of Insurance

For both individuals and firms, there may be a sociological explanation for the pattern of insurance purchases. Viviana Zelizer has argued that in the United States, life insurance was considered repugnant two hundred years ago, but late in the nineteenth century, there came a shift in attitudes, and life insurance became something that was considered proper and prudent to obtain. In fact, Zelizer argues that life insurance became part of the ritual of preparing for death.[14]

A family friend illustrates another sociological insurance phenomenon. Over the years, she has paid thousands of dollars in premiums for burial insurance, which guarantees that if she dies her funeral expenses will be paid. When it was suggested to her that this insurance was inordinately expensive and that she could achieve the same protection by building up a savings account, the woman said that while she understood the logic, she still preferred burial insurance. She indicated that her cohort of African-Americans considered it necessary to obtain insurance for funeral expenses. "It's what *we* do," she insisted.

Another sociological example comes from our own family. We belong to the American Automobile Association. This used to be a source of maps and trip planning, but those have become technologically obsolete. The sole use for AAA is to provide towing insurance. Towing is clearly an example of an event that causes only a trivial decline in our wealth. And yet, my parents always belonged to AAA, and I continue to belong to AAA. If you were to ask me to explain, I would say, "It's what *we* do."

Overall, the economic analysis of insurance does not produce very satisfying results in terms of predicting where insurance markets will emerge. We frequently have to appeal to behavioral economics or economic sociology in order to explain observed patterns of behavior.

Nonexistent Insurance Markets

Although the number of insurance markets has been growing over time, some insurance markets that seem to make sense nevertheless do not exist. Just as it is not easy to explain the decisions of some people to purchase insurance, it is not easy to explain why insurance is not prevalent for some risks. For example, a couple having a baby takes a risk that the child will have birth defects that impose very large costs on the parents, in terms of both time and money. One would expect to see prospective parents take out insurance against such a hazard. Instead, we have a poor approximation to that form of insurance, in that parents sometimes attempt to sue their obstetrician for malpractice when a baby is born with defects. If there were birth defect insurance, then fewer of these cases would be steered toward malpractice suits and more parents of health-impaired children would be protected from large financial losses.

Robert Shiller has proposed a number of innovative forms of social insurance. People could obtain insurance contracts tied to house prices, GDP growth, and income variability. For example, he proposes what he calls *inequality insurance,* meaning that income tax rates would become more progressive as income inequality widens, and conversely. His argument is that this would protect households against the risk of ending up in the bottom of the income distribution at a time when inequality is high.[15]

Government Provision of Insurance

In the United States, the government provides insurance directly in some cases. Flood insurance in high-risk areas is one example. Social Security provides an annuity, which insures the elderly against the risk of outliving their pensions. Medicare provides the elderly with health insurance. Instances in which state governments provide insurance for the riskiest customers are *high-risk pools* to cover automobile owners with bad driving records or health insurance customers with expensive pre-existing conditions. In a number of cases, although private forms of insurance have been available in the past, government policy presumes that private provision of insurance in not adequate. Deposit insurance is one example. Social Security, Medicaid, and Medicare are further examples. When government provides insurance, it is not clear whether the rationale is paternalism, redistribution, or a belief that there is a market failure that requires correcting. In any case, legislators determine that individuals facing certain sorts of risks ought to have insurance.

In the case of deposit insurance, the primary rationale is a concern with market failure. A bank with assets that exceed the value of its liabilities can nevertheless be subject to a panic or "run" from its customers. If too many customers seek to pull out their deposits at once, the bank will have to sell assets too quickly to obtain full market value. The intent of deposit insurance is to prevent such "runs" by convincing depositors that they have nothing to gain by rushing to pull out their funds before everyone else. Of course, a problem with deposit insurance is that it creates moral hazard. While deposit insurance takes away the incentive for depositors to "run," it also takes away their incentive to identify and punish banks that take excessive risks. Deposit insurance brings with it the responsibility of the insuring entity to regulate the risk-taking of banks.

Even if deposit insurance is a useful tool for preventing bank runs, a private entity could provide deposit insurance. Banks could join together in insurance pools, which in turn could set compliance standards that would mitigate moral hazard. Prior the Great Depression, such private risk pooling among banks did take place. One rationale for government-provided deposit insurance is that the risk is simply too large for the private sector to handle. An event could take place that causes such widespread banking losses that no private insurance company could remain solvent. That, in turn, means that if consumers become concerned that such an adverse event may be impending, they would have an incentive to engage in a bank "run" before the insuring entity becomes insolvent.

In the case of Medicare, it may also be the case that no private insurance company could offer equivalent long-term protection. If someone in their forties wishes to purchase health insurance that will cover them from retirement until death, the insurance company faces risks that include an overall increase in longevity or an unexpected increase in the cost of medical technology. This risk could overwhelm the effect of risk pooling, and any or all such private insurance companies could go bankrupt. (See David Cutler's paper, cited earlier.)

Of course, one can argue that even government-provided medical insurance can be subject to severe financial pressure. The United States and many other Western governments face unsustainable budget deficits, in part because of rising health care spending. Even the institution of government may not be able to absorb all of the risks posed by trends in health care technology and demographics.

For the purpose of retaining solvency, government has several advantages over private insurers. First, it is larger, and larger institutions can engage in more risk pooling. Second, government has the ability to redistribute costs. Particularly striking is the way that government can spread costs across generations. In the United States, young people absorb the costs and risks of health care spending and retirement income for the elderly. Social Security and Medicare are structured to redistribute income in this way. In fact, redistribution is one of the objectives of government-provided insurance. In addition to Social Security and Medicare, Medicaid combines elements of insurance, particularly in providing for nursing home care, with income redistribution.

There is also a strong element of paternalism in government-provided insurance. One possible justification for Social Security and Medicare is that policymakers treat retirement annuities and health care in old age as "merit" goods. If left to themselves, individuals will purchase too little of these services. Government provision ensures that people obtain more annuities and more health care in their old age than they would provide for themselves.

The theory of hyperbolic discounting, in which people underestimate their future concerns, might be used to justify the paternalistic provision of annuities and health insurance for the elderly. However, one worries that the political leaders responsible for this insurance are themselves subject to hyperbolic discounting, and thus, the conduct of fiscal affairs may be compounding risk rather than reducing it. Sudden fiscal crises, such as occurred in 2010 in Greece, can be viewed as the product of politicians' hyperbolic discounting.

Once government has taken over an insurance market, such as deposit insurance or health insurance for the elderly, it is difficult to evaluate private-sector alternatives. We do not know how deposit insurance might have evolved over the past seventy-five years without government involvement. Similarly, we do not know how the institutions related to retirement saving would have evolved over this period without Social Security. Nor do we know how health insurance for the elderly might have evolved over the past forty-five years, had Medicare not been enacted.

In the case of saving for retirement, the private sector has tended to move away from defined-benefit plans and toward defined-contribution plans. This seems to reflect the fact that as people live longer, insurance companies and private pensions funds have a more difficult time providing the sort of long-term risk management that defined-benefit plans require. This is yet another instance of David Cutler's observation that some long-term risks are not really diversifiable. Whether even the government is able to manage these long-term risks is still an open question. Again, the dire fiscal outlook of many governments raises doubts.

In many of its insurance programs, the government expects to take actuarial losses. What that means is that taxpayers subsidize the provision of insurance. Programs where actuarial losses are likely include flood insurance, high-risk pools for drivers with bad records, and high-risk health insurance pools for people with pre-existing conditions. The motivation for government provision of insurance in such cases appears to be redistribution, with the broader taxpaying public subsidizing people who are taking unusually high risk.

Regulation of Insurance

Insurance provision has natural economies of scale and scope. Within a single line of insurance, risk pooling increases with the number of participants in insurance. With multiple lines of insurance, as long as the risks are not perfectly correlated, the insurance company enjoys further diversification. This allows a given level of capital to support multiple insurance lines.

Natural economies of scale and scope mean that the insurance industry will tend to evolve toward a market structure with a few large companies. This natural industry structure invites regulation. It raises concerns about the ability of the market to be self-regulating through competition. Also, large firms are more likely to draw the attention of political activists.

When privately provided, insurance faces regulation from each of the fifty states (plus the District of Columbia) as well as the federal government. Regulation is intended to achieve a variety of objectives. One intended objective is to maintain the soundness of insurance companies. Regulators take over the role of trying to ensure that consumers do not lose insurance protection because the insurance company goes bankrupt. Regulation of insurance company soundness has economic justification, in that it can help prevent consumers from being effectively defrauded by companies writing insurance contracts that they lack the capacity to fulfill. However, there is a risk that large, incumbent insurance companies will encourage the use of soundness regulation as a means of stifling innovative competitors.

Sometimes, regulation forces people to carry insurance, as when drivers are required to carry automobile insurance. The intent of mandatory insurance is to prevent individuals from imposing uncompensated costs on other individuals. Regulators may intervene in the design and pricing of insurance policies, particularly with regard to health insurance. Regulators also intervene in the process of risk assessment. Insurance companies use a variety of factors to assess the risk of different customers. Regulators intervene when they believe that the use of certain factors unfairly discriminates against certain groups.

There is tension among these regulatory objectives. In particular, regulating insurance companies to achieve social purposes may undermine the companies' soundness. By the same token, the soundness of insurance companies suggests deep pockets, which can tempt politicians to impose burdens on insurance companies to achieve social objectives. The political pressures on Freddie Mac and Fannie Mae illustrate the potential problem. These companies achieved strong growth and high rates of return in the 1990s. Congress and federal regulators reacted by putting pressure on the companies to achieve their public mission. This pressure came in the form of explicit goals for lending in low-income neighborhoods, creating an incentive for the two enterprises to participate in the subprime mortgage frenzy.

Just as the financial strength of Freddie Mac and Fannie Mae induced policy-makers to steer the companies toward social objectives, the large financial reserves and strong capital base that insurance companies seek to maintain can offer a similar temptation to legislators. However, like Freddie Mac and Fannie Mae, insurance companies that are forced to subsidize certain classes of customers may consequently not have the capital to survive hard times.

We may be seeing this dynamic at work in the Massachusetts health reforms that were enacted in 2006. The reform included an insurance mandate, under which every citizen in the state is supposed to obtain health coverage. State regulations tightly restrict the nature of the policies that can be offered. Insurance companies are not allowed to refuse coverage. These reforms were intended to hold down health care costs in Massachusetts, by reducing the use of uncompensated care. Prior to the reforms, uninsured individuals could obtain care from emergency rooms, which were supported by taxpayer funds. The goal of the reform was to reduce the number of uninsured and thereby reduce uncompensated care.

What transpired was an increase in the demand for health care and in the demand for health insurance. This resulted in higher prices and higher spending. Under the reform, state taxpayers subsidize insurance coverage for moderate-income residents. As the cost of this rose, the state sought to impose price controls on the premiums that health insurance companies could charge. Whether the insurance companies will remain sound under this regime is not clear as of this writing.

In general, underwriting practices and pricing are a source of tension between insurance companies and politicians. The insurance company wants to align premiums to expected risk. If an insurance company finds that a certain factor is correlated with low risk, it will offer discounts based on that factor. For example, in automobile insurance, experienced drivers tend to be lower risk than young drivers. Also, some auto companies have found that people with good credit scores tend to have fewer car accidents. While higher prices for younger drivers is something that politicians can understand and accept, charging higher premiums to people with bad credit scores has created some political controversy.

Much economically questionable regulation of insurance appears to stem from confusion between risk pooling and cross-subsidization. To economists, these two issues are separate. A risk pool consists of people facing the same risk. If people face different risks, they should be charted different prices. In contrast, politicians act as if the role of insurance companies should be to even out the cost of insurance to people who pose different risks. For example, on health insurance, a mandate will be defended on the grounds that young, healthy people should be doing their part to pay for the cost of insuring people who are sick. Implicitly, this argument assumes that healthy people can and should be charged premiums above the actuarially fair amount, and that the profits from this can and should be redistributed to people who are sick.

Regulatory cross-subsidies are common with automobile and flood insurance. Insurance companies are prevented from charging appropriate premiums to high-risk drivers or homeowners in flood-prone areas. Instead, they are expected to subsidize the high-risk customers, presumably by charging higher rates for low-risk customers. Sometimes, this cross-subsidy takes the form of rate suppression. For example, some state governments force automobile insurance rates to be artificially low. This, in turn, makes many drivers uninsurable in the private market, forcing them into subsidized high-risk pools. Rate suppression creates an incentive for insurance companies to try to avoid offering policies at any price to high-risk consumers. It also provides an incentive for companies to exit states where rate suppression is particularly onerous.

Although cross-subsidies are a very common regulatory goal, there is little economic rationale.[16] Even the political basis is unclear, given that many in the general public are not aware of cross-subsidies and would not support them in many cases.[17] Nevertheless, this form of regulation is likely to be increasingly tempting in the future, as budget pressures constrain the ability of governments to provide subsidies directly.

The Future

As of late 2010, it would appear that the private insurance market is likely to expand. Government-provided insurance in many countries is constrained by adverse long-term budget prospects. Thus, it is more likely that government-provided insurance will be trimmed rather than expanded over the next several years. The focus of insurance protection may gradually shift from tangible property to intangible assets, such as human capital, intellectual property, and reputation. That is because as a share of wealth, such intangible assets are increasing.[18]

As the middle class expands in India, China, and other developing countries, we would expect their demand for insurance to increase. They will be acquiring more assets, and they will face more of the sorts of risks that are insurable. In the developed world, continued advances in information storage and processing should reduce the cost of providing insurance, in both new and existing forms. Insurance is likely to be a growing, innovative part of the world economy over the next few decades.

Given past practice and future budgetary constraints, the government is likely to pursue goals through regulation going forward. Cross-subsidization appears to provide the government with a tool for aiding specific constituents without explicitly having to fund the subsidies.

References

Cochrane, John. "Health-Status Insurance: How Markets Can Provide Health Security." Cato Institute Policy Analysis, February 2009. http://www.cato.org/pub_display.php?pub_id=9986.

Cutler, David. "Why Don't Markets Insure Long-term Risk?" (Harvard University, May 1996). http://www.economics.harvard.edu/files/faculty/13_ltc_rev.pdf.

Hamilton, Kirk et al., *Where is the Wealth of Nations? Measuring Capital for the 21st Century.* Washington, DC: World Bank, 2006.

Harrington , Scott and Gregory Niehaus. *Risk Management and Insurance,* 2nd ed. New York: McGraw-Hill/Irwin, 2003.

"Insurance to Cover Firms Against Celebrity 'Disgrace,'" *The Independent* (UK), November 16, 2010, http://www.independent.co.uk/news/people/news/insurance-to-cover-firms-against-celebrity-disgrace-2135001.html.

Kling, Arnold. "Insulation vs. Insurance," *Cato Unbound,* (January 8, 2007), http://www.cato-unbound.org/2007/01/08/arnold-kling/insulation-vs-insurance/.

Mayers, David and Clifford W. Smith, Jr. "On the Corporate Demand for Insurance," *Journal of Business* 55 (April, 1982): 181–296.

Pauly, Mark V., and Bradley Herring. *Pooling Health Insurance Risks*. Washington, DC: American Enterprise Institute, 1999.

Pociask, Stephen B. "Consumer Opinions on Insurance Price Regulation" (The American Consumer Institute, June 2007), http://insurancefederationnc.com/elements/media/msg_pdf/insurance20Survey20Study.pdf.

Roeder, Kerstin. "Hyperbolic Discounting and the Demand for Long-term Care Insurance" (paper presented at ECHE 2010, Helsinki, Finland, July 7–10, 2010), http://eche2010.abstractbook.org/presentations/162/.

Rothschild, Michael and Joseph Stiglitz. "Equilibrium in Competitive Insurance Markets: An Essay on the Economics of Imperfect Information," *Quarterly Journal of Economics* 90 (November 1976).

Shiller, Robert. *The New Financial Order: Risk in the 21st Century*. Princeton University Press, 2004.

Tabarrok, Alexander. "Genetic Testing: An Economic and Contractarian Analysis," *Journal of Health Economics* 13 (March 1994).

Zelizer, Viviana E. "Home Values and the Market: The Case of Life Insurance and Death in 19th-Century America," *The American Journal of Sociology* (November 1978). http://graphics8.nytimes.com/images/blogs/freakonomics/pdf/Zelizer InsuranceRepugnant.pdf (available on JSTOR).

3

Insurance Markets and Regulation

Case Studies in Failure

Martin F. Grace

Introduction

THE HISTORY OF insurance regulation is rife with examples of regulatory failure. To be fair, regulatory successes often go unnoticed, but the failures are generally spectacular. The numerous failures in insurance markets are often similar in their causes, nature, and scope and are worthy of special discussion. This chapter examines a number of regulatory failures in insurance markets, particularly where the state instituted strict price regulation. What will become evident in this discussion is a tension between economic efficiency and political views of fairness. Economic efficiency requires risk-based pricing, which means all insureds pay premiums based on their risk characteristics. In contrast, significant political coalitions occasionally have evolved to promote fairness and reduce the effect of risk valuations in pricing. By focusing on fairness and affordability, some states have hindered insurers' ability to set rates, which results in a series of ever-increasing subsidies to high-risk insureds.

A number of studies have indicated that price regulation can result in a significant lack of benefits. Harrington, for example, examines the historical data in auto insurance and finds that states with price regulation sometimes have lower prices than relatively competitive states, but other times these same states have prices higher than more competitive markets.[1] However, over a thirty-year period there was no statistical difference between regulated and unregulated market prices. Thus a simple query can be made: if there is no long-run difference, why spend the nontrivial regulatory resources on price regulation? Similarly, Bukame and Ruser, in their examination of deregulating workers' compensation markets, found two types of effects: lower prices as well as a reduction in injuries.[2] In particular, they found that price deregulation is associated both with reductions in long-run premiums of approximately 14 percent and with a reduction in injury rates of approximately 8 percent. A relevant question then arises—why do states regulate insurance prices? The answer has to do with the difference between the way insurance markets work and the way political markets work.

One of the benefits of federalism is the fact that states can engage in policy experiments, which will theoretically yield improved policy results. However, various states appear to make comparable disastrous policy decisions, yielding similar dismal results, and do not seem able to anticipate the predictable bad policy outcome. In fact, many regulators blame the insurance industry for failing to supply capital for state-regulated markets and raise the specter of collusion and bad faith. This, in turn, has the effect of hastening the insurance market's demise in these states. The political market is able to react quickly by introducing regulatory reform. Insurance markets, however, take much longer to recover from a shock. This mismatch in timing yields the dysfunctional markets that are the focus of the chapter.

Specifically, this chapter provides case studies in different states and lines of insurance, which hopefully will guide future policymakers when faced with insurance reform pressures involving price regulation. Each case study follows a typical pattern. First, a price shock occurs that disrupts the market, causing prices to increase dramatically. The price increase then makes the issue politically salient. Consumers, and therefore voters, upset about the higher prices and political coalitions, form to combat the higher prices. Governors, legislators, and insurance regulators then insert themselves into the political debate about what should be done. Inevitably, the politicians decide price regulation is the solution and legislate accordingly. This solution is a short-run fix with unintended long-run consequences.

In contrast to the short-run political process, insurance markets are focused on the long-term laws of supply and demand. Thus, while the politicians may decide that prices should fall, the market's response is a reduction in supply, which affects the highest-risk customers first. Then availability of coverage to the low-risk insureds becomes a politically salient issue as insurers increase underwriting standards to avoid losing money on those customers with the highest risk. Another short-run fix is proposed, and politicians and regulators respond by choosing to investigate and regulate more carefully. The form of this intervention comes in two main forms. First, the state might set up a high-risk pool that is explicitly subsidized by low-risk insurers. A second version has the state becoming a provider of insurance. Instead of a subsidy going from low-risk to high-risk insureds, the subsidy goes from taxpayers to high-risk insureds. In the first case, the subsidy is never enough to cover the costs of the high-risk consumers. In this case, insurers realize that it is not possible to make a profit in the market, and they withdraw. In the second case, the state can compete with the private market insurers and crowd them out. This also could lead private insurers to withdraw from the state.

What we observe from these case studies is that regulators forget that insurance is a voluntary transaction; that is, insurance firms will withdraw from a market if conditions are too onerous or normal economic profits are not likely to be obtainable in the long run. Insurers can exit markets at relatively low cost, and, even if the cost is higher for some, companies have given up their licenses for all insurance within a state. Aetna left Massachusetts over auto price regulation,[3] State Farm credibly threatened to leave Florida over homeowners' insurance regulation,[4] and almost every major workers' compensation carrier left Maine during its crisis.[5] The flight of capital cannot be fixed by further price regulation. Also, this leaves state residents bearing the entire cost of insurance risk rather than shifting it to national and international insurance and capital markets. The entire rationale behind insurance is undermined by strict price regulation if the taxpayers are left being the insurer.

A well-functioning insurance market occasionally experiences shocks, which increase prices, and then prices adjust as markets return to equilibrium. However state political cycles are often quicker to react to such economic shocks than insurance markets. As a result, intervention, while based upon notions of fairness, destroys the efficiency aspect of markets, causing them to fail—not from private decisions but from public decisions. Insurance markets generate prices that reflect the marginal cost of risk. These prices result from the interaction of long-run factors in the economic environment. An increase in medical care inflation can influence the cost of automobile insurance, as medical care is a key benefit of the insurance. Similarly, an increase in the frequency or severity of natural disasters causes the price of insurance to rise as the risk to the insureds has risen. These cost increases can be priced and then used to signal the market about the cost of risk in a particular line of business or geographic area.

The problem of pricing in response to a current shock is exacerbated by the political cycle's view. Insurers raising prices appear to be profiting (irrespective of the case) and so are prone to accusations of price gouging and the like. Politicians can use this saliency to create election opportunities. Thus, the political cycle's relatively short-term horizon can hinder the longer-term insurance market's viability. It is likely that, given the opportunity, the market's spike would return to a more traditional price level in a short period of time. Political changes sometimes occur before markets can adjust, potentially hurting the market for decades.

As a result of these crises, almost every state has returned to industry standards to some extent. The major exception is Florida, which has not yet finished its cycle. Thus, after destroying the market in these important insurance lines, the states have come full circle to restore some aspect of market discipline. To be fair, some states like South Carolina have gone further than others, such as Massachusetts, in allowing for market-based prices in the auto insurance arena.

A Brief Background

Price regulation, while historically present in most markets, has not been so strict as to limit market opportunities. From the 1940s on, most states allowed insurers to submit rates to rating bureaus, which would examine the rates to makes sure they were sufficient to prevent insolvency. Most rating bureaus have disappeared as ratemaking has become more of an actuarial effort and the industry has become more competitive. States later, in the 1970s, took on the direct power to regulate. At first, most states required that rates be submitted prior to approval for use. Other states adopted a competitive rating law. This implied that the insurer could employ a rate without prior approval, but the regulator could conceivably disapprove the rate at a later date. A third style of regulation was the state-made rate. Until recently, Massachusetts was the only state that set rates.

State-made rates are the most restrictive type of price regulation, followed by prior-approval regulation. On the other side of the regulatory spectrum is the absence of price regulation. Illinois, for example, has no rate or pricing regulation for personal lines but reserves the authority to regulate if the need arises. Since the law for open competition was passed in the early 1970s, Illinois has enjoyed a robust market without the political rancor and supply disruptions that characterize regulated insurance markets.[6]

Because of its special nature, workers' compensation insurance is mandatory in every state for companies with more than a given number of employees. This mandate makes it a condition for doing business, and states have been reluctant to allow the market to price employers out of business. The same problem has occurred with automobile insurance. As states made auto insurance a requirement for operating a motor vehicle, it became important to keep rates low enough for all drivers to be able to obtain auto insurance. In addition, while homeowners' insurance is not mandated by law like auto or workers' compensation, it is required to obtain and maintain a mortgage. Thus, in some states, to keep homeowners' insurance affordable, there is political pressure to keep rates low in certain geographic areas exposed to unique risk, such as wind risk.

All these insurance lines have become socialized to some extent as low-risk policyholders subsidize higher-risk policyholders. What is striking is that the rationale for subsidies has never really been addressed. Why do low-risk drivers need to subsidize high-risk drivers? If there are social benefits to driving, why should one sector of the economy pay for a subsidy? This seems to be the role of the state. Similarly, if there are benefits to having people live in high-risk zones, should not the entire state pay for this rather than other homeowners? Except for a few academic studies like those mentioned earlier, which looked at the effects of price regulation, there does not seem to be any examination of the benefits of subsidies, nor of the costs.

Figure 3.1 shows a series of automobile loss ratios for regulated states and relatively competitive states using the list of laws in Harrington[7] and updated to 2007. A loss ratio can be thought of as an index of insurer pricing; it reflects the amount of losses paid per premium dollar. Thus, if the ratio is high, the consumers are receiving relatively more in loss payments per premium dollar paid than are consumers in other states. Correspondingly, a low loss ratio implies that lower loss payments are being made per premium dollar to the consumer. So high loss ratios imply lower insurance prices, and low loss ratios imply higher insurance prices, all other things being equal. One test of how well price regulation works is to compare loss ratios in states with and without

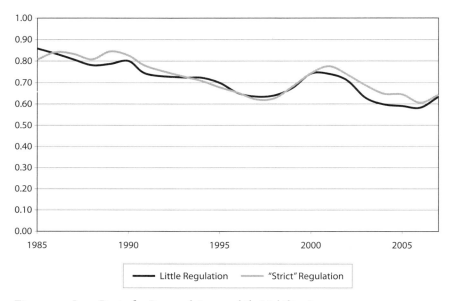

Figure 3.1. Loss Ratio for Personal Automobile Liability Insurance
(Losses Incurred to Premiums Earned) for Regulated and
Nonregulated States, 1985–2007.

strict price regulation. In Figure 3.1, we see that strict price regulation did not significantly reduce prices below those in the relatively unregulated states. In fact, significant state resources are spent on price regulation, but without any real benefit. Thus, while there is no difference between the average prices in states with regulation and those without, there are distributional effects. Price regulation causes insurers to underwrite more carefully. In doing so, they are more likely to reject relatively higher-risk customers. Since, as previously noted, auto insurance is compulsory in most states, some provision is needed for rejected high-risk drivers. As a result, nearly every state has used a residual market mechanism to deal with high-risk drivers.

The state administers this residual auto insurance market, which is apportioned to the insurance companies within the state, and the line of business is based on individual insurers' market share. The residual market generally loses money in any given year, and the losses must then be made up by a tax on the low-risk insureds' premiums in the following year. This pricing is dynamic and can be explosive, creating higher and higher prices every year in the low-risk markets. These higher prices make insurers underwrite more carefully, thus placing more drivers into the residual market. Low-risk drivers bear the tax via higher prices, and insurers bear the tax via lower profits. Further, the state's economy also bears a burden since high-risk policyholders do not have the proper incentives to reduce their risks. For example, if a driver is high risk and continues to obtain relatively inexpensive insurance, then there is no incentive to reduce his risky activities. As risk is subsidized, the lower-risk customers or the state taxpayers must make up the difference. The result of such price regulation is the eventual destruction of the private insurance market. As insurers have had difficulty pricing risks and earning a competitive rate of return, they have left the market.

While the states act as laboratories for policy reform, this chapter looks at a number of cases, focusing on the three main lines of insurance subject to strict price regulation: homeowners' insurance, automobile insurance, and workers' compensation insurance. In a number of these cases, the states significantly changed their regulatory approach to allow a freer market, with the result that prices stabilized and more insurers entered the market. It is interesting to note that these price regulation experiment results are predictable and have been observed in multiple insurance markets with almost exactly the same results. However, even in the face of numerous insurance pricing-policy disasters, there are those who believe that insurance markets need stronger price regulation. Regulators commonly express the feeling that if only we had the right regulatory approach, all of our insurance problems would go away. Nevertheless, the regulators cannot control market forces, and, as much as they believe their goals to be noble, the market will not accommodate them if there is no incentive to supply insurance capital to a state.

The first case presented here is the Florida homeowners' insurance market. This market is currently under strict price regulation, although the legislature is considering freeing it to some extent. The second and third cases concern the New Jersey auto insurance market and the Massachusetts auto market. The fourth case presents the market for automobile insurance in South Carolina, which deregulated in 1999 and showed an almost immediate turnaround. Finally, the fifth case presents a typical workers' compensation regulatory failure, which occurred in Maine.

Florida Homeowners' Wind Insurance Market I think that Floridians will be much better off without [State Farm]. My concern is that we have a good market for Floridians to get homeowners' insurance.[8]

[State Farm] probably charge[s] the highest rates in the state, anyway. Floridians will be much better off without them.[9]

—Governor Charlie Crist, on State Farm's decision to leave Florida (February 2009)

Hurricane Andrew was an unprecedented shock to the residents of Florida and to the insurance market. This catastrophic hurricane amounted to $23.6 billion (in 2007) in insurance loss and is the second highest, only to Hurricane Katrina, insurance loss in the last forty years. Since that event, the state of Florida has engaged in a massive intervention in state insurance markets, as described in Box 3.1.

As a result of the increased losses due to Hurricane Andrew, insurers raised prices to reflect their new understanding of the increased risk of loss due to

---

BOX 3.1. ABRIDGED TIMELINE OF FLORIDA HOME OWNERS INSURANCE REGULATION

1. 1992. Hurricane Andrew.
2. Eight Insurance company failures (mostly small single state companies).
3. Department of Insurance Regulation (DOIR) restriction on policy non-renewals to 5% or less.
4. 1993. Florida Hurricane Cat fund organized to provide reinsurance to Florida writers of homeowners insurance.
5. Mid-late 1990s. Single State Subsidiaries enter Florida from National Companies.
6. 1993–1997. Florida DOIR strictly regulates prices.
7. Industry drops customers—many going to state pools.
8. Legislature attempts to depopulate state pools by giving bonuses to start up companies, one of which is POE.
9. Merge of various state plans into Citizens Property Insurance Company (OIR (2005)).
10. 2005. State OIR (2005) regulation says we've done a good job of managing all of this. However, 20% of market was in state plans.

11. 2004–2005. Four major hurricanes impact the state. Prices are still regulated, but because of lack of major hurricanes in the recent past, there were no price pressures prior to 2005.

12. 2005. Five insurance companies failed after four hurricanes including POE which was the largest private insurer.

Price increases presented to OIR which were initial rejected, but eventually put in place.

1. New legislation setting up Florida Hurricane Cat Fund to provide reinsurance to risks in Florida. State believed international reinsurance market was overcharging for Florida risks. Ironically, Florida has to buy from international market because it cannot cover all states reinsurance risks.

2. Citizens can offer insurance but at 10 percent higher than other bids.

3. 2007. Florida builds its own Cat model, which provides for rates higher than private market models. (Begos, 2007)

4. 2007. Legislation—Citizens can compete with private market firms at below market rates. Citizen rate rollback of 10 percent. DOIR gets final authority over rate increases which it lacked previously.

5. 2007. Legislation provides bonuses for depopulating Citizens. 29 new companies start-up in since 2007 (Florida OIR, 2009).

6. 2007. Sixth hurricane related assessment put on Florida P& C premiums (Florida OIR, 2009b) currently at approximately 8.47 percent on most property-casualty insurance (Florida Insurance Council, 2009).

7. 2009. State Farm (2d largest insurer behind Citizens) announces a pullout of Florida after being denied 47 percent rate increase (Peliteir, 2009).

8. 2009. Legislation to allow greater pricing flexibility for private market insurers vetoed by Governor (Bender, 2009). Legislation enacted requiring Citizens will be raising rates 10 percent each year for the next five years to get closer to actuarially adequate prices.

Source: Grace, Klein, Kleindorfer and Murray (2003), Grace and Klein (2009) and Kunreuther et al. (2009) unless otherwise mentioned.

hurricanes. Some larger insurers announced intentions to reduce their presence in certain parts of the state, and still others announced they would restrict new writings until they better understood the risks facing the insureds. To stave off a mass insurance-availability problem, the state of Florida responded by passing legislation to prevent insurers from cutting more than 5 percent of their customers in a given year. In addition, the state became more aggressive in regulating prices. However, Florida did not cut rates uniformly, which meant subsidies had to be created from relatively low-risk areas to cover higher-risk areas.

Notably, rates in higher-risk areas ended up being lower than they should have been according to standardized methodology. The Insurance Services Office (ISO) assesses loss costs for properties so that insurers without the necessary actuarial data can price insurance. Analysis of loss costs that were used to justify rates for various territories in Florida showed that the highest-risk areas received the lowest price changes, when these areas should have received the greatest price changes. This was foreshadowing a significant problem that would develop as interregional subsidies created market distortions that required government intervention when firms left the regional markets.

Figure 3.2 shows relative loss costs by region in Florida in the mid 1990s. This chart shows three types of data. The first is indicated loss costs. The ISO calculates these to reflect the cost of an expected loss for a standard contract (e.g., homeowners' insurance for a house that is two stories, frame construction, in a city, with $200,000 of coverage, and with a $500 deductible). If we look at Figure 3.2, we see that the highest indicated loss costs are at the left of the figure, representing areas in the southern part of the state. These areas are the most exposed to wind risk. The second set of data in the chart represents prices that insurers filed with the state. These are the prices that insurers desired to offer for a contract in these territories. Notice that they are generally less than the indicated costs. Finally, we see the implemented costs (those the insurers actually used), which were substantially lower than the desired prices.

Note that the high-risk customers in the southern part of the state obtained the highest differential between what rates are indicated (which are recommended by supposedly objective standards) and what is allowed under state regulatory practice. In contrast, there is relatively little difference between the indicated and implemented costs across the regions of the state in 1992 (shown in Figure 3.3).

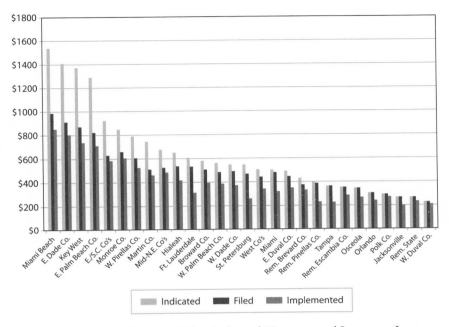

Figure 3.2. Insurance Services Office-Indicated Homeowners' Insurance Loss Costs versus Costs Filed and Implemented by Florida Territory, 1996.

We can also review Florida's homeowners' insurance market problems by looking at the presence and absence of hurricanes in the state. Insurers price insurance based upon expected losses. Therefore, if insurers believe storms will be small and occur infrequently in a particular region, then prices will be lower there than in areas where insurers believe that storms will be larger and relatively more frequent. Insurers and regulators differ when considering the likelihood of large and damaging storms, and this creates a tension regarding what prices will be allowed. Another problem for insurers is how long they are allowed to save up for a potential loss. For example, if an insurer will likely face a typical set of storms in a twenty-year period, then the insurer should be able to set prices that allow the company to break even over a twenty-year period. This pricing rule is not generally followed. There is concern that in years where there are no hurricanes, prices should be lower merely because there are no hurricanes. Insurers do not price insurance on the spot (immediate) market because they need to price over a longer horizon. In fact, if we look at the cumulative profitability of the Florida homeowners' market, it is negative, which suggests that

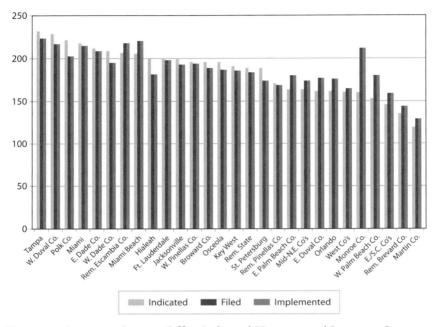

Figure 3.3. Insurance Services Office-Indicated Homeowners' Insurance Loss
Costs versus Costs Filed and Implemented by Florida Territory, 1992.

pricing is, indeed, a long-term problem.[10]

However, for political reasons, insurance regulators desire to keep prices low.
This has substantial effects on markets. Initially, it gives insurers an incentive
to reduce their writings in high-risk areas if they feel that they cannot obtain a
reasonable profit there. This leaves markets underserved. In Florida, as a result
of insurers leaving the area, the state became the insurer of last resort through
a state-run windstorm pool and a joint underwriting association (JUA). Florida
then attempted to cajole new insurers into writing business in high-risk areas by
offering them bounties when they removed insureds from the state-run entities.
Unfortunately, these replacement companies were not of the same quality as
their predecessors. After Florida's four hurricanes in 2004–2005, the largest of
these insurers, the POE Financial Group, which became the second-largest
homeowners' insurance company in the state (during the early 2000s), went
bankrupt due to exposure to hurricane risks. In addition, another three or four
insurers failed during this time period.

As a result of these market failures, a new state-run entity (created by the
merger of the windstorm pool and the JUA) was formed: the Citizens Property

Insurance Corporation. The state of Florida owns 100 percent of this company, and after the 2004–2005 hurricane seasons, it became the largest homeowners' insurance company in the state. Again, after the creation and growth of a state-run insurer, the state decided to depopulate Citizens Property Insurance Corporation by offering startup companies bonuses to take insurers out of the state pool. These are companies that cannot get A.M. Best ratings because of their relative immaturity, so their financial soundness is of concern.

Since Hurricane Andrew, Florida has experienced a number of hurricanes. The loss ratio during the period 1989–2007 shows the effects of Andrew in 1992 and of the four hurricanes in 2004–2005 (Figure 3.4). Losses have not been constant over the past two decades but were relatively lumpy. During the period of relatively low hurricane activity, the market seems to have been temporarily profitable with relatively low loss ratios compared to the United States as a whole, as shown in Figure 3.4. A large loss, however, can wipe out a number of years' or decades' worth of profits. We see the effects of Hurricane Andrew in 1992 and the vastness of the losses relative to the premiums collected. The 2004–2005 period also shows a distinctive increase in losses relative to premiums. What

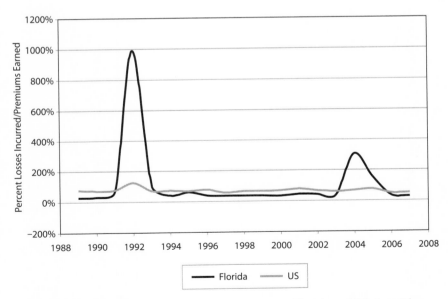

Figure 3.4. Loss Ratio for Homeowners' Insurance in Florida and Nationwide, 1989–2007.

Source: NAIC Profitability Report, 1998, 2007.

is important to note is that premiums were substantially higher in 2004 than they were in 1992, but the losses were quite high, too. Thus, while we do not see loss ratios the size of those for Hurricane Andrew, we do see significantly higher losses than in the past and significantly higher than those in the United States overall.

Another way of looking at what price regulation is doing to Florida's market is to consider the number of homeowners' companies operating in Florida over time and see what percentage of the market is being served by companies writing predominantly in Florida. Figure 3.5 shows that the number of insurers in Florida has fallen from about 219 in 1992 to 143 in 2007. In addition, the number of companies that write homeowners' premiums mostly in Florida has risen from 9 to 63 over the same time period. These companies are defined as those with 90 percent of their homeowners' premiums coming from Florida. The rates

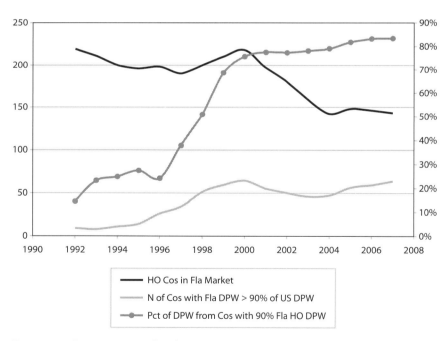

Figure 3.5. Companies in Florida Homeowners' Market, Number of Companies Writing More than 90 Percent of Their Homeowners' Premium in Florida, and Percent of the Market Served by Companies with 90 Percent or More of Their U.S. Premiums Written in Florida, 1992–2007.

in Florida have been kept low, and national companies have left the state, leaving it with some single-state companies that have national brand names (e.g., State Farm Florida or Allstate Floridian) and several startups. What is interesting is that the market share of these mostly Florida companies has risen from about 14.5 percent in 1992 to 83.3 percent of the homeowners' market in 2007. This massive change is consistent with other markets under stress, as discussed later.

In 2007, the state legislature enacted a new set of rules for insurers.[11] Price increases must be strictly prior approval, and the Office of Insurance Regulation is the final arbiter of insurance rates. Previously, companies could appeal rate orders to arbitration panels; now they are heard by administrative tribunals. Further, the state ordered Citizens Property Insurance Corporation to roll its rates back by 10 percent and froze proposed price increases; Citizens could now offer prices below private-market company rates. The new rules also increased the level of catastrophic reinsurance provided by the state and expanded the types of policies (except for workers' compensation and medical malpractice) that could be assessed to pay Citizens' or the Florida Hurricane Catastrophe Fund's losses. It is striking that the state legislature became involved in price setting of insurance without understanding the ramifications.

In February 2009, State Farm announced it was leaving Florida. The firm had asked for rate increases and had been repeatedly denied. State Farm was the second-largest insurer in the state behind Citizens, and it agreed to a multiyear withdrawal schedule. However, the state became concerned that even more insureds would be moving to Citizens as State Farm reduced its policy counts. Between Citizens and the Florida Hurricane Catastrophe Fund (which reinsures the other homeowners' insurers in the state), the state was becoming concerned about the increased concentration of hurricane risk for the Florida taxpayer. As a result of the perceived failure of the 2007 legislation, the financial crisis, and the concentration of catastrophe risk in the state, the legislature passed a bill that allowed price flexibility for the larger (non-startup) companies.[12] The governor vetoed the bill, claiming it was bad for Florida since it would let firms cherry-pick profitable customers.[13]

So while Florida, unlike the other states mentioned here, has not let market forces have more of a say in its homeowners' market, it has followed the rest of the price regulation cycle. A price shock caused political coalitions to form, which resulted in regulated prices. Regulated prices caused problems, including cross-subsidization and insurers leaving the market. Florida then created state-owned primary insurers and a reinsurer to keep prices lower. This had the effect of crowding out private-market providers.

In fact, Florida has so concentrated its risk in the hands of the taxpayers that a large hurricane could have a serious fiscal impact on the state.[14] Florida has focused on keeping prices low to the extent that it has forgotten why prices exist in the first place—they allocate scarce resources. Instead of transferring risk through the price system to investors and reinsurers worldwide, the state has undertaken a policy of undermining markets and destroying a profit incentive to supply risk capital to the state.

New Jersey Auto Insurance Market

No discussion of failed political solutions to the auto insurance crisis is complete without a look at New Jersey, the state with the most tangled auto insurance mess in history. Even the Soviet Union would be hard pressed to match this economic disaster.[15]

—Marjorie Bertie[16] (1991)

Like Florida, New Jersey has had a difficult time with its insurance markets. However, unlike Florida, as the result of recent changes regulating automobile insurance, that market has been revitalized. New Jersey legislators were concerned about providing insurance to drivers at reasonable prices. When auto insurance became mandatory, provision was made to cover those high-risk drivers who would otherwise not be able to afford insurance. Unfortunately, this makes things worse since checks were not put in place at the very beginning of the program to make high-risk drivers sensitive to the risks they place on the insurance system.

Box 3.2 contains a stylized timeline of important events in New Jersey's regulation of auto insurance. Essentially, we see a pattern similar to the one that occurred in Florida. A price shock resulted in political coalitions forming to obtain price regulation (and restrictions on profits). In this case, New Jersey saw an explosive growth in its joint underwriting authority (JUA), the state-run high-risk pool, followed by firms exiting the New Jersey auto insurance market.

BOX 3.2. ABRIDGED NEW JERSEY REGULATORY
        TIMELINE

1. New Jersey is a compulsory insurance state, which began the 1970s with a tort system.
2. 1972. Elective No Fault Introduced (unlimited PIP benefits and low monetary threshold)
3. 1983. Set up JUA and set caps on rates
4. 1988. Excess Profits Law causes problem when losses are abnormally low one year, set up flex rating, created a verbal threshold for no fault
5. 1990. The JUA ran up a deficit of $3 billion and then state switched to a state-run "market transition facility," which managed to accumulate a deficit of $1 billion in two years.
6. 1990s. Large suppliers withdraw from the market.
7. 1997. Tier Rating Put into Place
8. 1998. Insurance Reforms. 15 % rate reduction, Verbal Threshold for No Fault, Fraud reduction, new rating territories, lower mandatory limits,
9. 2001. Sate Farm and AIG announce withdrawals from NJ Market (Ress, 2001)
10. By 2003, 25 Carriers have left the state (Moroz, 2003).
11. Auto Insurance Reform 2003 removed the take all comers requirement, flex rating expanded to 7 percent, easier exit requirements.
12. 2003. Mercury enters market and is first entrant in 7 years. State Farm announces suspension of its program to leave market (2003, Lipka).
13. Insurers announce rate cuts (2003, Lipka).

Source: Worral (2002) unless otherwise noted.

Figure 3.6 shows the New Jersey and U.S. loss ratio over time, and Figure 3.7 shows the average expenditure on auto insurance for New Jersey compared to the U.S. average during this same period (1992–2007). While the New Jersey loss ratio is higher than the U.S. ratio during this period, which implies lower prices in the state, it is misleading to think the market was healthy for consumers or producers. Losses were high in New Jersey due to the size of the residual market

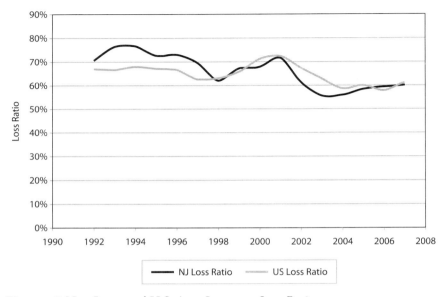

Figure 3.6. New Jersey and U.S. Auto Insurance Loss Ratio, 1992–2007.

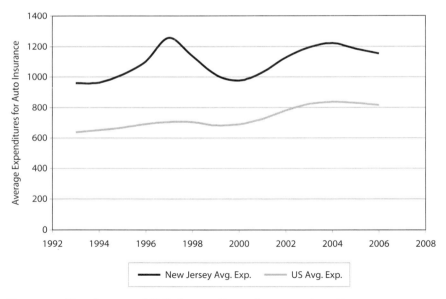

Figure 3.7. New Jersey and U.S. Average Expenditures on Auto Insurance, 1992–2007.

in the 1980s and early 1990s. Figure 3.7 shows that the average expenditures in New Jersey were higher than the U.S. average during the entire period, and for all but two years, New Jersey had the highest auto insurance expenditure in the nation.[17] This was caused by the effect that low prices had on the JUA residual market and the eventual residual market deficits. Figure 3.8 shows the residual market for New Jersey over time (1985–2007).

As seen in Figure 3.8, the residual market was quite large in the 1980s and through the early 1990s, when the state closed its JUA and set up a state-run Market Transition Facility (MTF), which was supposed to transfer high-risk policies back to the private market. Companies had to take the high-risk drivers but were not allowed to charge them market-based prices. While the MTF was operating, it still ran deficits, and the private market insurers, taxpayers, and auto insurance consumers had to pay for these deficits. This, in turn, caused insurers to leave the market. With the removal of the MTF, the number of cars in the residual market declined over time.

Since 1992, the number of insurers writing in auto in New Jersey has changed (see Figure 3.9). A significant number left the state during the 1990s. Most

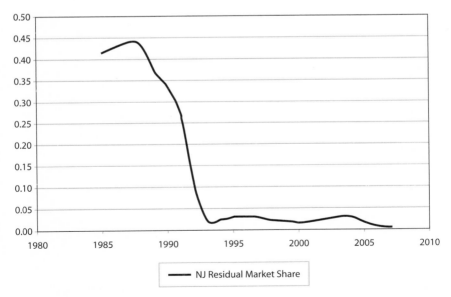

Figure 3.8. New Jersey Residual Auto Insurance Market Share, 1985–2007.

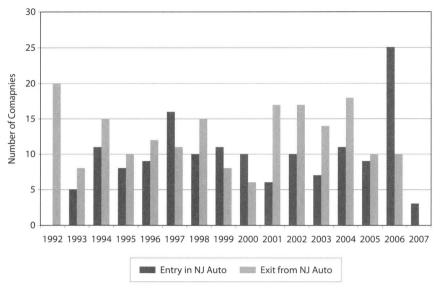

Figure 3.9. Entry and Exit in New Jersey Auto Insurance, 1992–2007.

years, the number of exits was greater than the number of entrants. However, the reforms in 2003 led to a large uptick in entrants in 2006. While there is not enough evidence to say the reforms were causing entry and reducing exits, former Banking and Insurance Commissioner Holly Bakke stated that she believed the activity was due to the reforms.[18] In addition to the entry of national insurers, other insurers that had been dropping customers in preparation for leaving the state started to affirmatively market to new customers. In fact, some insurers voluntarily lowered prices.[19]

Two years after the reform was adopted, 64 percent of auto policyholders had received premium reductions.[20] By 2006, Esurance, Mercury, Progressive, AMEX, Progressive, Unitrin, GEICO, and 21st Century had entered the market, and others such as State Farm, AllState, and AIG had expanded their market presence, employing agents and claims processors.[21] By 2007, approximately 75 percent of New Jersey drivers had lower premiums, and insurers were advertising for new customers, something not seen in the past.[22] New Jersey still has high loss costs relative to other states, in part due to its urban nature and high density of autos. Thus, New Jersey will always likely have high premiums. However, the market is functioning to attract insurance capital, when before it was causing companies to exit. More drivers are paying risk-based prices, which is a sign of a healthy market.

Massachusetts Auto Insurance Market

Massachusetts is a mess. . . . If you tried to sit down and devise a dumber system, you couldn't.[23]
—Clifford Fraiser, a deputy regional vice president for State Farm

Like Florida and New Jersey, Massachusetts has had a set of highly interventionist policies regulating insurance prices in the state. Box 3.3 presents an abridged history of auto insurance regulation in Massachusetts. The state has significantly intervened in insurance markets since the advent of automobile insurance regulation (1927). In the early 1970s Massachusetts was the first state to introduce no-fault insurance in an attempt to keep the price of auto insurance relatively low. The idea behind no-fault was to reduce costly small-claims litigation. However, due to an easily breached no-fault threshold and relatively generous insurance benefits, insurance costs increased dramatically. Massachusetts also introduced compulsory insurance laws and a mandatory-offer rule that required insurers to take all comers. Massachusetts, interestingly, has a procompetitive insurance-pricing law. However, the same law also allows the insurance commissioner to find that the market is insufficiently competitive and then impose state rates. Since 1977, the insurance regulator found insufficient competition each year for ten years, thus setting the stage for continued regulated rates in Massachusetts.[24] This changed in late 2007, when the insurance commission proposed a departure from the status quo and for the first time allowed firms to offer their own policy forms and prices.[25]

Because of the finding that the market was not competitive, the state mandated rates. The political solution was to keep rates artificially low for higher-risk drivers or for those in higher-risk geographical areas. The resulting rate structure led to subsidized rates in two ways: from rural to urban areas and from low-risk drivers to high-risk drivers. Geographical rating territories were set up, and rates were not allowed to reflect higher costs in urban areas. The political coalition that arose protected city dwellers and high-risk drivers from

BOX 3.3. ABRIDGED TIMELINE FOR MASSACHUSETTS AUTO INSURANCE REGULATION

1. 1927. Massachusetts introduces state administered auto insurance prices because of mandatory nature of auto insurance.
2. 1970s. Massachusetts becomes the first state to mandate no-fault auto insurance.
3. 1977. Move to competitive based rates.
4. 1977. competitive based rates deemed failure and return to administered rates.
5. 1980's. Nationwide cost shocks to medical care and auto repair. No good driver discounts, 'wrong" coverage levels, no fault threshold that was too low given inflation since 1970 (Gooderham, 1989).
6. 1987. Industry claims loss of $840 million since 1978 in auto markets (Lewis, 1988).
7. 1987. Companies exit market (including nationwide companies like State Farm and Aetna).
8. 1987. Auto insurance reform focusing on assigned risk pool and rates (Gooderham, 1989).
9. Assigned risk pool had over 50 percent of states drivers. Insurers were worried about having to pay deficits from high-risk drivers. Some started to leave to avoid assessments.
10. 1988. Massachusetts motorists file claims at rates twice that of either New York or Connecticut (Lewis, 1988).
11. 1990s. Focus is on fighting fraud. With nationwide downward claims occurring in Massachusetts, price increases were moderated. However, Massachusetts still had rates in the top 2 nationwide.
12. 2000. Subsidies in pricing were being paid by low risk rural drivers and commercial companies to the benefit of urban areas.
13. 2000. Number of groups represented in auto market is 20 down from 70 in 1992.
14. 2005. Protectionist state companies fight reform due to fears of competition from larger national companies (Donohue, 2005).
15. 2007. Insurance commissioner moves to a managed competition environment. New entry occurs almost overnight with the addition of Progressive and GEICO.

Source: Tennyson et al. (2000) unless otherwise noted.

high rates. This cross-subsidy resulted in a residual market deficit, which was passed on to low-risk drivers in their premiums.

Figure 3.10 shows the auto insurance loss ratio in Massachusetts and the United States from 1992 through 2007.[26] We can see that this ratio reflects how much a dollar of incurred losses comes from written premiums each year. The higher the loss ratio, the better the price for insurance. The Massachusetts loss ratio is higher than the U.S. loss ratio about half the time during this period. This is consistent with the literature in general; that is, automobile price regulation does not necessarily mean lower prices for insurance. In high loss states like New Jersey and Massachusetts, consumers pay real prices, too. This loss ratio does not show the distribution of losses and premiums between high- and low-risk drivers. Thus, we cannot see the effect of subsidies that low-risk drivers pay to high-risk drivers or that drivers in rural areas pay to urban drivers. In an analysis of Massachusetts policies in 2000, Tennyson et al. found that inexperienced and urban drivers received significant cross-subsidies, which tended to come from commercial insurance consumers.[27] Looking at the data on average automobile insurance expenditures provided by the National Association of Insurance Companies (NAIC), Massachusetts was almost always ranked as one

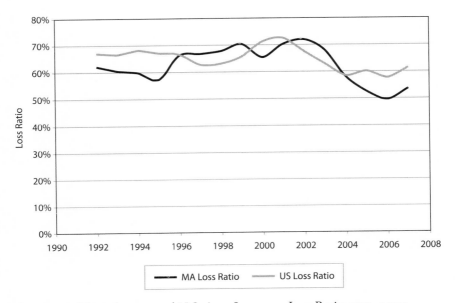

Figure 3.10. Massachusetts and U.S. Auto Insurance Loss Ratio, 1992–2007.

of the most expensive states. This was, in part, caused by a rapid growth in loss costs. In turn, increased regulatory scrutiny kept premiums too low.[28] This put more drivers in the residual market and caused companies to leave the market.

Massachusetts, like Florida, reacted to a price shock by making prices lower and imposing a de facto subsidy scheme. This scheme had longer-run effects, such as fewer people in high-risk pools and fewer private market participants. Figure 3.11 shows the Massachusetts residual market over time. While exploding in the late 1980s, the residual market for auto insurance gradually decreased over time, in part because the state was pushing high-risk drivers to the private market. In the mid 2000s, however, even the relatively low level of 5 percent was still high compared to a state like Illinois, which has competitively set prices. In Illinois, for comparison, the residual market ranged from .02 percent to .23 percent, while Massachusetts residual markets ranged from 72.73 percent in 1989 to 4.78 percent in 2006.

Massachusetts was becoming a state without a significant presence of any national automobile insurance companies. Since 1990, Massachusetts saw the

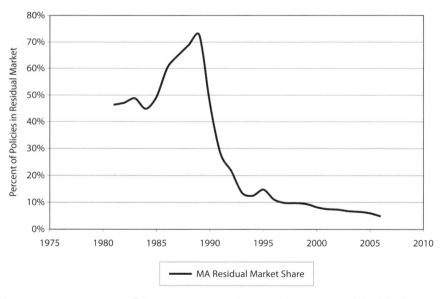

Figure 3.11. Percentage of Auto Insurance Policies in Massachusetts' Residual Market, 1980–2006.

number of auto insurers decline from thirty-five to nineteen.[29] Further, the remaining companies were mostly "Massachusetts only" companies, many of which were able to sell insurance because the rates were regulated and there was no real competition.

In 2007, the governor of Massachusetts formed a study group to examine the regulation of insurance markets. Among other things, the group recommended allowing more flexible rating and streamlining the regulatory approval process.[30] The insurance commissioner set up a process by which the state could move to a more competitive environment. In essence, the insurance commissioner was looking at the law that stated the commissioner should make a determination each year regarding market competitiveness. By permitting what was called "managed competition," the commissioner allowed insurers to set rates on their own policy forms. As a result, nine new firms entered the market, including GEICO and Progressive; the residual market continues to shrink; and prices have fallen on average by 8.2 percent. Further, consumer coverage levels have not decreased, and those who did change their coverage levels were twice as likely to increase coverage as decrease it.[31]

While not yet offering a freely competitive market such as the one in Illinois, the Massachusetts insurance regulator has removed the one-size-fits-all regulatory approach and allowed competition, which has led to lowered prices. The Massachusetts story confirms that keeping prices low to hide the cost of risk to drivers is folly. This only makes losses worse. In fact, Massachusetts, like New Jersey, has densely populated urban areas and thus a high level of accident frequency, and this by itself will keep prices relatively high (compared to other states). Also like New Jersey, the reforms in Massachusetts are just starting, but the initial results are quite promising.

South Carolina Auto Market

South Carolina is the 48th state in which Progressive has opened business, and it's because of the new law. We wouldn't be here otherwise.[32]
—Mark Arnell, general manager for Progressive's Carolinas business unit

South Carolina has had insurance price regulation for a long time. Like other states that experienced cost inflation in the 1970s and 1980s, South Carolina was increasingly scrutinizing insurance prices. The state did not have to pass new laws in order to regulate prices; it just had to strictly enforce the ones it had. Rates were politically salient, and regulators responded by keeping prices below what insurers believed were adequate for long-run profitability. South Carolina was a strict prior-approval state, and Grace et al. report that by many objective standards, it was one of the most restrictive pricing regimes in the nation.[33]

Like other states, South Carolina requires drivers to have auto insurance, and it created an insurance risk facility to provide coverage for high-risk drivers. However, this assigned risk facility was deficit ridden from the beginning. Losses from high-risk drivers were greater than the premiums collected. A recoupment fee paid by drivers in the low-risk voluntary market financed the deficit (Gaston 1998). In 1988, the recoupment fee was listed separately on insurance bills, and this allowed consumers to see the exact effect high-risk drivers in the state had on their insurance premiums.[34]

Figure 3.12 shows the South Carolina auto insurance loss ratio over time as compared to the U.S. loss ratio. From 1992 through 1999, South Carolina had a greater loss ratio than the United States overall, but after 2000, the state's ratio was slightly lower than the national average. Again, this use of the loss ratio to talk about prices is suspect when significant subsidies were going from low-risk to high-risk customers. What is more important is how the residual market behaved, which is shown in Figure 3.13. The percentage of drivers in the residual market was quite high during the 1990s and fell to zero after the introduction of insurance reform in the state.

In 1997, the state of South Carolina enacted insurance market reforms, which took effect in 1999. Essentially, the state permitted flex rating (no prior approval needed for rate changes less than 7 percent), and insurers were allowed greater freedom in geographic underwriting. As a result, new writers came into South Carolina. Figure 3.14 shows the number of insurers writing in South Carolina from 1985 to 2007. It is evident that the 1997 reform had an effect, as the number of firms writing auto insurance more than doubled just after the effective date of the reform (1999). In addition, as shown in Figure 3.13, the residual market fell to zero, eliminating the need to cross-subsidize high-risk drivers.

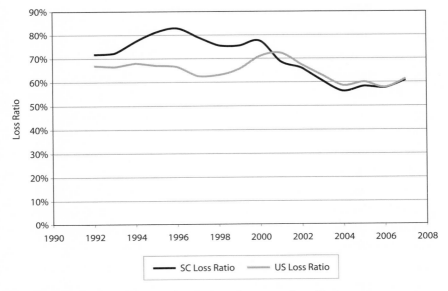

Figure 3.12. South Carolina and U.S. Auto Insurance Loss Ratio, 1992–2007.

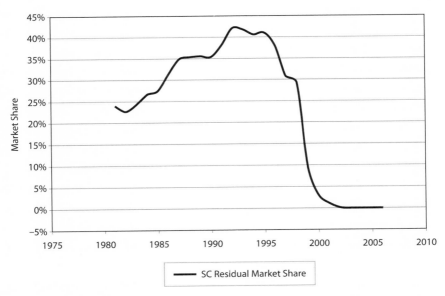

Figure 3.13. South Carolina Auto Insurance Residual Market Share, 1980–2006.

> ### BOX 3.4. ABRIDGED HISTORY OF SOUTH CAROLINA
> ### AUTO INSURANCE REGULATION
>
> 1. SC was a prior approval state.
> 2. SC over time allowed deviations from uniform bureau rates.
> 3. 1974. State makes auto insurance compulsory (Gaston, 1999).
> 4. 1975. legislation mandated compulsory insurance, mandatory coverage by auto insurers, establishment of a reinsurance facility, mandated a uniform risk rating plan.
> 5. 1975–1987. Growth of residual market.
> 6. 1987. Recoupment fee charged to policyholders to cover residual market (JUA).
> 7. 1988. Recoupment fee listed separately on insurance bill.
> 8. 1997. Legislation takes effect in 1999 allows flex rating, eased underwriting restrictions, depopulated the JUA and phased out subsidy to JUA.
>
> *Source:* Grace, Klein and Phillips (2002) unless otherwise mentioned.

Since 1999 when the reforms took place, the overall auto insurance market in South Carolina has stabilized. Average expenditures on auto insurance were ranked twenty-fourth in 2006, and right before the reforms, the state was ranked twenty-sixth. While not as urban as New Jersey or Massachusetts, which means fewer high-frequency events, South Carolina suffers from a high number of highway fatalities. For example, in 2007, there were 1,045 auto fatalities in South Carolina, compared to 429 in Massachusetts and 771 in New Jersey.[35] Given their respective populations, this comes to 233 auto-related deaths per million residents in South Carolina compared to 66 deaths per million in Massachusetts and 89 deaths per million in New Jersey. Thus, South Carolina's high auto insurance costs are the result of state-specific factors, and placing the cost of risk on those who are likely to be high-risk drivers will encourage better long-run accident-avoidance behavior.

In the previous auto insurance case studies, increases in loss costs caused prices to increase, and the increased prices became important to voters. What is interesting about South Carolina's story is that premiums for low-risk drivers became politically salient when the recoupment fee, or subsidy to high-risk

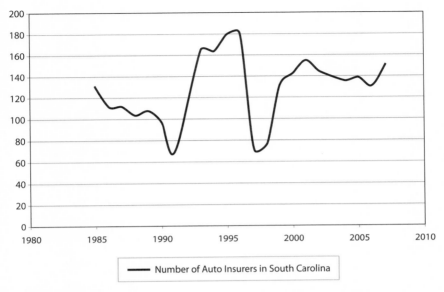

Figure 3.14. Number of South Carolina Auto Insurers Writing Private Passenger Liability and Physical Damage Coverages (with Positive Loss Experience), 1985–2007.

drivers, was made explicit on the consumers' automobile insurance bills. In Massachusetts, a political coalition of urban drivers and high-risk drivers was enough to overcome the political power of low-risk and rural drivers. However, in South Carolina, when the low-risk drivers gained more political clout than the high-risk drivers, the subsidy scheme could not stand.

Maine Workers' Compensation Market

What if the law required everybody to buy insurance, but no one wanted to sell it?[36]
    —Peter Kerr, *New York Times* newspaper reporter

The availability of insurance coverage is a major issue for private auto insurance markets, where coverage is mandated. The same is true for workers' compensation insurance, which all states require for businesses with more than a certain number of employees. Ordinarily, as in auto insurance, private workers' compensation insurers are not compelled to write policies for all those who

---

BOX 3.5. ABRIDGED TIMELINE FOR MAINE WORKERS COMPENSATION MARKET

1980s. Small business are unable to obtain workers compensation insurance due in part to increased costs for litigation, medical care, fraud and abuse.

1. Regulatory practice changes from risk-based pricing to social pricing (how much can business afford).
2. There were no rate increases from 1981 to 1987 even when costs were increasing.
3. WC insurers leave market including the largest U.S. workers comp carrier, Liberty Mutual.
4. 1987. Reforms lowered benefit payouts, shifted share of assigned risk pool to employers and insurers equally.
5. 88 companies reentered the market after '87 reforms. (J Commerce, 88)
6. Price Suppression starts again. Regulators claim insurers were filing bloated premium requests. Later admit prices allowed were too low.
7. 1989. Companies again leave the market because of a concern of a growing assigned risk pool and fewer and fewer insurers willing to write WC implies that the remaining insurers will be assessing a greater portion of the pool's deficit.
8. 1992. Maine WC prices were highest in nation.
9. 1993. Major reform capped legal fees to 30 percent of employee benefits, allowed rates to be set more freely. Reform set up new state mutual insurance company to cover workers compensation. (Harris, 1992 & Campbell, 1997 and Fletcher, 1993)
10. 1995. Legislation financed residual market deficits from 1988–1992. Gilbert (1996)

Source: Kerr (1992) unless otherwise noted.

---

desire coverage. The result is that some employers are left outside the private market and must obtain coverage for their employees from self-insurance or from some alternative plan generally provided by the state. If the alternative market grows due to price suppression and then there is a potential deficit—and if that deficit is severe—it can drive a workers' compensation system into crisis, as happened in Maine in the early 1990s.[37]

This story follows the same pattern as the stories about auto insurance markets (see Box 3.5 for a short history of the Maine workers' compensation regulations). Supply dried up as companies left the market. The problem was even more severe in Maine, as just one significant company remained in the market.[38] Figure 3.15 shows the loss ratio from 1985 to 2007 for workers' compensation in Maine. What is noticeable is that Maine's loss ratio was over 100 percent for a great deal of the time under consideration. Auto insurance loss ratios even in the most-regulated states never show this type of loss relative to premiums earned. The economic dislocation caused by a failure in the workers' compensation market was more troublesome than a typical auto market failure. It is possible for drivers to illegally opt out of the insurance market, but it is much more difficult for employers to do so. Further, if employers closed their doors when unable to provide insurance, this could lead to increased unemployment. Employees, employers, and politicians in Maine focused on the availability of

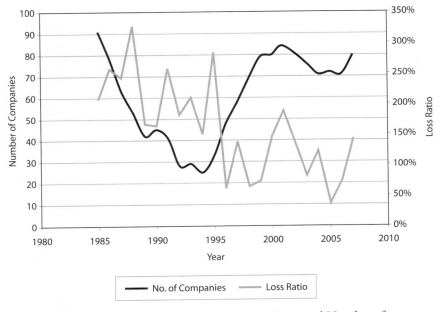

Figure 3.15. Maine's Workers' Compensation Loss Ratio and Number of Companies, 1985–2007.

relatively inexpensive workers' compensation insurance. This coalition was able to influence the direction of prices until the market was nearly destroyed.

As a result, regulators would not allow premium increases to account for medical cost inflation during the 1980s, and the Maine workers' compensation market suffered from price compression. This forced out national insurers. Reforms in 1987 attempted to reduce the benefit payouts, which were generous, and shifted the residual market liability to employers and insurers. This led to increased confidence in the market, and some eighty-eight companies reentered the market. However the Maine insurance department refused to allow rate increases for the next few years. The damage was done. The residual market liability became more oppressive as fewer and fewer insurers were left in the state. Insurers were afraid of being the last remaining company in the state and having to bear the entire industry portion of the deficit. This provided an incentive for more companies to exit.

In 1992, the state again reformed its workers' compensation market by creating a new mutual insurer that would cover high-risk customers. The new mutual company was to be competitive and was given the power to set terms and conditions so that it could compete in the voluntary and residual market. Prices were adjusted to include incentives for employers that reduced costs for making safety improvements. Additional benefits were trimmed, and the length of time one could receive benefits was decreased. Other changes reduced the incentive to litigate by restricting fee payments and limiting a benefit to 80 percent of an individual's actual salary rather than 80 percent of the average salary in the state. Incentives were also put in place to use mediation rather than litigation.[39]

By 1997, the state had reduced workers' compensation insurance rates for six years in a row,[40] and thirty new insurers had entered the state. Four firms that dominated the industry with 79 percent of the market in 1993 had fallen to 68 percent by 1997. Thus, we see again the effect of price deregulation on a market's health. However, the deregulation in Maine was a bit more complicated than just allowing prices to be set based on market competition, as there was a structural change in the relationship between workers, management, and safety. The system for compensation became less adversarial following the institution of mediation and legal fee limits. The use of an employers' mutual company also reduced system costs as the company could insist on safety improvements in exchange for lower premiums. The safety issue is quite interesting because under a highly regulated price environment, an insurer is unlikely to contract for price reduction in exchange for safety improvements if there is a rational fear that increasing future prices to match market increases will not be allowed. In Maine, however, deregulation allowed firms to feel comfortable about lowering prices.

Like the other state markets discussed here, Maine's insurance market suffered a disconnect from the political coalitions that arose to keep prices low in the face of increasing costs. It took a long time for regulators to see that it was their policies rather than a market failure that were causing firms to exit the state. It was only when no firms were left in the industry that real reform became possible.

Conclusions

A number of case studies have been provided here to show a commonality in some states' approaches to insurance price regulation. State regulation often becomes stricter when relatively short-term cost pressures increase the price of insurance. In the automobile and workers' compensation markets presented, regulation was predominately due to medical cost inflation; in Florida's homeowners' market it was due to the increased frequency and severity of hurricanes. Regulators have little influence over medical cost inflation and no influence over natural disasters, but they can regulate prices in response to demand. Consumers may demand regulatory protection from higher prices, and various political coalitions may form to influence state government and regulators to provide stable prices. The resultant price regulation comes at a cost, though: cross-subsidization or taxpayer-based intervention into a market. Since regulation does not really address the costs of the price pressure, a market's long-run incentives still operate. If insurers cannot earn profits, they will rationally exit from a market. The only solution to this problem is for states to let the market work.

There are significant benefits to letting the market work. On the other hand, when we regulate markets, such as by pricing insurance too low for high-risk drivers, there is no price signal to the consumer to alter his or her driving behavior. Or if wind insurance is subsidized, it is cheaper for someone to build in a risky area. Both of these subsidies end up increasing losses and increasing the tax on the low-risk insured.

In each of these case studies, the state would have been better off not regulating prices and letting the market adjust to a new equilibrium. In fact, each time price regulation has been tried, we can point to an outcome like those observed here. This is because there is a distinct difference between the political market for regulation and the economic market for insurance. The benefits of regulation accrue quickly to politicians who provide the regulatory power and to consumers in the first year or two of the new regulatory regime. The costs, however, take years to fully evolve and are much higher.

References

Barkume, Anthony J., and John W. Ruser. "Deregulating Property-Casualty Insurance Pricing: The Case of Workers' Compensation." *The Journal of Law and Economics* 44 (2001): 37–63.

Baurer, Todd. "Augusta Georgia: business@ugusta: Auto Insurance Reform at Hand." *Augusta Chronicle,* February 28, 1999. http://chronicle.augusta.com/stories/022899/bus_MPS-4716.000.shtml.

Begos, Kevin. "Hurricane Model Sized Up." *Tampa Tribune,* June 13, 2007. http://www2.tbo.com/content/2007/jun/13/me-hurricane-model-sized-up/.

Bertie, Marjorie M. *Hit Me—I Need the Money: The Politics of Auto Insurance Reform.* San Francisco: ICS Press, 1991.

Campbell, Richard. "Prevail a Pandora's Box." *Bangor Daily News,* May 17, 1997.

D'Arcy, Stephen P. "Insurance Price Deregulation: The Illinois Experience." In *Deregulating Property-Liability Insurance: Restoring Competition and Increasing Market Efficiency,* edited by J. David Cummins. Washington, DC: Brookings–AEI Joint Center on Regulation, 2002. http://www.aei-brookings.org/publications/abstract.php?pid=221.

Derrig, Richard. "Price Regulation in U.S. Automobile Insurance: A Case Study of Massachusetts Private Passenger Automobile Insurance 1978–1990." *Geneva Papers on Risk and Insurance* 18 (1993): 158–73.

Donohue, John F. "Beware Romney's Insurance Scam" (op-ed), *The Boston Globe,* August 22, 2005, p. A-11.

Fletcher, Meg. "Maine Law Could Prevent Comp System Collapse." *Business Insurance,* October 26, 1992.

Gaston, Elaine. "Low-Risk Drivers May Get a Break in South Carolina Insurance Reform." *Knight Ridder/Tribune Business News,* October 28, 1998. http://www .accessmylibrary.com/coms2/summary_0286–5610261_ITM?email=mgrace@ gsu.edu&library=.

Gilbert, E. "ITT Hartford Renters Maine Workers' Compensation Market" (PC ed.). *National Underwriter,* March 11, 1996.

Gooderham, Mary. "Massachusetts Battles Monster Created by Car Insurance Reform." *Globe and Mail (Toronto),* April 3, 1989.

Grace, Martin F., and Robert W. Klein. "The Perfect Storm: Hurricanes, Insurance, and Regulation." *Risk Management and Insurance Review* (2009) 81–124.

Grace, Martin F., Robert W. Klein, Paul Kleindorfer, and Michael Murray. *Catastrophe Insurance.* Norwell, MA: Kluwer Academic, 2003.

Grace, Martin F., Robert W. Klein, and Richard D. Phillips. "Auto Insurance Reform: Salvation in South Carolina." In *Deregulating Property-Liability Insurance: Restoring Competition and Increasing Market Efficiency,* edited by J. David Cummins. Washington, DC: Brookings–AEI Joint Center on Regulation, 2002. http://www.aei-brookings.org/publications/abstract.php?pid=221.

Harrington, Jeff, and Jennifer Liberto. State Farm Bails on Us. *St. Petersburg Times,* January 28, 2009.

Harrington, Scott. "Effects of Prior Approval Rate Regulation on Auto Insurance." In *Deregulating Property-Liability Insurance: Restoring Competition and Increasing Market Efficiency,* edited by J. David Cummins. Washington. DC: Brookings–AEI Joint Center on Regulation, 2002. http://www.aei-brookings.org/ publications/abstract.php?pid=221.

Harrington, Scott E., and S. Travis Pritchett. "Automobile Insurance Reform in South Carolina." *Journal of Insurance Regulation* 8 (1990): 422–45.

Harris, Norma and Kathleen Kisner. "Maine Reforms Workers' Compensation— State Report." *Business & Health,* November 1992. http://findarticles.com/p/ articles/mi_m0903/is_n13_v10/ai_13359848/.

Hunt, Alan, and Robert W. Klein. "Workers' Compensation Insurance in North

America" (Technical Report No. 96–010). Kalamazoo, MI: W. E. Upjohn Institute for Employment Research, 1996.

"It's Time We Got Straight Answers on Insurance" (editorial). *St. Petersburg Times*, October 19, 2007. http://www.sptimes.com/2007/10/19/Opinion/It_s_time _we_got_stra.shtml.

Kerr, Peter A. "A Showdown on Workers' Compensation in Maine." *New York Times,* August 9, 1992. http://www.nytimes.com/1992/08/09/us/a-showdown-on-workers -compensation-in-maine.html.

Kunreuther, Howard, and Erwann Michel-Kerjan. *At War with the Weather: Managing Large-Scale Risks in a New Era of Catastrophes.* Cambridge: MIT Press, 2009.

LaModa, Bill. "Insurance Veto: Florida Governor Charlie Crist Vetoes Bill That Would Deregulate Big Property Insurers." *Orlando Sentinel,* June 25, 2009. http://www .orlandosentinel.com/features/smartliving/home/sfl-insurance-veto-062409, 0,5630620.story.

Lewis, Dianne. "Driving: Don't Give an Inch and Pay Through the Nose." *The Boston Globe,* October 28, 1988, 1.

Lipka, Mitch. "NJ's Changes Get Auto Insurers to Yield." *The Philadelphia Inquirer,* October 29, 2003, A01.

Massachusetts Division of Insurance. "Executive Summary: Results of the Survey of the Auto Insurance Market After One Year of Managed Competition" (2009). http://www.mass.gov/?pageID=ocamodulechunk&L=4&L0=Home &L1=Government&L2=Our+Agencies+and+Divisions&L3=Division+of+ Insurance&sid=Eoca&b=terminalcontent&f=20090702executivesummary &csid=Eoca.

Moroz, Jennifer. "Assembly Passes Auto-Insurance Bill." *The Philadelphia Inquirer,* May 16, 2003, B1.

National Association of Insurance Commissioners. Various years. *Annual Automobile Expenditures.* Kansas City: NAIC.

National Association of Insurance Commissioners. Various years. *Profitability Report.* Kansas City: NAIC.

National Highway Traffic Safety Administration. "2007 Traffic Safety Annual Assessment—Alcohol-Impaired Driving Fatalities" (DOT HS 811 016). *Traffic Safety Facts. Research Note.* http://www-nrd.nhtsa.dot.gov/Pubs/811016.Pdf.

New Jersey Department of Banking and Insurance. "Auto Insurance Reform Continues to Produce Results," March 1, 2004. Retrieved July 2, 2009, from http://www.newjersey.gov/dobi/pressreleases/pr040301.htm.

New Jersey Department of Banking and Insurance. 2004. "Ready, Set, Go! New Jersey Auto Insurance Reforms Are Moving Ahead." http://www.state.nj.us/dobi/pressreleases/040609report.pdf.

New Jersey Department of Banking and Insurance. "More Savings for New Jersey Drivers," May 18, 2005. http://www.newjersey.gov/dobi/pressreleases/pr050518.htm.

New Jersey Department of Banking and Insurance. "New Jersey Welcomes New Auto Insurance Company," October 12, 2006. http://www.state.nj.us/dobi/press releases/pr061012.htm.

Office of Consumer Affairs and Regulation. "The Massachusetts Automobile Insurance Study Group," 2007. http://www.mass.gov/Eoca/docs/autoinsurance report20070315.pdf.

Office of Insurance Regulation. *Assessments.* Tallahassee: Florida Office of Insurance Regulation, 2009. http://www.floir.com/Assessments.aspx.qq.

Office of Insurance Regulation. *Fast Facts.* Tallahassee: Florida Office of Insurance Regulation, 2009. http://www.floir.com/pdf/OIR_FastFacts_0508.pdf.

Ress, David. "Second Top Car Insurer Pulling Out." *The Star Ledger* (New Jersey), June 20, 2001, 1.

Roth, Alex, Dan Fitzpatrick, and Paulo Prada. "Florida Braces for Storm's Economic Blow." *Wall Street Journal,* August 19, 2008. http://online.wsj.com/article/SB1219 10444634651453.html?mod=googlewsj.

St. John, Paige. "Florida's Hurricane Catastrophe Is Fund in Jeopardy." *Herald Tribune,* February 7, 2009. http://www.theledger.com/article/20090207/NEWS/902070 346/1410?Title=Fla__s_Hurricane_Catastrophe_Is_Fund_in_Jeopardy.

Tennyson, Sharon, Mary A. Weiss, and Laureen Regan. "Automobile Insurance Regulation: The Massachusetts Experience." In *Deregulating Property-Liability Insurance: Restoring Competition and Increasing Market Efficiency,* edited by J. David Cummins. Washington, DC: Brookings–AEI Joint Center on Regulation, 2002. http://www.aei-brookings.org/publications/abstract.php?pid=221.

Treaster, Joseph. "Where Drivers Are Now Courted." *New York Times,* August 24, 2006. Retrieved July 2, 2009, from http://query.nytimes.com/gst/fullpage.html ?res=9806E5DB133EF937A1575BC0A9609C8B63.

"Workers' Comp Still on the Upward Track." *Portland Press Herald*, December 5, 1997. http://global.factiva.com/ha/default.aspx.

Worrall, John D. "Private Passenger Auto Insurance in New Jersey: A Three-Decade Advertisement for Reform." In *Deregulating Property-Liability Insurance: Restoring Competition and Increasing Market Efficiency*, edited by J. David Cummins. Washington, DC: Brookings–AEI Joint Center on Regulation, 2002. http:// www.aei-brookings.org/publications/abstract.php?pid=221.

Yelen, Suzanne. "Withdrawal Restrictions in the Automobile Insurance Market." *Yale Law Journal* 102 (1993): 1431–55.

4

The Effects of Credit-Based Insurance Scoring on Insurance Markets

Lawrence S. Powell

Insurance Pricing and Insurance Scoring

AN INSURANCE COMPANY facilitates risk pooling, reducing the uncertainty of individual pool members. Uncertainty decreases because the ultimate value of a group's losses is more predictable than the value of an individual's losses. Swiss mathematician Jacob Bernoulli first proved this phenomenon, known as the law of large numbers, around 1690. Relying on the law of large numbers, members of a risk pool can each pay the average or expected loss of the group, rather than paying for a much less predictable and potentially larger individual loss on their own.

Risk pooling is most effective when all members of the pool have the same distribution of expected loss. Insurance companies rely on risk classification systems to ensure that groups of insureds pay premiums commensurate with their exposures to risk. When insurers pool exposures with unequal expected losses, the low-risk group must subsidize the high-risk group. This creates an incentive for low-risk pool members to purchase less insurance than high-risk pool members, a scenario called adverse selection. Adverse selection can break down the risk-pooling mechanism and, in extreme cases, lead to insolvency of the pool. Furthermore, suppressing rates for high-risk insureds dampens their incentives to take care, increasing total losses.[1]

Insurance companies use information about insurance applicants to classify them into groups with very similar expected loss. Of course, no risk classification system is perfect. In addition to other restrictions, insurers can use rating information only if it is cost-effective, meaning the cost of obtaining the information is less than the difference in expected loss between groups.

For example, assume there are only two types of drivers, low-risk and high-risk. The low-risk group has expected loss of $500, and the high-risk group has expected loss of $700. If it costs more than $100 to classify a driver, it will be more cost-effective to simply pool the groups and charge both $600. However, if an insurer can identify low-risk drivers for, say, $20, it benefits the low-risk drivers to charge them $520, while charging the high-risk drivers $720. On the other hand, insurers can be more precise in risk classification if they hire private investigators to follow each driver for six months before offering an insurance policy. Obviously, this would cost more than $100 and raise privacy concerns. To generate enough money in the risk pool to cover expected losses, low-risk drivers would have to pay more than $600. In this case, there is no justification for such classification.

Insurers use many variables to classify drivers based on expected loss. These include, but are not limited to, geographic location, age, gender, marital status, miles driven, type of vehicle, use of vehicle, driving record, and insurance score. An insurance score is a numerical prediction of propensity for loss, which is estimated using certain information from a driver's credit history. The actuarial literature shows it is one of the most accurate and cost-effective loss predictors available.[2]

There are several apparent misconceptions about insurance scores. To understand why insurance scores are beneficial to insurance systems, it is important to start with an accurate description that is free of incorrect assumptions. The variables commonly used to estimate insurance scores include measures of performance on credit obligations, credit-seeking behavior, use of credit, length of credit history, and types of credit used.[3] They do not include income, wealth, race, ethnicity, or any other prohibited factor.

Insurance scores and credit scores are calculated using some of the same information, but they are not equivalent. The important difference is that credit scores use these variables (and others) to estimate the probability of a borrower defaulting on a financial obligation, while insurance scores estimate the probability of having insured losses.

An important fact often overlooked in the insurance scoring debate is that including insurance scores in an insurance rating model can result in higher premiums only if the sample population with lower scores has more insured losses. As I describe in more detail later, any deviation from using the most accurate, cost-effective predictors results in unfair outcomes and damage to the insurance mechanism.

One observed barrier to understanding insurance scoring is manifest in the common criticism that an intuitive link between insurance scores and driving ability does not exist. While several studies develop potential causal links between insurance scores and driving, it is perhaps more compelling to recognize an alternative relation. The use of insurance scores does not rely on a link between credit information and driving ability. Rather, it is a link between insurance scores and insured losses.

Many factors unrelated to driving ability can increase the likelihood of insured losses. For example, someone who always makes debt payments on time to avoid higher interest rates the next time they borrow may also choose not to file a small insurance claim to prevent future increases in insurance premiums. Insurance scores may also measure hazards other than lack of driving ability.

Predictive Accuracy of Insurance Scores

The correlation between driving outcomes and credit information appears in academic literature as early as 1949.[4] Over time, evidence of the empirical relation between automobile insurance losses and insurance scores has developed to address not only the simple correlation between insurance costs and insurance scores, but also the additional predictive power and accuracy insurance scores contribute to insurance pricing models containing traditional pricing variables. In this section, I review methods and results from several studies investigating the relation between insurance scores and insurance losses. The findings consistently and conclusively demonstrate that insurance scores are highly correlated with losses. The studies also show that insurance scores supply information about insurance losses not contained in other underwriting and rating variables.

More than a dozen studies related to insurance scoring have appeared in the public domain in the last decade. To improve the exposition of information, I present evidence from various studies in order of increasing complexity. This does not match the exact temporal order in which they were released.

Furthermore, many of these studies produce very similar evidence and reach nearly identical conclusions. I make an effort to report from the most recent and clearest studies.

The most basic result is the simple correlation between insurance scores and losses. A study conducted by the Texas Department of Insurance in 2004[5] firmly establishes the simple correlation between insurance scores and losses. Using data representing about 2 million insurance policies, the authors group exposure units by deciles of credit scores and graph the coinciding average loss frequency and loss amount.

Figure 4.1 shows that average loss per vehicle declines steadily across deciles of credit scores, based on data from the Texas Department of Insurance. Those with the lowest scores average about $360 per vehicle, while those with the highest scores average about $175 per vehicle. Similarly, Figure 4.2 shows number of claims per 1,000 exposures decreasing from about 110 for those with the lowest credit scores to just over 60 for those with the highest scores. These results are

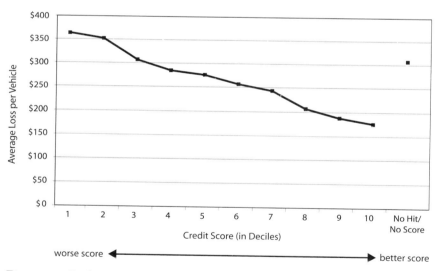

Figure 4.1. Credit Score and Average Loss per Vehicle: Personal Automobile Insurer Group F, Pure Premium vs Credit Score.

Note: Includes BI (bodily injury) and PD (property damage). Losses are capped at basic limits ($20,000/$40,000/$15,000).

Source: Texas Department of Insurance, "Use of Credit Information by Insurers in Texas" (report to the 79th Legislature, 2004), Chart 7.

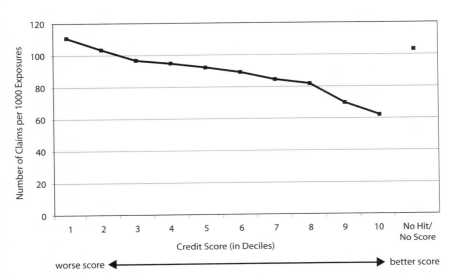

Figure 4.2. Figure 2. Credit Score and Number of Claims per 1000 Vehicles: Personal Automobile Insurer Group B, Claim Frequency vs Credit Score.

Note: Includes BI (bodily injury) and PD (property damage).

Source: Texas Department of Insurance, "Use of Credit Information by Insurers in Texas" (report to the 79th Legislature, 2004), Chart 9.

qualitatively similar across all of the companies reporting automobile insurance data for the study. Other studies reach similar conclusions using data from nationally representative samples,[6] rather than the single-state sample used by the Texas Department of Insurance.

Critics of these findings, including the Texas Department of Insurance itself, point out that simple correlation between a rating variable and losses is neither necessary nor sufficient to establish its validity as a predictor of losses. This is true because no variable alone can produce a more accurate prediction of losses than a combination of accurate predictors of losses. Therefore, in addition to simple linear correlation between predictors and losses, one must also consider the interactions among a group of predictor variables. To do so requires multivariate analysis.

Multivariate analysis, as the name implies, involves analysis of two or more predictor variables at the same time. EPIC Actuaries, the Federal Trade Commission (FTC), and a second study by the Texas Department of Insurance employ multivariate analysis to determine if insurance scores are risk related.[7] I summarize the analysis and primary findings of these studies below.

The Texas Department of Insurance[8] examines a large database of personal automobile and homeowners insurance policies in Texas. The authors performed multivariate analysis considering the interaction of insurance scores and several other common predictors of insurance losses. They find that the strong correlation between insurance scores and losses persists, even when controlling for other underwriting factors. The report concludes that "credit scoring provides insurers with additional predictive information, distinct from other rating variables, which an insurer can use to better classify and rate risks based on differences in claim experience." The authors also find that "use [of insurance scoring] is justified actuarially and it adds value to the insurance transaction."

Conducting a study for EPIC Actuaries, Miller and Smith examine a nationally representative sample of insurance scores, underwriting data, and policy outcomes (losses).[9] The study produces four primary findings. First, insurance scores are correlated with risk of loss, even after controlling for relationships with other variables. The correlation is due primarily to loss frequency rather than loss severity. Second, insurance scores are correlated with some other common risk factors; however, even after controlling for other factors, insurance scores significantly increase the accuracy of the risk assessment process. Third, insurance scores are very powerful predictors of loss relative to other common risk factors. Finally, results from the study apply generally to all states and regions.

The FTC also examines a large, nationally representative database to determine the relation between insurance scores and losses.[10] The study finds that "even when non-credit variables are included in the analysis, credit-based insurance scores continue to predict the amount that insurance companies are likely to pay out in claims to consumers." More specifically, they find insurance scores are effective predictors of risk under automobile policies. They are predictive of the number of claims consumers file and the total cost of those claims. The use of scores is therefore likely to make the price of insurance better match the risk of loss posed by the consumer. Thus, on average, higher-risk consumers will pay higher premiums, and lower-risk consumers will pay lower premiums.

These recent studies represent a spectrum of backgrounds and data sources. Private groups and government agencies conduct them; they represent single-state and national samples; they employ different measures and methodologies.

Nonetheless, they all reach the same general conclusion: Insurance scores are highly predictive of losses, even when controlling for other factors. As noted at the outset, insurers are unique in the U.S. economy, as they do not know the ultimate cost of their product when they sell it. Having a tool to more effectively predict losses helps insurers price their products more fairly, benefiting all consumers.

Effects of Insurance Scoring on Insurance Markets

Because insurance scoring is an accurate and inexpensive predictor of insured losses, it should lead to more fair and efficient outcomes in insurance markets. However, critics of insurance scoring claim it is detrimental to consumers. While several studies test the accuracy of insurance scoring, very little has been done to test its effects on insurance markets.

The FTC study briefly explores comparisons of states that allow insurance scoring to states that do not.[11] Unfortunately, results are inconclusive. Indeed, data problems, confounding events, and measurement error make testing such hypotheses difficult.

In this section, I expand the current literature by presenting evidence of market outcomes in relation to the use of insurance scoring. In doing so, I test two hypotheses regarding effects of insurance scoring on insurance markets. The first hypothesis is that scoring reduces the size of residual markets. The second hypothesis is that scoring does not increase the average cost of insurance. When considered in tandem, results from these two hypotheses provide clear evidence applicable to the most important effects insurance scoring could have on insurance markets.

Empirical Analysis

Prior studies struggle to estimate the extent to which insurance scoring was used to price insurance. For example, the FTC[12] assumes that insurance scoring entered the market around 1997 and uses a time trend to measure effects of scoring on various market measures. To mitigate this problem, I use market penetration of Progressive Insurance Company and its subsidiaries (Progressive) by state to proxy for the use of scoring. Progressive was the first insurance company to use insurance scoring in automobile insurance. The company's website (http://www.progressive.com/progressive-insurance/first.aspx) indicates Progressive began using insurance scores to price insurance in 1991. As Progressive gained market share with lower prices and higher profits, its competitors followed suit. Therefore, Progressive's market share by state is at least a decent proxy for the volume of insurance scoring taking place in the market, and certainly improves on the time trend method.

Figure 4.3 presents my analysis as a graph. Premium and loss data are collected from the National Association of Insurance Commissioners (NAIC) InfoPro database (1994–2004). The number of insured vehicles and the number of vehicles insured by a residual market mechanism are collected from *AIPSO Facts* (various years). Each number is calculated using state data summed to the national level.

The solid blue line represents market share of Progressive by premium volume. From 1994 until 2004, Progressive's market share grew from 2.1 percent to 7.7 percent. During the same time, the share of vehicles insured by residual market mechanisms (solid gray line) decreased from 4.0 percent to 1.4 percent. Thus, as the proxy for insurance scoring increases, the percentage of vehicles in

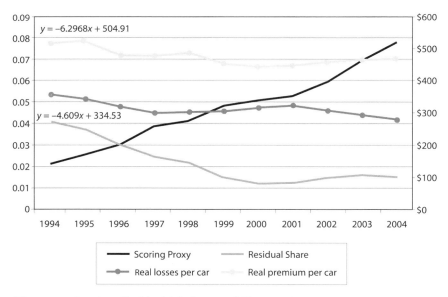

Figure 4.3. Scoring, Residual Markets, and Cost: 1994–2004.

the residual market exhibits a sharp decrease. This is consistent with the hypothesis that the improved accuracy from scoring allows the voluntary market to underwrite risks that were previously insured by residual market mechanisms.

The two dotted gray lines near the top of Figure 4.3 represent real premiums and real losses per car (in 2004 U.S. dollars) during the same period. The top line is premium per car. It decreases from $507 in 1994 to $462 in 2004. The straight line splitting this curve indicates the linear trend of these data. The equation ($y = -6.3x + 505$) is the mathematical representation of the trend. The coefficient estimate for x (−6.3) indicates that premium per insured vehicle decreased by an average of $6.30 per year. Similarly, losses per vehicle dropped from $354 to $281, with a slightly smaller linear trend of $4.61 per year.

It is important to note that this analysis does not prove conclusively that insurance scoring was the cause of either change in insurance markets. Other events certainly influenced residual markets, premiums, and losses. However, it is instructive to witness the increasing fairness achieved by reducing explicit cross-subsidies created by residual markets, as well as the decreasing cost of insurance while the use of credit scoring more than quadrupled in the market.

Appropriateness of Insurance Scores

Regulators require insurance rates to meet three criteria. They must not be inadequate, excessive, or unfairly discriminatory. A rating criterion is unfairly discriminatory if it does not bear a reasonable relationship to the expected loss and expense experience among insured exposures. Given the evidence presented here, insurance scores clearly meet the third criterion. However, some people remain uncomfortable with the application of credit information in insurance rating. In this section, I describe the individual and societal benefits of insurance scoring. Finally, I present evidence that competition in insurance markets prevents discrimination based on any factor other than expected losses.

Insurance scoring benefits society in several ways. All of the benefits accrue from improved efficiency and accuracy of risk estimates. The first benefit is that insurance scores provide a very high level of accuracy for a relatively small cost. Using insurance scores reduces cost for insurance companies. Because the market for insurance is competitive, this savings is passed through to consumers as lower premiums. Data from a recent report by the Arkansas Insurance

Department indicates that if insurance scoring were eliminated as a rating factor, nearly 91 percent of automobile and homeowners insurance consumers would incur a rate increase. Using a slightly different method, the FTC study estimates that insurance scoring results in a decrease in insurance premiums for 59 percent of drivers.[13]

The next benefit of insurance scoring is that improved accuracy may make insurers more willing to offer insurance to high-risk consumers for whom they would otherwise be unable to determine an appropriate premium.[14] For example, insurance scoring information can allow an insurer to offer coverage to drivers living in a geographic area with high traffic density at a price the driver can afford. Without information from insurance scores, insurers would not be able to differentiate sufficiently among these drivers. Therefore, they would not be able to offer the coverage at a lower price to lower-risk drivers living in the area. Consistent with this assertion, the FTC finds limited evidence that the advent of credit scoring in automobile insurance coincided with substantial decreases in residual market mechanisms.[15] This suggests insurers, with the benefit of credit information, are more willing to offer coverage to high-risk drivers (at a risk-based price) than they were before the introduction of insurance scores.

Another advantage of using insurance scores is that it improves accuracy of information used to classify drivers. In addition to calculating more accurate loss predictions, the scores themselves are less likely to contain material factual errors than several of the driving history variables used to underwrite insurance. Studies by Associated Credit Bureaus and TransUnion report material errors in credit information in only 0.2 percent of credit records.[16] In striking contrast, a study by the Insurance Research Council found public information available on only 40 percent of a sample of known automobile losses.[17] Under-reporting of traffic citations also appears problematic. IRC indicates less than a third of all traffic citations are accurately reported in state driving records.[18] Furthermore, consumers have a strong incentive to correct inaccurate credit information, whereas the opposite incentive exists for driving records, since recorded driving events can only be adverse events. Data describing instances in which drivers avoid collision by defensive driving and alertness are not collected.

The final benefit of insurance scoring is that because scoring produces more accurate loss estimates, it results in outcomes that are more equitable for individuals and society as a whole. As noted earlier, insurance scoring is likely to make the price of insurance more closely match the risk of loss posed by the consumer. Thus, on average, higher-risk consumers will pay higher premiums, and lower-risk consumers will pay lower premiums.[19] This addresses a very common problem in the insurance mechanism called cross-subsidization.

When insurers cannot accurately classify applicants for insurance, they must either decline applications or charge the same premium to high-risk and low-risk drivers. The latter case obviously leads to cross-subsidization—when low-risk drivers must overpay to make up for underpaying high-risk drivers. However, declining applications for insurance ultimately leads to the same outcome. This type of cross-subsidization is facilitated by residual markets for insurance.

Each state has a residual market mechanism to make insurance available to drivers whom the voluntary market will not cover. Residual market mechanisms effectively set a maximum price that insurers may charge for insurance. If insurers are not willing to offer coverage at this price, consumers may purchase coverage at this price from the residual market. However, if the premium is not enough to cover losses and expenses, insurers in the voluntary market must make up the deficit in proportion to their market shares. The FTC shows that as insurance scoring has become more common in ratemaking models, the populations of states' residual markets have decreased.[20] This suggests insurance scoring results in more equitable or fair outcomes compared to less accurate rating models that do not use insurance scores.

Another way to address the appropriateness of insurance scoring is to consider the level of competition occurring in insurance markets. If insurance markets are competitive, insurers will not be able to charge excessive or unfair prices. If an insurer tries to set prices based on anything other than expected losses and costs, it will either suffer substantial losses if the price is too low, or, if the price is too high, it will lose market share as its competitors offer a lower price to the same consumers.

Effective competition is a fundamental characteristic observed in U.S. insurance markets. Competition prevents insurers from charging excessive or unfair prices. For 2005, NAIC data show an average of 157 insurance companies underwriting the private passenger automobile cover in each state.[21] It is, therefore, reasonable to believe that an insurer cannot systematically overcharge a group of drivers because any one of the other 156 existing companies, or perhaps a new company, has an opportunity to cover that group of drivers at an equilibrium price.

While competitive markets are very effective at making the goods and services consumers want available to them, critics have voiced concerns that, when a drop in credit is unrelated to insurance risk, some individuals could be mistreated by insurance scoring. In response to such concerns, almost every state has regulations in place to recognize the benefits of insurance scoring while limiting its use in certain scenarios. It is worth noting that many insurers offered the same protections before the laws were enacted. This is another example of competitive markets creating an optimal outcome.

Conclusion

Setting reasonably accurate prices for insurance is a difficult task because insurers must establish prices without the benefit of knowing all of the costs involved. To offset this hardship, actuaries have developed complex pricing models using applied economic and statistical tools. While this complexity is necessary, it unfortunately leads to a lack of understanding among people who have not developed such specific expertise.

Insurance scoring is an often misunderstood example of a beneficial tool used in ratemaking. Insurance scores are relatively powerful and accurate predictors of losses, even when controlling for other factors known to be correlated with losses. When insurers use insurance scores to improve the accuracy of predicted losses, it benefits individuals and society. It increases the equity or fairness in insurance pricing outcomes because, on average, premiums are more closely related to consumers' risk of loss. Insurance scoring also adds value to insurance transactions. It reduces the overall cost of providing insurance because insurance scores are accurate and inexpensive rating variables.

Insurance scoring appears to have a beneficial effect on insurance markets. Empirical evidence suggests scoring improves availability in the voluntary market without increasing price. This prevents harmful cross-subsidies that lead to increased losses and inherently unfair redistribution of money from low-risk drivers to high-risk drivers. It is important to note that these results hold in both univariate and multivariate statistical tests.

Finally, the vigorous competition exhibited by the property and casualty insurance industry suggests that pricing of insurance based on anything other than expected losses is nearly impossible. Insurance markets show strong signs of effective competition, including a large number of suppliers and low barriers to entry.

References

Danzon, P., and S. E. Harrington. "Workers' Compensation Rate Regulation: How Price Controls Increase Costs." *Journal of Law and Economics* 44 (2001): 1–36.

Federal Trade Commission. *Credit-Based Insurance Scores: Impacts on Consumers of Automobile Insurance.* Report to Congress, 2007.

Insurance Research Council. "A Survey of Public Attitudes on Insurance Fraud, Workers' Compensation, Traffic Violations and Driver Improvement Courses, Financial Stability and Insolvency, and Other Insurance Topics." *Public Attitude Monitor,* October 1991.

Miller, M. J., and R. A. Smith. "The Relationship of Credit-Based Insurance Scores to Private Passenger Automobile Insurance Loss Propensity" (Actuarial study, EPIC Actuaries, LLC, 2003). http://www.epicactuaries.com.

Texas Department of Insurance. "Use of Credit Information by Insurers in Texas." Report to the 79th Legislature, 2004.

Tillman, W. A., and G. E. Hobbs. "The Accident-Prone Automobile Driver: A Study of the Psychiatric and Social Background." *The American Journal of Psychiatry* 106 (1949): 321–331.

5

Catastrophes and Performance in Property Insurance Markets

A Comparison of Personal and Commercial Lines

Patricia H. Born

Barbara Klimaszewski-Blettner

Introduction

HURRICANES KATRINA, RITA, AND WILMA made the year 2005 the most expensive year for property insurers since 1906, the year of the San Francisco earthquake. With total losses of $45 billion, Katrina alone claimed 7.5 percent of U.S. non-life premium volume. Rita and Wilma each caused another $10 billion in losses for the property insurance industry.[1] The natural disasters of 2005 cannot be seen as unusual outliers but reflect the continuing trend of increasing frequency and severity of losses from natural catastrophes during the last decades. Figure 5.1 shows the striking trend of an increasing number of such events worldwide.

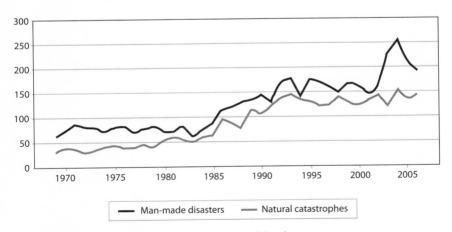

Figure 5.1. Number of catastrophic events worldwide, 1970–2007.

Source: Swiss Re (2008).

Catastrophic property risks pose a variety of problems for insurers, thus affecting the supply of insurance coverage for such perils. Limitations on the availability of coverage mainly result from insurability constraints, most notably the characteristic lack of independence between insured units and the serious loss potential of catastrophic risks.[2] Moreover, although insureds cannot directly influence loss probabilities, they may certainly affect loss size by deciding on loss prevention and mitigation measures such as investments in adequate building materials or protective dams in flood areas. So, there is potential for moral hazard if prevention efforts are not observable by insurers and/or if risk-dependent premiums do not reward loss prevention via an adequate premium reduction. Furthermore, the insurability of catastrophic risks is aggravated by the difficulty in predicting the probability of loss, compared to other "high frequency, low severity risks" (for example, auto accidents). Besides the fact that these are "low frequency, high severity, and strongly dependent" perils, increased construction activity in high-risk areas, climate change, and apparent cycles of storm activity complicate the determination of insurability of these risks.

Catastrophic events resulting in large unexpected property losses may induce insurers to take a variety of actions to stabilize their underwriting performance. Immediate attempts to control losses are limited to accurate appraisals of damage and investigation of possible fraud. But subsequent activities may include a re-evaluation of the portfolio of risks borne by the insurer, leading to changes in premiums, changes in coverage levels, exit from some markets, and perhaps entry into others.

The need for regulatory intervention in the property insurance market hinges on private insurers' ability to adapt to changes in the risks they choose to bear and, consequently, to meet the demand for coverage. Conversely, the ability of private insurers to adapt to changes in the underlying risk exposure is affected by the regulatory regimes in which they operate. The homeowners insurance market receives much more public policy attention than does the commercial property market; this differential treatment by regulators provides a natural experiment in which to evaluate and compare personal and commercial insurers' behavior in response to unanticipated events. In this project, we evaluate insurers' responses to unexpected catastrophic events over a long time period in an effort to discover the more successful private strategies for dealing with these risks.

Our empirical analysis addresses some fundamental aspects of how catastrophic events affect property insurance markets. We use information on losses incurred and premiums earned, by firm and by state, for all U.S. personal and commercial property insurers for the period 1984 to 2007. We supplement the data with information on state regulatory requirements and the incidence, by state, of natural catastrophes, as compiled from the Swiss Re Sigma reports. This comprehensive dataset enables us to analyze the effects of catastrophic events on insurance company performance and behavior in subsequent years.

We begin our analysis with an evaluation of the market structure, focusing on changes in the number of insurers and market concentration over the period of observation.[3] We consider two main segments of the property insurance market—the personal lines (homeowners) and the commercial lines (fire, allied lines, commercial multiperil)—and explore the extent to which insurers operate in one or both of these segments. Next, we shift our analysis to the performance and conduct of insurers in response to natural disasters.[4] Following Born and Viscusi,[5] we evaluate the role of *unanticipated* catastrophes (number of catastrophic events relative to the number *expected* based on previous years) as they affect the underwriting performance of property insurance markets. We suspect insurers operating in the personal lines will respond differently than those operating in commercial lines due to differences in the size of exposures, treatment under state regulation, and the nature in which contracts are negotiated.

Our paper proceeds as follows: In the next section, we provide an overview of the personal and commercial property insurance markets with a special focus on regulatory issues. Then we outline our data and the methodologies we apply to assess the differential performance of personal and commercial property insurers. We conclude with a discussion of our findings, implications for regulatory reform, and a motivation for further research.

Background

Insurance regulation has two main targets: financial performance and market conduct.[6] Financial regulation attempts to protect policyholders against the risk of financial distress or insolvency of the insurance company which endangers the fulfilment of the financial obligations toward the insured. The main goal of market regulation is to protect insurance consumers from unfair insurance prices, products, and trade practices. Efforts for solvency and market regulation are intended to protect insurance consumers, but often the goals of different regulatory activities may conflict. For example, affordability and availability issues aggravate solvency considerations if regulators suppress insurers' rate levels or impose other tying obligations, such as exit restrictions or policy renewal duties following catastrophic events. Florida, for example, has imposed severe pressure on the financial viability of its insurance markets by instituting restrictive rules for operating within the state. Following Hurricane Andrew, insurers were forbidden to raise premiums and reduce their insurance portfolio in coastal areas. After Hurricane Wilma, regulators imposed restrictions on cancelling or refusing to renew policies and imposed rules that compel insurers to exit all lines of business if they seek to exit a line subject to availability problems. Such regulatory actions, like premium limitations or exit restrictions, may cause severe market distortions, resulting in an inadequate supply of insurance coverage against catastrophic threats in the long run. The balancing of financial and market regulatory objectives, therefore, seems to be an important issue in catastrophe insurance.[7]

In discussing how to adequately prepare for catastrophic events, it is necessary to consider how binding regulatory constraints influence insurers' performance and their decisions with respect to supplying insurance and structuring their underwriting portfolios. We expect insurers to raise rates following catastrophes if such events indicate a higher rate of catastrophes in the future. Such increases are justified by an enhancement of the actuarial risk. If regulators, however, impose restrictions on premium adjustments aimed at guaranteeing the affordability of insurance coverage for consumers, insurers may instead choose to exit the market if rates are not adequate to maintain solvency. This, in turn, prompts regulators to impose exit restrictions or cancellation bans that force insurers to retain a larger amount of high-risk exposure than they might choose in the absence of such constraints.

Another regulatory response to ensuring the availability of insurance coverage is through residual market solutions offering insurance at affordable prices below competitive premiums. Such approaches can create severe market distortions and incentive-incompatible structures, resulting in further crowding out of private insurers who cannot compete with the cheap residual insurance products but are consequently penalized through an assessment for the losses of these insurance programs according to their market share.[8] Such chain reactions, whereby one regulatory intervention establishes the necessity of another, might not only influence insurers' underwriting performance but also expose insurance consumers and taxpayers to significant risk and assessments when catastrophes occur. We specifically address the former aspect in our empirical investigation.

In a recent study, Grace and Klein suggest that the most prominent and criticized policy is rate regulation.[9] They note that the homeowners insurance market is especially subject to stringent rate regulation, and although most state regulators do not attempt to impose severe price constraints, severe conflicts might occur if cost pressures compel insurers to raise prices while regulators do not allow insurers to risk-adjust premiums according to an increase in the faced risk exposure. If the market is competitive, such regulation should not be needed because insurers would be forced to compete at the premium that just allows a fair profit. A great deal of empirical research affirms that insurance markets are competitive.[10] Authorizing regulators to regulate rates invites political pressure and interference.[11] Although premium and policy regulations are to be favored from the insured's perspective at a first glance, such restrictions can force insurers to tighten their coverage offers if expected losses increase but premiums cannot be adjusted accordingly.

Unexpected catastrophic events should elicit similar responses by all property insurers to the extent that such events call for a change in underwriting policy. However, we might observe certain features of personal and commercial lines to intervene. A first important difference between personal and commercial insurance business lies in the underlying risk exposure. Commercial risks are usually smaller in number but bigger in size and more heterogeneous than personal ones (that is, typically many small homogeneous risks, such as homes and automobiles). As a higher number of insured risks normally corresponds with a smaller deviation between actual and estimated expected losses, premiums calculated on the basis of expected losses more often cover actual losses. Thus, we might expect homeowners insurers' underwriting performance (that is, their loss ratios) to be more stable. On the other hand, accumulation risk seems to be a bigger problem in the personal-lines insurance market, aggravating the balance within the portfolio and adversely affecting insurers' performance.

Another difference between the homeowners and commercial insurance business results from distinct levels of regulation intensity. Premiums, policy forms, and contract terms are more intensely regulated in the homeowners insurance context than among commercial property insurers. Regulators assert this is generally justified because the personal insured is less sophisticated in insurance matters than the commercial client, who is more likely to be a professional insurance consumer. However, rate regulation that constrains insurers from setting adequate rates may actually exacerbate losses, as consumers have less incentive to manage risk when rates cannot increase.[12]

On the other hand, especially large commercial consumers have more alternative risk-transfer mechanisms at their disposal if insurance premiums increase significantly. They are sometimes able to access alternative markets that allow them to transfer part of their risk to the capital markets (for example, by issuing catastrophe bonds) or form their own internal insurance companies by so-called captive solutions. This reduces incentives for large commercial clients to insist on regulatory premium limitations. In addition, the heterogeneity of risk exposure and coverage needs aggravates standard regulation of premiums and coverage terms.[13] Rejda discusses an obvious trend toward rate deregulation for commercial lines.[14] Our compilation of state statutes confirms Rejda's observation: Although there are some deregulation efforts in homeowners insurance markets, the commercial lines are less regulated, especially for large commercial risks. Our data on rate regulation in the U.S. property lines is provided in the Appendix.

Closely related to a differing degree of regulation are different habits in insurers' pricing and underwriting decisions. As a result of business clients' heterogeneous coverage needs, products are much less standardized in this insurance context. Especially large commercial clients negotiate both prices and coverage terms with their insurers (mostly with the help of brokers),[15] for example, *ex post* premium adjustments depending on the actual loss development at the end of the contract year. Thus, commercial underwriters are much more flexible in their underwriting conditions, which should lead to more risk-adjusted premiums in the commercial insurance context.[16] We examine this further in our empirical investigation.

Data

For our analysis we compiled an especially large and detailed dataset, starting with the annual statement data from the National Association of Insurance Commissioners (NAIC), which contains underwriting and financial information for all U.S. property insurers for the period 1984 to 2007. We consider two main segments of the property insurance market: personal (homeowners)[17] and commercial lines (fire, allied, and multiperil).[18] In particular, we use information on losses incurred and premiums earned by firm, by line, and by state over this twenty-three-year period. We supplement the data with information on state rate regulations and the incidence, by state, of natural catastrophes. Regulation data are obtained from state statutes. Catastrophic events are compiled from figures reported in the annual Swiss Re Sigma reports on catastrophic events, which are based on data from the Property Claims Service (PCS), a division of the Insurance Services Office (ISO). The PCS currently defines catastrophes as "events that cause $25 million or more in direct insured losses to property that affect a significant number of policyholders and insurers." This comprehensive dataset enables us to analyze the effects of catastrophic events over time on insurance company behavior and performance in subsequent years.

Figure 5.2 shows the number of catastrophes over our time period. To be consistent with our empirical approach, we account for these events on a state-by-state basis. Thus, for each catastrophic event noted in the Swiss Re reports,

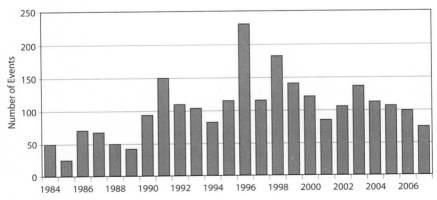

Figure 5.2. State-level catastrophic events, by year.
Source: Swiss Re Sigma Reports (1984–2007) and NAIC.

we may have multiple state-level events if the event spanned multiple states. In other words, an insurer that writes in two states that are hit by the same hurricane is assumed to have been hit by two separate catastrophes, each affecting losses in a particular state market. While the number of state-level events appears to have increased and then decreased through our sample, the data do not indicate whether these changes are necessarily due to changes in the number of catastrophes, changes in the scope of events, on average, across states, or both. Other data from Swiss Re, presented in Figure 5.1, show more distinctly that the number of such events worldwide has increased rather substantially since the mid 1980s.

Market Overview

We start our analysis with a short overview of the personal and commercial property insurance markets. The *structure* of the overall property market can be described by examining the number of insurers that focus on the personal lines segment, the commercial lines segment, or both. Figure 5.3 shows that a small

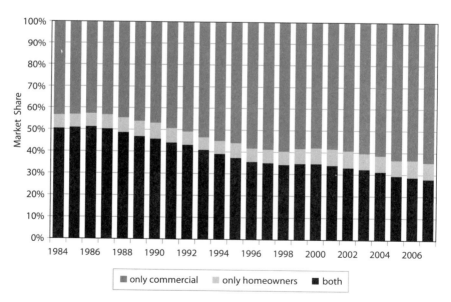

Figure 5.3. Distribution of all property insurers, by market segment focus. *Source:* NAIC annual statement data.

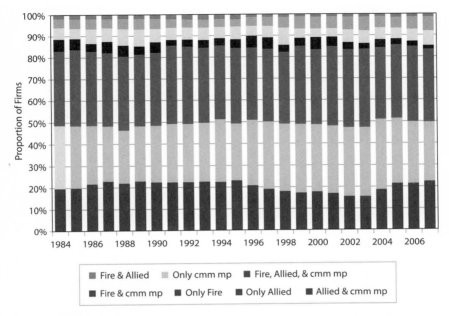

Figure 5.4. Distribution of commercial property insurers, by line combinations.
Source: NAIC annual statement data.

number of insurers write only homeowners insurance coverage, while many companies offer only commercial insurance or both lines of business. The figure shows that the proportion of insurers selling only commercial insurance grew during the period of observation. A possible reason for this is reduced regulatory requirements as well as more flexible underwriting conditions. Figure 5.4 shows the most common combinations of the different lines of commercial business for insurers writing only commercial insurance coverage. The most favored offer combinations are "fire & allied," "only commercial multiple peril," and "fire & allied & commercial multiple peril."

The number of insurers writing business in the different lines allows for a comparison of *market concentration* in each line for the period of observation. It can be seen in Figure 5.5 that market concentration, measured simply by the number of firms providing coverage, seems to be quite constant in commercial lines whereas there is a downside trend in the average number of insurers per state in the homeowners market supporting a trend toward consolidation. Furthermore, the average number of insurers offering homeowners coverage

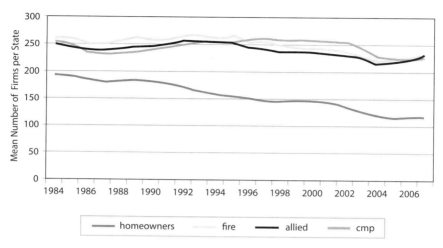

Figure 5.5. Average number of firms per state, 1984–2007.
Source: NAIC annual statement data.

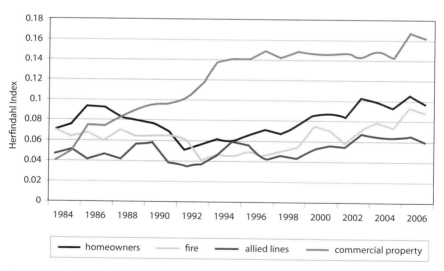

Figure 5.6. Line of business concentration, 1984–2007.
Source: NAIC annual statement data.

per state is substantially lower throughout the time period, which confirms a higher concentration in this market.

Increased concentration is also evident when the line of business concentration is calculated by market shares. Figure 5.6 presents the market concentration, measured by the Herfindahl Index, for each line of property business based on premiums written. We see that premium volume in the homeowners line is typically more concentrated than in the commercial lines, which corresponds to our previous observations.

We complete our market overview by examining the development of premiums written (as a measure for the volume of business) as well as total surplus of all U.S. property insurers over the period of observation. The data on premiums and surplus, shown in Figures 5.7 and 5.8, suggest substantial variation over time.[19] We will measure correlation of this variable with catastrophic events.

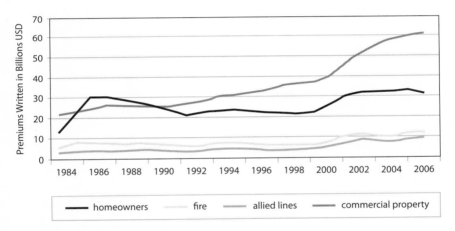

Figure 5.7. Total premiums written, by line, 1984–2007.

Source: NAIC annual statement data.

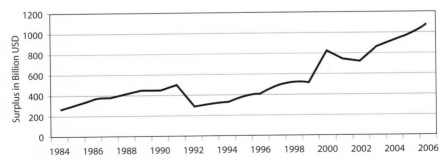

Figure 5.8. Total surplus of U.S. property insurers, 1984–2007.

Source: NAIC annual statement data.

The exact statistical impact of catastrophes on insurers' performance is examined with the help of regression analysis in the following parts of this report.

Empirical Analysis of Insurer Performance

We now turn to the performance and conduct of insurers in response to natural disasters, with a special focus on loss ratios, losses, and premiums, and then we provide some preliminary remarks on insurers' market exit and entry decisions. We expect short-run responses to catastrophes to include reduced total premiums[20] and increased exits from markets experiencing unanticipated events, although such reactions may be limited by state regulations. We suspect that insurers operating in personal lines will respond differently than those operating in commercial lines due to the reasons described previously. Homeowners insurers might not raise their premiums to the same extent as commercial ones because of a higher degree of rate regulation, whereas commercial insurers are more flexible regarding their premium (and coverage) design. Commercial premiums are more loosely regulated and sometimes result from unique negotiations between insurers, brokers, and firms. This flexibility may imply that commercial premiums are more risk-adequate than homeowners prices and might also lead to a greater reduction of policies written following unanticipated catastrophic events if these insurers have greater flexibility in avoiding the underwriting risk (for example, via exit). Altogether, the consequence should actually be lower commercial loss ratios following catastrophic events.

We start our analysis with a series of regressions to assess the relationship between catastrophic events and three measures of underwriting performance: loss ratios, losses incurred, and premiums earned. The sample characteristics of these and the other variables included in our regressions are shown in Table 5.1. As hurricanes in Florida and tornadoes in the Midwest should not take insurance companies entirely by surprise, we calculate an *unexpected catastrophes* variable that comprises the actual number of catastrophic events per state minus the average number of catastrophic events, by state, for the prior four years as a measure for the expected number of events.[21] From our calculation, insurers through this sample period faced an average of just 0.086 unexpected events each year across all states, but the value ranges from −6.667 to 7.667.[22]

Table 5.1. Sample statistics, 1984–2007 (N=429.692)

Variable		Mean	Std. Dev.
Panel A. Line of Business Comparison			
Total Premiums Written	Fire	318,503.10	2,216,548.00
	Allied Lines	226,720.90	1,484,221.00
	Commercial MP	1,259,419.00	5,789,978.00
	Homeowners	1,730,053.00	16,434,250.00
Panel B. Firm Characteristics			
Total Assets		1,200,000,000.00	3,410,000,000.00
Total Surplus		369,000,000.00	1,120,000,000.00
Organizational Form (Omitted: Stock)	Mutual	0.136	0.343
	Reciprocal	0.022	0.146
	Lloyds	0.004	0.067
Unexpected Catastrophic Events		0.086	2.000
Number of States in Which Insurer Operates		35.515	16.506
Total Property Premiums Earned		3,425,918.00	19,600,000.00
Total Property Losses Incurred		2,157,646.00	17,700,000.00
Loss Ratio on All Property Business		0.789	1.362

Source: NAIC annual statement data.

We include *interactions* of this variable with dummies for firms writing only homeowners, only commercial, or both kinds of coverage so that we can compare the effects of catastrophes across the different types of insurers. Specifically, these terms allow us to analyze the impact of unexpected catastrophes on the dependent variable, given the firm is writing only homeowners, only commercial, or both types of coverage.

We claim that the main reason for differences in the intensity of responses to catastrophic events across personal and commercial insurers is due to their different regulatory environments. Thus, we also test if rate regulation has a significant impact on insurers' underwriting performance. To control for distinct regulatory environments, we therefore include a dummy variable for *restrictive rate regulation* as a proxy for regulatory intensity in a certain state. If a state's premiums are subject to prior approval, we refer to this as restrictive rate regulation. In these states, firms must obtain prior approval before using or changing their insurance rates. As we especially want to test whether insurers respond differently to catastrophes if they are constrained by strict rate regulation, we add *variables capturing possible interactive effects* of the regulatory regime with the effect of the unexpected catastrophe variable. We also lag these interactions one and two years, so that we may assess a possible lingering influence of above-average catastrophic events.

Finally, we include in our analysis several variables to control for other factors affecting insurers' underwriting. In particular, we add three variables that reflect the overall size of the insurance companies' operations. The national measures are the *number of states* in which the insurer operates[23] and the *total national premiums* written by the insurance company in all lines of insurance. We also include *total premiums in state in all lines of insurance* as a measure of the scale of the firm's operations within the state. We expect smaller firms to be more susceptible to shocks than larger firms, and we anticipate that firms with a substantial presence in the state will be more reluctant to substantially reduce their volume of business (or leave the state) after a catastrophic event because of the losses associated with other lines.[24]

Analysis of Loss Ratios

We start with a regression of the natural logarithm of loss ratios on the set of explanatory variables described above. In general, unexpected catastrophes should increase firms' *loss ratios* in the year of the catastrophic event(s). Given potential lags in the ability to increase rates for subsequent years due to the delay in receiving accurate loss information and any restrictive rate filing rules, this effect may linger for one or more years following the event(s). If commercial lines insurers are less regulated and thus more flexible regarding their premium design, such that premiums reflect more precisely the actuarial risk compared to homeowners lines, we expect that this positive effect on loss ratios would be less intense among commercial insurers. For firm i in state s at year t, we estimate:

$$Ln(loss\_ratio)_{ist} = \alpha_1 + \beta_1 UnexpCat_{ist} + \beta_2 UnexpCat_{is,t-1}$$

$$+ \beta_3 UnexpCat_{i,s,t-2} + \beta_4(cm\_only*UnexpCat_{ist})$$

$$+ \beta_5(both*UnexpCat_{ist}) + \beta_6(cm\_only*UnexpCat_{i,s,t-1})$$

$$+ \beta_7(both*UnexpCat_{is,t-1}) + \beta_8(cm\_only*UnexpCat_{is,t-2})$$

$$+ \beta_9(both*UnexpCat_{i,s,t-2}) + \beta_{10} RateReg_{st}$$

$$+ \beta_{11}(UnexpCat_{ist}*RateReg_{st}) + \beta_{12}(UnexpCat_{i,s,t-1}*RateReg_{s,t-1})$$

$$+ \beta_{13}(UnexpCat_{i,s,t-2}*RateReg_{s,t-2}) + \beta_{14} LnPrems_{is,t-1} + \beta_{15} LnNumsts_{ist} +$$

$$\beta_{16} LnStatePrems_{ist} + \beta_{17} LnNatPrems_{ist} + \sum_{j=1}^{23} \delta_j Y_j + \sum_{i=1}^{n} \eta_i F_i + \varepsilon_{ist} \qquad (1)$$

Where Y_j are dummy variables for each year, j = 1989–2007 and F_i are dummy variables for each firm included to capture firm-specific effects.[25]

Our hypotheses regarding insurers' loss ratios are the following:

Hypothesis (1): Unexpected catastrophic events lead to an increase in loss ratios.

Hypothesis (2): This effect is less intense among commercial insurers compared to insurers writing only homeowners insurance (due to different regulatory constraints and underwriting flexibility).

Hypothesis (3): Loss ratios are higher if insurers operate in a strict rate regulation regime, especially following unexpected catastrophic events.

The results from estimating equation (1) are shown in Table 5.2. First, unexpected catastrophic events lead to an increase in the contemporaneous loss ratios, which confirms Hypothesis (1). The results suggest that, all else being equal, an increase by one in the number of unexpected catastrophic events corresponds to a 6.5 percent increase in insurers' loss ratios (on average). Next, we find that the response among commercial insurers is lower than that for insurers writing only homeowners insurance. The results show the expected positive effect of the current value of the unexpected catastrophe variable, but the coefficient on the first interaction term (firm writes only commercial property) is negative. In other words, for commercial insurers, an increase by one in the number of unexpected catastrophic events corresponds on average with a 2.4 percent increase in the loss ratio, compared to the 6.5 percent increase experienced by firms writing only homeowners insurance. Thus, loss ratios for commercial insurers seem to increase less intensely than those for homeowners insurers, which supports Hypothesis (2) and fits with our theory that commercial insurers are more risk-adequate in their underwriting decisions.

The significantly positive coefficient on the *strict rate regulation* variable confirms Hypothesis (3), postulating that loss ratios are higher if insurers operate in a strict rate-regulation regime. The interaction terms for unexpected catastrophes and strict premium regulation in equation (1) allow us to compare the impact of regulation on insurers' performance following catastrophic events. The results indicate that in years when unexpected catastrophic events strike (and even two years after), the loss ratios of insurers are significantly higher if they operate in a strict rate regulation regime.[26] This also confirms Hypothesis (3) and suggests that restrictive premium regulation might aggravate risk-adequate underwriting behavior, with the consequence of higher loss ratios. These results support our assumption that differing regulatory regimes among personal and commercial insurers might be a sound reason for differences in insurers' performance following catastrophic events.

Interestingly, the results do not indicate much of a lingering effect of unexpected catastrophes. The previous year's unanticipated events have a significant positive effect on current year loss ratios, but the effect is quite small compared to that of the current year events, and the lagged line of business interactions reveal no significant effect across the types of insurers. Given the especially random nature of catastrophic events, this result is not surprising. Furthermore, if the number of such events is increasing over time, we expect insurers to make premium adjustments in order to provide sufficient coverage in case of future disasters. We explore the potential for any lingering effect on premiums and losses later and simply note here that two years after the unexpected catastrophe, there appears to be no statistically significant evidence of any effect on loss ratios.

We can also derive some conclusions regarding diversification and economies of scale from the regression: The number of states in which an insurer operates can be interpreted as a measure of geographical diversification. Our results indicate that loss ratios decrease as the number of states in which insurers write business increases. Similarly, we can confirm our hypothesis that larger firms should be less susceptible to shocks than smaller firms, as higher

Table 5.2. Regression Results for Insurer Loss Ratios

Explanatory Variable	Coefficient (Standard Error)
Unexpected Catastrophic Events$_t$	0.065***
	(0.005)
Unexpected Catastrophic Events$_{t-1}$	0.015***
	(0.005)
Unexpected Catastrophic Events$_{t-2}$	0.000
	(0.005)
UnexpCat$_t$ * (Insurer writes commercial lines only)	−0.041***
	(0.006)
UnexpCat$_t$ * (Insurer writes both homeowners & commercial lines)	−0.023***
	(0.006)
UnexpCat$_{t-1}$ * (Insurer writes commercial lines only)	−0.005
	(0.006)
UnexpCat$_{t-1}$ * (Insurer writes both homeowners & commercial lines)	0.005
	(0.006)
UnexpCat$_{t-2}$ * (Insurer writes commercial lines only)	−0.003
	(0.006)
UnexpCat$_{t-2}$ * (Insurer writes both homeowners & commercial lines)	−0.001
	(0.006)
Strict Rate Regulation$_t$	0.091***
	(0.016)
UnexpCat$_t$ * strict rate regulation$_t$	0.017***
	(0.003)
UnexpCat$_{t-1}$ * strict rate regulation$_{t-1}$	−0.008***
	(0.003)
UnexpCat$_{t-2}$ * strict rate regulation$_{t-2}$	0.011***
	(0.003)
Ln(number of states in which the insurer writes property coverage)	−0.261***
	(0.013)
Ln(insurer's total premiums in state)	−0.085***
	(0.004)
Ln(firm's total premiums in U.S.)	−0.067***
	(0.006)
Intercept	2.603***
	(0.093)
Adjusted R^2	0.021

Note: Regression includes year and firm fixed effects, not shown.

*, **, and *** denote significance at the 90 percent, 95 percent and 99 percent level, two-tailed test.

total premiums written on state and national levels are associated with lower empirical loss ratios.

Analysis of Losses Incurred

We now turn to the separate analysis of losses and premiums to better understand the changes in property markets following catastrophic events. Controlling for the scale of the insurer's operations by including the total premium volume on the righthand side of the equation, unexpected catastrophes should clearly boost the contemporaneous losses incurred by the insurance company. Table 5.3 shows the results of estimating the following equation:

$$
\begin{aligned}
Ln(Losses\_inc)_{ist} = {} & \alpha_1 + \beta_1 UnexpCat_{ist} + \beta_2 UnexpCat_{is,t-1} \\
& + \beta_3 UnexpCat_{is,t-2} + \beta_4(cm\_only*UnexpCat_{ist}) \\
& + \beta_5(both*UnexpCat_{ist}) + \beta_6(cm\_only*UnexpCat_{is,t-1}) \\
& + \beta_7(both*UnexpCat_{is,t-1}) + \beta_8(cm\_only*UnexpCat_{is,t-2}) \\
& + \beta_9(both*UnexpCat_{is,t-2}) + \beta_{10} RateReg_{st} \\
& + \beta_{11}(UnexpCat_{ist}*RateReg_{st}) + \beta_{12}(UnexpCat_{is,t-1}*RateReg_{s,t-1}) \\
& + \beta_{13}(UnexpCat_{is,t-2}*RateReg_{s,t-2}) + \beta_{14} LnPrems_{is,t-1} + \beta_{15} LnNumsts_{ist} \\
& + \beta_{16} LnStatePrems_{ist} + \beta_{17} LnNatPrems_{ist} + \sum_{j=1}^{23}\delta_j Y_j + \sum_{i=1}^{n}\eta_i F_i + \varepsilon_{ist}
\end{aligned}
\tag{2}
$$

Our hypotheses regarding insurers' losses are the following:

Hypothesis (4): Unexpected catastrophic events boost the losses incurred by the insurers.

Hypothesis (5): Controlling for the firm's premium volume, this effect is less intense among commercial insurers compared to insurers writing only homeowners (due to more flexible/risk-adequate underwriting).

Hypothesis (6): Controlling for the firm's premium volume, losses of insurers increase even more in a strict rate regulation regime, especially following catastrophes.

We can conclude from the regression of losses incurred that both homeowners' and commercial insurers' losses are higher in the years with positive unexpected catastrophic events. This confirms Hypothesis (4). An increase by one in unexpected catastrophic events results on average in a 6.2 percent increase in losses for the homeowners insurers and about a 2.4 percent increase for commercial insurers, all else being equal. The lower increase of commercial insurers' losses supports Hypothesis (5). Besides the argument of differences in the regulation intensity among the different insurer types, these different intense reactions might also be explained by a higher accumulation risk or portfolio issues in the homeowners market. But since we control for total premium volume in our regression, such effects should be captured otherwise. As in the results for the loss ratio equation (above), previous years' unexpected catastrophes do not have a consistent effect on current year losses, although the significant effects are all positive.[27]

The results also confirm Hypothesis (6), that—controlling for total premium volume—the losses of insurers operating in a strict rate-regulation regime seem to be more affected by catastrophic events, which supporting our theory that strict rate regulation matters to insurers' performance and allowing us to draw the conclusion that differences in the intensity of personal and commercial lines insurers' reactions might at least partly be explained by differences in the way they are regulated.

Analysis of Premiums Earned

The results so far fit our theory quite well. Finally, we investigate the relationship between unexpected catastrophic events and premiums earned. Specifically, we estimate the following equation:

$$Ln(Prems\_earned)_{ist} = \alpha_1 + \beta_1 UnexpCat_{ist} + \beta_2 UnexpCat_{is,t-1}$$

$$+ \beta_3 UnexpCat_{i,s,t-2} + \beta_4(cm\_only * UnexpCat_{ist})$$

$$+ \beta_5(both * UnexpCat_{ist}) + \beta_6(cm\_only * UnexpCat_{i,s,t-1})$$

$$+ \beta_7(both * UnexpCat_{is,t-1}) + \beta_8(cm\_only * UnexpCat_{is,t-2})$$

$$+ \beta_9(both * UnexpCat_{i,s,t-2}) + \beta_{10} RateReg_{st}$$

$$+ \beta_{11}(UnexpCat_{ist} * RateReg_{st}) + \beta_{12}(UnexpCat_{i,s,t-1} * RateReg_{s,t-1})$$

$$+ \beta_{13}(UnexpCat_{i,s,t-2} * RateReg_{s,t-2}) + \beta_{14} LnPrems_{is,t-1} + \beta_{15} LnNumsts_{ist}$$

$$+ \beta_{16} LnStatePrems_{is,t-1} + \beta_{17} LnNatPrems_{ist} + \sum_{j=1}^{23} \delta_j Y_j + \sum_{i=1}^{n} \eta_i F_i + \varepsilon_{ist} \qquad (3)$$

Table 5.3. Regression results for insurer losses

Explanatory Variable	Coefficient (Standard Error)
Unexpected Catastrophic Events$_t$	0.062***
	(0.005)
Unexpected Catastrophic Events$_{t-1}$	0.013**
	(0.005)
Unexpected Catastrophic Events$_{t-2}$	−0.003
	(0.005)
UnexpCat$_t$* (Insurer writes commercial lines only)	−0.038***
	(0.005)
UnexpCat$_t$* (Insurer writes both homeowners & commercial lines)	−0.019***
	(0.005)
UnexpCat$_{t-1}$* (Insurer writes commercial lines only)	−0.002
	(0.005)
UnexpCat$_{t-1}$* (Insurer writes both homeowners & commercial lines)	0.007
	(0.005)
UnexpCat$_{t-2}$* (Insurer writes commercial lines only)	0.001
	(0.005)
UnexpCat$_{t-2}$* (Insurer writes both homeowners & commercial lines)	0.003
	(0.005)
Strict Rate Regulation$_t$	0.070***
	(0.015)
UnexpCat$_t$* strict rate regulation$_t$	0.016***
	(0.003)
UnexpCat$_{t-1}$* strict rate regulation$_{t-1}$	−0.007**
	(0.003)
UnexpCat$_{t-2}$* strict rate regulation$_{t-2}$	0.010***
	(0.003)
Ln(premiums earned)$_{ist}$	0.806***
	(0.003)
Ln(number of states in which the insurer writes property coverage)	−0.092***
	(0.013)
Ln(insurer's total premiums in state)	0.080***
	(0.004)
Ln(firm's total premiums in U.S.)	−0.041***
	(0.006)
Intercept	1.669***
	(0.092)
Adjusted R^2	0.380

Note: Regression includes year and firm fixed effects, not shown.
*, **, and *** denote significance at the 90 percent, 95 percent, and 99 percent level, two-tailed test.

Our hypotheses regarding insurers' premiums are the following:

Hypothesis (7): Insurers increase premiums and/or reduce their exposure following unexpected catastrophic events.

Hypothesis (8): Commercial insurers increase premiums more than homeowners insurers and also reduce their business more intensely (due to different regulatory constraints and underwriting flexibility).

Hypothesis (9): Strict rate regulation has a negative impact on total premiums written by insurers.

The results of estimating equation (3) are shown in Table 5.4. In this equation, we include the lagged value of premiums earned in order to capture any autoregressive character to insurance underwriting, as firms that write a large number of premiums in the state in a given year will tend to continue to do so in subsequent years.

We do not expect that current catastrophic events will have an influence on contemporaneous premiums, since such events occur in the aftermath of the establishment of premiums. However, we are curious to determine any lingering effect of these events on premiums in subsequent years. We would expect firms to increase premiums following catastrophes if insurers anticipate a higher rate of catastrophes to continue. Thus, for any given number of policies written, the total premiums should rise. On the other hand, major catastrophes may also reduce the quantity of insurance business because of higher rates, insurance rationing, and the exit of firms from the state.

What we see in our results is therefore a combination of two issues: increases in the price of coverage and reductions in the volume of insurance provided. To the extent that these effects balance out, we might not observe a significant relationship between past events and premiums. However, we do get a significant result for the two years lagged unexpected catastrophe variable. The coefficient allows us to make a statement on the combined effects described in Hypothesis (7): The significant positive relation might be the result of rising premiums following catastrophic events dominating the opposite effect of a possible reduction of the quantity of insurance written, and also the consequence of a rising number of firms offering additional coverage being attracted by the usually growing demand for insurance in the immediate aftermath of catastrophic events.[28]

Table 5.4. Regression results for insurer premiums

Explanatory Variable	Coefficient (Standard Error)
Unexpected Catastrophic Events$_t$	−0.001
	(0.003)
Unexpected Catastrophic Events$_{t-1}$	0.002
	(0.003)
Unexpected Catastrophic Events$_{t-2}$	0.005*
	(0.003)
UnexpCat$_t$* (Insurer writes commercial lines only)	0.002
	(0.003)
UnexpCat$_t$* (Insurer writes both homeowners & commercial lines)	0.000
	(0.003)
UnexpCat$_{t-1}$* (Insurer writes commercial lines only)	−0.003
	(0.003)
UnexpCat$_{t-1}$* (Insurer writes both homeowners & commercial lines)	−0.001
	(0.003)
UnexpCat$_{t-2}$* (Insurer writes commercial lines only)	−0.002
	(0.003)
UnexpCat$_{t-2}$* (Insurer writes both homeowners & commercial lines)	−0.006*
	(0.003)
Strict Rate Regulation$_t$	−0.008
	(0.008)
UnexpCat$_t$* strict rate regulation$_t$	−0.002
	(0.002)
UnexpCat$_{t-1}$* strict rate regulation$_{t-1}$	0.001
	(0.002)
UnexpCat$_{t-2}$* strict rate regulation$_{t-2}$	−0.001
	(0.002)
Ln(Premiums earned)$_{t-1}$	0.627***
	(0.001)
Ln(number of states in which the insurer writes property coverage)	0.329***
	(0.007)
Ln(insurer's total premiums in state)	0.413***
	(0.002)
Ln(firm's total premiums in U.S.)	0.048***
	(0.003)
Intercept	−3.339***
	(0.047)
Adjusted R^2	0.675

Regression includes year and firm fixed effects, not shown.
*, **, and *** denote significance at the 90 percent, 95 percent and 99 percent level, two-tailed test.

If we look at the lagged unexpected catastrophe variables for commercial lines insurers, we can see that the effect of catastrophes on total premiums seems to be changed. The issue of insurers reducing their business following catastrophes appears to be dominant in the commercial insurance context. Besides simply reducing their coverage offers, insurers might also decide to leave the market. Homeowners insurers might not be able to do that to the same extent because of regulatory constraints forcing them to renew policies and forbidding them to cancel contracts as well as compelling them to exit all lines of business if they decide not to offer homeowners insurance. Unfortunately, the results for the insurer-type interactions are not statistically significant, so we cannot draw general valid conclusions regarding these issues and therefore cannot confirm or reject Hypothesis (8).

Furthermore, insurers' total premium volume seems to be negatively influenced by a strict premium regulatory environment, especially following catastrophic events, supporting Hypothesis (9). The reasons for a reduced total premium volume might be a reduced total coverage offer by insurers combined with a restricted ability to adjust prices as a result of regulatory constraints. But since these results do not come in statistically significant, we are not allowed to make a general empirical statement.

Market Structure Following Unexpected Catastrophic Events

Our previous analysis documents the effects of unexpected catastrophic events on insurers' losses and loss ratios but does not clearly explain insurance companies' responses. The regression results for loss ratios suggest that insurers adjust their premiums following catastrophic events, especially if they are not constrained by restrictive rate regulation: While unexpected catastrophes increase insurance companies' loss ratios during the year when the catastrophe strikes, the boosting effect does not hold to the same extent for one and two years later. This may be the result of lower losses in these years, but it might also be evidence that insurers increase premiums in anticipation of a new expected exposure to catastrophic events. The results of the premium regression also imply an adjustment of insurers' premiums following catastrophes.

Nevertheless, we are not able to separate price and quantity effects in our data and therefore cannot make general conclusions on insurers' actual responses.

In order to comment on the availability and affordability of property insurance coverage, we might therefore have to consider whether, and to what extent, these events affect the structure of state property insurance markets. Our preliminary analysis suggests that opportunities to obtain affordable property coverage may have changed significantly over the considered time period. In particular, Figure 5.6 shows that market concentration increased greatly in the homeowners property line relative to that of the commercial lines. This higher market concentration might be a consequence of a trend towards insurer consolidations, but may also result from insurers exiting from the homeowners property insurance market. The correlation between increasing market concentration, market exits, and catastrophic events is a subject for further work.

With the goal of improving the market of insurance for catastrophic risks, current public policy is largely focused on creating reinsurance mechanisms and various methods of securitizing catastrophe risk. Also, we note that some states are experimenting with measures to encourage private insurers to enter their

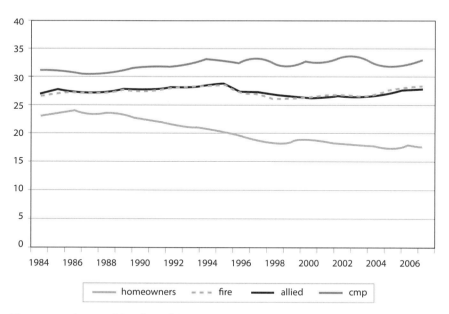

Figure 5.9. Average Number of States Per Firm, 1984–2007.
Source: NAIC annual statement data.

markets.[29] If regulatory requirements are impacting insurers' ability to diversify geographically, regulatory reform aimed at reducing the duplication of licensing and reporting activities might be given more consideration. For example, allowing insurers to opt for a federal charter could greatly reduce these barriers to diversification.[30] As shown in Figure 5.9, our preliminary analysis indicates that the average number of states in which an insurer operates has slightly increased for the commercial lines but has declined for the homeowners line. This is preliminary proof that diversification may be easier for commercial lines due to less binding regulatory requirements, and we use this as our primary motivation for exploring constraints on geographic diversification in our future research.

Conclusion

In the aftermath of several years of large catastrophic losses, it is not surprising that property insurance issues remain at the top of public policy agendas in Washington and in many states. The importance of achieving consensus on how best to prepare for the "next big one" is elevated even more with the spate of failures in the financial services industry in general. Surely, the ability to absorb large losses is only more dubious and calls for increased attention. Regulatory intervention, however, might entail a loosening of those regulations that may have distorted incentives for insurers to develop effective private solutions.

In this report, we highlight changes in the U.S. property insurance industry over the past twenty-three years. We show trends in the number and types of firms providing property coverage and assess changes in the market structure that might have important implications for the availability and affordability of coverage. More important, our analysis establishes a significant difference in the way that personal and commercial insurers respond in the aftermath of unexpected catastrophes. We show that such events have a stronger boosting effect on losses and loss ratios of homeowners insurers, which should be a consequence mainly of distinct regulatory treatment. We also provide evidence that rate-filing restrictions on insurers constrain their ability to maintain underwriting profitability following catastrophic events. The regression results suggest that restrictive premium regulation aggravates risk-adequate underwriting behavior resulting in higher loss ratios, which supports the necessity and importance of further deregulation in this context. The relatively smooth operation of less intensely regulated commercial lines insurers over our sample period suggests that successful strategies for responding to catastrophic events may call for less, not more, regulation of insurer activities. Deregulation of insurance prices would be a first step to improve the efficiency of insurance markets, enabling insurers to deal with mega-catastrophes.

In the discussion about alternative regulatory systems, there are a number of possible ways to restructure and improve efficiency and competition while at the same time enhancing consumer protections. Feldhaus and Klein discuss various suggestions for the commercial market: "We recommend not deregulation *per se,* but a shift in regulatory emphasis from review and approval of rates and forms and other restrictions, to increased emphasis on market monitoring and strategic intervention only when necessary."[31] By reviewing state statutes, we observed a trend toward deregulation, but further changes may be warranted. Options such as a reform of residual market solutions should be top priorities on the regulatory agenda, with emphasis on allowing market forces to operate more freely in responding to insurance needs and avoiding severe incentive conflicts that endanger successful private solutions for dealing with catastrophic events.[32] "Regulatory chain reactions," noted earlier as the phenomenon in which one regulatory intervention induces the necessity of another, might not only influence insurers' underwriting performance, but also expose insurance consumers and taxpayers to significant risk and assessments when catastrophes occur. If regulators attempt to solve availability and affordability issues by suppressing rates or imposing tying obligations, such as exit restrictions or policy renewal duties, following catastrophic events they may exacerbate the problem in the long run.

More freedom in underwriting, which results in more accurate risk adjustment, can of course aggravate goals for achieving more universal coverage for property risks. Some insureds in high-risk areas may simply not be able to afford the price of coverage and cannot be expected to move or invest in other loss-control mechanisms. A possible solution might be direct state subsidization of these premiums for low-income people. This way of subsidizing premiums seems preferable to artificially low and thus indirectly subsidized premiums, as this allows market forces to continue to work.[33] However, incentive-incompatible subsidization of premiums—for example, for new buildings in high-risk areas—has to be strictly avoided in order to prevent people from building new houses in these areas and externalizing a portion of the risk.

While our study is limited to an analysis of readily observable responses to catastrophic events, that is, insurers' underwriting performance, we propose that further investigation into the actual responses of commercial and personal property insurers (for example, insurers' decisions to exit the market or enter into others) will yield important insight for the discussion on regulatory reform in the property insurance lines.

References

Berliner, Baruch. *Limits of Insurability of Risks.* Englewood Cliffs, NJ: Prentice Hall, 1982.

Born, Patricia H., William Gentry, W. Kip Viscusi, and Richard Zeckhauser. "Organizational Form and Insurance Company Performance: Stocks vs. Mutuals." In *The Economics of Property-Casualty Insurance,* edited by David F. Bradford, 167–192. Chicago: The University of Chicago Press, 1998.

Born, Patricia H. and W. Kip Viscusi. "The Catastrophic Effects of Natural Disasters on Insurance Markets," *Journal of Risk and Uncertainty* 33 (2006): 55–72.

Coomber, John R. "Natural and Large Catastrophes—Changing Risk Characteristics and Challenges for the Insurance Industry." *The Geneva Papers* 31 (2006): 88–95.

Cummins, J. David. "Reinsurance for Natural and Man-Made Catastrophes in the United States: Current State of the Market and Regulatory Reforms." *Risk Management and Insurance Review* 10 (2007): 179–220.

Feldhaus, William R., and Robert W. Klein. "The Regulation of Commercial Insurance: Initial Evaluation and Recommendations" (working paper, Center for Risk Management and Insurance Research, Georgia State University, 1997).

Grace, Martin F., and Robert W. Klein. "After the Storms: Property Insurance Markets in Florida" (working paper, Center for Risk Management & Insurance Research, Georgia State University, 2006).

Grace, Martin F., and Robert W. Klein. "Efficiency Implications of Alternative Regulatory Structures for Insurance" (working paper presented at the American Enterprise Institute, Conference on Optional Federal Chartering and Regulation of Insurance, 1999).

Grace, Martin F., and Robert W. Klein. "Hurricane Risk and Property Insurance Markets" (working paper, Center for Risk Management & Insurance Research, Georgia State University, 2007).

Grace, Martin F., and Robert W. Klein. "Overview of Catastrophe Insurance Markets in the U.S." (working paper, 1998).

Grace, Martin F., and Robert W. Klein. "Overview of Recent Developments in Residential & Commercial Property Insurance" (Final report, Prepared for the National Association of REALTORS', 2003).

Grace, Martin F., and Robert W. Klein. "The Past and Future of Insurance Regulation: The McCarran-Ferguson Act and Beyond" (Unpublished manuscript, Searle Center Research Symposium on Insurance Markets and Regulation, April 14, 2008).

Grace, Martin F., Robert W. Klein and Zhiyong Liu. "Increased Hurricane Risk and Insurance Market Responses." *Journal of Insurance Regulation* 24 (2005): 3–32.

Harrington, Scott E., and Patricia Danzon. "Workers' Compensation Rate Regulation: How Price Controls Increase Costs." *Journal of Law & Economics* 44 (2001): 1–36.

Harrington, Scott E., and Gregory R. Niehaus. 2003. *Risk Management and Insurance,* 2nd ed. New York: McGraw Hill, 2003.

Klein, Robert W. "Catastrophe Risk and the Regulation of Property Insurance: A Comparative Analysis of Five States" (working paper, Center for Risk Management & Insurance Research, Georgia State University, 2007).

Klein, Robert W. "Insurance Regulation in Transition," *The Journal of Risk and Insurance,* 62 (1995): 363–404.

Klein, Robert W. "Managing Catastrophe Risk: Problems and Policy Alternatives," (working paper, presented at "Rethinking Insurance Regulation 1998," Competitive Enterprise Institute, Washington, DC, 1998.

Klein, Robert W. "Regulating Insurer Solvency in a Brave New World" (working paper, Center for Risk Management & Insurance Research, Georgia State University, 2000).

Klein, Robert W. and Paul R. Kleindorfer. "The Supply of Catastrophe Insurance Under Regulatory Constraints" (working paper 99–25, The Wharton School of Pennsylvania, 1999).

Klein, Robert W., and Shaun Wang. "Catastrophe Risk Financing in the U.S. and the EU: A Comparative Analysis of Alternative Regulatory Approaches" (working paper presented at the SCOR-JRI Conference on Insurance, Reinsurance and Capital Market Transformations, 2007).

Kunreuther, Howard C. "Guiding Principles for Mitigating and Insuring Losses from Natural Disasters." *Risk Management Review* (2006): 2.

Kunreuther, Howard C., and Erwann O. Michel-Kerjan. "Managing Large-Scale Risks in a New Era of Catastrophes." *Journal of Reinsurance* 15 (2008).

Kunreuther, Howard C., and Mark Pauly. "Rules Rather Than Discretion: Lessons From Hurricane Katrina." *Journal of Risk and Uncertainty* 33 (2006): 101–116.

Mercer, Oliver Wyman. "Study of Homeowner, Commercial Property, Liability, and Marine Insurance" (Prepared for the Government of Newfoundland and Labrador, 2004).

NAIC. 2005. "Rate Filing Methods for Property/Casualty Insurance," NAIC's Compendium of State Laws on Insurance Topics.

Rejda, George E. *Principles of Risk Management and Insurance*, 10th ed. Boston: Pearson/Addison Wesley, 2008.

Swiss Re. "Natural Catastrophes and Man-made Disasters 2005: High Earthquake Casualties, New Dimension in Windstorm Losses." *Sigma* 2 (2006). *www.swissre.com*.

_____. "Natural Catastrophes and Man-Made Disasters in 2007: High Losses in Europe." *Sigma* 1(2008), *www.swissre.com*.

Appendix. Rate Regulation in the Property Lines

State	Premium Approval System: Commercial Lines	Changes and Comments: Commercial Lines	Premium Approval System: Homeowners	Changes and Comments: Homeowners
AL	FR	changed from PA in 2001	PA	
AK	FR	changed from PA in 2005	FR	changed from PA in 2005
AZ	U&F	NF for industrial insured	U&F	
AR	F&U/NF	F&U for small commercial risks; NF for large commercial risks	F&U	
CA	PA		PA	
CO	F&U	NF for exempt commercial policyholders	F&U	
CT	F&U		F&U	
DE	F&U	NF for certain large risks	F&U	
DC	F&U	from 2001 on NF for exempt commercial risks	F&U	
FL	F&U/U&F	optional for insurers	F&U/U&F	
GA	F&U/NF	NF for large commercial risks	F&U	
HI	PA		PA	
ID	U&F		U&F	

State	Premium Approval System: Commercial Lines	Changes and Comments: Commercial Lines	Premium Approval System: Homeowners	Changes and Comments: Homeowners
IL	U&F/NF		U&F	
IN	F&U/NF	NF for large commercial insured	F&U	
IO	PA		U&F	
KS	F&U/NF	NF for large commercial insured	F&U	
KY	FR	NF for industrial insured and exempt commercial policyholders	FR	
LA	FR/NF	NF for exempt commercial policyholders; changed from PA to FR 2004; change to NF 2006	FR	changed from PA 2004
ME	F&U/NF	NF for large commercial risks	F&U	
MD	F&U		F&U	
MA	F&U/NF	NF for large commercial policyholders	F&U	
MI	PA or F&U	optional for insurers; NF for exempt commercial policyholders	F&U	
MN	F&U		F&U	
MS	PA		PA	

State	Premium Approval System: Commercial Lines	Changes and Comments: Commercial Lines	Premium Approval System: Homeowners	Changes and Comments: Homeowners
MO	NF	commercial casualty and property are filed for informational purposes only	U&F	
MT	F&U		F&U	
NE	F&U/NF	NF for large commercial policyholders	F&U	changed from PA 2005
NV	NF		PA	
NH	U&F/NF	NF for large commercial risks	F&U	
NJ	U&F	NF for special risks	PA	
NM	F&U	change to NF 2007	PA	change to F&U 2007
NY	F&U/FR		F&U	
NC	F&U		PA	
ND	PA		PA	
OH	PA/F&U	property: PA; commercial multiple peril: F&U	F&U	
OK	U&F/NF	NF for special large commercial risks; changed from F&U 2004	U&F	changed from F&U 2004
OR	F&U	FR (15% increase/ decrease for commercial casualty)	F&U	

State	Premium Approval System: Commercial Lines	Changes and Comments: Commercial Lines	Premium Approval System: Homeowners	Changes and Comments: Homeowners
PA	FR/NF		FR	
RI	F&U/NF	NF for large commercial risks	FR	changed 2005
SC	NF	NF for exempt commercial policies	FR	changed from PA 2004
SD	F&U/NF	NF for large commercial risks	F&U	
TN	U&F		PA	
TX	F&U		F&U	
UT	U&F	NF for commercial excess and umbrella liability	U&F	
VT	U&F		U&F	
VA	F&U		F&U	
WA	U&F/NF	NF for large commercial property casualty accountschanged from PA 1997	PA	
WV	F&U		PA	
WI	U&F		U&F	
WY	NF		NF	

Sources: Feldhaus and Klein (1997), Mercer Oliver Wyman (2004), NAIC (2005), Wharton (2008). Changes of regulations over time are obtained from state statutes.

6

"Watery Marauders"

How the Federal Government Retarded the Development of Private Flood Insurance

Eli Lehrer

AMERICA'S LITTORAL COMMUNITIES face a crisis. Years of land mismanagement, the destruction of wetlands, a pattern of increasing storm intensity likely to last for some time, the potential of global climate change, and the ongoing expansion of state-run and state-mandated residual insurance markets have resulted in a massive increase in the risks of flooding.

The National Flood Insurance Program, the topic of this chapter, is the major government response to flooding. Insofar as it functions, underwrites risks, and encourages flood-resistant construction in some places, it can be said that the program works.

In many important ways, however, the program has reached a point of crisis. Incentivized partly by the availability of inexpensive, implicitly subsidized flood insurance, states like Florida, South Carolina, North Carolina, Mississippi, and Louisiana have created residual wind insurance mechanisms that create further incentives for development. The result has been enormously increased coastal development and greater damage from hurricanes. While North Carolina, South Carolina, and Louisiana have made significant progress in rationalizing these markets and reining in their size, far too many Americans still live in dangerous areas. And they do so, in part, because of the National Flood Insurance Program, which has been a political creature intended, over the years, to pursue a variety of goals rather than simply making flood insurance available. What applies to all insurance regulation applies to the National Flood Insurance Program as well: As Kenneth Meier writes, "the goals of insurance regulation must be viewed as multiple and political rather than just in terms of correcting market failures."[1]

• • •

Since civilization first arose in the fertile river valleys of the Middle East, humans have always clustered near water. Water irrigates fields, quenches the thirst of livestock, and, of course, provides drinking water for humans. Nearly all major bodies of water overflow their banks at one time or another—major rivers tend to flood yearly, oceans and major lakes less often. But, in time, nearly all of them flood. Since the dawn of civilization, therefore, humans have had to deal with floods.

Before the twentieth century, however, society simply could not afford flood insurance or accomplish the technical tasks needed to underwrite it. From the time of the Romans—who built enormous breakwaters to prevent the Tiber from flooding—some efforts to control floods existed. But the great bulk of the population worked in subsistence agriculture and lived in crude structures that the occupants themselves often built. The wealthy, to vastly oversimplify things, either lived in areas unlikely to flood with any regularity or built flood protection mechanisms. When individuals, corporations, and governments erected flood control measures, they did so with the goal of preventing floods altogether: A mix of public and private efforts built floodwalls around much of the Netherlands, raised the city of Chicago above Lake Michigan's water table, and erected walls to protect the Port of Boston.[2]

Flood insurance, broadly, represents a confession that human efforts cannot prevent floods altogether but, instead, should transfer and pool the risk in a particular way. Any risk transfer vehicle provides a form of flood insurance. Lloyd's associations, catastrophe bonds, and reserving practices all provide flood insurance of a sort. For a variety of reasons stemming from marketing, regulation, and wealth—reasons that lie beyond the scope of this chapter—these vehicles have not proved viable for providing the types of insurance policies most American consumers seek to purchase.

Instead of exploring these options, this chapter deals with *conventional admitted market flood insurance*. Using conventional insurance, people overwhelmingly insure their homes, automobiles, and valuable property against a variety of risks, such as fire, theft, and pests. It is reasonable to believe that they should be able to insure against floods in much the same way.

How Should Flood Insurance Work?

Conventional flood insurance transfers the risk of floods in the same manner as conventional homeowners' insurance transfers the risk of fires. Although policies may be slightly different, for purposes of this chapter, a conventional flood insurance policy works this way: A corporation or cooperative prices a risk-transfer contract for flooding in a predictable fashion based on standardized rating mechanisms and maintains a large degree of price consistency between similarly situated insureds. The policy, furthermore, is offered under the conditions normally associated with the "admitted market" in the United States.

Insurance does not represent charity or government-provided welfare: It involves a mutually beneficial financial arrangement to transfer risk. Insurance providers—government or private—that fail to operate in a financially self-sustaining fashion convert themselves into conduits for relief payments. Following major floods, it is inevitable that some groups and people will need relief, particularly in the short term. Such provision of relief does not provide the risk-transfer inherent in insurance and is largely disconnected from the topic of this chapter. Our premise is that flood insurance should function in much the same manner as other insurance from the consumers' perspective. This functioning should extend to pricing, availability, financial responsibility, its impact on patterns of development, and status in the market economy.

Flood insurance should have six attributes. To begin with, flood insurance should price similar risks similarly and different risks differently. People who have less risk of flood should pay less for flood insurance. People who live at great risk of flood, on the other hand, should pay significant premiums for flood coverage.[3] Second, people who want flood insurance should have few problems buying it at reasonable prices. Such "reasonable prices" may be quite high—a house built on a sand dune will face severe flooding and erosion with some frequency—but they should provide a good insurance value for people who buy them. In other words, the expected claim payouts, along with the value of risk reduction, will be worth the premiums. Third, people who face increased risks of floods as a result of the places where they live should pay for those risks themselves. In other words, people who live far away from areas that flood frequently should not have to pay the bills for those who live in areas that flood all the time. Fourth, flood insurance pricing in a market economy will almost certainly provide incentives to do some combination of these three things: (1) discourage development in areas likely to flood, (2) encourage mitigation against flooding, (3) pay for a portion of the costs of periodic rebuilding in places where people can afford the cost *and* where mitigation is impossible. Fifth, flood insurance should impact patterns of development in a way that either increases society's resistance to floods or creates a mechanism by which society finances rebuilding. Last, if flood insurance is to work like other types of insurance, it should work largely through private means. Governments might provide certain types of subsidies for the poor (insofar as they engage in any income transfer programs at all) and even set up some sort of residual market for areas that society believes should be inhabited but are not insurable at rates that allow them to be inhabited. However, in theory, flood insurance should work through the same private market mechanisms that provide other types of property and casualty insurance.

Finally, this conventional flood insurance should be offered within the confines of the *admitted market*.[4] Admitted market insurance has two major qualities: It is guaranteed, and it exists on the basis of utmost good faith contracts. Within the admitted market, an entity that is almost always governmental or quasi-governmental guarantees insurance. It assures consumers that even if a given company engages in mismanagement or fraud, or has an enormous string of bad luck, legitimate claims will still be paid. Second, admitted market insurance has utmost good faith contracts. In other words, policyholders do not have to read or understand every piece of policy language in order to have an assurance that their polices will be followed.

Like consumers, insurance companies want the environment for providing flood insurance to look like the environment they experience for other types of insurance. In particular, they seek the opportunity to remain financially solvent, to subject themselves to a proper level of regulatory oversight, and to set prices based on risk. First, therefore, insurance companies cannot be forced to operate at a long-term financial loss when insuring against floods. Insurance on dwellings does not always produce underwriting profits (in other words, insurance companies typically pay out more in claims than they receive in premiums). Much of the time, insurance companies make money on homeowners' insurance by investing money they receive in premiums. Many insurance companies operate as nonprofit mutual insurers, but even these companies cannot stay in business if they cannot make profits. Nevertheless, in all circumstances, insurers need to make money to continue their work. Second, like all other economic activity, insurance cannot operate in a vacuum: external forces such as the market and government discipline modify the way it works. Because of the nature of the insurance business—companies promise to provide coverage against events that may or may not happen—it is vital to have someone make sure that companies remain solvent enough to pay likely claims made against them. Insolvent companies engage in fraud if they sell insurance. Therefore, mechanisms (although not necessarily governmental ones) must exist to make sure that insurance companies remain solvent. Other types of regulation ranging from provisions specifying the nature of paperwork involved with insurance to the manner in which insurance companies set rates also may prove advantageous in certain cases. Insurance companies want a regulatory "sweet spot" that provides the appropriate level of regulation, no more and no less.

Finally, insurance companies want to price based on risk. Risk-based pricing insures the most efficient and largest market for insurance and makes the largest number of people able to afford adequate insurance. Pricing on a basis other than risk (by, say, reducing prices for favored groups) almost always leads to corresponding increases for other groups. Externally mandated insurance rate cuts for given groups almost never save money for society as a whole. Instead, they tend to redistribute wealth from people who incur risks to those who do not. In the case of flood insurance—in modern times, people living near water are almost always wealthier than average—it is worth noting that the wealth redistribution implicit in non-risk-based pricing will rarely serve egalitarian goals. Although individual consumers may benefit from pricing on a basis other than risk, it is highly likely that risk-based pricing does the most to advance overall consumer welfare.

The United States has ended up with a flood insurance system that is quite a long distance from what either consumers or insurance companies would expect in a free market situation. Exploring it requires a look at how the federal government took over responsibility for managing America's floods.

Although one might trace the history of America's flood insurance program back to early nineteenth-century efforts to provide disaster relief, the analysis that follows begins with the events that resulted in the system the United States has today. The following section describes how the federal government took on responsibility for protecting all Americans from flooding, provides theories as to the manner in which political forces and factors intrinsic to the industry made the development of flood insurance difficult, outlines the first U.S. efforts at establishing flood insurance, and describes how these efforts further suppressed private market participation. Finally, the chapter outlines the manner in which government agencies added a measure of ris awareness to U.S. flood planning, established floodplain zoning, and thus set the stage for the adaptation of a politically palatable federal flood insurance program.

Setting the Tone

The path that leads to the current U.S. national flood insurance regime began in 1936 with a 932-word policy statement called the National Flood Control Act. This handful of words from Congress would have enormous consequences for the entirety of America's costal and riverine landscape. The most important section—the one that would set the tone for national flood insurance—reads as follows:

> It is hereby recognized that destructive floods upon the rivers of the United States, upsetting orderly processes and causing loss of life and property . . . that it is the sense of Congress that flood control on navigational waters or their tributaries is a proper activity of the Federal Government in cooperation with States, their political sub-divisions and localities thereof; that investigations and improvements of rivers and other waterways, including watersheds thereof, for flood-control purposes are in the interest of the general welfare; that the Federal Government should improve or participate in the improvement of navigable waters or their tributaries including watersheds thereof, for flood-control purposes if the benefits to whomsoever they may accrue are in excess of the estimated costs, and if the lives and social security of people are otherwise adversely affected.[5]

As Gilbert Fowler White describes, this rather momentous act federalizing the entire risk of flood appears to have passed Congress as an afterthought: a few words attached to a laundry list of flood control proposals of the sort Congress passed every year.[6] A massive flood in New England, White recounts, gave an extra push to write an overall policy into law. At the time, it did not appear to be a major change. The Army Corps of Engineers had engaged in flood control efforts since the early nineteenth century, and Congress had appropriated disaster relief as early as 1803.[7] Torrential, deadly floods on the Mississippi-Missouri system in 1927 had destroyed enormous amounts of property, swept away many flood control measures, and resulted in a massive and then-unprecedented flood relief effort under Herbert Hoover's leadership.[8] The Corps gained enormous new authority in the flood's wake and used it widely.

While it passed with little debate, the Act does signal a clear dividing line. Before the 1936 Act, Congress provided relief but considered floods a largely local matter. Afterwards, it made an implicit promise: The federal government would prevent floods so long as "the benefits to whomsoever they may accrue are in excess of the estimated costs." (The Act, in a sign of things to come, neither specifies nor requires any particular type of cost-benefit calculus.) Its text—by calling for "flood control" rather than "management" or "mitigation"—implicitly endorses what the Corps already did: treat floods as "watery marauders which do no good, and against which society wages a bitter battle."[9] Every single one of the 250 projects funded following the policy statement involves either "bank protection works" or "levees" along America's major river systems. In other words, the Corps and the government would battle floods.

The 1936 Act had an immediate impact. Spending on flood control mechanisms doubled in the four years after the report came out, predictably declined during World War II as resources became scarce, and then skyrocketed in 1946 as soon as the war ended.[10] Relief efforts moved forward at a similar pace. Each time cropland flooded, each time people died in a flood, each time a town found its doom in the waters of a rising river, the federal government would step in with help. There was no cost sharing from property owners and, with each major flood, the risk to the federal treasury grew larger.

Amid this background, flood insurance did not develop the way one might have expected. The following section addresses three sets of factors that retarded the development of flood insurance: federal regulation, state regulation (about which little information is available), and the intrinsic nature of flood risk between the 1930s and 1950s.

Why Private Industry (Mostly)
Did Not Develop in the 1930s or 1940s

Federal efforts retarded the development of flood insurance by building
breakwaters that reduced the value of flood insurance over the life of a typical
mortgage by implicitly encouraging development in frequently flooded areas
and by implicitly preempting the need for private insurance.

By shielding much of the country against minor floods, the Army Corps of
Engineers moved floods outside of ordinary experience. Neither the Corps nor
any other agency gave an explicit guarantee that the projects would guard against
catastrophic losses, however, they did reduce the risk of floods in any given year.
This made it harder for the private sector to write insurance policies that it could
market. An example can illustrate this point. Let us assume that, in a given town,
the Corps of Engineers builds flood walls that engineers believe waters will
breach only once in a hundred years. After the wall goes up, a flood insurance
policy purchased over the life of a thirty-year mortgage would have only a 30
percent chance of ever proving useful. While some people might still buy such
a policy, their willingness to pay a given premium will decline significantly
since the event has becomes much less likely. For insurers, however, the risk of
a catastrophic flood resulting in the maximum claim does not decrease. This
makes flood insurance much harder to market; the product remains similarly
priced, but over a given mortgage term, it becomes much less useful.

Floodwalls create moral hazards and make it relatively more attractive for
private parties to build on land likely to flood. Over a period of years, this moral
hazard modifies the built environment a good deal. While developers and property owners may take calculated risks building behind "hundred-year" floodwalls, insurers have little upside in insuring such properties. Vigorous federal
efforts to build floodwalls thus resulted in construction that a private insurance
industry could not insure using conventional insurance policies that it could
market successfully.

Finally, federal relief efforts reduced the need for insurance. Certain types
of floods certainly mandate external relief, and in many cases, preserving lives
may require federal relief. However, any relief beyond short-term efforts to
meet basic human needs will likely reduce some amount of insurance. As John
Barry documents, from the 1920s on, the federal government typically helped

white Americans get back on their feet after floods while doing only the bare minimum to meet basic needs for African Americans. Since nearly all people with assets significant enough to buy insurance were white, this further reduced the need for insurance.

A preliminary literature review did not prove sufficient to determine the consequences of state regulation. It remains undetermined to what extent state regulations impeded or facilitated the development of private flood insurance. It is unclear to date what impact state regulatory environments had (or failed to have) on flood insurance: According to one source, at least 46 states had some form of insurance price regulation in 1951—the earliest compilation the author can find.[11] It is unclear what flood insurance programs, if any, existed before 1936: John M. Barry does not mention any particular insurers in his massive study of the 1927 Mississippi floods but this is not determinative. More research is needed in all of these areas. We can safely say, however, that the general climate in insurance was heavily regulatory during the 1930s and 1940s: Nearly all states passed laws of one sort or another (43 had them by 1952) to regulate rates, and this discouraged risk-based pricing. The McCarran-Ferguson Act of 1945 required that insurance companies subject themselves to state regulation in return for antitrust provisions.[12]

Even so, a small handful of private flood insurance programs—all single-state domestic insurers—did exist. White himself found that "more than 31 organizations wrote some type of policy covering flood damages."[13] But coverage was scanty in one massive Los Angeles flood, private flood insurance paid benefits of $320,000 to cover gross damages of $25 million.[14] Still some evidence exists that the market was growing: In 1956 (after the first proposals to offer flood insurance were made), at least five more companies were offering flood products than had been ten years earlier during White's review.[15] In a limited sense, private flood insurance did exist and people did buy it, but by the late 1930s, a number of political factors were already suppressing the development of private flood insurance.

Flood Insurance and the First Mover Disadvantage

Politics played a major role in the suppression of flood insurance, and the intrinsic nature of the market also made it relatively unattractive for insurers to enter. The nature of flood insurance's risk profile, weather patterns, and the nature of the insurance market all retarded the development of flood insurance.

Quite simply, the distribution of flood risk is different from the exposures against which most people buy insurance. Flood risks are highly correlated and knowable while other risks are not. Although it's possible for a single home to flood, most floods impact dozens of different homes in some same area at a different time. Entire river systems can flood, spreading devastation over multistate areas. The result is that flood risks are highly correlated, and providing indemnity for a certain quantity of flood risk requires much larger capital reserves and a more significant catastrophe load than writing other types of insurance. Since homeowners' insurance in general produces scant underwriting profits—insurers make money largely through investments of premium payments—flood insurance is simply not an attractive business to enter in any circumstances. It requires lots of capital and does not provide a large chance for earning a good return on that capital.

Weather may have also had an impact. Most major floods correlate with hurricanes, and severe hurricanes appear to come in cycles. Between 1944 and 1954, the years when one might have expected a private flood insurance market to develop, no major hurricanes struck anywhere on the U.S. mainland.[16] This further reduced the apparent market for flood insurance. Disasters provide very good advertising for insurance and, for a ten-year period, the United States avoided major flood disasters.

Finally, flood coverage simply presents a smaller market than other types of property and casualty coverage. Nearly every home runs a risk of damage from fire, wind, and falling trees. Some homes, however, have a much smaller chance of flooding than others. Although even homes in desert areas can sometimes fall victim to flash floods, a house near a lake, the ocean, or a river is at much greater risk of flooding than one far from these things. A rational insurance company would likely work to exploit these other opportunities before spending profits to enter a flood market. Between the beginning of the Depression in 1929 and the end of World War II in 1945, Americans had few opportunities to buy many types of consumer goods. In the late 1940s and mid-1950s, the nation had enormous unmet consumer needs. Millions of new housing units were built, and Americans bought new cars in droves. These things needed insurance, and the mechanisms for writing this insurance already existed. Because people had not lived near water in significant numbers, however, no unified mechanism existed for writing flood insurance across the country. Offering it simply was not a priority for insurance companies, who saw growth opportunities elsewhere. This further retarded the development of a market for flood insurance.

A First Failed Effort

In 1951, following a particularly severe flood season in the Southwest, President Harry Truman laid down the first serious national proposal for flood insurance, intended to force property owners to pay a portion of their own relief bills. "At present," the president claimed, "insurance against flood damage is . . . unobtainable from private insurance companies."[17] Truman, as discussed above, wasn't entirely correct—about 40 companies did offer flood insurance. Partly as a result, the proposal went nowhere. Although the Senate held some brief hearings on Truman's proposal, it never received a committee vote and never moved forward.

Four years later, however, Truman's successor made a similar proposal; this time Congress acted. In the wake of a particularly active 1955 hurricane season that saw 12 tropical cyclones hitting the eastern seaboard and causing a record amount of damage, Congress created America's first residential flood insurance program at the request of President Dwight D. Eisenhower.[18] In his January 10, 1957, State of the Union address, Eisenhower explicitly presented flood protection as a part of a plan for cooperative water use planning:

> The whole matter of making the best use of each drop of water from the moment it touches our soil until it reaches the oceans, for such purposes as irrigation, flood control, power production, and domestic and industrial uses clearly demands the closest kind of cooperation and partnership between municipalities, States and the Federal Government. Through partnership of Federal, state and local authorities in these vast projects we can obtain the economy and efficiency of development and operation that springs from a lively sense of local responsibility.
>
> Until such partnership is established on a proper and logical basis of sharing authority, responsibility and costs, our country will never have both the fully productive use of water that it so obviously needs and protection against disastrous flood.[19]

Eisenhower's other communications never explicitly mention the word *insurance* (although they use the term *indemnity* once). Nonetheless, the bill that resulted from Eisnehower's policy—largely shaped through the efforts of Sen. Prescott Bush—set up what appeared to be an actual insurance program.

Congress, however, left things vague, and the program never even named a director. The bill Eisenhower signed provided little guidance and offered short-term borrowing authority rather than appropriations; it required Congress to approve funding after the agency established a premium structure.[20] Written in very broad language, the bill authorizes the creation of a Federal Flood Indemnity Administration to "make available flood insurance." The Act offers a flat 40 percent subsidy to homeowners on "risk-based insurance premiums" and requires that states wanting to participate put up half of the money for that subsidy.[21] It requires the federal government to pay the program's overhead in full and contains no provision for allowing private companies to sell or service policies. It sets caps for coverage but allows the housing and home finance administrator to set premiums and "provide for floodplain management." The bill promises to encourage the private sector to write insurance policies above its statutory cap of $10,000—according to the bill's preamble, a sum that covered the structure value of about 75 percent of all homes standing in 1957. It does not, however, provide any inducement for the private sector to do so. While it gives borrowing authority to stand up the administration and begin operations, it does not actually authorize the sale of products or provide operating funds.

With a vague mandate and no assurance for its future, the Federal Flood Indemnity Administration nonetheless set up office space and began developing its approach; the plan it proposed—but never even published in the Federal Register—had severe flaws.[22] Under the 1957 plan, all property owners desiring insurance would be subject to a so-called "postage stamp" premium—a flat even-rate premium within each state. The only adjustments would exist for construction type and properties directly abutting a stream or river.[23] Given that the legislation did not authorize it, no mapping would take place.

As David Grossman—a Kentucky floodplain administrator in the 1950s—explains, this system is rather absurd on its face: It takes only two risks (construction type and immediate proximity to water) into account and then only very crudely. Such a program would almost certainly attract only the people facing the greatest risks. In other words, it would have had an enormous adverse selection bias. It seems impossible that this system could ever achieve the self-sufficiency the legislation promised.

Even worse from the standpoint of those who favored the program, many states, Grossman observes, could not have participated at all due the mandatory subsidy structure that provided direct subsidies to individual homeowners and would thus violate state prohibitions on appropriating public money for private purposes. While the guidelines did anticipate land use planning efforts going forward, the program would launch, the Housing and Home Finance Administration (HHFA) decided, without any such land use guidelines in place. The HHFA, furthermore, proposed no mechanisms to implement them.

The insurance industry opposed this plan for practical and self-interested reasons. Edward Overman, at the time a leading spokesman for the insurance industry in his capacity as the assistant dean of the Institute for Property and Liability Underwriters, explained the industry's position:

> The [insurance companies'] argument [against the program] is somewhat paradoxical. They are in general agreement that private carriers cannot provide insurance against the peril of flood on fixed property. At the same time, they object to the government's entry into the field. The objection is based not only on the fact that the flood peril is such that it cannot be insured properly by any institution. They contend also that the government's entry into the field marks a step in a movement towards greater government activity in what has been recognized as the private sector of the economy.[24]

One insurance industry-supported study attacked the very idea of such insurance. Flood insurance, the study concluded, could never work under the plan and would, in fact, amount to "relief in the guise of insurance."[25] Political support ebbed quickly once the specifics of the bill became clear. The author's partial review of U.S. Senate floor debates in the period before the bill received approval shows three speeches against the bill and only one (from Prescott Bush) for it. Thanks in large part to the insurance industry's persistent lobbying against it as well as the plan's self-evident absurdity, no funding bill for the program ever made it to the House or Senate floor. But Congress never repealed the statute creating it.[26]

Insurers Ask: Why Bother?

Although it did nothing to begin the federal provision of flood insurance, the 1956 flood act surely chilled the market. By 1960, Best's shows that only 21 companies were writing flood policies; a decline of almost 50 percent (from a very low base). A portion of this may have resulted from a general trend toward consolidation in the industry but, in any case, flood coverage remained unavailable in most of the country. When Gilbert White again surveyed the flood insurance landscape in 1962, he found that things had gotten worse for those seeking insurance. In one town he studied *nobody* had flood insurance or could find anyone besides Lloyds of London willing to write it: "Although a few . . . thought they were covered under all risk policies, none was supported by the fine type of his policy."[27]

This likely happened for a simple reason: Not only did companies continue to face all the risks described above, but they knew that an existing law would let the federal government take away all of their resources at any moment. Hydrologic data collection to support the setting of premiums must have also looked particularly unattractive after 1956: Even with the vast resources of the federal government, the HHFA had decided that it would not compile any risk data before it began writing policies.

Of course, creating a feasible flood insurance program without the manifest flaws of the 1956 proposal was difficult. To make a program politically palatable, Congress needed some assurance that the program would have a relationship to the risk involved and thus needed to collect some risk data.

Making Flood Insurance Feasible

Just as the 1956 flood insurance proposal was failing on the floor of Congress, a series of government actions created a body of risk data that would later facilitate the creation of a non-postage-stamp premium system. Although government agencies developed some useful scientific methodologies, these efforts did not improve the nation's resistance to hydrologic disasters. Instead, they replaced efforts to calculate the actual risk of flooding with mapping efforts that avoided collecting data that would prevent development. Rather than improving risk transfer mechanisms, thus, these new calculations existed to facilitate economic development goals, disconnected from the risks they were creating. In all these efforts, the Tennessee Valley Authority led the way while local and other federal efforts helped build the necessary body of data.

The Tennessee Valley Authority, a federally charted power company with a broad social mission, represented the high-water mark for explicit regional economic planning in the United States. It appears obvious in retrospect that government efforts at massive land use planning would begin at the TVA. Through the 1950s, a variety of TVA projects both coined the term *floodplain management* and contributed a great deal to the environment that made flood insurance feasible.[28] Beginning in 1953, the TVA funded an all-out effort to map the floodplains of 150 frequently flooded communities in its service area.[29] At first, TVA efforts, although free of direct cost, faced enormous resentment from local communities, which saw them as federal meddling in local land use decisions.

TVA managed to overcome this resistance by changing its methodologies in a manner that likely reduced the nation's resistance to floods. In the beginning of their efforts, the TVA's engineers used a "maximum probable flood" standard drawn from the Army Corps of Engineers. This calculation essentially consisted of an engineering estimate of the worst-possible-case scenario flood, whether or not such a flood had actually taken place.[30] Although the creation of such a model provided the best estimate of what a community had to do to actually protect against itself against flooding, its widespread use in planning would have almost certainly foreclosed development in many towns that those communities wanted to see developed. As an agency with the political charge of improving a region's economy, the TVA found its mandates conflicting: It could not simultaneously promote as much short-term economic development as it wanted to and act to reduce flood risk.

Thus, in catering to local opinion and promoting its own economic development goals, TVA decided on another model: Rather than calculating hypothetical future flooding, it would make planning estimates based on regional floods that had actually taken place during recorded history within sixty or one hundred miles of areas where development was proposed. As James Wright notes, this flood area was almost always "significantly smaller and [thus] . . . became the standard for floodplain regulations."[31] Through the 1950s and 1960s, the TVA produced flood studies for most of its service area. While these reports had no legal force, communities throughout the TVA service area as well as the TVA itself began to make use of these maps in zoning and planning. In 1959, the TVA itself even submitted a report to Congress calling for a national floodplain management agenda.[32]

On balance, the TVA's mapping effort made it harder to write actual, useful, financially viable insurance policies: The TVA wanted to transfer water rather than risks. Since mechanisms used for flood control tend to move water rather than making it vanish, they simply reduce the risks of flooding in some areas while increasing it in others. They do not transfer risks in any real sense. Flood insurance, on the other hand, shifts the financial risks associated with flooding rather than moving water itself. Although the maps could be used in setting relative insurance premium levels—they included risk data—they were not developed using the methodologies an insurer would use.

Coincident with the TVA's work—and partly supported by the regional flood techniques it developed—communities both inside and outside of its service area began implementing formal floodplain zoning ordinances. These laws, today virtually universal in littoral settlements, specify when, how, and even if development can take place in an area likely to flood. Their enforcement by definition requires mapping where floods would take place. Thanks to the TVA's efforts, many communities now had these maps. Between 1955 and 1958, the number of governmental jurisdictions with floodplain zoning rose from eight to forty-nine.[33] Beginning with Washington State legislation in 1962, furthermore, states began implementing statewide flood control policies.[34] The growth of these mechanisms and the techniques for replicating them made it possible for more and more communities to implement floodplain ordinances.

At the same time, the U.S. Geological Survey, in cooperation with the Corps of Engineers, began producing a series of flood atlases and maps for areas outside of the TVA's service area.[35] Although presented in a different form, these maps followed the TVA's pattern of basing predictions on floods that had actually taken place rather than floods that might one day take place. While maps did include "500-year floods" roughly equivalent to the Army Corps' "maximum probable flood," the related analysis always emphasized mitigations against the "100-year" regional flood. This was essentially the same standard that the TVA used.[36]

By the mid-1960s, the combination of these efforts quickly gave the United States the rudiments of a national floodplain map for its high-risk areas. Localities had data on which they could write useful zoning ordinances to keep structures away from the worst flooding. Experts, furthermore, had calculated the relative risk of a variety of different types of floods. Based on this data, the government could write flood insurance without resorting to the impractical and uniform "postage stamp" premiums. Apparently, however, the data did nothing to germinate the creation of a private market.

Government Failure

On its face, the mapping effort provided fatally flawed data, distorted development patterns, and made market entry even more unattractive for private insurers. Because they stemmed from the TVA's regional flood model, nearly all risk data compiled by the mid-1960s and the floodplain zoning ordinances they inspired had a laughably fatal flaw: They assumed that flooding would never get worse than it had in the past. While government data existed, in other words, the great bulk of it was worse than useless for private insurers, who were worried about whether risks were declining or increasing. A different data collection effort might have jump-started private insurance, but the existing data collection effort actually retarded it.

These mapping projects also created a false sense of security on the part of builders, businesses, and homeowners. While they impeded the most obviously unwise development—development that few lenders, even public ones, would have funded in the first place—early TVA-inspired efforts at floodplain zoning introduced a significant moral hazard problem. In many cases, they encouraged development in areas where it otherwise would not have happened. An enormous number of people moved into floodplain areas.

The data, furthermore, presented insurers with a massive political risk if they did enter the market. Even if an insurer were willing to spend millions of dollars to redo the TVA's work mapping floodplain areas, it would face major political problems if it sought to price risks in ways that differed markedly from the government data. Hit with high rates to insure property that the government had said was "safe," homeowners would likely have protested and quite probably managed to secure rate regulation favorable to their own interests. Because the zoning ordinances were new, furthermore, no useful experience-based risk data existed anyway, so insurers would have had to charge sizeable risk premiums to secure a return on investment. This made the market even more difficult to enter.

In a different situation, insurers might well have entered the market and priced policies using a variety of deductibles, risk premiums, and the like to protect themselves and market the product. But, as discussed above, given the nature of the regulatory climate, the growth the general insurance market was experiencing anyway, and the risks associated with government data collection, it became far less attractive for insurers to enter the flood insurance market. Thus, the market remained greatly underserved.

The System We Have

The modern flood insurance system emerged in the wake of the TVA's mapping efforts. Its forms, as this section discusses, come from two major studies: one, written largely by Gilbert F. White, which proved prophetic about its likely problems, and the other, a far more political document, that proposed the specifics of the program. As initially passed, the National Flood Insurance Program required the use of a fair amount of risk-based data but, in the first four years of the program's existence, a series of actions gutted the program's risk-based character altogether. Even potentially effective flood maps, required under the program, were essentially ignored. The program that exists today resulted: a program that takes risk into account but does so in a way far different from the probable private-sector approach.

Toward the National Flood Insurance Program

In 1965, Hurricane Betsy scoured the Gulf Coast, leaving $1.42 billion ($9 billion in 2006 dollars) of damage in its wake. In a foreshadowing of 2005's much more severe Hurricane Katrina, "billion dollar Betsy" dumped millions of gallons of water into Lake Pontchartrain, breaching several levees and inundating much of New Orleans. Very soon after the hurricane, the Army Corps of Engineers began to focus explicitly on hurricanes, creating its own hurricane protection programs.[37] Congress, following a long-established pattern, quickly appropriated more than $500 million to repair the damage through the Southeast Hurricane Disaster Relief Act of 1965.[38] In his signing statement for the bill, President Lyndon B. Johnson described what he saw as its objectives: immediate relief "to those victims of the hurricane who suffered losses for which no insurance was obtainable" and study of "programs which could be established to help provide financial assistance in the future to those suffering property losses in floods and other natural disasters, including but not limited to disaster insurance or reinsurance."[39]

In fact, two studies emerged from the bill: one by a Presidential Commission of floodplain management experts and the other by a Department of Housing and Urban Development commission operating under the direction of the Senate's Committee on Banking and Insurance. Both groups considered the creation of flood insurance programs and came to strikingly different conclusions. The former report proves prophetic about the problems of flood insurance; the latter had enormous impacts on the policies that Congress approved. Both merit exploration.

The White Commission

Under the leadership of the omnipresent Gilbert White, the presidential commission far exceeded its legislative mandate and proposed a major rethinking of floodplain management policy, one that did not include a national flood insurance program in the short term.[40] Rather than simply considering the flood insurance question the president emphasized, the commission issued sixteen recommendations. Among other things, the White Commission called for greater attention to flood hazards in nearly all land-related federal programs, increased state and local cost-sharing for flood control projects, and land acquisition efforts to prevent unwise floodplain development.[41] Its report emphasizes personal responsibility. "Floods are acts of God," the commission writes. "Flood damages result from the actions of men."[42] Further, the White Commission expresses skepticism about the Corps' work. "Individual beneficiaries from engineering protection do not, in many instances, bear an adequate share of the cost," it writes. On page after page, in fact, the report attacks the Corps' efforts to prevent floods, pointing out that, since the 1936 Flood Control Act, the nation had spent nearly $6 billion of federal money on levees and less than $500 million on other measures to prevent erosion and redirect development.

Addressing the topic of flood insurance, the White Commission report says that a flood insurance system (implicitly private) is "theoretically ideal" but that "further study must be completed" before taking any concrete action.[43] In particular, the commission recommends a five-phase program to pilot flood insurance, beginning with the construction of new flood risk models based on "hydrological and statistical studies [that] evaluate average annual damages and their variance, geographic distribution and required rates." The studies, the commission notes, "also should investigate differences in land use, age of structures, type of hazard, local planning, and other factors as they affect the feasibility of insurance coverage."[44] Only after rigorous measures to verify these studies with "a range of areas, types of structures, and other conditions," the commission said, it would be wise to "recommend a course of action."[45] Contrary to what some authors say, the White Commission *does not* recommend that the government fund a program of national flood insurance. It proposes that the government simply begin collection of the data the private sector likely would have eventually collected, absent the Corps' persistent flood control efforts and the TVA's poorly conceived mapping schemes.

If implemented and coupled with land use policies that moved away from the TVA's regional flood model, it appears quite possible that the White Commission's proposal could have encouraged a private or largely private market for flood insurance in states where the regulatory climate allowed it.[46] Although the existence of the federal statutes creating a federal flood of insurance program as well as ongoing Corps of Engineers efforts to prevent floods would have certainly retarded market entry, no federal regulation seems to have stood in the way of the creation of a private market. Some states almost certainly had regulations that might have retarded market entry, but somewhere, it appears likely that market entry would have been possible. The studies envisioned—which included a long period of testing—would have allowed the setting of true risk-based premiums on floodplain land.

As White himself had noted two years earlier, any flood insurance system would work best if information about flood coverage is "available and known to financial officers, [so that] they will automatically inquire about it each time a property is transferred or that a mortgage is negotiated. [And thus] force direct decision on flood adjustment."[47] Today's flood insurance system still lacks an effective way to do just this.

Although it proves prescient in many respects, White's Commission had rather little influence in the short term. The nature of the U.S. building environment and the public demand for some sort of flood insurance made its leisurely proposed timetables and ambivalence about flood insurance a political nonstarter.

The Evans Commission

Instead, the national flood insurance program found itself shaped by a far more political commission under the leadership of resource economist Marion Evans. The commission, supervised by the Senate Committee on Banking and Insurance, came to a strikingly different conclusion than White's Commission.[48] Issued the same year as the White Report, the Evans Commission report recommends "a national system of flood insurance . . . with government assistance or participation to the extent necessary" on the fourth page and then devotes the bulk of its length to exploring its theoretical benefits and detriments. Whereas the White Commission cautioned that numerous studies would be required to determine risk-based flood premiums, the Evans report simply says "it has been estimated that the Corps of Engineers with the assistance of other Federal and State agencies, could [map] all flood prone areas (coastal as well as riverine) in ten years at a total cost of $60 million."[49] The report cites a passage on page 22 of the White Commission report that makes this estimate. In the context of the White Report, however, it is quite clear that the maps produced are intended as a preliminary tool to help localities improve floodplain zoning and move away from the TVA-influenced model, *not* as a tool for setting insurance premiums, which the White Commission believed wasn't possible in the short term. The Evans report, however, assumes that these maps would be useful for setting risk adjusted premiums, while the White Commission— which included actual flood plain management experts—knew that they would provide little more than a rough baseline. The Evans report also suggests that the program be limited to communities that adopt floodplain zoning. Although it does not explicitly recommend a particular way of administering the program, the report's text has the most favorable assessment of the option that Congress would adopt in the end: "Private Insurance Industry Operates a Federal Flood Insurance Program."

The Program

The 1968 federal legislation[50] that passed in the wake of the Evans report established the outlines of the program that still exists today: what Rutherford Platt has aptly called "two programs rolled into one."[51] One part of the flood program (Section 1331 and 1332 of the original Act) provides federally backed insurance against flooding; the rest of the Act encourages municipal, county, and occasionally state-level "permanent land use and control measures"—floodplain zoning—intended to direct flooding away from high-risk areas. The two parts work in tandem: Only communities with floodplain zoning ordinances that meet administratively determined federal standards can get insurance. Although the statutory language allows the program to cover nearly anything, the 1968 legislation and all updates since then make the program's primary objective the coverage of single-family homes and apartment buildings with four or fewer units.[52] With a few small exceptions, this is all the program has ever covered. The legislation also sets a structure coverage limit ($30,000 in 1969, $250,000 today). The flood insurance program's initial authorizing legislation lets the administrator contract out nearly all sales and servicing activities: Through what is today called the "write your own" program, private insurers market and service policies that the National Flood Insurance Program prices and underwrites.

The program had a number of limitations and flaws that seem obvious in retrospect. Neither the initial legislation nor any succeeding legislation places substantial limits on the number of times a property could be rebuilt. Structures built before 1970 in floodplain zoning communities were grandfathered into the program. Under the original program, the Corps of Engineers would produce data about the relative risk of property, codified into Flood Insurance Rate Maps (FIRMs).[53] Although existing FIRMS have some serious problems, there's no reason to think that they are particularly biased. The methodologies used to create them, in fact, offer a reasonable semblance of those that private insurance companies would use, and at least in the short term, it's likely that insurance companies would contract with the same private companies that currently work for the National Flood Insurance Program. Rather than attempt to interfere with the FIRMs themselves, forces seeking to create less stringent floodplain zoning have simply substituted other, less rigorous methods of determining flood risk. FIRMs themselves, however, have remained reasonably scientific. Within the last decade, in fact, staff at the Federal Emergency Management Agency (FEMA) have stood against the FEMA director's efforts to modify FIRMs to appease a politically connected developer.[54]

Although the Evans report had said that floodplain studies for the nation could be completed within ten years, the Act's section 1361 offered a leisurely fifteen-year timetable for preliminary mapping of the nation's floodplain. To pay for the insurance coverage, the Act deposits premiums into a special fund at the Treasury while authorizing an initial borrowing limit of $1 billion to cover whatever premiums couldn't (currently $22.3 billion). States and localities must enact zoning codes to take part but do not have any actual financial responsibility for the program.[55] To encourage purchase, section 1314 of the Act denies any federal disaster relief to people who are eligible to purchase flood insurance and do not do so.

From an administrative standpoint, the program appears rather clever: It creates a strong local interest in floodplain zoning throughout the country without having the federal government impose it. Communities that did not want to take part in the program could avoid enacting ordinances but would thus leave their citizens without any viable flood insurance coverage options. Since the program was voluntary and did not explicitly require any tax revenue or local matching investment, nobody had a vested interest in opposing it.[56] In theory, the program contains a strong enforcement mechanism: the denial of disaster relief to anyone who can purchase flood insurance but does not.

This approach had obvious appeal and, in the main, had broad support in 1968. Although congressional testimony suggested dozens of minor modifications, executives from the National Association of Independent Insurers, State Farm, the National Association of Mutual Insurers, Travelers, the Hartford Insurance Group, and dozens of other companies and organizations all expressed support for the program's broad outlines, as described above. T. Lawrence Jones, the President of the American Insurance Association, offered a typical comment: "The need for flood insurance is too great," he said. "and the present governmental flood relief programs too costly, wasteful, and inefficient to permit further delay."[57] Among the rare opponents of the program was G. Richard Challinor, the president of a wholly private Missouri flood insurance mutual insurer, which he said had only 50 policy holders. He warned that the subsidy structure proposed could "make it very much like running a national lottery or gambling at Las Vegas."[58] Only two private flood insurers testified, and, according to Jones, none of the AIA's large members were writing flood insurance for homeowners in 1967.

Although the program probably would have had to either borrow from Treasury or engage in the profit-seeking investments common to private insurance carriers, well-designed FIRMs based on research of the sort White had recommended and the legislation envisioned could have made risk-based pricing a reality. White himself later expressed regrets about the program, but the 1968 legislation is potentially consistent with his vision of piloting flood insurance toward true risk-based pricing. The National Flood Insurance Program could have simply delayed the issuance of FIRMs and refused to write policies until it had sufficient risk data. Political forces would have made things much messier in reality but, in its outlines, the original 1968 program appears as sound as one could reasonably expect. But politics, of course, quickly got in the way.

The Flight from Risk

As might be expected given its heavy requirements for risk-based pricing and the need to enact special ordinances and create special maps, the National Flood Insurance Program began with a whimper. In 1968, the first year of the program's existence, only sixteen property owners purchased policies and only four sizeable communities (Fairbanks, Alaska; Alexandria, Virginia; Metairie, Louisiana; and Mobile, Alabama) developed the maps and zoning ordinances needed to take part. All, not surprisingly, were among the nation's most flood-prone areas. Progress seemed slow, and in August of that year, Hurricane Camille slammed the Gulf Coast. Causing over $1 billion in damage and killing 250, the storm resulted in another legislative frenzy: Nobody with flood insurance suffered any storm damage, and the program had done nothing to mitigate the damage.

In addition to sending a by-then-customary relief package, Congress also changed the flood insurance program in Camille's wake. These reforms gutted the risk-based nature of the 1968 programs. Through Section 408 of the Housing and Urban Development Act of 1969 (PL 91-152)—passed without detailed hearings—Congress backed off the fundamental financial attributes of the 1968 design while leaving the insurance legislation intact. Under the law, Flood Hazard Boundary Maps (FHBMs) replaced FIRMs on a temporary basis to let communities enter the program without risk programs. Although they have a slightly different form, FHBMs are essentially updated versions of the TVA regional flood estimates: Rather than modeling potential future floods, they simply record boundaries of past floods. They provide an element of risk awareness but, unlike FIRMs, do not even vaguely resemble the types of data private companies might use. Deadlines for moving away from FHBMs and mapping the nation's entire floodplain were repeatedly extended and, even in 2007, some communities continue to use them FHBMs rather than FIRMs.[59] Many FIRMs, furthermore, remain significantly out of date, and efforts to update them have fallen behind. Although a series of reforms in the 1990s limited communities' ability to do so, buildings and insured under FHBMs can still typically qualify for flood insurance indefinitely, even if the FIRMS make them uninsurable. This creates just what the insurance industry feared in 1957: a charity—an open-ended entitlement to be made whole after a flood—in the guise of insurance.

Even with these changes, flood insurance remained slow to catch on. Premiums in communities that drew FIRMs were almost always high, largely because the first communities to enter the program were among those most at risk for flooding. In smaller communities, the cost of compiling FIRMs themselves also added to the premiums. In the first three years of the program's existence, only about 500 communities signed up and all but seventeen used FHBMs. In July 1972, the National Flood Insurance Program simply cut premiums across the board by 37.5 percent to encourage participation.[60] Thus, even in communities using FIRMs, prices of flood insurance are no longer correlated with risk in a fashion that resembles what the private sector would use. In the wake of this rate cut, not surprisingly, participation soared; by the end of 1973, more than 2,850 communities had joined the National Flood Insurance Program.[61] Over 80 percent used FHBMs.[62] The program had lost its risk-based character altogether.

Although the program had begun to expand nicely, Congress again revisited it in 1973 and passed a series of reforms that proved the last gasp for the risk-based pricing model of five years earlier. Under the 1973 reforms (PL 93-288), Congress extended the emergency program allowing the use of FHBMs until 1980 and removed the provisions denying emergency relief to people eligible to purchase flood insurance who did not do so.[63] The following year, the flood program again cut insurance rates—an additional 10 percent for most policy holders but as much as 20 percent for some to encourage participation in communities where few had signed up.

Although created as a reasonable insurance product in 1968, by 1973, the flood insurance program had given up its risk-based character altogether. By using FHBMs, ending the denial of relief to people who failed to purchase flood insurance, and engaging in reckless across-the-board premium cuts, the program transformed itself from an insurance product to a voluntary tax intended to fund some portion of relief efforts. While private "write your own" carriers—private companies that serviced policies and reaped profits (or at least broke even) doing so while still leaving actual risks and pricing decisions to the government—continued to provide a patina of free market participation, the 1973 reforms snuffed out the last possibility that the private market would ever take an interest in the product.

The program's evolution over the subsequent three decades would result in numerous changes and even some moves toward greater risk awareness. But flood insurance would remain a largely political creature disconnected from risk calculations.

Conclusion: Government Failure

A recent study's definition of *government failure* provides a good summary of how the National Flood Insurance Program emerged in the manner that it did:

> Government failures appear to be explained by the self-correcting nature of some market failures, which makes government intervention unnecessary; by the shortsightedness, inflexibility, and conflicting policies of government agencies . . . officials initiate and maintain inefficient policies.[64]

The simple fact that insurance has become a political game also played a major role in the type of political structure that emerged. As Kenneth Meier notes, insurance in general is a high-complexity, low-salience issue: It's difficult to understand and isn't relevant to many people.[65] Since most people do not live in areas where flood is a major factor in daily life, furthermore, flood insurance simply doesn't matter to a large number of people one way or the other and, even for those who it does impact, the issue is often too complex and tangential to spend much time on. The resulting system, therefore, probably does not reflect the will of a large number of people but, rather, those groups that decided they had some particular interest: the TVA, communities interested in development, and insurers that did not want to write flood insurance.

A real market failure—of a sort—did slow the emergence of flood insurance. The very nature of the market, its reasonably small size, and the need to prepare complex hydrologic studies in order to price conventional insurance meant that flood insurance would emerge more slowly than other types of insurance. Although it's impossible to know for certain, these problems do not appear irremediable: In the long term, with the right database, no enormous problems seem to exist with writing flood insurance. Today, in fact, Chubb writes flood insurance policies that cover damages above the $250,000 limit of the National Flood Insurance Program and USAA offers renters insurance that covers flood damages. In the long term, floods are not uninsurable.

Instead, four major factors resulted in this government failure: the Army Corps of Engineers' massive levee-building project, the TVA's mapping efforts and the spin-off zoning ordinances they spawned, market suppression via an enacted-but-unfunded flood insurance statute, and Congress's decision to remove risk-based pricing from the flood program to encourage participation.

To begin with, the Army Corps of Engineers levee system gave Americans living in frequently flooded areas a sense that they had a right to near-total freedom from flooding: that the government could always keep them safe from the worst of Mother Nature. This same system of levees often served to reduce the value of insurance without resulting in a significant reduction in the premiums that insurance companies would have to charge to break even on underwriting. Simultaneously, it encouraged development that would not have taken place absent the levees. Congress's heavy use of earmarking to decide where levees were built—the 1936 Flood Control Act named 250 particular projects—ensured that nearly all levees got built as a result of political pressures rather than economic or scientific concerns. The U.S. built landscape thus changed drastically with little regard to the danger of flooding involved.[66]

The Tennessee Valley Authority's regional flood modeling and the FHBMs that followed made an already bad situation worse. Rather than mapping based on the best possible hydrological engineering estimates, the TVA distorted mapping to achieve its economic development objectives. This created an even larger moral hazard and resulted in even more development in areas that market forces probably would not have developed on their own. The spread of the TVA's own methods across the nation resulted in floodplain zoning ordinances that, in many cases, replicated the worst aspects of the TVA's efforts.

The 1956 Flood Insurance Act further discouraged private participation in flood insurance markets. Since Congress never actually repealed the Act, its very existence on the books made the expensive, risky process of market entry much less likely. Companies would not enter the market because they needed to invest a lot to enter in the first place, and since government was involved, they had good reason to think that any investments they made would be replaced by a government program.

The TVA's efforts, while useless from the standpoint of private insurance, also made possible the setting of risk-aware policy premiums for the National Flood Insurance Program. These premiums made the program politically palatable for Congress while simultaneously making it a foregone conclusion that the program would lose money year after year. While the initial program passed in 1968 required superficially strong risk-based pricing, Congress quickly gutted the program's risk-based character by allowing the use of deeply flawed FHBMs, removing penalties for failing to purchase flood insurance, and allowing across-the-board premium cuts that undermined the program's financial stability.

It's impossible to know for certain, of course, how or even if the private market would have developed flood insurance products. The evidence relating to flood policy, however, indicates that the government efforts made the emergence of private flood insurance—or even the slow development of a private system—more problematic. The political system saw a small market failure and greatly overcompensated. The failures of flood insurance, ultimately, are political rather than purely a matter of policy. The United States ended up with a system of political insurance that has placed an enormous burden on the Treasury and created a moral hazard. The creation of such a system, this chapter has argued, did not result from inevitable, unavoidable market failures but rather from several deliberate, interconnected political actions.

References

American Institute for Research, et al. "A Chronology of Major Events Affecting the National Flood Insurance Program." Washington, DC: FEMA, 2002.

American Insurance Institute. *Studies of Floods and Flood Damage, 1952–1955.* New York: American Insurance Institute, 1956.

Barry, John M. *Rising Tide.* New York: Simon and Schuster, 1998.

Best's Directory of Insurers and Underwriters. Oldwick, NJ: A.M. Best and Company, 1953.

Brouwer, Greg. "The Creeping Storm," *Civil Engineering* 73 (June 2003). http://www.pubs.asce.org/ceonline/ceonline03/0603ce.html.

Eisenhower, Dwight D. "Annual Message to Congress on the State of the Union" (January 10, 1957). http://www.presidency.ucsb.edu/ws/index.php?pid=11029.

Floods of the Kansas River, Topeka, Kansas, in 1935 and 1951: U.S. Geological Survey Hydrologic Investigations, Atlas HA-14. Washington, DC: Government Printing Office, 1959.

Grossman, David. "Flood Insurance: Can a Feasible Program Be Created?" *Land Economics* 34 (November 1958): 352–357.

Grunwald, Michael. "For S.C. Project, a Torrent of Pressure; Developer Wins Reprieve From FEMA on $4 Billion Project in Columbia Flood Plain." *The Washington Post,* July 13, 2001.

Jarrell, Jerry D., et al. "The Deadliest, Costliest, and Most Intense Hurricanes from 1900 to 2000." National Oceanic and Atmospheric Administration, 2001. http://www.aoml.noaa.gov/hrd/Landsea/deadly/index.html.

Johnson, Lyndon. "605 - Statement by the President Upon Signing the Southeast Hurricane Disaster Relief Act of 1965." November 8, 1965.

National Oceanic and Atmospheric Administration. "Hurricane History, 2007." http://www.nhc.noaa.gov/HAW2/english/history.shtml.

Overman, Edward. "Flood Peril and the Federal Flood Insurance Act of 1956." *The Annals of the American Academy of Political and Social Science* 309 (1957): 98–106.

Platt, Rutherford H. *Land Use and Society: Geography, Law, and Public Policy.* Washington, DC: Island Press, 2004.

Robertson, Willis, et al. "Insurance and Other Programs for Financial Assistance to Flood Victims: A Report from the Secretary of HUD as required by the Southeast Hurricane Disaster Relief Act of 1965." Washington: Government Printing Office, 1966.

Task Force on Federal Flood Control Policy. *A Unified National Program for Managing Flood Losses.* Washington: Government Printing Office, August 10, 1966.

Truman, Harry. "119—Special Message to the Congress Transmitting Proposed Legislation on a National System of flood Disaster Insurance," May 5, 1952.

U.S. Congress. *Insurance and Other Programs for Assistance to Flood Victims: A Report from the Secretary of Housing and Urban Development as required by the Southeast Hurricane Disaster Relief Act of 1965.* 89th Congress, Second Session. Washington: U.S. Government Printing Office, 1966.

U.S. Congress, Committee on Banking and Insurance. *Hearings Before the Subcommittee on Banking and Insurance on H.R. 11197,* Ninetieth Congress, First Session, 166.

U.S. Senate. "A Program for Reducing the National Flood Damage Potential: Memorandum of the Chairman to Members of the Committee on Public Works." U.S. Senate, 86th Cong., 1st Sess., 31 Aug. 1959.

White, Gilbert. "Choice of Adjustment to Floods." Chicago: University of Chicago, Department of Geography, Research Paper No. 93, 1964.

White, Gilbert Fowler. *Human Adjustment to Floods: A Geographical Approach to the Flood Problem in the United States.* Chicago: University of Chicago, Department of Geography, 1942.

Winston, Clifford. *Government Failure Versus Market Failure: Microeconomics Policy Research and Government Performance.* Washington, DC: AEI-Brookings Joint Center for Regulatory Studies, 2006.

Wright, James M. "The Nation's Responses to Flood Disasters: A Historical Account." Association of State Floodplain Managers," 2000. http://www.floods.org/PDF/hist_fpm.pdf.

7

Alternative Frameworks for Insurance Regulation in the United States

Martin F. Grace
Robert W. Klein

Introduction

INSURANCE REGULATION IN the United States is at a cross-roads. The states have regulated the industry for 150 years. During this long history, the states—with strong industry support—have successfully repelled several federal challenges to their authority. However, as the insurance industry has evolved, its support for state regulation has eroded, and many insurers now support the creation of an optional federal charter (OFC) that would preempt state regulation for insurers and agents regulated by the federal government and also modify antitrust law for insurers. The U.S. Department of the Treasury's blueprint for financial regulatory reform also envisions a much greater federal role in the industry's oversight.[1] Subsequent federal actions associated with the recent crisis in financial markets have spurred further discussion of federal oversight of the industry. The states, as well as certain industry groups (for example, independent agents) with a vested interest in preserving the existing system, strongly oppose an OFC, and a fierce debate continues over the restructuring of the insurance regulatory framework and its policies.

Despite this strong opposition, the push for some form of federal regulation is unlikely to diminish and may intensify. Change is clearly in the wind, but how things will evolve is uncertain, given the interplay of many forces. While large segments of the industry continue to prefer an OFC, other institutional arrangements may surface as the debate continues. Some of these alternatives may be viewed as incremental steps to a more comprehensive federal framework while others may be proposed as ultimate solutions. Further, a number of issues arise with the specific design and implementation of any particular arrangement, including the regulatory policies that would be adopted within a given framework. In this context, it is important to develop an understanding of the key features of the most viable alternative frameworks and their potential advantages and disadvantages.

This chapter examines the merits of alternative frameworks for insurance regulation in the United States and their implications for regulatory and market efficiency. This examination is founded on a review of the historical foundations of the current system as well as its present structure. It is helpful to understand how insurance regulation has evolved and its present configuration in considering how it might be improved. This naturally leads to a discussion of the limitations of the current U.S. regulatory system and the potential benefits and pitfalls of alternative arrangements. We also address issues concerning how insurance should be regulated (that is, regulatory policies) that are inevitably intertwined with the locus of regulatory authority.

The chapter begins with a brief historical overview of insurance regulation in the United States. The next section outlines the current framework for insurance regulation and state efforts to improve its efficiency. This is followed with an examination of alternative frameworks for insurance regulation, their relative advantages and disadvantages, and their implications for rationalizing regulatory policies and enhancing the efficiency of the insurance industry. Finally, we summarize and conclude our analysis.

A Brief History of Insurance Regulation

Insurance regulation in the United States has a long history, one that is relevant to the current debate about how it should be reformed. Several attempts to establish a greater federal role in insurance regulation have been thwarted by the states, often with strong industry support. Further, the state regulatory framework has evolved in response to developments in the industry as well as issues that led to threats of greater federal intrusion. However, significant segments of the industry have become disenchanted with state regulation within the last two decades, believing that it is an antiquated system that is incapable of achieving the efficiency that a single federal regulator would provide. Hence, it is important to weigh the progress of initiatives implemented by the states against the arguments made by the proponents of federal regulation.

Early Origins

State insurance regulation dates back to the early 1800s, when insurance markets were generally confined to a particular community.[2] At that time, property insurers were formed as stock companies or mutual protection associations to provide fire insurance for a particular town or city. The high concentration of exposures and the occurrence of large conflagrations led to considerable market instability. Pricing was highly cyclical, and there were periodic shakeouts when a number of insurers would fail after a major fire.[3] During this same period, life insurance companies also were formed, but some became notorious for high expenses, shaky finances, and abusive sales practices.[4] The fact that insurance markets were local in nature led municipal and state governments to establish the initial regulatory mechanisms for insurance companies and agents.

Local governments made the first attempts to assert some industry oversight, but their efforts proved to be inadequate as the industry grew and market problems persisted.[5] Various states (beginning with New Hampshire in 1851) then formed insurance commissions to license companies and agents, regulate policy forms, set reserve requirements, police insurers' investments, and administer financial reporting. Price regulation was essentially confined to limited oversight of property-casualty industry-rate cartels. At that time, uniform pricing was viewed as the solution to "destructive competition," and regulators' expected role was to ensure that this system was not abused to extract excessive profits from consumers.[6]

The states soon realized the need to coordinate their regulatory activities as insurers began to cross state boundaries and common issues arose. This led to the formation of the predecessor organization to the National Association of Insurance Commissioners (NAIC) in 1871. Initially, it focused on developing common financial reporting requirements for insurers. State regulators also began using the NAIC as a vehicle for discussing common problems and developing model laws and regulations that each state could modify and adopt (or not) according to its preferences.

Through the years, insurance department responsibilities and resources grew in scope and complexity as the industry evolved. Two major trends appear to have heavily influenced the evolution of regulatory functions and institutions.[7] One trend has been the significant growth of the industry and the increasing diversity of insurance products and the types of risks that insurers have assumed. The other trend is the geographic extension of insurance markets with a number of carriers operating on a national and international basis. Other important trends include significant consolidation within the industry, new types of firms offering insurance coverage and/or services, changes in distribution channels, convergence of financial services markets, alternative risk transfer and financing vehicles, and systemic financial and economic risks. Tables 7.1 and 7.2 summarize basic trends in the property-casualty and life-health insurance sectors that document some aspects of the industry's transformation.

Arguably, such developments have increasingly challenged the state regulatory framework. Every state has had to increase its resources and expertise to oversee a more complex and geographically extended industry. The states' reliance on the NAIC also has necessarily increased as it has become a vehicle to pool resources and augment their regulatory activities. Consequently, the NAIC has been transformed into a major service provider as well as a mechanism for coordinating state actions and centralizing certain regulatory processes. These measures have been developed, at least in part, to address growing externalities among states as well as to achieve greater economies of scale in performing certain regulatory functions.[8] Although the states have substantially increased their resources and the sophistication of their regulatory mechanisms, their critics raise concerns about the inherent inefficiency of a state-based framework and its ability to keep pace with the industry and the broader economic environment in which it operates.

The State versus Federal Regulation Debate

The states and the federal government have been engaged in battles over insurance regulation since the mid-1800s. An inherent tension exists between state and federal authorities, which is fostered by the interstate operation of many insurers and their significant presence in the economy. In several instances, the federal government has sought to exert greater control over the industry, and the states, backed by the insurance industry, have successfully defended their authority. The economic and political stakes are high for both sides.

The primacy of the states' authority over insurance was essentially affirmed in various court decisions until the U.S. Supreme Court decision in *U.S. v.*

Table 7.1. Property-Casualty Insurance Trends: 1960–2006

	1960	1970	1980	1990	2000	2006
No. of Companies	NA	2,800.00	2,953.00	3,899.00	3,215.00	2,648.00
Assets ($M)	30,132.00	55,315.00	197,678.00	556,314.00	1,034,090.00	1,483,013.00
Revenues ($M)	15,741.00	36,524.00	108,745.00	252,991.00	341,590.00	501,106.00
New Premiums Written (%)	95.1	94.3	89.6	86.9	87.7	89.3
Investment Income (%)	4.9	5.7	10.4	13.1	12.3	10.7
Market Share of 10 Largest Insurer Groups (%)	34.4	36.8	38.2	40.3	43.7	48.5
Premiums/Surplus (%)	125.5	210.2	183.4	157.6	75.6	89.7
Return on Net Worth (%)	NA	11.6	13.1	8.5	6.5	13.4

Source: Insurance Information institute, A.M. Best.

Table 7.2. Life-Health Insurance Market Trends: 1950–2006

	1950	1960	1970	1980	1990	2000	2006
No. of Companies	649	1,441	1,780	1,958	2,195	1,268	1,072
Assets ($M)	64,020	119,576	207,254	479,210	1,408,208	3,185,945	4,882,884
% 10 Largest Insurer Groups	NA	62.4	57.7	52.5	36.7	41.7	NA
Income ($M)	11,337	23,007	49,054	130,888	402,200	826,660	883,597
% Life Insurance Premiums	55.1	52.1	44.2	31.2	19.1	15.8	16.9
% Annuity Considerations	8.3	5.8	7.6	17.1	32.1	36.7	34.3
% Health Insurance Premiums	8.8	17.5	23.2	22.4	14.5	12.8	16.0
% Investment Income	18.3	18.7	20.7	25.9	27.8	25.2	27.1
% Other	9.5	5.8	4.4	3.3	6.5	9.5	5.9
Policy Reserves ($M)	54,946	98,473	167,779	390,339	1,196,967	2,711,420	3,607,743
% Life	NA	71.9	68.8	50.7	29.1	27.4	30.8
% Annuities	NA	27.2	29.1	46.5	68.1	69.1	65.0
% Health	NA	0.9	2.1	2.8	2.8	3.5	4.2
Net Rate of Investment Income (%)[1]	3.1	4.1	5.3	8.1	9.3	7.1	5.4
Capital Ratio (%)[2]	NA	NA	9.7	9.2	8.5	11.1	10.0
Return on Equity (%)	NA	NA	NA	13.9	10	10.0	12.0

Source: American Council of Life Insurance, Insurance Information Institute, A.M. Best.

1. Net investment income divided by mean invested assets (including cash) less half of net investment income.

2. Capital plus surplus plus Asset Valuation Reserve divided by general account assets.

South-Eastern Underwriters in 1944.[9] In that case, the Court ruled that the commerce clause of the Constitution did apply to insurance and that the industry was subject to federal antitrust law. This decision prompted the states and the industry to join forces behind the passage of the McCarran-Ferguson Act in 1945, which delegated regulation of insurance to the states, except in instances where federal law specifically supersedes state law.[10] The Act also granted a limited antitrust exemption to insurers tied to compensating regulatory oversight by the states.

Despite the passage of McCarran-Ferguson, federal interest in insurance regulation has continued to grow over time for several reasons. First, the insurance industry plays an increasingly important financial role in the nation's economy. Second, the performance of insurance markets affects interstate commerce and a number of areas of public policy of interest to the federal government, such as health care, the availability of liability insurance, natural disasters, and terrorism risk, among others. Third, periodic crises, such as the spike in insurer insolvencies in the 1980s and the current crisis in financial markets (including the federal bailout of the American Insurance Group), have raised concerns about the ability of state regulators to adequately oversee the industry.[11] These crises and concerns have prompted debates about whether federal intervention is warranted to remedy market failures. Fourth, the lines between financial services markets have become blurred as insurers compete with other financial institutions in the sale of products with similar characteristics, a development that has been aided by the passage of the Gramm-Leach-Bliley Act in 1999. Finally, considering the vast resources commanded by the industry, one might expect that some members of Congress would favor a stronger federal role in insurance in order to increase their authority and influence.

Historically, the industry strongly supported state over federal regulation. However, in recent years, this has changed as the industry has continued to evolve. Increasingly, many insurers—especially those that operate on a national basis—have come to favor some form of federal regulation, such as an OFC.[12] These insurers have become increasingly frustrated with the additional costs and burdens that they associate with the state system. They perceive that it would be less costly and more efficient for them to deal with one central regulator than with fifty-six jurisdictions.[13]

The reality is that most of the insurance purchased in a typical state is sold by insurers that are not domiciled in that state, as indicated by Tables 7.3 and

7.4.[14] Insurers advocating federal regulation have not been satisfied with the states' efforts to harmonize and streamline their regulation, which can only go so far before they undermine the basis for preserving a state-based system. We should note, however, that the industry is not unanimous in its support of federal regulation. Many state and regional insurers, along with local agents, continue to support a state framework, albeit with policy reforms.[15]

Table 7.3. Direct Premiums by Non-Domestic Property-Liability Insurers by State in 2006

State	Domestic Companies	Premiums Written by Non-Domestic Companies	Non-Domestic Market Share (%)
Alabama	960,140,814	5,633,368,769	85.4
Alaska	199,073,287	1,326,309,523	86.9
Arizona	784,507, 535	7, 684,470,329	90.7
Arkansas	225,406,700	3,687, 605,735	94.2
California	18,476,141,444	41,325,400,747	69.1
Colorado	318,006,417	7, 414,151,021	95.9
Connecticut	1,159,681,584	5,892,575,976	83.6
Delaware	293,658,907	2,069,795,401	87.6
Dist. f Columbia	34,573,764	1,499,298,480	97.7
Florida	10,703,312,702	28,341,801,727	72.6
Georgia	1,525,419,120	12,380,639,913	89.0
Hawaii	727, 497, 055	1,597, 694,859	68.7
Idaho	286,125,255	1,567, 678,247	84.6
Illinois	9,279,732,130	11,874,180,974	56.1
Indiana	1,363,404,594	7, 150,200,213	84.0
Iowa	1,146,817, 315	3,425,251,422	74.9
Kansas	488,023,038	4,052,269,830	89.3
Kentucky	984,111,055	4,821,562,698	83.0
Louisiana	1,661,060,873	7, 090,655,905	81.0
Maine	457, 457, 203	1,515,481,541	76.8
Maryland	1,236,942,435	7, 719,661,243	86.2
Massachusetts	5,243,218,893	6,639,899,899	55.9
Michigan	7, 205,703,810	8,114,813,197	53.0

State	Domestic Companies	Premiums Written by Non-Domestic Companies	Non-Domestic Market Share (%)
Minnesota	924,741,008	7, 745,520,222	89.3
Mississippi	502,048,337	3,670,694,377	88.0
Missouri	1,097, 599,585	7, 956,990,523	87.9
Montana	27, 744,210	1,530,069,650	98.2
Nebraska	382,761,886	2,789,080,106	87.9
Nevada	243,628,746	4,351,300,716	94.7
New Hampshire	278,220,809	1,877, 017, 495	87.1
New Jersey	5,017, 772,536	12,339,873,743	71.1
New Mexico	154,322,435	2,410,956,362	94.0
New York	8,613,369,469	26,104,575,059	75.2
North Carolina	1,836,157, 736	9,977, 224,870	84.5
North Dakota	163,328,226	1,142,870,091	87.5
Ohio	5,049,116,034	8,265,064,920	62.1
Oklahoma	751,286,657	4,499,132,418	85.7
Oregon	1,380,962,536	4,052,242,598	74.6
Pennsylvania	4,953,341,519	15,013,047,840	75.2
Rhode Island	361,172,066	1,581,234,985	81.4
South Carolina	370,493,137	6,218,784,461	94.4
South Dakota	75,346,971	1,381,121,923	94.8
Tennessee	1,174,449,321	7,216,198,614	86.0
Texas	14,760,141,813	19,960,335,380	57.5
Utah	430,183,750	2,846,911,603	86.9
Vermont	122,420,815	988,759,500	89.0
Virginia	333,919,068	10,287,049,724	96.9
Washington	1,629,453,680	7,198,468,407	81.5
West Virginia	892,213,671	2,189,954,125	71.1
Wisconsin	3,673,436,736	4,343,889,876	54.2
Wyoming	60,703,862	775,488,036	92.7
Guam	100,803,619	17,461,504	14.8
Puerto Rico	1,793,660,730	245,922,413	12.1
U.S. Virgin Islands	37,680,482	52,579,647	58.3
Total	120,020,352,549	361,538,625,273	75.1

Source: NAIC data, authors' calculations.

Table 7.4. Premiums Written by Non-Domestic Life-Health Insurers by State in 2006

State	Domestic Companies	Premiums Written by Non-Domestic Companies	Non-Domestic Market Share (%)
Alabama	298,066,325	5,233,207,341	94.6
Alaska	—	834,760,555	100.0
Arizona	117,100,491	7,818,979,186	98.5
Arkansas	88,049,707	2,779,417,289	96.9
California	76,601,008	51,420,393,745	99.9
Colorado	328,631,440	8,353,159,748	96.2
Connecticut	8,968,009,457	6,870,054,939	43.4
Delaware	2,041,820,825	19,148,123,831	90.4
Dist. Of Columbia	2,917,207	1,824,003,522	99.8
Florida	117,188,109	29,349,453,410	99.6
Georgia	94,096,665	10,892,022,010	99.1
Hawaii	32,534,630	2,329,902,873	98.6
Idaho	11,343,082	1,804,368,678	99.4
Illinois	1,503,515,928	19,126,798,445	92.7
Indiana	1,463,279,671	8,315,296,615	85.0
Iowa	3,588,079,498	3,709,342,923	50.8
Kansas	271,151,674	6,762,640,085	96.1
Kentucky	40,642,575	4,095,718,603	99.0
Louisiana	189,099,358	6,346,594,741	97.1
Maine	20,841,111	1,819,432,785	98.9
Maryland	82,953,614	13,559,717,706	99.4
Massachusetts	1,256,082,604	11,917,921,901	90.5
Michigan	2,227,779,994	13,784,728,642	86.1
Minnesota	1,855,673,642	8,873,038,300	82.7
Missouri	274,013,875	8,715,275,174	97.0
Missouri	86,937,283	2,521,007,968	96.7
Montana	4,653	941,542,572	100.0

State	Domestic Companies	Premiums Written by Non-Domestic Companies	Non-Domestic Market Share (%)
Nebraska	482,479,999	3,146,838,231	86.7
Nevada	—	2,711,936,563	100.0
New Hampshire	3,895,969	2,138,005,891	99.8
New Jersey	3,997,113,346	23,774,433,526	85.6
New Mexico	149,672	1,822,502,902	100.0
New York	28,191,295,409	18,763,361,604	40.0
North Carolina	230,361,030	13,120,640,035	98.3
North Dakota	10,876,876	917,750,343	98.8
Ohio	2,078,124,424	16,121,765,181	88.6
Oklahoma	67,781,186	3,803,658,441	98.2
Oregon	319,696,672	4,195,542,367	92.9
Pennsylvania	451,254,503	21,565,944,160	98.0
Rhode Island	28,844,603	1,707,491,388	98.3
South Carolina	110,067,752	4,969,509,836	97.8
South Dakota	1,130,649	1,105,132,252	99.9
Tennessee	319,837,470	8,215,414,510	96.3
Texas	3,685,963,076	25,560,975,825	87.4
Utah	228,460,797	3,048,828,855	93.0
Vermont	19,631,888	953,128,301	98.0
Virginia	2,451,603,347	10,743,862,258	81.4
Washington	198,817,990	7,992,753,296	97.6
West Virginia	635,249	1,875,780,064	100.0
Wisconis	789,986,198	8,523,553,424	91.5
Wyoming	—	695,590,887	100.0
Guam	808,328	59,418,880	98.7
Puerto Rico	243,252,558	577,431,857	70.4
Virgin Islands	—	43,791,513	100.0
Total	68,948,483,417	447,301,945,977	86.6

Source: NAIC Data, authors' calculations.

Although the primary regulatory authority for insurance still resides with the states, the federal government has affected state insurance regulatory policy and institutions in several ways. In a number of instances, Congress has instituted federal control over certain insurance markets or aspects of insurers' operations that were previously delegated to the states. In other cases, the federal government has established insurance programs that are essentially exempt from state regulatory oversight. Even the threat of such interventions has spurred the states to take actions to forestall an erosion of their regulatory authority.

The federal government also has set regulatory standards for certain insurance products (for example, Medicare supplement insurance), which the states are expected to enforce. In addition, the Congress also has significantly constrained state regulatory control over certain types of insurance entities, such as risk-retention groups and employer-funded health plans, in order to increase coverage options in markets where the cost of traditional insurance is high. Finally, federal policies in a number of other areas, such as antitrust, international trade, law enforcement, taxation, and the regulation of banks and securities, have significant implications for the insurance industry and state regulation.

The most recent manifestations of the push for federal regulation are proposals for federal regulatory standards and an OFC for insurers that choose to be federally regulated. The states oppose both proposals, with their strongest opposition aimed at an OFC, which is receiving the most attention. They likely perceive that many insurers, especially larger companies, would choose an OFC, which would effectively remove a large part of the industry from state oversight.[16] State-oriented insurers and agent groups also strongly oppose an OFC, recognizing that it would reduce state entry barriers and enhance the competitive position of national insurers and producers. The OFC proposal is now the central focus of the state versus federal regulation debate.

While the OFC proposal remains controversial, the Congress and the administration have continued on the path of more incremental changes. For example, legislation has been introduced in the Congress that would establish an Office of Insurance Information within the Treasury. The office's purpose would be to provide the Treasury with expertise on insurance markets and to assist in developing international standards. The NAIC is supporting the legislation and has pledged its cooperation in working with the federal government to establish and maintain such an office. Other proposed federal bills would ease state regulatory constraints on reinsurance and surplus-lines insurers, facilitate reciprocal licensing of nonresident agents and brokers, and expand risk-retention groups to property insurance. There is considerably less political opposition to this legislation than to an OFC.

Views differ on what these measures would portend if enacted. Some state regulators might believe that these steps would ease the pressure for and imminence of broader federal insurance regulation. Others may see these measures as laying a pathway for a true federal insurance regulator.[17] Indeed, while OFC supporters have stated that this kind of legislation helps to address specific problems, it does not obviate the need for broader insurance regulatory reform.[18]

The Evolution of State Insurance Regulation

As noted above, insurance regulation has been greatly affected by and compelled to evolve in response to changes in the industry and its economic and financial environment. One wave of reforms, which began in the late 1980s, was primarily aimed at strengthening solvency regulation. A large spike in the number and cost of insurer insolvencies (see Figure 7.1) in the mid-1980s led to an intensive congressional investigation and a number of state regulatory initiatives. These initiatives included strengthening insurer financial standards, establishing risk-based capital requirements, improving financial monitoring systems, and developing a program for certifying the adequacy of each state's solvency regulation.[19] As insurer insolvencies fell, congressional scrutiny diminished and the immediate threat to the state system seemed to subside.

However, growing industry complaints about the inefficiency and high cost of outmoded state regulatory policies warranted attention. This led to a second wave of state and NAIC initiatives, which continues through the present.[20] The objective of these initiatives has been to streamline and harmonize state regulatory policies and practices to lessen regulatory cost burdens on insurers (and coincidentally ease the pressure for federal regulation). Other measures have been aimed at enhancing the effectiveness of state regulation in several key areas.

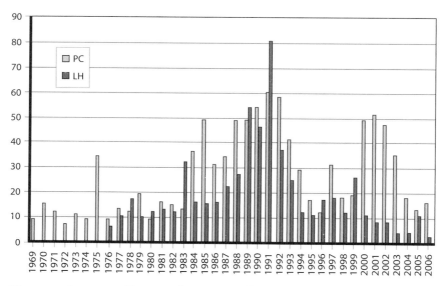

Figure 7.1. Insurance Company Impairments Property-Casualty and Life-Health Insurers.

During this period, several initiatives ensued or gained increased momentum, including:[21]

- Commercial insurance deregulation
- Enhanced consumer protection, reflected in the Consumer Information Source (CIS) website
- More efficient market regulation, articulated in the *Market Analysis Handbook*
- "Speed to Market for Insurance Products," encompassing the Interstate Insurance Product Regulation Commission and the System for Electronic Rate and Form Filing
- Uniform forms and processes for producer licensing, reflected in the National Insurance Producer Registry
- Standardized insurance company licensing, represented in the Uniform Certificate of Authority Application
- Improved solvency regulation, encompassing the NAIC Financial Data Repository and other enhanced solvency monitoring measures
- Streamlined changes of insurance company's control, reflected in the Form A database[22]

While these initiatives are impressive and some may be enhancing regulatory and market efficiency, they have failed to satisfy many insurers' demand for a true national regulatory system. It is difficult to see how insurers' desire for one regulatory system can be reconciled with the states' desire to retain their individual authorities to regulate insurers and insurance markets. Indeed, the states face a dilemma as they move toward more uniform regulation. If the states took the concept of uniform regulation to its ultimate limit, it would beg the question of why regulatory authority and enforcement should continue to reside at the state level. A more realistic scenario is reflected in the current state and NAIC initiatives, which appear to take uniformity only to a certain point. This would retain state discretion on certain rules and regulatory enforcement, which would seem fundamental to arguments for maintaining a state-based framework. However, such a scenario would be unacceptable to large segments of the industry that seek a truly singular regulatory system. In essence, even if the natural limit of harmonizing regulation is reached, it still does not solve many insurers' problems associated with duplicative and conflicting regulation.

The Current Framework for Insurance Regulation

To inform our discussion of alternative frameworks, we review the current system of insurance regulation in terms of its structure, functions, and policies. Many (although not necessarily all) current regulatory functions might be assumed by a new regulator or divided among different authorities depending on the proposed framework. How these functions would be performed raises significant issues and considerations. The orientation and specific design of regulatory policies could change dramatically under different institutional arrangements, and this also raises a number of questions. Hence, it is helpful to have some understanding of the current system of insurance regulation in considering how it might be reformed.

Structure

The current regulatory framework is not confined to insurance departments per se but extends to all levels and branches of government. The major authorities in this system are (1) state insurance departments, (2) the courts, (3) state legislatures and the Congress, and (4) the executive branch at the state and federal level. Involving both federal and state government authorities in insurance regulation adds complexity and also leads to potential conflicts.[23]

The legislature establishes the insurance department in each state, enacts insurance laws, and approves the regulatory budget. Each insurance department is part of the state executive branch, either as a stand-alone agency or as a division within a larger department. Commissioners often must utilize the courts to help enforce regulatory actions, and the courts, in turn, may restrict regulatory action. The insurance department in a given state must coordinate with other state insurance departments in regulating multistate insurers and must also rely on the NAIC for advice as well as some support services. The federal government overlays this entire structure, currently delegating most regulatory responsibilities to the states, while retaining an oversight role and intervening in specific areas.[24]

In most states, the governor (or a regulatory commission) appoints commissioners for a set term or "at will," subject to legislative confirmation. Typically, the governor and other higher administration officials do not interfere with daily regulatory decisions but may influence general regulatory policies and become involved in particularly salient issues. Twelve jurisdictions elect their insurance commissioners, who are more autonomous in the sense that they are not appointed by their governors, but they must still cooperate with the administrations and legislatures in their states in order to achieve their objectives. The insurance commissioner and the administrative branch, the legislature, and the courts collectively determine regulatory policy.

Regulatory Functions

Insurance regulatory functions can be divided into two basic areas: (1) financial or solvency regulation and (2) market regulation. Beyond these two basic areas, state insurance departments engage in certain other activities to facilitate competition and better market outcomes, such as providing consumer information. Such activities can be important in promoting regulatory objectives and potentially lessening the need for more intrusive regulatory constraints and mandates. However, the states do not view these activities as substitutes for active regulatory oversight and enforcement actions. The most important aspects

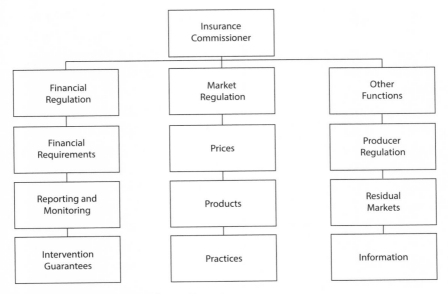

Figure 7.2. Insurance Regulatory Functions

of the different regulatory functions are summarized below and diagrammed in Figure 7.2.

Financial Regulation

Arguably, the primary goal of insurance regulation is to protect policyholders and the general public against excessive insurer insolvency risk.[25] This goal is accomplished by requiring insurers to meet certain financial standards and to act prudently in managing their affairs. To perform this task, insurance regulators are given authority over insurers' ability to incorporate and/or conduct business in the various states. State statutes set forth the requirements for incorporation and licensure to sell insurance. These statutes require insurers to comply with minimum capital standards and financial reporting requirements and authorize regulators to examine insurers and take other actions to protect policyholders' interests. Solvency regulation involves a number of areas of insurers' operations, including (1) capitalization, (2) pricing and products, (3) investments, (4) reinsurance transactions, (5) reserves, (6) asset-liability matching, (7) transactions with affiliates, and (8) management. It also encompasses regulatory intervention with insurers in financial distress, management of insurer receiverships (bankruptcies), and insolvency guaranty mechanisms, which cover a portion of the claims of insolvent insurers. These functions are similar in many respects to the financial regulation of banks, with some differences that are specific to insurance companies.

The primary responsibility for the financial regulation of an insurance company is delegated to the state in which it is domiciled. Other states in which an insurer is licensed provide a second level of oversight, but, typically, non-domiciliary states do not take action against an insurer unless they perceive the domiciliary state is failing to fulfill its responsibility. The states use the NAIC to support and coordinate their solvency oversight and compel domiciliary regulators to move more quickly in dealing with distressed insurers, if this proves necessary. This helps to remedy (but may not fully correct) the negative externalities associated with solvency regulation. An insurer's domiciliary state tends to reap the lion's share of the direct economic benefits of its operations (such as employment and payrolls), but the costs of its insolvency are distributed among all the states in which it operates. Economic and political considerations could cause a domiciliary regulator to exercise more forbearance in dealing with a distressed insurer than what regulators in other states might believe is warranted.

The states rely heavily on a number of reports that insurers are required to file, including annual and quarterly financial statements. Insurer financial reports are subject to *statutory accounting principles*, which differ somewhat from the *generally accepted accounting principles*. Regulators review these reports at in-house bench audits, and insurers' financial data are analyzed using various automated tools and monitoring systems. Financial monitoring occurs at the state level for all insurers, and the NAIC also performs financial monitoring of larger companies that write business in a significant number of states. This analysis can trigger further investigation of an insurer if there are concerns about its financial condition. Insurers are subject to both periodic on-site examinations (conducted every three to five years) and targeted exams to address particular questions or issues.

Insurers are subject to both fixed minimum and risk-based capital requirements. Each state sets fixed-minimum standards, which average in the area of $2 million. Each company's requirement is determined through formulas developed by the NAIC, which apply various factors to accounting values. It is essentially a static system; U.S. regulators do not require insurers to perform any kind of dynamic risk modeling.[26] An insurer's total adjusted capital—its actual capital with minor adjustments—is compared to its risk-based capital to determine whether any company or regulatory actions are required. The risk-based capital model law, adopted by the states, specifies certain authorized or mandatory regulatory actions that are tied to specific ratios between total adjusted capital and risk-based capital, which start at 200 percent and become progressively more severe as lower ratio triggers are reached.

Insurers that fail to comply with regulatory financial standards and/or are deemed to be in hazardous financial condition are subject to informal or formal regulatory intervention. Formal interventions typically involve regulators seizing control of a company and can constitute conservation, rehabilitation, or liquidation, depending on the condition of the insurer and its prospects. It is not uncommon for an insurer's financial statement to be revised when regulators step in, and hence, regulatory measures can progress rapidly from simply controlling an insurer's transactions to liquidating the company if restructuring or rehabilitation is infeasible.

The domiciliary regulator is primarily responsible for administering remedial actions or sanctions taken against an insurer, including managing its receivership, and can exercise a fair degree of discretion with court approval. However, other states in which the insurer is licensed can bring pressure to bear on the domiciliary regulator to act more quickly and decisively if warranted. While this dual layer of financial monitoring has likely improved the states' regulation of insurer solvency, there is still empirical evidence that domiciliary regulators have been allowed to exercise too much forbearance in some instances.[27]

Every state has separate state guaranty associations for property-casualty insurers and life-health insurers. These associations cover a portion of the unpaid claims obligations of insolvent insurers in their respective states. These associations cover only certain lines of insurance, and there are maximum dollar limits on the amount of coverage for each claim, with the exception of workers' compensation insurance. Generally, insurance products purchased by individuals and small businesses receive greater coverage than those purchased by larger commercial insurance buyers. Guaranty association costs are assessed back against licensed insurers. The ultimate burden of these assessments falls on insurance buyers, taxpayers, and the owners of insurance companies.[28]

Market Regulation

The regulation of an insurer's market practices is principally delegated to each state in which it operates. Hence, each state effectively regulates its own insurance markets. The scope of market regulation is broad (potentially encompassing all aspects of an insurer's interactions with consumers), and the states' policies can vary significantly.[29] State regulation of insurers' prices or rates is a particularly visible and controversial topic. The rates for personal auto insurance, homeowners insurance, and workers' compensation insurance are subject to some level of regulation in all the states.[30] The extent of price regulation for other commercial property-casualty lines tends to vary inversely with the size of the buyer. The rates for certain types of health insurance may be regulated, but the prices of life insurance, annuities, and related products are only indirectly regulated through the product approval process.

Insurers' policy forms and products also tend to be closely regulated with the exception of products purchased by large firms. Other aspects of insurers' market activities—for example, marketing, underwriting, and claims adjustment—generally fall within the area of *market conduct* regulation. A state may impose some specific rules regarding certain practices, such as constraining an insurer's use of certain factors in underwriting or mandating that the insurer offer coverage to all applicants. Beyond this, regulation tends to be aimed at enforcing fair practices based on regulators' interpretation of what this means. Monitoring and enforcement activities are typically implemented through investigating consumer complaints and market conduct examinations.

The states also regulate producers or insurance agents. Producers must be licensed in each state in which they sell insurance and are required to pass tests to demonstrate their competence. They must also comply with continuing education requirements and are subject to sanctions if they violate regulations governing their conduct. The close relationship between insurers and agents can sometimes blur the line between who is responsible for certain market conduct problems and the targets for regulatory sanctions.

Not surprisingly, market regulatory policies and practices are complex and also subject to the greatest criticism by insurers and economists. Further, this is an area where the states most strongly defend their individual authorities and prerogatives. A number of factors influence a given state's policies, including the cost of risk and its political climate, among many others. Economists tend to have greater confidence than regulators and legislators in the ability of competitive insurance markets to produce efficient outcomes. Perhaps more important, political interests and social preferences are often at odds with the outcomes that a competitive insurance market would produce, such as risk-based prices. This difference in perspectives contributes to the fierce debate about insurance regulatory policies and the prospects for their reform.

It should be noted that while financial regulation and market regulation are often discussed separately, they are necessarily intertwined. Regulating an insurer's financial condition and risk has implications for its market practices and vice versa. This is an important consideration in discussing alternative regulatory frameworks and policy reforms. Proposed frameworks and other structural options vary in terms of the extent to which financial and market regulatory authority is vested in one entity or divided between federal and state governments. The potential for contradictory financial and market regulatory policies must be evaluated for different regulatory schemes. This observation also applies to the relationship between the stringency of financial regulation and insolvency guarantees.

Alternative Frameworks for Insurance Regulation

Debate continues over expanding the federal government's role in insurance regulation. Various proposals for some form of federal regulation (or greater federal involvement in state regulation) have been vetted over the years. The concept that is currently receiving the greatest attention and industry support is the establishment of an OFC, which would allow an insurance company or agent to choose to be federally regulated and exempt from state regulation. Another concept that has been proposed but has received less attention is the enactment of federal standards for state regulation, which would impose greater uniformity on the current system. Other institutional arrangements have been discussed but have not garnered significant legislative attention.

Each alternative raises a number of issues that warrant discussion. In theory, consideration of the institutional features of any particular framework might be separated from the regulatory policies that it would adopt and enforce. In reality, institutions and policies become intertwined in the proposals that have been offered and how they might be implemented. Some policies may be more feasible and/or more likely under one framework versus another. Hence, our evaluation considers both the institutional features of alternative systems as well as the policies that one might associate or anticipate with these systems.

Status Quo

We begin with the current system of state regulation for several reasons. The first reason is that some form of the current system may remain dominant for a considerable period of time, while it continues to evolve. To many observers, some form of federal insurance regulation may be inevitable, but strong political opposition to this concept could delay its implementation. Second, discussion of any alternative framework must consider the functions it would inherit from the current system as well as how its policies may be similar or different. Third, the current system may coexist with an alternative framework, and this could have implications that warrant consideration. For these reasons, it is useful to contemplate how the current system may evolve, with or without the creation of a new institutional arrangement.

As discussed earlier, both industry pressures and the threat of federal intervention have compelled the states to embark on a set of ambitious policy and institutional reforms. The stated intent of these reforms is to streamline, harmonize, and rationalize the current system of state regulation while preserving certain state prerogatives. In essence, the states are seeking to reduce as much of the inefficiency that has been associated with the state-based framework as politically and logistically possible.

This is an important qualification. Fundamentally, if the states wish to retain a significant amount of discretion in how they regulate insurers, especially in the area of market practices, then there is a limit as to how far harmonization can go. For example, if a state insists on retaining rate regulation, mandated coverages, and prohibitions on certain underwriting factors, no force other than the federal government or market pressures can compel it to do otherwise.

Further, the NAIC's centralized systems for filing rates and policy forms, agent licensing, and other processes must accommodate differing state requirements, and each state determines regulatory approvals and compliance, not the NAIC. The interstate commission for life insurance products (to which thirty-three states belong) is an exception to this observation, in that all members agree to a common set of standards. Beyond this exception, there is still considerable variation in state market regulations. Finally, the policy reforms supported by the majority of states fall far short of what the industry and many experts advocate. It is difficult to envision that this difference in perspectives will ever be resolved to the satisfaction of both sides.

There are some positive aspects of this picture. One is that the states have made substantial strides, even if they fall short of what could be achieved under an alternative framework. A second observation is that the threat of federal intervention has tended to push the states in the right direction. It is likely that the states' efficiency initiatives will continue to move forward. The operative questions are how far forward and how quickly this further evolution will occur. Arguably, the states will never be able to fully replicate the efficiency of a single regulatory authority.

That said, state regulation advocates have several arguments in their quiver that may resonate with some stakeholders and legislators. For example, while state inertia may thwart or delay beneficial policy reforms, it also can discourage nationwide shifts in the opposite direction. In other words, it may be easier to fight excessive price regulation in a few states than to try to counter a federal regulator bent on implementing price regulation in all states. Another consideration is that state regulators are geographically closer to the consumers they are sworn to protect, and this may offer some benefits to the industry as well as to consumers. The states further argue that this proximity allows them to craft and enforce regulations that are better tailored to the circumstances in their specific jurisdictions. This may be the most challenging argument that advocates of federal regulation or single-regulator systems will need to address.

There are also issues involved with the financial regulation of insurance companies under the current system. Generally speaking, the states have adopted fairly uniform financial standards, so uniformity per se is not the predominant concern. The more significant issues lie with the underlying approach and standards that the states have adopted and their ability to enforce these standards.

As discussed by Grace and Klein and Klein and Wang,[31] the states are still wedded to a prescriptive approach to insurance financial regulation that is falling behind the more progressive principles-based systems being developed by the European Union (EU) and other countries.

The states would not be precluded from moving to a true principles-based system that employs the most modern methods, such as dynamic modeling to determine insurers' capital requirements. However, beyond a few general statements and limited initiatives (for example, principles-based reserving for life insurers' reserves), there are no indications that the states are seriously contemplating a major paradigm shift. Further, even if the states desired to move to an EU type of system or something comparable, there would be serious questions as to their ability to implement it, given the division of resources among fifty-six regulatory agencies. Arguably, a federal regulator would be better positioned to adopt and implement a modern financial regulatory system for insurance companies (consistent with the regulation of other financial institutions) with the concentration of resources and expertise within one agency.

Hence, the current system, while inherently inefficient and still driven by local political winds, is still evolving and improving. Ironically, the strong push for federal regulation plays a significant role in driving this evolution. Like it or not, this is the system that insurers may have to live with for some time to come. In such a scenario, regulatory reform is likely to incur [occur?] incrementally both at the state and federal level. Such incremental changes are reflected in proposed legislation to establish a federal Office of Insurance Information and other small steps that seek to remedy specific problems, such as regulating agents, surplus lines insurers, and reinsurance transactions. Some might view these measures as paving the way to a broader federal role while others may be concerned that they will undermine the impetus for a single regulatory system. Time will tell which scenario becomes the reality.

Federal Standards

One approach to increasing the federal role in insurance would involve creating federal standards for state regulation. This concept was embodied in a draft legislative proposal released in 2004—the State Modernization and Regulatory Transparency (SMART) Act—by representatives Michael Oxley

(R-OH) and Richard Baker (R-LA).[32] The proposed legislation would establish minimum standards to govern various aspects of state insurance regulation. Federal rules would preempt state regulations that fail to comply with the minimum standards after specified time periods. At the time it was released, the SMART proposal attracted some attention, but it appears that interest in this approach has diminished as the OFC concept has garnered significant support among certain industry segments. Still, the SMART concept warrants some discussion. There is the possibility that it could resurface in some form as an alternative to an OFC, or some of its elements may be included in other proposals.

The areas of insurance regulation encompassed by the SMART Act include, but not limited to:

- Market conduct
- Rates and policy forms
- Insurer and produce licensing
- Surplus lines
- Reinsurance
- Financial surveillance
- Receiverships

Essentially, the Act would cover all lines of insurance and industry sectors. A state-national insurance coordination partnership would be charged with determining state compliance with the federal standards and resolving disputes among government agencies.

This proposal has two principal objectives. One, it would compel the states to achieve a level of regulatory uniformity that they might not otherwise achieve. Two, it would dictate insurance regulatory policies in a number of areas. The dual nature of the proposal—framework reform and policy reform—is also characteristic of other proposals for federalizing insurance regulation. The notion of establishing federal standards for state regulation has some precedent. It is currently reflected in federal standards for state regulation of Medicare supplement insurance. The concept of federal standards also was broached as a potential remedy to the significant increase in insurer insolvencies in the late 1980s and early 1990s, when the Congress raised concerns about the adequacy of the states' financial regulation of insurance companies.[33]

Some might view the SMART concept as less intrusive and ambitious than other proposals that would establish a federal regulator, although states and consumer groups still oppose it.[34] Under SMART, the states would still be responsible for insurance and regulatory oversight and enforcement and would still retain some discretion in regulatory policy within the limits of the federal standards. As Harrington observes, SMART would avoid the establishment of a federal regulator and its associated bureaucracy.[35] Further, it could avoid significant policy swings that would undermine market efficiency and harm consumers. The word *could* is an important qualifier, as the enactment of the SMART Act would not preclude subsequent congressional changes to its minimum standards.

At the same time, Harrington identifies a number of potential disadvantages to SMART.[36] From a framework perspective, one of the principal concerns is that SMART could prove to be an administrative, monitoring, and enforcement nightmare. Some states might seek to circumvent the standards, raising the prospect of protracted and costly disputes regarding states' compliance with the standards. SMART could be simplified and its scope narrowed, but this would also undermine its objectives of greater uniformity and policy reform. This reflects the fundamental tension between uniformity and the states' prerogative to regulate insurance as they see fit.

The policy changes contemplated under SMART are broad in scope and, arguably, its principal objective. The thrust of these reforms is to substantially deregulate many areas of insurance and lessen regulatory constraints in others. The states and consumer groups oppose a number of these changes, arguing that they gut essential consumer protections. The proposed reforms are outlined at a relatively high level in the draft document. Any legislative version that would be seriously considered by the Congress would likely be much more detailed and specific and subject to intensive discussion and modification.

It seems that SMART's principal advantages would be greater uniformity in state regulations than what would likely be achieved by the states acting on their own. The Congress would determine what policies the states would be required to implement. Further, the policy reforms embodied in SMART, particularly deregulation in several key areas, would likely go farther than what the states would choose to adopt. On the other hand, regulatory enforcement would still be left to fifty-six regulators, and SMART would not offer the efficiencies that could be achieved by concentrating regulatory activities within one central agency. Further, SMART would not offer the optional characteristics of an OFC that would allow insurers and agents to choose their regulator. Finally, as noted above, enforcing the SMART standards could prove to be very difficult.

At this time, it appears unlikely that any version of the SMART Act will receive significant legislative consideration as the industry is placing its support behind OFC legislation. Still, some of the concepts and policies embodied in SMART could emerge in an OFC bill as it proceeds through its legislative gauntlet.

Optional Federal Charter

The concept of an OFC has received the greatest support among significant segments of the industry and attracted the greatest interest. It continues to be the focus of attention in the current state versus federal regulation debate. The original vehicle for the optional federal charter approach was the National Insurance Act (NIA)—S. 40—introduced on May 24, 2007, by Senators John Sununu (R-NH) and Tim Johnson (D-SD).[37] A companion bill was introduced in the House at the same time—H.R. 3200—cosponsored by Representatives Melissa Bean (IL) and Edward Royce (CA). The two bills were referred to the Senate Committee on Banking, Housing, and Urban Affairs and the House Committee on Financial Services, and there has been no further action on either bill, although a number of hearings have been held on the proposed legislation. While many details may or may not be in a final bill enacted by Congress, a number of important provisions in the proposed legislation are likely to be present in any law that is enacted.[38]

The NIA would set up the Office of the National Insurance (ONI) regulator within the Department of the Treasury. This agency would be similar to the Office of the Comptroller of the Currency (OCC), the agency that regulates national banks operating in the United States. Indeed, the entire proposed federal insurance regulatory system is modeled on the OCC. Like the OCC, the ONI's functions would be funded by an assessment on the insurers it regulates.

The NIA allows both life and property-casualty insurance companies to apply to the ONI for a charter and license to sell particular products in all states. It further permits the ONI to regulate the solvency and market conduct of insurers within its jurisdiction. In addition, it authorizes a commissioner of national insurance to establish a comprehensive insolvency resolution scheme, which includes the state guaranty associations (funds) that meet minimum qualifications. Thus, the ONI would oversee solvency, policy forms, other aspects of market conduct, and insurer insolvencies. It would not regulate prices (except that prices and reserves would have to be based upon sound actuarial principals) or underwriting standards.[39] States would not be able to discriminate against national insurers (those companies receiving a national charter) or national insurance agencies (those agencies with a national license).

Certain state prerogatives would be preserved under the OFC legislation. States would still be permitted to tax insurers under current tax law—again with the qualification that no national insurer or national agency would be taxed differently than insurers domiciled in a state. This would preserve both state premium taxes and the special aspects of their retaliatory taxes. Federal insurers also would be subject to state compulsory auto and workers' compensation laws and also could be required to participate in state residual market mechanisms. Further, national insurers would participate in a state's insolvency guaranty association if a state's guaranty system were deemed to be adequate.[40] If a state plan did not qualify, a federal plan would cover insolvent OFC insurers' obligations in the state.

National insurers or agencies would also be allowed, under the NIA, to choose their state of domicile, which could be different from the state where the company has its headquarters if the company so desires. In addition, the NIA would permit insurers to choose the law under which their insurance contracts are to be interpreted. Finally, the NIA would subject the industry to the antitrust provisions specifically exempted under the McCarran Ferguson Act. The major exception to the antitrust exemption repeal would be that insurers would still be able to share information about losses or claim payments.[41] Finally, the NIA allows lawsuits in a federal court if a state attempts to interfere with the operation of a national insurer or agency.

Theoretically, federal regulation would offer greater structural efficiencies than the current state regulatory system. Economies of scale could be achieved by consolidating insurance regulatory functions in one central agency. Presumably, the coordination and communication problems faced by state insurance departments would also disappear, but such problems can arise even within a single federal agency, albeit to a lesser extent. Insurers and producers would be subject to one uniform set of laws and regulations nationwide, reducing barriers to interstate operations and facilitating greater competition. This should significantly reduce the regulatory costs borne by insurers (and ultimately their policyholders) in dealing with fifty-six regulatory jurisdictions. Overall, a fairly strong case can be made that a federal system, properly designed and administered, would offer the most efficient and effective framework for regulating insurance.

Proponents of an OFC also are hoping that it would result in significant policy reforms. Most important, rate regulation would be eliminated (under the proposed legislation) for OFC-regulated insurers—a major concern of property-casualty insurers. OFC policies in other areas are more difficult to predict, but additional reforms are possible. For example, the standards for and regulation of insurance products could be rationalized, and unnecessary and inefficient constraints could be avoided. A federal regulator could also establish and enforce more reasonable and efficient oversight of other aspects of insurers' market practices. Finally, a more progressive principles-based approach could be employed in the financial regulation of insurers. This would be consistent with the Treasury's blueprint for financial regulatory reform, which envisions a more coordinated and advanced system for the oversight of financial institutions.

The carve-outs for state residual market mechanisms and guaranty associations are understandable from a political perspective but potentially problematic if an OFC were established. Excessive state regulatory constraints can cause residual market mechanisms to balloon and incur large deficits, a problem that mismanagement of these mechanisms can exacerbate. This could pose a significant burden on national insurers, which might be viewed as a lucrative target for extracting cross-subsidies. It is difficult to predict whether this would prove to be a significant problem or an unusual occurrence.

The participation of national insurers in state guaranty associations could present a more significant dilemma. Excluding national insurers would likely significantly reduce the capacity of state guaranty associations, and we presume this is why the existing state guaranty association system is preserved in the current OFC proposal. However, under this arrangement, poor regulation of state insurers could expose national insurers to large assessments. Conversely, inadequate regulation of national insurers could expose state insurers to large assessments. The bifurcation of solvency oversight and insolvency guarantees between different government authorities invites moral hazard on the part of financial regulators.[42] This issue may generate further discussion if OFC legislation moves forward.

Questions also have been raised about modifying the industry's antitrust exemption as contemplated in OFC legislation. Grace and Klein concluded that such modifications would likely have a minor impact on the industry, if any.[43] Arguably, the industry's current practices already comply with antitrust rules that apply to firms generally. Sharing loss data and analysis could be justified as pro-competitive and economically beneficial and hence would pass broader antitrust scrutiny. The carve-out for this activity in the current OFC proposal would further reaffirm the legality of this practice. The only concern might be that changing insurers' antitrust exemption could create some legal uncertainty, at least in the short term, but this concern could dissipate over time, and any problems could be remedied through further tweaking of insurance antitrust provisions.

Beyond these issues, there is no assurance that the federal government would establish and sustain a more reasonable and efficient set of policies than the states.[44] In a number of instances, Congress has intervened and required the states to impose additional regulatory constraints on insurers in certain areas such as health insurance. For example, during the Clinton administration, the Department of Housing and Urban Development sought to extend Community Reinvestment Act requirements to homeowners' insurers. Some members of Congress are currently calling for tighter regulation of property insurance in hurricane-prone areas. Consumer advocates and economists can debate whether such policies would be welfare enhancing, but the federal government is not immune from interest group pressures and excessive and unsound regulatory actions. National insurers might hope to opt out of federal regulation in such a worst-case scenario, but "regulation hopping" would probably not be a viable strategy.[45]

Despite a strong push from many segments of the insurance industry for an OFC, the states and certain industry groups—independent insurance agents and state and regional insurance companies—present a formidable opposing force, and no significant action could occur before the 2008 elections. The Treasury Department under the Bush administration also supported an insurance OFC.

It is reasonable to expect that insurance will be included in the financial regulatory plan that will be developed by the Obama administration, but its specific recommendations for federal insurance regulation are unknown at this time. Hence, the prospects for moving the OFC legislation will need to be reassessed as the new administration and Congress digest a formidable agenda. While they are preoccupied with many pressing issues, it is unclear how OFC legislation (or something akin to it) will fare in this environment. Indeed, new issues have emerged about the need for strengthening federal regulation of banks and financial markets. The Treasury Department's proposal for revamping the regulation of financial institutions included a component for federal regulation of insurance companies and is likely to resurface in any revised plan put forward by the new administration.[46] Hence, insurance is being drawn into a broader reconsideration of financial regulation that could aid or hamper OFC efforts.[47] Regardless of the political climate, OFC advocates will continue to push the issue.[48]

There is a possibility that OFC proposals will surface for specific industry sectors. For example, some believe that the issues associated with establishing an OFC for life insurers are less significant than they are for property-casualty insurers. Hence, there is a distinct possibility that a life-insurance-only OFC proposal will surface with better political prospects than an OFC for all insurers. Another possibility is an OFC for insurers that sell commercial insurance. While these options might be viewed as "half a loaf" to OFC advocates, they might gain traction in an incremental journey to a broader OFC.

A Single-State Regulatory System

An alternative framework that has been discussed (although no legislative version has been introduced) would allow an insurer to choose one state as its regulator.[49] There are several potential advantages to such an approach. One is that an insurer would be subject to a single regulator and one set of rules. A second advantage is that it would make use of the existing state insurance regulatory agencies and avoid the need for creating a new federal bureaucracy. A third advantage envisioned by those favoring such an approach is that it would promote healthy regulatory competition among the states. The states would have an incentive to establish good regulatory systems to attract or retain insurers within their jurisdictions.

This kind of approach shares some similarities with the current rules governing risk retention groups.[50] Some might raise the concern that it would induce a "race to the bottom," in the sense that states would be induced to go too far in creating lax regulatory systems to attract insurers. Grace and Klein offer counterarguments to this concern.[51] In essence, they argue that insurers would be most attracted to good regulators, as this would enhance their reputation and ultimately contribute to firm value. Consumers could learn who the good regulators were and be willing to pay a premium for products from companies who had good regulators. Grace and Klein point to the banking industry, where regulatory competition has tended to lead to better regulation as well as to benefits for consumers. Still, one might want to insert some safeguards so that low-quality insurers would not abuse such a system. Rating agencies could take regulatory quality into account in their assessments of insurers. Unfortunately, not all insurers are rated, and consumers (and their agents) do not always pay attention to insurers' ratings when they buy insurance. A single-state regulator would also need to be able to address market conduct issues wherever its insurers operated.

This proposal to allow a single-state regulator to oversee insurers in other states has an existing analogue. Corporate regulation is undertaken by the state that incorporates a company. Any disputes involving shareholders and management are interpreted under the law of the incorporating state. State legislation affects only those corporations that have chosen to incorporate under those rules. Insurance regulation is different from corporate law, in part, due to the fact that injured third parties are bound by the terms of a contract even though they played no role in its negotiation. With the adoption of a single-state regulatory system, these third parties possibly would be subject to remedy limitations that they could not influence. This is already true under the current system when an out-of-state person is injured by a state resident. Thus, some minimum level of state protections might be in order under the single-state regulator model.

The major benefit of this style of regulation is that there would be the possibility of true regulatory competition among the states. If we look at the banking model with state and federal regulators, one might suggest that there is competition between the federal and state regulators. However, in practice, most states emulate federal regulators so as not to provide national banks with advantages over state banks. In addition, the switching costs between a state and federal regulator are high and make such threats to leave less credible. However, with a single-state regulator, the cost of compliance is much lower, as an insurer need comply with only one set of standards. So if a state were thinking of imposing a costly type of regulation on the industry, it would be able to move to a competitor state.

Other Options

A number of other potential regulatory frameworks have been discussed or might be considered. One such system would delegate solvency regulation to the federal government and market regulation to the states. The appeal of this kind of system is that a single federal regulator might be best positioned to oversee the financial condition and risk of multistate insurers, and some might believe that the states are best positioned to deal with other consumer protection issues within their respective jurisdictions. Further, there is some precedent for this kind of federal-state system in the financial services industry as well as in certain other countries, such as Canada and Australia.

However, there are some potential concerns with this kind of system. One is that state regulatory constraints and actions could have implications for an insurer's financial condition. For example, the states may have an interest in keeping prices of insurance low. This can increase the likelihood for insurer insolvency, thus setting up a conflict between state and federal regulatory authority. Further, such a proposal would not address most of the complaints about the current system, which have more to deal with market regulation than financial regulation. Hence, while this model has some attributes, it is unlikely to satisfy proponents of federal regulation nor induce the states to drop their opposition to a greater federal role in insurance regulation.

Our discussion has omitted other proposals that have been offered. These include the Insurance Consumer Protection Act, a mandatory federal charter for insurance companies, and an insurance information office. There may be others we have failed to mention. While these other proposals are not in the forefront of current discussions with the exception of an Office of Insurance Information, some of their elements could appear in future initiatives to reform the framework for insurance regulation.

Summary and Conclusions

In sum, the economic and political context surrounding proposals for insurance regulatory reforms is complex. Proponents of federal regulation believe they have a strong case, and a number of arguments can be made in support of a federal framework. However, the real world is messy, and advocates of federal regulation face formidable political opposition that has so far stymied OFC legislation. Further, even academic experts are not uniformly in favor of the kind of federal system that the largest insurers advocate, although most support significant reforms. Fortunately, from our point of view, the changes contemplated for the industry's antitrust exemption should not be problematic and may prove to be the least controversial.

Unfortunately, the same cannot be said for other institutional and policy reforms. Both practical considerations and politics will encumber efforts to rationalize insurance regulation. Hence, a major revamping of the current system is unlikely to occur in the near future. What we are likely to see are smaller incremental changes at both the state and federal level that have been the industry's historical legacy. These changes will not achieve the objectives of reformists, but they may help set the stage for more substantive reforms under more favorable political conditions. The topic of insurance regulation and its transformation will continue to provide rich ground for research and discussion by scholars and practitioners.

References

A.M. Best. *Best's Insolvency Study, Property/Casualty.* Oldwick, NJ: A.M. Best, 2008.

Barrese, J., and J. M. Nelson. "Some Consequences of Insurer Insolvencies." *Journal of Insurance Regulation* 13 (1994): 3–18.

Brown, E. F. "The Fatal Flaw of Proposals to Federalize Insurance Regulation." Paper presented at the Searle Center Research Symposium on Insurance Markets and Regulation, Chicago, 2008.

Butler, H. N., and L. E. Ribstein. "A Single-License Approach to Regulating Insurance." Northwestern Law and Econ Research Paper No. 08–10, 2008.

Day, J. *Economic Regulation of the Insurance Industry.* Washington, DC: U.S. Department of Transportation, 1970.

Detlefsen, R. "Potential Consequences of Dual Insurance Chartering." Paper presented at The Future of Insurance Regulation Conference. Washington, DC, 2008.

Grace, M. F., and R. W. Klein. "The Effects of an Optional Federal Charter on Competition in the Life Insurance Industry". SSRN, working paper series. 2007. http://papers.ssrn.com/sol3/papers.cfm?abstract_id=1027135.

Grace, M. F., and R. W. Klein. "Efficiency Implications of Alternative Regulatory Structures for Insurance." In *Optional Federal Chartering and Regulation of Insurance Companies*, ed. by Peter Wallison. Washington, DC: American Enterprise Institute, 2000.

Grace, M. F., and R. W. Klein. "Insurance Regulation: The Need for Policy Reform." Paper presented at The Future of Insurance Regulation Conference, Washington, DC, 2008.

Grace, M. F., and R. W. Klein. "The Past and Future of Insurance Regulation: The McCarran-Ferguson Act and Beyond." Working paper, Georgia State University, 2008.

Grace, M. F., R. W. Klein, and R. D. Phillips. "Managing the Cost of Property-Casualty Insurer Insolvencies." Report to the National Association of Insurance Commissioners, 2002.

Grace, M. F., and H. Scott. "Optional Federal Chartering of Insurance: Rationale and Design of a Regulatory Structure." Paper presented at the "Future of Insurance Regulation Conference, Washington, DC, 2008.

Hall, B. J. "Regulatory Free Cash Flow and the High Cost of Insurance Company Failures." *Journal of Risk and Insurance* 67 (2000): 415–438.

Hanson, J. S., R. E. Dineen, and M. B. Johnson. *Monitoring Competition: A Means of Regulating the Property and Liability Insurance Business*. Milwaukee, WI: NAIC, 1974.

Harrington, S. E. "Federal Chartering of Insurance Companies: Options and Alternatives for Transforming Insurance Regulation." Networks Financial Institute Policy Brief 2006-PB-02: March 2006.

Insurance Information Institute. *The Fact Book 2008*. Washington, DC: 2008.

Keating, F. "Letter to Secretary of the U.S. Treasury," 2008. http://insurancenewsnet.com/article.asp?a=top_pc&q=0&id=98423.

Klein, R. W. "Insurance Regulation in Transition." *Journal of Risk and Insurance* 62 (1995): 263–404.

Klein, R. W. *A Regulator's Introduction to the Insurance Industry*, 2nd ed. Kansas City, MO: National Association of Insurance Commissioners, 2005.

Klein, R. W. and S. Wang. "Catastrophe Risk Financing in the United States and the European Union: A Comparison of Alternative Regulatory Approaches." Paper presented at the New Forms of Risk Sharing and Risk Engineering: A SCOR-JRI Conference on Insurance, Reinsurance, and Capital Market Transformations, Paris, 2007.

Lilly, C. C. "A History of Insurance Regulation in the United States." *CPCU Annals* 29 (1976): 99–115.

McCarran-Ferguson Act. 15 U.S. Code §§ 1011–1015.

Meier, K. J. *The Political Economy of Regulation: The Case of Insurance.* Albany: SUNY Press, 1988.

Munch, P., and D. E. Smallwood. "Theory of Solvency Regulation in the Property and Casualty Insurance Industry." In *Studies in Public Regulation*, edited by Gary Fromm, Cambridge, MA: MIT Press, 1981.

Pottier, S. W. "State Insurance Regulation of Life Insurers: Implications for Economic Efficiency and Financial Strength." Report to the ACLI, University of Georgia, 2007.

Regan, L. *The Optional Federal Charter: Implications for Life Insurance Producers.* Washington, DC: American Council of Life Insurers, 2007.

Rusboldt, R. "AIG Failure Doesn't Justify Federal Charter for Insurers" (Letter to the Editor). *The Hill*, 2008. http://thehill.com/letters/aig-failure-doesnt-justify -federal-charter-for-insurers-2008–09–25.html.

Scott, H. "Optional Federal Chartering of Insurance: Design of a Regulatory Structure." Paper presented at the Searle Center Research Symposium on Insurance Markets and Regulation, Chicago, 2008.

"Study of the Decision to Act Against Distressed Insurers." *Journal of Risk and Insurance* 67 (2000): 593–616.

Sununu, J., T. Johnson, M. Bean, and E. Royce. "Insurance Companies Need a Federal Regulator." *Wall Street Journal*, September 23, 2008. http://online.wsj.com/article/SB122212967854565511.html?mod=article-outset-box.

U.S. Department of the Treasury. *Blueprint for a Modernized Financial Regulatory Structure.* Washington, DC, 2008.

U.S. House of Representatives, Subcommittee on Oversight and Investigations of the Committee on Energy and Commerce. *Failed Promises: Insurance Company Insolvencies.* Washington, DC: Government Printing Office, 1990.

U.S. v. South-Eastern Underwriters. 322 U.S. 533 (1944).

Willenborg, M. "Regulatory Separation as a Mechanism to Curb Capture: A Study of the Decision to Act Against Distressed Insurers," *Journal of Risk and Insurance* 67 (2000): 593–616.

8 | A Comparison of Insurance Regulation in the United States and the European Union

Martin Eling

Robert W. Klein

Joan T. Schmit

Introduction

THE UNITED STATES (U.S.) and the European Union (EU) offer an interesting and important contrast in their respective approaches to insurance regulation. In 1994, the EU enacted its first joint insurance regulations for member countries. Important elements of this first endeavor include pricing, products, and consumer protections. Solvency issues were formally addressed with the implementation of Solvency I in 2004—a set of rules focused mostly on minimum capital requirements. Following Basel II in the European banking industry, Solvency II will establish principles-based, risk-based capital standards when implemented, which is now scheduled for 2012. The lengthy and involved analysis phase associated with Solvency II, as well as the influence of insurers affected by it, has generated significant global interest. It may well be that Solvency II yields a model for international insurance regulation, particularly as we see movement toward international accounting standards. Insurance regulation in the United States has been guided by a different philosophy, and this raises significant issues in terms of its place in the global marketplace.

The purpose of this chapter is to present similarities and differences between the U.S. and EU insurance regulatory frameworks, focusing primarily on solvency, but also extending to product, price, and other consumer protection elements. We discuss the pertinent elements of each system and review the literature that assesses their efficiency and effects on insurance markets. Our focus follows the current emphasis on solvency and enterprise risk management. First, we review existing regulations and then discuss the details of the proposed Solvency II regulations. We also summarize the current knowledge about the effectiveness of various solvency regulations in limiting financial risk and insolvency costs, as well as other aspects of regulation. In some sense, our chapter presents a contrast between the old and the new in insurance regulatory systems.

During the past fifteen years, most major economies around the globe have moved from fixed capital standards for their solvency regulation to some form of risk-based capital (RBC) standards. Canada and the United States were among the first to introduce these risk-based standards, in 1992 and 1994, respectively. Japan followed with the *solvency margin standard* in 1996 and Australia with the *general insurance reform act* in 2001. Europe is relatively late in developing RBC requirements; however, some EU countries already have implemented first approaches: the United Kingdom (UK) introduced its concept of enhanced capital requirement and individual capital assessment in 2004, and Switzerland enacted the *Swiss solvency test* in 2006. Currently, the EU is working toward harmonizing risk-based methods across member countries, in what is known as Solvency II. While the EU may seem to be "late to the table," it has the advantage of being able to develop a system based on the evolution of financial risk management and the innovations of some of its members.

The timing of the EU approach is relevant in that we know much more about how to incorporate dynamic cash flow analysis into solvency regulation now than we did in 1994, when the U.S. formula-based system was devised. Further, existing empirical investigations of the U.S. system raise questions about its accuracy and stringency, suggesting the need for improvement. Furthermore, the influence of qualitative, as well as quantitative elements in supporting solvency are better understood today than in 1994. The size and historical independence of the U.S. insurance industry have likely contributed to its regulatory inertia and reluctance to embrace new methods. This position is becoming less tenable in the context of the insurance industry's and insurance markets' evolution, not just in the United States but also around the globe, as well as the growing importance of international trade in insurance.

The research suggests that the type of regulatory standards and monitoring systems employed in the United States are deficient and could be improved by using more advanced methods. The best systems appear to employ dynamic financial analysis, as well as qualitative methods that are more common in prudential frameworks. Hence, we may be able to use the U.S. experience to anticipate how Solvency II will produce a better regulatory system. In turn, Solvency II may well offer insights that could be used to improve U.S. regulation.

In reviewing recent regulatory solvency approaches and related literature, three main trends can be observed: (1) a movement toward an integrated *total balance sheet* approach that takes into account the interdependencies between assets and liabilities; (2) a greater focus on a flexible, principles-based setting instead of fixed rules (for example, many regulators allow the use of individual risk models instead of standard models to calculate the target capital requirements); and (3) the inclusion of qualitative aspects, such as assessment of management, in the regulatory framework. We will highlight these elements in our discussion.

Under Solvency II, insurance regulation is organized in three pillars. The first pillar addresses quantitative regulations for capital requirements. The second pillar focuses on the qualitative elements of supervision and incorporates regulatory principles on internal risk control, pricing, and product design. To the third pillar belong considerations about market transparency and disclosure requirements, which aim at promoting market discipline. Both the Basel II accords for banking regulation and the evolution of international insurance regulatory standards embrace the three-pillar framework.

We follow the three pillars for our analyses of the U.S. and EU insurance regulatory systems, first presenting the quantitative aspects and then following with the qualitative. We also discuss issues of market transparency, including an overview of product and price regulation as well as other elements of consumer protection. Empirical evidence of regulatory effects, particularly associated with solvency regulation, is also provided. Following this review of the U.S. and EU systems, we present a discussion of differences and similarities. Because we hope that our chapter's primary audience will include those in a position to affect insurance regulatory mechanisms, we conclude the chapter with a discussion of policy implications and future research.

Insurance Regulation in the United States

U.S. insurance regulation has its historical origins in the early 1800s.[1] While the regulation of other financial institutions has been largely federalized, insurance continues to be regulated by the states. Each state retains the principal responsibility for regulating insurance; the federal government has the authority to supersede state regulation when it chooses but has done so only selectively to date. Principal responsibility for the financial regulation of an insurer is delegated to its domiciliary state, but nondomiciliary states also perform some financial monitoring of all insurers licensed to operate in their jurisdictions and can suspend or revoke their licenses.[2] Each state also retains the principal responsibility for regulating the market practices of all insurers operating in its jurisdiction. The states use the National Association of Insurance Commissioners (NAIC) to coordinate and support their regulatory activities. There have been proposals to increase the federal role in insurance regulation, for example, through an optional federal charter (OFC) for insurance companies and agents, but the prospects for federal regulation in the near term are daunting.[3]

The NAIC promulgates model laws and regulations, but the states are not required to enact them. In some areas, such as RBC standards, all the states have adopted NAIC model laws and related technical specifications. In many aspects of solvency regulation, the states have adopted uniform standards developed by the NAIC, but they may differ somewhat in terms of their specific rules.[4] In the area of market regulation, there is much less uniformity, and the states may or may not use NAIC models or modify them according to their specific preferences. States may also adopt their own laws or regulations for which there is no related NAIC model.

It is important to understand the U.S. philosophy and approach to insurance financial regulation, which contrast sharply with the EU paradigm. The states apply a prescriptive or rules-based approach to regulating insurers' financial conditions and market practices that is oriented by an accounting perspective. This is reflected in numerous laws, regulations, rules, and other measures that govern virtually every aspect of insurers' activities and financial structure. Regulators focus on insurers' compliance with these prescriptions rather than the competence and prudence of their management and their overall financial risk. Insurers' reported accounting values and financial statements are the principal measures by which their regulatory compliance is determined. This approach permeates all aspects of solvency oversight, including capital requirements.

In earlier times, the U.S. paradigm might have been considered appropriate, given the state of the science of financial risk analysis and management. However, in our opinion, it appears to be increasingly antiquated, inefficient, and potentially irrelevant in light of the evolution of the insurance industry and management methods. It is also lagging far behind the evolution of solvency oversight in the EU and the development of international standards. This raises serious concerns about the efficiency and effectiveness of U.S. regulation. It also will have significant, adverse implications for U.S. insurers competing in a global marketplace.

The states have been slow to adopt anything resembling a principles-based approach (despite statements to the contrary), and this is unlikely to change without significant economic and/or political pressure or a regime change. To their credit, U.S. regulators have sought to increase their emphasis on risk assessment within their monitoring systems and associated tools. For example, the NAIC created the Risk Assessment Working Group to guide the development of financial monitoring activities. It appears that examiners and analysts are encouraged to think about risk when they perform their tasks, but it is not clear what this means in a U.S. context. The NAIC also has established the Principles-Based Reserving Working Group to assess changes in policies and practices. The group has initially focused on principles-based reserve requirements for life insurance companies, but the group's ultimate mandate is to expand its study to other aspects of regulating life-health and property-casualty insurance companies.[5] Still, it is unclear as to how far and how fast U.S. regulators would be willing to embrace a principles-based approach to insurer financial regulation. Without using dynamic financial analysis and employing other practices associated with a principles-based approach guided by a prudential philosophy, there are limits to what U.S. regulators are likely to do in terms of true risk assessment.

Quantitative Regulations for Capital Requirements

The states impose two types of capital requirements on insurers. Each state has its own fixed-minimum requirement.[6] Insurers are also subject to uniform RBC requirements based on a complex formula developed by the NAIC. There are different formulas for property-casualty, life, and health insurers. An insurer is required to have capital that meets or exceeds the higher of the two standards. In the RBC formula, selected factors are multiplied times various accounting values (for example, assets, liabilities, or premiums) to produce RBC charges or amounts for each item. The charges are summed into several "baskets" and then subjected to a covariance adjustment to reflect the assumed independence of certain risks. The basic formula for property-casualty insurers is shown below:

R0: Investments in affiliates

R1: Fixed-income assets (interest rate and credit risk)

R2: Equity assets (market value risk)

R3: Credit (risk associated with reinsurance recoverables)

R4: Loss reserves (risk associated with adverse loss development)

R5: Premiums (risks of underpricing and rapid growth)

$$RBC = 0.5 [R0 + \sqrt{R1^2 + R2^2 + R3^2 + R4^2 + R5^2}]$$

The RBC formula accounts for asset risks (components R1, R2, and R3) and insurance risks (components R4 and R5). There is also a component for the risk of default by affiliates and off-balance-sheet items, such as derivative instruments and contingent liabilities (R0). R1 accounts for the primary risks associated with fixed-income investments—the risk of default (that is, credit risk) and the risk of declines in asset values due to interest rate changes. In calculating R1 charges, assets are categorized by *credit quality,* and the factors applied vary inversely with quality. R2 models the risk associated with the decline in the values of other investments, such as stocks or real estate and assigns selected factors. R3 accounts for the credit risk associated with reinsurance recoverables and other receivables. R4 reflects the risk associated with adverse loss reserve development, and different factors are assigned for different lines of business based on their historical loss development patterns. Finally, R5 accounts for *underwriting risk,* which is the risk that premiums collected in a given year may not be sufficient to cover the corresponding claims that arise from the business that is written. Different factors are also assigned in the R5 calculation for different lines of business, based on historical loss ratios. The formula is much more complex than this simplified description indicates, but delving into its complexities is beyond the scope of this discussion.[7]

The covariance adjustment assumes that the R1 through R5 risks are independent but that the R0 risk is correlated with the other risks. This is an arbitrary assumption that is not necessarily consistent with reality.[8] Multiplying the summed RBC amounts by 0.5 might raise the curiosity of some readers. This adjustment was simply intended to increase insurers' reported RBC ratios. As discussed later, an RBC ratio of less than 200 percent requires company action. Hence, the operative RBC amount is twice the formula result, which negates the effect of the 0.5 adjustment in terms of regulatory compliance. The result is a framing issue and not a substantive outcome.

The RBC formulas for life and health insurers are similar, but they contain some differences to reflect the specific kinds of risks they face. The NAIC's life RBC formula encompasses five major categories of risk: (1) asset risk—affiliates (C0); (2) asset risk—other (C1); (3) insurance risk (C2); (4) interest rate risk, health credit risk, and market risk (C3); and (5) business risk (C4). In 2005, the NAIC adopted a modeling approach to assessing the market risk, interest rate, and expense-recovery risk of variable annuities, which are reflected in the C3 component. Insurers can use prepackaged scenarios developed by the American Academy of Actuaries or their own internal models. The RBC formula for health insurers includes: (1) asset risk—affiliates (H0); (2) asset risk—other (H1); (3) underwriting risk (H2); (4) credit risk (H3); and (5) business risk (H4).

An insurer's calculated RBC amount is compared to its actual total adjusted capital (TAC) to determine its RBC position.[9] Under the RBC model law, certain company and regulatory actions are required if a company's TAC falls below a certain level of RBC.[10] Four RBC levels for company and regulatory action have been established, with more severe action required for companies coming in at the lower levels (see Table 8.1). An insurer falling between the highest level (company action level) and the second-highest level (regulatory action level) is required to explain its financial condition, and how it proposes to correct its capital deficiency to regulators. When an insurer slips below the second level, regulators are required to examine the insurer and institute corrective action, if necessary. Between the third level (authorized control level) and fourth level (mandatory control level), regulators are authorized to rehabilitate or liquidate the company. If an insurer's capital falls below the lowest threshold, regulators are required to seize control of the insurer.

The fact that an insurer's failure to meet specified RBC levels results in certain mandatory or authorized actions has important implications. For example, this limits a regulator's discretion to some degree. Arguably, this has contributed

Table 8.1. RBC Action Levels

Action Level	Percent of ACL	Requirements
Company Action	200	Company must file plan.
Regulatory Action	150	Commissioners must examine insurer.
Authorized Control	100	Commissioner authorized to seize insurer.
Mandatory Control	70	Commissioner required to seize insurer.

to regulators' caution in setting the RBC bar fairly low to avoid being compelled to take actions against an insurer that would not be warranted based on a more thorough and specific analysis of its financial condition and risk.[11]

While there has been some tweaking of the RBC formulas over the years, some of their components and factors have not been modified since their original construction. For example, the property-casualty R4 and R5 factors have not been changed since the formula was developed in 1993. In September 2007, an American Academy of Actuaries committee presented its recommendations to the NAIC for updated and refined factors for reserving and underwriting risks.[12]

The complexity of the U.S. RBC formula gives a false sense of accuracy. Most important, the U.S. RBC formula takes a static approach based on historical, reported accounting values. Unlike systems that use some form of dynamic financial analysis, the U.S. approach does not look forward to consider how an insurer might fare under a range of future scenarios. Regulators rejected proposals to incorporate dynamic financial analysis when the formulas were being developed. Also, accounting values can either be erroneous or manipulated to obtain more favorable regulatory assessments. For example, Cummins, Harrington, and Klein observe that the formula encourages insurers to lower their loss reserves to reduce the associated RBC charge.[13] As noted later, similar issues have existed in the EU.

Further, while not all risks can be quantified, the formula omits some that can be, for example, operational risks, using methodological tools now available. It is also important to note that the U.S. RBC formula contains no explicit adjustment for an insurer's size or its catastrophe exposure.[14] Factors for both were proposed in the initial development of the property-casualty RBC formula but were rejected. The NAIC is currently considering adding a catastrophe component to RBC, but this initiative is bogged down in a debate that is unlikely to be resolved any time soon.

The U.S. RBC formula could benefit from using better methods to model some of the risks the formula attempts to measure or from developing improved factors for the formula.[15] Yet, while some elements of the formula could be improved, a more fruitful strategy would be to move toward some form of dynamic analysis that is tailored for a particular insurer's characteristics. Of course, there are limits to what any kind of quantitative methods can reveal, which underlines the importance of qualitative assessments in the overall solvency monitoring process. Such factors would include management competence, corporate governance, and internal risk management.[16]

Qualitative and Other Elements of Supervision

Capital standards are only one component of an extensive framework for the financial supervision of U.S. insurers. This framework includes detailed rules governing virtually all aspects of insurers' financial structures and transactions, substantial financial reporting requirements, extensive monitoring, intervention against troubled insurers, receiverships, and insolvency guaranty associations. Here we primarily focus on the system of financial monitoring that augments capital standards and how regulators deal with companies that are in hazardous financial condition. While many of these elements might not be normally associated with the second pillar of solvency regulation, they play an important role in augmenting capital standards in the United States.[17]

One element of U.S. insurance regulation that is receiving considerable attention is the accounting treatment of reinsurance purchased from non-U.S. reinsurers. Under current statutory accounting rules, non-U.S. reinsurers must post collateral in order for U.S. insurers to receive accounting credit for the risk transferred. The current U.S. rules have been criticized for being unreasonable and inefficient.[18] After a long debate, the NAIC recently adopted a new framework for determining reinsurers' collateral requirements. Under this new framework, U.S. insurers may qualify as national reinsurers regulated by their home state. Non-U.S. reinsurers may qualify as port of entry (POE) reinsurers by using an eligible state as a port of entry. A POE reinsurer will be subject to oversight by its POE supervisor. Both national reinsurers and POE reinsurers will be subject to collateral requirements that will be scaled according to something resembling a financial strength rating. Reinsurers receiving the highest rating will not be required to post collateral. U.S. and non-U.S. reinsurers that do not become qualified as national or POE reinsurers will remain subject to current state laws and regulations governing credit for reinsurance. An NAIC Reinsurance Review Supervision Division will be established to implement the new framework, including determining those states that will qualify as the supervisors for national and POE reinsurers.

Issues such as the treatment of foreign reinsurance become intertwined with solvency monitoring and regulators' assessment of an insurer's financial condition. Fundamentally, the objective of solvency monitoring is to ensure that insurance companies meet regulatory standards and to alert regulators if actions need to be taken against a company to protect its policyholders. Solvency monitoring encompasses a broad range of regulatory activities, including financial reporting, early-warning systems, financial analysis, and examinations.[19] In the United States, insurers file annual and quarterly financial statements, which serve as the principal sources of information for the solvency monitoring process, but a number of other special reports are filed and used in regulatory monitoring.[20] Accounting rules take on added importance because accounting values become the principal measures that determine whether an insurer is complying with regulatory standards. Regulators also have broad authority to compel insurers to provide other information deemed necessary to assess their financial condition.[21]

The reports filed by insurers are subject to a bench or desk audit by an in-house financial analyst or examiner, who assesses the information's accuracy and reasonableness and determines whether an insurer requires further investigation.[22] Typically, an insurer's domiciliary regulator performs the most extensive review of its financial information, but an insurer must file financial reports with every state in which it is licensed, and nondomiciliary regulators also may review these reports. In addition, the NAIC scrutinizes insurers' financial statements and disseminates its analysis to state insurance departments.[23] This reflects the multilayered nature of financial regulation and monitoring of U.S. insurers—the domiciliary regulator constitutes the first layer, and nondomiciliary regulators and the NAIC constitute successive layers. Some might question whether this multilayered regulation and monitoring is redundant, but in the

U.S. system, it is viewed as essential to assure that domiciliary regulators are taking appropriate actions against insurers in financial distress.

U.S. regulators rely heavily on early-warning systems and other financial analysis tools in their monitoring activities. The fact that RBC standards are relatively low makes financial monitoring particularly important because an insurer could be in financial distress and still exceed its RBC requirement. For the most part, these systems and tools are based on static quantitative financial ratios. The use of qualitative information appears to be limited and also may vary among the different states. The linchpins of U.S. monitoring are the Insurance Regulatory Information System (IRIS) and the Financial Analysis Solvency Tools (FAST) system. IRIS is comprised of twelve to thirteen financial ratios (depending on the type of insurer), and its results are made available to the public. Normal ranges are set for each ratio. Ratio results that fall outside these ranges and other criteria can trigger further regulatory investigation.

In the early 1990s, U.S. regulators concluded that IRIS was inadequate, which led to the development of the FAST system. In the NAIC's explanation of its systems, FAST comprises the full array of its solvency monitoring tools (including IRIS), but its heart is a computerized analytical routine called the scoring system. The scoring system consists of a series of approximately twenty financial ratios based on annual and quarterly statement data, but, unlike the IRIS ratios, the FAST ratios are assigned different point values for different ranges of ratio results. A cumulative score is derived for each company, which is used to prioritize it for further analysis. These scores are provided to all regulators but are not available to the public.[24]

It is important to note that NAIC analysts use these scores and other information to identify companies that deserve special attention.[25] This can lead to a process in which the NAIC's Financial Analysis Working Group will query a domiciliary regulator about a company's status and steps being taken to address any problems it may have. If the NAIC group determines that a domiciliary regulator is taking all appropriate actions, then the group will either close the file or continue to monitor the company. If the working group determines otherwise, it can compel the domiciliary regulator to take the actions the group deems necessary. The working group's power does not stem from any direct regulatory authority. Rather, its power stems from the authority of nondomiciliary regulators to suspend or terminate an insurer's license to write business in their jurisdictions. This could effectively force the domiciliary regulator's hand, as license suspensions and terminations would quickly lead to a company's demise and propel it into receivership.

Regulators use additional tools and information in their financial monitoring activities. They can use the NAIC's insurer profiles system and may also develop their own customized financial ratios. Both periodic (every three to five years) and targeted company financial examinations are conducted; targeted exams are performed to address specific questions or concerns that arise from bench audits and analysis.[26] Additional sources of information may be tapped, including Securities and Exchange Commission filings, claims-paying ability ratings, complaint ratios, market conduct reports, correspondence from competitors and agents, news articles, and other sources of anecdotal information. While a wide array of information sources are available, it appears that U.S. regulators rely primarily on quantitative data and tools, as well as financial examinations. This is consistent with a prescriptive, rules-based approach, as most rules are stated in quantitative terms. U.S. regulators tend not to engage in consultations with an insurance company's management to assess its competence and future plans. Further, regulators do not perform any kind of dynamic financial analysis nor require companies to do so.[27]

There are two categories of regulatory actions with respect to troubled companies: (1) actions to prevent a financially troubled insurer from becoming insolvent and (2) delinquency proceedings against an insurer for the purpose of conserving, rehabilitating, reorganizing, or liquidating the company. Actions within the first category include hearings and conferences, corrective plans, restrictions on activities, notices of impairment, cease and desist orders, and supervision. Some of these actions may be conducted informally; others require formal measures. Similarly, some actions against companies may be confidential, and others may be publicly announced. Regulators can negotiate sales or mergers of troubled insurers in order to avoid market disruptions. This is often more feasible for life-health insurers because of the embedded value of their long-term contracts.

If preventive regulatory actions are too late or are otherwise unsuccessful and an insurer becomes severely impaired or insolvent, then formal delinquency proceedings will be instituted. These measures can encompass conservation, seizure of assets, rehabilitation, liquidation, and dissolution. For many insurers, these actions are progressive. A regulator may first seek to conserve and rehabilitate a company to maintain availability of coverage and to avoid adverse effects on policyholders and claimants, as well as lower insolvency costs. The regulator, however, ultimately may be forced to liquidate and dissolve the company if rehabilitation does not prove to be feasible. This is often the case with property-casualty insurers that have already dug themselves into a deep hole by the time regulators seize control.

One question that is difficult to answer is how much leverage regulators can exercise in compelling an insurer to lower its financial risk if it greatly exceeds its RBC requirement and complies with all regulations from a quantitative perspective. In theory, regulators can act against any company deemed to be in hazardous financial condition. However, regulators would bear the burden of proof if an insurer resisted corrective action, and the dispute ultimately would have to be resolved in court. In practice, when regulators initiate formal actions, an insurer's problems are sufficiently obvious that the courts typically approve such actions. What we cannot observe is regulators' power to impose their will in informal actions that are not subject to public disclosure.

Insurer receiverships involving liquidation can be long and protracted affairs that are largely controlled by the domiciliary regulator. An in-house or outside receiver is appointed to manage all aspects of the receivership, including the disposition of claims and the marshalling and selling of assets. Further, receiverships are typically administered through state rather than federal courts. Historically, receiverships have tended to be opaque to outsiders, and very little information is conveyed to stakeholders and the public. Significant concerns have been raised that receivers sometimes unnecessarily prolong and milk their receiverships for their own financial gain. It is difficult to assess the severity of this problem because of the lack of public information and oversight, but research suggests that the receivership system increases insolvency costs.[28]

An insurer's liquidation can trigger the involvement of insurance guaranty associations (GAs). Each state has separate guaranty associations for property-casualty and life-health insurers. These associations cover a portion of the insolvent insurer's unpaid claims obligations. Each state's GA covers the unpaid claims in that state, regardless of where the insolvent insurer is domiciled.[29] Only certain lines of insurance are covered, and there are limits on the amount of coverage for each claim.[30] Insurance policies purchased by individuals and small businesses tend to have greater coverage than insurance purchased by large commercial buyers.[31] Those with unpaid claims and other creditors stand in a long queue to seek recovery against the estate of an insolvent insurer and inevitably will receive only a portion of their claims, if anything.

All licensed insurers are required to belong to the GAs in the states in which they operate and to cover GA claims payments. Depending on state laws and the type of insurance, insurers may be able to recoup all or a portion of these assessments through rate surcharges and premium tax credits; these recoupment provisions vary by state and the type of insurer. Insurers also may deduct residual costs in calculating their federal income taxes. Baresse and Nelson estimated that the burden of GA assessments is distributed among different groups as follows: taxpayers, 54 percent; policyholders, 21 percent; and equity holders, 25 percent.[32]

GAs have been criticized for creating moral hazard among insurance buyers and reducing market discipline.[33] It is difficult to determine how severe this problem is. Personal lines buyers may be unaware of GA coverage or simply may assume that the government will make them whole if their insurer goes bankrupt. Commercial insurance buyers, presumably, are savvier and understand their exposure. Arguably, market discipline should be stronger in commercial lines markets where GA coverage is limited or nonexistent and buyers are better positioned to assess the financial risk of insurers.[34] Some have proposed that U.S. GA assessments (or premiums) should be risk based to diminish the moral hazard problem. However, these proposals have been rejected by regulators, who question their feasibility and likely benefits.

Transparency and Market Regulation

In the United States, transparency is variable. Insurers' financial statements and certain other reports are available to the public; however, any regulatory assessments of an insurer's financial condition and risk are confidential, and there is no distribution of any internal analysis a company may have performed. At the same time, rating agencies play an important role in informing buyers, intermediaries, and other stakeholders about insurers' claims-paying ability. Rating agencies use reports filed with regulators and other information provided by insurers to grade their financial conditions. They also employ qualitative methods to a greater degree than regulators. The agencies' ratings and analysis are made available to the public in a form that is easier to interpret than insurers' financial statements. Hence, the rating agencies are critical facilitators of market discipline. However, a significant number of insurers are not rated by a major rating agency (for example, A.M. Best provides only letter grade ratings for two thirds of the companies listed in its *Best's Key Rating Guide*).

Regulating insurance markets (such as prices, products, and trade practices) is fairly extensive in the United States. Regulating an insurer's market practices is principally delegated to each state in which it operates. Hence, each state effectively regulates its insurance markets. The scope of market regulation is broad (potentially encompassing all aspects of an insurer's interactions with consumers), and the states' policies vary significantly. State regulation of insurers' prices or rates is a particularly visible and controversial topic. The rates for personal auto insurance, homeowners insurance, and workers' compensation insurance are subject to some level of regulation in all the states, but the degree to which regulators seek to constrain prices differs.[35] The extent of price regulation for other commercial property-casualty lines tends to vary inversely with the size of the buyer; markets populated by large buyers are subject to less regulation. The rates for certain types of health insurance may be regulated, but the prices of life insurance, annuities, and related products are only indirectly regulated through the product approval process.

Insurers' policy forms and products also are closely regulated, with the exception of products purchased by large firms. Regulators must pre-approve most policy forms (except those for large buyers) before they are offered in the market. Other aspects of insurers' market activities—such as marketing, underwriting, and claims adjustment—generally fall within the area of market conduct regulation. A state may impose some specific rules regarding certain practices, such as constraining an insurer's use of certain factors in underwriting or mandating that they offer coverage to all applicants.[36] Beyond this, regulation tends to be aimed at enforcing fair practices based on regulators' interpretation of what this means.[37] Further, intermediaries must obtain a license in every state in which they sell insurance and are subject to certain regulations regarding their conduct and continuing education requirements.

The scope, nature, and variety of market regulations raise questions about their necessity, efficiency, costs, and benefits. Most experts agree that some level of market conduct regulation is warranted, such as rules and sanctions against abusive marketing practices. Beyond that, there is considerable disagreement about other market regulations. Insurers and economists generally agree that price regulation is unnecessary (and potentially harmful) given the highly competitive nature of insurance markets, but many regulators have a different view. Excessive constraints on insurance products, including mandated benefits or coverages, raise costs and stifle choice as well as innovation. Intrusive interference with other aspects of insurers' activities, especially underwriting and claims adjustment, create additional problems. Some of these policies may arise from regulators' and legislators' sincere belief that they are necessary to protect consumers. Others are likely politically motivated to appeal to consumers or other interest groups.

Some efforts have been made to lessen and streamline market regulation. For example, many states have deregulated commercial lines insurance rates and products that buyers, as well as insurers, have advocated. More states, in recent years, have moved to competitive rating systems for personal lines insurance. Further, the NAIC has established centralized filing systems for property-casualty rates and policy forms and life insurance policy forms. While these steps have been helpful, many insurers believe they are inadequate. Each state still retains its authority to impose its specific rules as well as approve the rates and policy forms that insurers are required to file.[38] This reality has motivated many insurers to advocate some form of federal regulation.[39] Even insurers that do not support federal regulation advocate deregulation of insurance prices and other aspects of their market activities.

Empirical Evidence on the Effectiveness of Regulation and Market Discipline

Empirical research and evidence on the effectiveness of insurance regulation fall into several categories. A handful of studies have looked at the effect of regulation on insolvency costs. Many more studies have tested the ability of RBC and/or regulatory early warning systems to predict insolvencies, separately or in conjunction with other predictors. And extensive research has considered the effects of price regulation in personal auto insurance and workers' compensation insurance. A full literature review is beyond the scope of this chapter, but we can briefly summarize research findings and other empirical evidence.

Studies have found that the relative cost of insolvencies is much higher for insurance companies than for banks. Grace, Klein, and Phillips estimated the average cost of property-casualty insurer insolvencies (over the period 1986–1999) to be $1.10 per $1 of pre-insolvency assets.[40] Non-regulatory factors probably account for some of the disparity; the operative question is whether regulatory policies also contribute to higher insurer insolvency costs. Willenborg and others point to the problem that regulators' ability to tap guaranty associations to cover insolvency costs could induce excessive forbearance in their dealings with troubled insurance companies.[41] Grace et al. found evidence of three major factors contributing to higher insurer insolvency costs: (1) the financial condition of an insurer prior to insolvency and its managers' moral hazard incentives; (2) regulatory forbearance; and (3) regulatory management of insurer receiverships.[42] They suggest that improved financial monitoring and greater transparency surrounding domiciliary regulators' intervention and receivership management could reduce insolvency costs.[43] Some might also argue that measures that would facilitate greater market discipline would be beneficial and potentially would reduce the need for stricter regulatory standards, at least in certain markets.[44]

This brings us to the question of the accuracy of RBC and regulatory financial monitoring systems. Numerous studies have tested various indicators or predictors of insurer insolvencies. Some of these studies have found that RBC ratios make a marginal contribution to insolvency prediction, at best. Although an insurer's RBC ratio is not intended to be an insolvency predictor, this research raises questions about the accuracy and effectiveness of RBC standards.

Using logit analysis, Cummins, Harrington, and Klein tested alternative models that employed RBC in some form to predict insolvent (and solvent) property-casualty insurers and their tradeoffs with respect to Type 1 errors (failed insurers not predicted to fail) and Type 2 errors (surviving insurers predicted to fail).[45] They found that less than one-half of the companies that became insolvent had TAC less than the company action level one to three years prior to its failure. They also found that a model that allowed the weights of the RBC components to vary and that included firm size and organizational form produced a material improvement in the Type 1/Type 2 error tradeoff relative to a model that used an insurer's RBC ratio as the sole independent variable. Cummins et al. developed further empirical evidence of the deficiencies of the RBC formula.[46]

The NAIC's FAST scoring system has faired better than RBC in these studies, which is not surprising but is still important in assessing their relative contributions to solvency oversight. Grace, Harrington, and Klein found that FAST scores are more accurate than RBC ratios in identifying property-casualty insurers that become insolvent.[47] The FAST system had a success rate of between 40 and 91 percent in predicting property-casualty insolvencies, depending on the data sample used and the specified Type 1 error rate (ranging from 5–30 percent).[48] In a second study, Grace, Harrington, and Klein found that the FAST system was somewhat less accurate for life-health insurers, but its performance might be improved by adjusting the FAST scoring system based on empirical analysis.[49]

These and other studies have found that financial monitoring could be further improved by incorporating more information and better methods, such as financial strength ratings and cash-flow testing.[50] The cash-flow simulation used by Cummins et al. comes closest to the dynamic financial analysis approach we discuss; its significant explanatory power in insolvency prediction tests lends support to its consideration in determining capital adequacy and financial monitoring.[51] It is difficult to estimate the effect of using more qualitative methods and information, as these things do not lend themselves as easily to empirical testing. The predictive value of claims-paying ability ratings comes closest to indicating the potential contribution of qualitative analysis, which is a part of the rating process.

The empirical case against insurance price regulation is strong. A long line of studies evaluates the effects of rate regulation in personal auto insurance, dating back to the 1970s. The whole of the literature indicates that regulation does not benefit consumers by providing them with consistently lower premiums.[52] However, the evidence also shows that regulators can cause significant market distortions if they seek to substantially constrain insurers' rates. The negative effects of such policies include cutbacks in the supply of insurance, coverage availability problems, diminished quality of service, and higher claim costs.

For example, a recent study by Derrig and Tennyson found that Massachusetts's strict rate controls for auto insurance increased claims costs by 44 to 50 percent and regulation-imposed cross-subsidies increased claims costs in towns that were subsidy receivers.[53] Danzon and Harrington found similar effects in the regulation of workers' compensation insurance rates.[54] A study by Klein, Phillips, and Shiu also found that stricter price regulation induces insurers to hold less capital that would be subject to regulatory expropriation.[55]

When these kinds of regulatory policies are taken to the extreme, they can create severe market problems. Several state auto insurance markets experienced severe problems before the resulting crises compelled regulatory reforms. Consequently, studies have shown that deregulating prices in such markets have greatly improved the supply of insurance and their overall efficiency.[56]

Broader studies that consider the full scope of U.S. insurance regulation and its effects are harder to come by. A number of studies have looked at the efficiency of U.S. property-casualty insurers and life-health insurers, but most have not attempted to assess the effect of regulation on insurers' efficiency. Ryan and Schellhorn found that efficiency levels in the life insurance industry did not change after RBC standards were implemented.[57] This is not necessarily surprising, as the vast majority of insurers already met the new standards when they were implemented.

A more recent study by Pottier found that life insurers' efficiency decreases as the number of states in which they operate increases.[58] This inefficiency arises from several sources, including compliance costs, delays in introducing new products, regulatory barriers to entering state markets, and other constraints that inhibit competition. It also reflects the combined effects of state regulatory policies and a state-based framework. Pottier also found that a significant number of life insurers are operating below the minimum efficient scale for the industry, consistent with the findings of prior studies. It appears that most of the higher costs associated with this inefficiency are passed on to consumers through higher premiums. Grace and Klein concluded that creating an optional federal charter for life insurers would increase the industry's competitiveness and efficiency and facilitate greater consolidation, which would enable more companies to achieve higher economies of scale.[59]

Insurance Regulation in the European Union

Since the mid-1990s, the EU financial services markets have undergone significant deregulation. Specific to the insurance industry, a fundamental market change resulted from the introduction of the EU's Third Generation Insurance Directive in 1994. Prior to the directive, the European insurance business was mostly embedded in a dense regulatory network. Insurers were subjected to significant requirements on contractual characteristics, leading to uniformity in products and limiting competition.[60] Implementing the 1994 deregulation, however, yielded intensive price competition, margin erosion, and cost pressure.[61]

Quantitative Regulations for Capital Requirements

The Third Generation Insurance Directive of 1994 did not directly address solvency issues. Instead, the directive recommended that the rules-based set of minimum capital requirements introduced in the 1970s be reviewed. The European Commission, the body responsible for proposing legislation in the EU, responded with a framework for action for financial services. According to this plan, EU solvency regulation was to be harmonized and reformed in two steps, called Solvency I and Solvency II. Solvency I regulations went into effect for member nations by January 2004, slightly modifying the existing solvency margin requirements, and mostly focusing on coordination issues.[62] A limitation of these requirements is that they are derived by volume numbers such as premiums or claims, rather than being based on the insurer's specific risk situation, often leading to undesired incentives. For example, through underpricing, an insurer lowers its capital requirements because its premiums are lower even though its risk has grown, all else equal. Volume-based requirements are easy to apply, but as has been mentioned often in the literature,[63] they tend to be too crude and their theoretical foundation too weak to achieve good risk management.

Largely in response to these problems, the European Commission initiated Solvency II, with the primary goal of developing and implementing harmonized RBC standards across the EU. The intent is to focus on an enterprise risk management approach toward capital standards, meaning that it will provide an integrated solvency framework that covers all relevant risk categories and the dependencies across them. Solvency II's current schedule is as follows: In July

2007, the European Commission published a framework directive,[64] which is now under discussion in the parliament and industry. The next step is for each member country to implement the EU rules into national law. Solvency II should then become the general norm for insurance regulation in the EU by 2012. Most parts of Solvency II are already in place, and although modifications are still possible, major changes seem very unlikely. The implementation of Solvency II is well organized and on schedule, but as the political process is not predictable, there still might be a number of obstacles that the EU regulators have to overcome before Solvency II will be the new standard. However, compared to the situation in the United States, where a major reform currently seems far away, there is a broad consensus among the EU countries that it is time for a broad reorganization of the solvency standards. This consensus is shared not only by regulators but also by politicians and in the industry.[65]

A number of institutions are involved in setting Solvency II standards. Most notable is the Committee of European Insurance and Occupational Pension Supervisors (CEIOPS), which is responsible for managing the entire process. Among other efforts, CEIOPS is undertaking comprehensive consultations with all market participants, in which suggestions for future solvency rules are collected and discussed. They are also undertaking quantitative impact studies, in which the proposed rules are tested. Our view is that the institutions are providing mechanisms for interested parties to participate in rule development, as well as mechanisms to anticipate the effects of the ultimate outcomes.

All indications are that the final Solvency II regulation will be very similar to the corresponding regulation in the banking industry, Basel II.[66] Both are based on three pillars: (1) quantitative requirements, (2) qualitative requirements and supervision, and (3) supervisory reporting and public disclosure. Under the first pillar—the quantitative requirements—each insurer's available capital is compared to standards. The first level is the minimum capital requirement (MCR), a minimum amount of equity capital that an insurer must hold. The second level is the solvency capital requirement (SCR), also called "target capital," which is intended to represent the economic capital the insurance company needs to run its business within a given safety level. In the context of Solvency II, the economic capital is derived by value-at-risk at a 99.5 percent confidence level over a one-year time horizon. In determining the SCR, all relevant risk categories are covered, that is, insurance, market, credit, and operational risk.

Furthermore, risk mitigation techniques applied by insurers (such as reinsurance and securitization) are taken into account. The MCR will be a fraction of the SCR, although the precise value is not yet determined. One option is for the MCR to equal one-third of the SCR, the so-called compact approach. A second option is for the MCR to be measured as value-at-risk, similar to the SCR, but calibrated at a 90 percent confidence level instead of 99.5. This second method is called the modular approach.[67] A minimum floor for the MCR is also established at about €2 million for life insurers and €1 million for non-life and reinsures.[68]

Regulators are considering several methods to calculate MCR and SCR. One is to use a standard model that is given by the regulator. Another is to use an internal model, which the insurer itself develops and which might be used for the target capital calculation after being approved by the regulator. Internal models offer a number of advantages, including that they are individualized and therefore can be made to fit the insurer's specific needs, rather than a one-size-fits-all standard model. Another advantage is that internal models might trigger innovation in insurer risk management practices. Furthermore, the option to use internal models provides the insurer an opportunity to integrate regulatory requirements into its risk management process. Regulatory and business objectives then go hand in hand and lead to more efficient regulation and risk management.[69] For all these reasons, large insurers are likely to use internal models. Some small insurers, however, might not have sufficient personnel and financial resources to develop such internal models, leading them to prefer a standard model. Yet even standardized models allow for some use of personalized parameters while providing standardized simplifications for small and medium-size enterprises.[70]

Both with standard models and internal models, assets and liabilities must be estimated at market values. Relying on market values should ensure a realistic picture of an insurer's risk capacity, especially compared to a situation where balance sheet values are used for regulatory purposes. As can be seen in the left part of Figure 8.1, two values need to be estimated: the market value of the liabilities and the market value of the assets. The market value of the assets minus the market value of the liabilities gives the available solvency margin. Estimating these market values is not trivial, especially if no market prices are available. In this context, determining the market value of the assets is

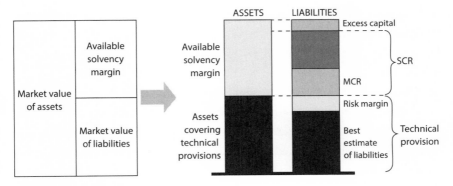

Figure 8.1. Pillar I of Solvency 2

easier than estimating the market value of the liabilities. The market value of liabilities, referred to as the *technical provisions,* is based on their current exit value, that is, the amount necessary to transfer contractual rights and obligations today to another undertaking.[71] The technical provisions are then given as the best estimate of the liabilities plus a risk margin based on cost of capital. A market-consistent valuation of risk requires the implementation of sound financial methods that account for the relevant sources of uncertainty in the cash flows. Future cash flows, therefore, must be estimated and risk adjusted, either by reducing the cash flow and discounting with a risk-free interest rate or by discounting with a risk-adjusted discount rate. Estimations of future cash flows are complicated by the number of options in the insurance contracts, often requiring the use of option-pricing methods to incorporate these in the estimation process. Solvency II thus supports the use of modern financial tools in insurer risk management processes.

After estimating the market values of assets and liabilities, adequate estimators to describe the risk of loss or of adverse change in the value of assets and liabilities need to be found. Under the Solvency II SCR standard formula, individual risk modules cover different risk types, that is, one module estimates underwriting risk (with three submodules for life, non-life, and health), a second estimates market risk, and a third estimates counterparty default risk. These three risk modules are aggregated to the so-called basic solvency capital requirement (BSCR). A capital requirement for operational risk (OpRisk) and an adjustment for the loss-absorbing capacity (LAC) of technical provisions and deferred taxes are added to the BSCR, yielding the SCR formula seen in Figure 11.3:[72]

$$SRC = BSCR + OpRisk + LAC = \sqrt{\sum_i \sum_j Corr_{ij} \cdot SCR_i \cdot SCR_j} + OpRisk + LAC$$

The factor Corrij denotes different items in a correlation matrix given by the regulator.[73] Underwriting risk, market risk, and counterparty default risk are thereby correlated among each other, but these three are independent of operational risk. All risk modules are further subdivided; for example, the underwriting risk modules for non-life and health are subdivided in two submodules:[74]

- Premium and reserve risk: the risk of loss, or of adverse change in the value of insurance liabilities, resulting from fluctuations in the timing, frequency, and severity of insured events and in the timing and amount of claim settlements.
- Catastrophe risk: the risk of loss, or of adverse change in the value of insurance liabilities, resulting from significant uncertainty of pricing and provisioning assumptions related to extreme or exceptional events.

For life insurers, submodules such as mortality, longevity, disability-morbidity, or lapse risk are considered. The market risk module contains submodules for interest rate risk, equity risk, property risk, spread risk, concentration risk, and currency risk. When appropriate, the SCR standard formula also allows the use of insurer-specific parameters and standardized simplifications for small and medium-size insurers.

Depending on the relationship between the amount of available capital to the SCR and MCR, there are three levels of regulatory intervention. When the available capital is above the SCR, there is no intervention. If the available capital is below the SCR but above the MCR, the regulator will take action aimed at restoring the insurer to a healthy condition. If the available capital is below the MCR, the regulator will revoke the insurer's license. This will be followed either by liquidating the insurer's in-force business or by transferring the insurer's assets and liabilities to another insurer.[75]

It is important that Solvency II follows a principle-based approach instead of using strict rules such as those required in the U.S. RBC standards. A major drawback of standard rules-based models is their lack of flexibility to handle individual situations, limiting the ability to assess the wide range of insurance risk profiles. Rules-based approaches also increase the possibility of a systemic problem arising from the entire industry responding to a condition in the same or similar way. Principles-based regulation should encourage greater levels of individuality, but these advantages do not come without drawbacks. Relying upon principles increases the complexity and costs of regulation, both for the insurer, who needs time and resources to implement the principles into a model, and for the regulator, who needs sufficient resources to control all the individual models instead of one standard model. Furthermore, a lack of precise guidelines could create inconsistencies in the application of standards across organizations and thereby reduce comparability.[76] This problem is especially relevant if principles are not properly enforced.[77]

Qualitative Elements of Supervision

The developers of Solvency II recognize the need for qualitative assessment in addition to the quantitative capital requirements described in the last section.[78] This need is highlighted by results from a study of twenty-one insurer failures (and a larger set of near failures) in the EU, which demonstrated that the fundamental causes of insurer insolvencies are management error rather than undercapitalization.[79] Based on these findings, Ashby et al. recommend a number of regulatory responses to bolster internal controls, most of which involve providing on-site inspections, offering expert advice, and taking similar actions that respond to specific situations rather than imposing universal requirements.[80]

Such qualitative requirements represent the second pillar of the Solvency II framework and thus one of the building blocks of the new regulatory framework. The underlying theory of the second pillar is that the risks recognized by quantitative models in the first pillar must be handled with appropriate processes and decisions in the context of a management system. Quantitative models alone are insufficient. The central instrument of the second pillar is the supervisory review process.[81] This supervisory review comprises an evaluation of the strategies, processes, and reporting procedures established by the insurer as well as the risks the insurer faces or may face and its assessment ability. The regulator also reviews the adequacy of the insurer's methods and practices to identify possible events or future changes in economic conditions that could have unfavorable effects on its overall financial standing.

An example of the requirements within the second pillar is that all insurers should have a regular practice of assessing their overall solvency needs with a view to their specific risk profile.[82] The supervisory authority reviews results of this internal assessment process as a part of the supervisory review process. The review process also includes outsourced activities. To do that, the supervisor must have a right to access all relevant data held by the outsourcing service provider as well as the right to conduct on-site inspections of the outsourced activity, even if the outsourcing service provider is an unregulated entity in a third country.

In order to make this supervisory process efficient, regulators again need to have sufficient resources, including a follow-up process to review their findings. Furthermore, effective regulation requires appropriate monitoring tools that enable deteriorating financial conditions to be identified and remedied. As a result of the supervisory review process, the regulator might require the insurer to hold more capital than the SCR determined under pillar one of Solvency II. The regulators can thereby compel an insurer to undertake remedial actions if the qualitative analysis reveals problems, even if the insurer exceeds its SCR. This is especially relevant when the standardized formula does not entirely reflect an undertaking's specific risk profile.[83] The capital add-on must be reviewed at least once a year.

Although EU regulators are working diligently to prevent insolvencies, a fundamental principle of Solvency II is that regulators will not prevent insolvencies at any price. As shown, the capital requirement is based on a ruin probability of 0.5 percent. In reverse, this means that the insurer will fail on average once in two hundred years (or one out of every two hundred insurers will fail this period). Of course, increasing these requirements to 0.1 percent would increase the insurer's capital requirement and its costs. To assess the benefit of increasing capital requirements, these costs should be compared to the costs of a failure. The use of guaranty mechanisms must also be considered. Solvency II does not cover guaranty mechanisms, but they are generally available in the EU member countries. An example is the Protector and Medicator Fund in Germany (for life and health insurance contracts) and the Financial Services Compensation Scheme in the United Kingdom (which covers life and most general insurance policies, such as motor, home, and employers' liability insurance; reinsurance, marine, aviation, transport business, and credit insurance is not covered).[84] Existing guaranty schemes are not affected by the introduction of the Solvency II rules.

Market Entry, Rate Regulation, and Profit Distribution

Beyond solvency regulation, other classic fields of supervision include market-entry regulation, rate regulation, and profit regulation. Regulating market entry, premiums, and profits was very common in the EU until the 1994 deregulation. Today most of these regulations do not exist, although differences continue among the EU member countries and across some regulated fields in the national markets.

With the 1994 introduction of the so-called "country-of-destination principle," market entry regulation has been simplified significantly throughout the EU. Once an insurer receives a license from a regulator to sell insurance products, that license is valid for all other member countries. To obtain a license, insurers must fulfill certain requirements, such as holding the absolute minimum capital required (€2 million for life, €1 million for non-life and reinsures) and submitting a business plan covering the next three years. Life insurers are also required to hire an actuary responsible for calculating premiums and reserves in line with regulations.

Direct rate regulation, which was common in the EU until 1994, was then eliminated with the introduction of the Third Generation Insurance Directive. Some member countries, however, still regulate other conditions that affect the determination of insurance premiums. An example is the automobile insurance bonus-malus system in France.[85] While there are no regulations governing the pricing of a contract, the premiums are adjusted by a bonus-malus coefficient that takes into account the driver's past experience. These bonus-malus coefficients are set by law. Even though they set barriers on insurers, these rules are completely known; insurers can anticipate them and therefore incorporate them into the pricing process, so the competition in French automobile insurance continues, even if constrained.

Many country-specific differences in the EU emerge from the fact that the individual states still regulate contract law. EU legislators tried to harmonize contract law, but due in large part to the divergent histories and underlying theories of the legal systems in the EU member countries, insurance contract law has not yet been harmonized. A number of differences in contract terms, therefore, can be found in the EU countries. Examples are the right of withdrawal, disclosure requirements, and documentation requirements. In some lines of business, the freedom of contract is restricted. An example is that in Germany, Denmark, and Italy, automobile third-party liability insurers are obliged to enter into a contract with the customer; that is, they are not allowed to refuse an applicant. Nor are insurers in these countries allowed to discriminate among customers in order to separate good risks from bad risks. Such an obligation to enter into a contract is not known in other EU automobile third-party liability insurance.[86]

Another example is surplus participation, a kind of profit regulation that still exists in the German life insurance industry.[87] According to *surplus participation,* life insurers are obliged to share their annual profit between the policyholders and the shareholders in designated ways. At least 90 percent must be paid out to the policyholders, while shareholders can take no more than 10 percent. Contract terms are also strictly regulated in the German automobile insurance market, limiting competition to pricing differentials rather than to contractual distinctions. Yet, even with these various regulatory constrictions, regulation in the EU insurance industry is not too extensive, especially compared to the situation before the deregulation in 1994.

Insurer receivership is another field not yet harmonized in the EU. Although the EU developed receivership rules in 2000, insurance undertakings and credit institutions were excluded from the regulation. Justification for excluding insurance and credit organizations was based on the extremely wide-ranging powers of intervention held by national supervisory authorities, as well as on the existence of special arrangements for insurance and credit institutions within country-specific legislation.[88] Considering German law as an example, the receivership process is comparable to that in the United States, especially in the dominant role of the domiciliary regulator. A major difference, however, is that the process runs through the court of bankruptcy rather than the insurance supervisor. The court nominates a representative, who manages all aspects of the receivership in the case of an insurer's failure.[89] We are unaware of any research on the relative efficiency of the receivership system in the EU.

Empirical Evidence on the Effectiveness of Regulation and Market Discipline

While numerous studies test the U.S. solvency model and consider other aspects of U.S. supervision, very few studies employ European data to analyze supervision-related questions. One exception is the field of efficiency analysis (data envelopment analysis, stochastic frontier analysis)[90] where a number of studies test the influence of regulation in the European insurance markets:

- Rees et al. found modest efficiency gains from deregulation for the United Kingdom and German insurance markets for the period from 1992 to 1994.[91]
- Mahlberg identified decreasing efficiency for Germany, considering life and property-liability insurance for the period of 1992 to 1996, but an increase in productivity.[92]
- Diacon et al. observed decreasing efficiency for the years 1996 to 1999, considering non-life insurers from fifteen different countries.[93]
- Ennsfellner et al. established strong evidence that deregulation had positive effects on the production efficiency of Austrian insurance companies for the period of 1994 to 1999.[94]
- Cummins and Rubio-Misas found evidence of total factor productivity growth in Spain for the years 1989 to 1998, with consolidation reducing the number of firms in the market.[95]
- Hussels and Ward did not identify clear evidence for a link between deregulation and efficiency, again for the United Kingdom and German insurance markets during the period 1991 to 2002.[96]
- Fenn et al. observed decreasing costs and increasing returns to scale for a large number of EU insurance companies. They concluded that mergers and acquisitions, facilitated by the liberalized EU market, have led to efficiency gains.[97]

The aim of the 1994 deregulation in the financial services sector was to improve market efficiency and enhance consumer choice through more competition. As can be seen from this discussion, the evidence on efficiency gains due to deregulation is quite mixed. The limited evidence for single countries and the limited number of years of data to study, however, indicates that much future research is needed to provide general evidence regarding European systems and/or experiences that would provide useful input in developing an appropriate European solvency regime.

Another aspect of efficiency that has been analyzed in academic literature is the efficiency of the French pricing system, including the previously discussed bonus-malus regulation. Dionne showed that the variables used under the bonus-malus system (such as age, sex, and driving experience) efficiently deal with adverse selection.[98] Moreover, he demonstrated that the resulting bonus-malus variable is significant in explaining both the individual distribution of accidents and the individual choice of insurance coverage. He concludes that it represents a valuable source of information, one that should create appropriate incentives in this market.[99]

One new and important aspect of insurance regulation under Solvency II is market transparency via disclosure requirements. The Solvency II rules require insurers to disclose annually a report covering essential and concise information on their solvency and financial condition.[100] Public disclosure constitutes the third pillar of the Solvency II framework. A transparent process with public disclosure requirements is expected to result in market participants forcing appropriate behavior. Market discipline is expected to encourage a strong and solvent insurance industry. Today's evidence of market discipline in the EU insurance markets is still limited. For example, Eling and Schmit found some market discipline in the German insurance market, but their evidence is less clear than that for other insurance markets or other fields of the financial services industry.[101] The new disclosure requirement under Solvency II could be a valuable data source for market participants, perhaps increasing market discipline. The new data might also be useful to analyze the success of the new solvency rules in the coming years.

Comparison of United States and European Union Insurance Regulation

The prior detailed discussion on insurance regulation in the United States and the EU illustrates the various ways in which the two regimes are similar to and different from one another. Here we offer a brief outline of several general themes that emerge from that discussion. In doing so, we highlight both the differences between the United States and EU as well as their relationship to economic principles of efficient regulation.

Insurance regulation has long been justified by its proponents based on what constitutes good public policy or serves the public interest. Because insurance aids economic development, the argument goes, its fair operation is crucial to society. Furthermore, a competitive market may be hampered by informational limitations. Within the domain of solvency regulation, many economists have argued that agency problems and costly information offer a general rationale for governmental intervention.[102] When a market is hampered by agency problems and costly information, it is believed subject to risk-shifting moral hazard, whereby equity holders have incentives to extract value from debt holders through excessive risk taking. In the insurance context, equity holders have an incentive to take more risk than is optimal for policyholders. Although risk-taking behavior may be mitigated by the existence of franchise value,[103] the problem is particularly acute in insurance because of the long-term nature of many insurance contracts, which allows management to increase risk after entering into contractual arrangements with its policyholders. The regulatory role in this situation is to "limit the degree of insolvency risk in accordance with society's preference for safety."[104] Regulators have performed this role historically by imposing minimum capital and various other financial requirements.

Until the 1990s, solvency regulation in both the United States and the EU set fixed minimum capital standards. With the introduction of RBC in the United States, a move began toward using individual insurer characteristics to determine its capital requirement. While the United States moved in this direction earlier than the EU and had a shorter distance to travel, the EU appears to have caught up and surpassed the United States, with its recent focus on principles-based solvency regulation. RBC standards in the United States remain somewhat static and focused on accounting data. In contrast, the EU is developing models that utilize dynamic financial analysis and add flexibility in incorporating individual insurer characteristics.

As presented above, most studies of the U.S. RBC system indicate that it is a relatively poor predictor of solvency. While the U.S. RBC formula is not intended to be a solvency predictor, its relatively subpar performance in empirical testing raises questions about its accuracy in determining capital requirements. These results suggest that using dynamic financial analysis and qualitative methods could improve current solvency regulatory tools in the United States substantially. In this sense, then, the likely results of Solvency II, which incorporate those tools, will be to improve regulators' ability to anticipate financial weaknesses and take action early. Solvency II also is expected to encourage insurers to manage their financial risk more prudently. What is less clear is whether or not the benefits of these new rules will outweigh the costs of additional complexity.[105] This question arises when considering the rules that will determine whether insurers will be compelled to use an internal model versus a standard model that could apply to all insurers. The standard model could incorporate dynamic financial analysis.

Beyond capital requirements, the United States imposes many additional financial requirements in numerous forms, including many rules governing insurers' financial structure and transactions, expectations for an array of financial ratios, extensive reporting of financial results, regular financial audits, and participation in guaranty associations. These requirements are costly and sometimes opaque. In both jurisdictions, we believe that market transparency through easily accessible information could be improved. In the United States, rating agencies and the NAIC offer extensive financial information regarding most insurers. Commercial policyholders are particularly aided by such information. Still, public information available on U.S. insurers may not provide accurate indications of their financial risk. This same type of information has not been the standard throughout the EU, but it is being considered as part of the Solvency II requirements. Indeed, with the implementation of Solvency II, the quality of information available on European insurers could be superior to that available for U.S. insurers. Given that the economic rationale for regulatory intervention rests on informational and agency problems, a focus on removing informational barriers and supporting market discipline would appear to serve solvency objectives.

In addition to solvency requirements, the United States continues to impose a variety of strict pricing regulations in many state jurisdictions. The economic justification for price regulation is much more tenuous than that for solvency regulation. Competition precludes the need for regulation to prevent excessive prices. Further, effective solvency oversight and market discipline are better vehicles to address underpricing that would threaten an insurer's solvency. Hence, there is no credible economic basis for insurance price regulation.

Prior to 1994, most pricing regulation in the EU focused on assuring prices sufficiently high to protect against insolvency. Since 1994, most price regulation has been abandoned in the EU. Today, regulation in the EU tends to allow competition to set prices. The initial change in philosophy was accompanied by numerous insolvencies in several jurisdictions, but it seems now to have settled into equilibrium.[106] A negative reaction such as this can be a common initial scenario when price floors are eliminated. Markets tend to stabilize as insurers adjust to a competitive environment. Again, an effective risk-based financial regulatory system combined with market discipline is likely to discourage chronic underpricing as well as other high-risk behaviors.

Numerous additional regulations associated with policy forms, advertising restrictions, licensing, and so on can be found across the United States. Some are also found within the EU. In both systems, variations across jurisdictions are being considered. The Optional Federal Chartering (OFC) concept in the United States is receiving considerable attention and support, although it has detractors.[107] Within the EU, a desire to harmonize appears hampered primarily by larger issues, such as the more extensive question of contract law across borders. It may well be that within the EU, insurance regulations will harmonize more quickly than the general national contract laws.

Policy Implications and Future Research

What is the impetus for the striking difference between the static accounting system used in the United States and the holistic management approach found under Solvency II? Answers to this question can be found in variations across the two markets and cultures, as well as in the timing of each system's introduction. Creators of Solvency II are able to take advantage of research that has generated a broad consensus among academics, practitioners, and policymakers that neither the European regulatory rules from the 1970s nor the current regulatory framework in the United States is meeting regulatory objectives most effectively. They also have the advantage of advanced computer systems that allow for development and use of more complex models. We perceive, therefore, that much can be learned from the process being implemented under Solvency II.

The conceptual framework for and methods to accomplish risk management within financial institutions have evolved considerably in the past two decades. We see a movement toward enterprise risk management and the use of internal risk models with emphasis placed on dynamic financial analysis. An important facilitator of this development is the improvement in computing power that was not as readily available twenty years ago. Other facilitators are the increase in the speed of communication and the amount of data that can be transferred across business parties. Such technical progress is reflected in differences between the U.S. and EU standards.

Yet, not only has technology seen massive changes in the last twenty years, but the competitive environment in the EU has undergone tremendous modification with extensive deregulation leading to increased competition.[108] Improved market transparency and the entrance of foreign competitors led to intensive price competition, margin erosion, and cost pressure. There also were substantial changes in capital market conditions, such as the stock market crash from 2000 to 2003 and the historical low interest rates. Furthermore, the convergence in the financial services sector and developments in other fields of financial services, such as Basel II in banking, have influenced the new EU regulation.

The length of the process in the EU, however, also provides a good example of how difficult it is to introduce a new, innovative system of regulation. The disadvantages of the old EU regulatory rules have been widely discussed and understood in academia and practice for many years,[109] yet thirty years passed between the old and new systems. Political decision-making takes time, and in most cases, a trigger is needed to push the development forward. In the EU this has been the formation of the common financial services market. The current financial market crisis that reveals the need for a regulatory reform might be such a trigger for the United States.

Despite the ease with which we compare developments in the EU and the U.S. insurance regulatory systems, we also acknowledge the environmental differences that must be considered in evaluating regulatory success. The U.S. and EU insurance markets operate in distinct economies and cultures, both of which affect regulatory approaches. Any true evaluation of the potential influence of different regulations requires focus on the respective market, limiting our ability to draw direct and clear conclusions about the two regulatory approaches.

Nevertheless, we encourage U.S. regulators to keep in mind a variety of ideas that emerge from the Solvency II process when revising the U.S. system. One of these is the notion of a principle-based approach. While U.S. regulators have indicated interest in exploring the broad application of a principles-based approach, there is no indication that they are poised to pursue a comprehensive set of reforms such as those being developed in the EU. A drawback of standard rules-based models as found in the United States is that these have only very limited flexibility to handle individual situations. Therefore, the U.S. model might not be very effective in assessing the wide range of insurance risk profiles.[110] In comparison, the principles-based approach found under Solvency II is flexible and captures individual risk profiles, for example, using the insurer's parameters instead of those determined by the regulator. A principles-based approach could trigger innovation, as insurers are encouraged to develop and use their own risk models in order to determine the regulatory target capital. We anticipate competition among insurers to develop the best risk model in the market.

Another advantage in this context is that the principles-based approach allows the insurer to integrate regulatory requirements into its management process. Business and regulatory objectives then go hand in hand, which could lead to efficient regulation and risk management.[111] Therefore Solvency II has the potential to improve management practices. Overall, Solvency II might create a superior atmosphere for innovation in EU insurance markets, which might also result in a competitive advantage for EU insurers compared to their U.S. competitors.

These advantages, however, do not come without drawbacks. Relying upon principles could increase the complexity and costs of regulation, both for the insurer, who needs time and money to implement the principles into a model, and for the regulator, who needs sufficient resources to evaluate all the individual models instead of one standard model. A major effort by regulators will be to assure that internal models are appropriate for the situation, and not methods to hide concerns specific to individual reasons. Such effort is costly in time and resources. For that reason, we do not argue that there is a need for a centralized regulatory authority. Most academic experts believe that the efficiency of U.S. regulation could be improved by creating a federal regulatory authority;

however, the retention of a state-based system would not preclude more effi-cient and harmonized regulation. We should note that the idea of creating an EU-wide insurance authority with independent country (state) regulators has been discussed periodically and then abandoned. Of course, it is important to recognize that the United States consists of states within one nation whereas the EU consists of sovereign countries within a unified framework. In either setting, what can be improved is the coordination between the different regula-tors; they therefore need to work on a mutual basis using the same principles, and they need a fast and efficient connection to transfer information.

We therefore argue for a flexible scheme, one in which RBC standards are used as guidelines to assist insurers in managing their risk structures rather than as absolute requirements.[112] Flexibility is likely to yield a variety of risk strategies, limiting the possibility of systemic risk inherent in using a single standard model for all or even most insurers. Model arbitrage would be less effective, too, given that the requirements are flexible rather than rigid. U.S. regulators might also consider forming something akin to the CEIOPS, which has been given the task to redesign the EU regulatory framework and is con-ducting public forums in which suggestions for future solvency rules are being collected and discussed. In the United States, the closest analog to a structure that would have any kind of real authority would be an interstate compact. An interstate compact has been used to harmonize the regulation of U.S. life insurance products, and such a vehicle could be used to advance and harmonize other aspects of U.S. insurance regulation.

Throughout this chapter, we have presented specifics of a variety of insur-ance regulatory controls in the United States and the EU. We further presented existing empirical evidence of the performance of some of those controls. Much additional research is warranted to assess the effects of recent and soon-to-be-implemented changes to those regulatory systems. We encourage research on the effectiveness of various solvency models, the ability of market discipline to substitute for government intervention, and the ways in which insurance supervisors will be most effective in employing qualitative analyses of insurer practices. Implementation of Solvency II offers us a rich opportunity for a natu-ral experiment on these open questions.

References

American Academy of Actuaries. "An Update to P/C Risk-Based Capital Underwriting Factors." September 2007 report to the National Association of Insurance Commissioners P/C Risk-Based Capital Working Group, Washington, DC.

Ashby, S., P. Sharma, and W. McDonnell. "Lessons about Risk: Analyzing the Causal Chain of Insurance Company Failure." *Journal of Insurance Research and Practice* 18(2003): 4–15.

BaFin. *German Insurance Supervision Act (Versicherungsaufsichtsgesetz)*. 2009. http://www.bafin.de.

Barkume, A., and J. W. Ruser. "Deregulating Property-Casualty Insurance: The Case of Workers' Compensation." *Journal of Law and Economics* 44 (2001): 37–63.

Barrese, J., and J. Nelson. "Some Consequences of Insurer Insolvencies." *Journal of Insurance Regulation* 13 (1994): 3–18.

Basedow, J., and T. Fock. *Europäisches Versicherungsvertragsrecht I*. Tübingen: Mohr Siebeck, 2003.

Basel Committee on Banking Supervision. "The New Basel Capital Accord." Bank for International Settlements, 2001. http://www.bis.org.

Black, J., M. Hopper, and C. Band. "Defining Principles-Based Accounting Standards," *Law and Financial Markets Review* 1(2007): 191–206.

Butsic, R. P. "Report on Covariance Method for Property-Casualty Risk-Based Capital." *Casualty Actuarial Society Forum* summer (1993): 173–202.

CEIOPS. "Draft Advice to the European Commission in the Framework of the Solvency II Project on Pillar I Issues—Further Advice." Consultation paper 20, 2006. http://www.ceiops.org.

Chiappori, A., and B. Salanié. "Testing for Asymmetric Information in Insurance Markets." *The Journal of Political Economy* 108 (2000): 56–78.

Conference of Insurance Supervisory Services of the Member States of the European Union. "Prudential Supervision of Insurance Undertakings." Report prepared under the Chairmanship of Paul Sharma, Head of the Prudential Risks Department of the UK's Financial Services Authority, 2002.

Cummins, J. D., ed. *Deregulating Property-Liability Insurance: Restoring Competition and Increasing Market Efficiency*. Washington, DC: Brookings Institution Press, 2002.

Cummins, J. D. "Reinsurance for Natural and Man-Made Catastrophes in the United States: Current State of the Market and Regulatory Reforms." *Risk Management and Insurance Review* 10 (2007): 179–220.

Cummins, J. D. "Risk Based Premiums for Insurance Guaranty Funds." *Journal of Finance* 43 (1988): 823–839.

Cummins, J. D., M. Grace, and R. D. Phillips. "Regulatory Solvency Prediction in Property-Liability Insurance: Risk-Based Capital, Audit Ratios, and Cash Flow Simulation." *Journal of Risk and Insurance* 66 (1999): 417–458.

Cummins, J. D., S. E. Harrington, and R. W. Klein. "Insolvency Experience, Risk-Based Capital, and Prompt Corrective Action in Property-Liability Insurance." *Journal of Banking and Finance* 19 (1995): 511–527.

Cummins, J. D., and M. Rubio-Misas. "Deregulation, Consolidation, and Efficiency: Evidence from the Spanish Insurance Industry." *Journal of Money, Credit, and Banking* 38 (2006): 323–355.

Danzon, P. M., and S. E. Harrington. "Workers' Compensation Rate Regulation: How Price Controls Increase Costs." *Journal of Law and Economics* 44 (2001): 1–36.

Derrig, R. A., and S. L. Tennyson. "The Impact of Rate Regulation on Claims: Evidence from Massachusetts Automobile Insurance" (2008). http://ssrn.com/abstract=1115377.

Diacon, S. R., K. Starkey, and C. O'Brien. "Size and Efficiency in European Long-Term Insurance Companies: An International Comparison." *Geneva Papers on Risk and Insurance* 27 (2002): 444–466.

Dionne, G. "Commitment and Automobile Insurance Regulation in France, Quebec and Japan." Working paper, HEC Montreal, 2001.

Distinguin, I., P. Rous, and A. Tarazi. "Market Discipline and the Use of Stock Market Data to Predict Bank Financial Distress." *Journal of Financial Services Research* 30 (2006): 151–176.

Downs, D. H., and D. W. Sommer. "Monitoring, Ownership and Risk-Taking: The Impact of Guaranty Funds." *Journal of Risk and Insurance* 66 (1999): 477–497.

Duverne, D., and J. Le Douit. "IFRS for Insurance: CFO Forum Proposals." *Geneva Papers on Risk and Insurance* 32 (2007): 62–74.

Eling, M., N. Gatzert, and H. Schmeiser. "The Swiss Solvency Test and Its Market Implications." *Geneva Papers on Risk and Insurance* 33 (2008): 418–439.

Eling, M., and M. Luhnen. "Frontier Efficiency Methodologies to Measure Performance in the Insurance Industry: Overview and New Empirical Evidence." Working paper, University of St. Gallen, 2008.

Eling, M., and T. Parnitzke. "Dynamic Financial Analysis: Conception, Classification, and Implementation." *Risk Management and Insurance Review* 10 (2007): 33–50.

Eling, M., H. Schmeiser, and J. T. Schmit. "The Solvency II Process: Overview and Critical Analysis." *Risk Management and Insurance Review* 10 (2007): 69–85.

Eling, M., and J. T. Schmit. "Market Discipline in the European Insurance Industry: The Case of Germany." Working paper, University of St. Gallen/University of Wisconsin-Madison, 2008.

Ennsfellner, K. C., D. Lewis, and R. I. Anderson. "Production Efficiency in the Austrian Insurance Industry: A Bayesian Examination." *Journal of Risk and Insurance* 71 (2004): 135–159.

Epermanis, K., and S. Harrington. "Market Discipline in Property/Casualty Insurance: Evidence from Premium Growth Surrounding Changes in Financial Strength Ratings." *Journal of Money, Credit, and Banking* 38 (2006): 1515–1544.

Esson, R., and P. Cooke. "Accounting and Solvency Convergence—Dream or Reality?" *Geneva Papers on Risk and Insurance* 32 (2007): 332–344.

European Commission (EC). "Directive of the European Parliament and the Council on the Taking-Up and Pursuit of the Business of Insurance and Reinsurance—Solvency II, COM: 361." Brussels, 2007.

European Commission (EC). "Frequently Asked Questions" (MEMO/07/286). Brussels, 2007.

European Union. "Council Regulation (EC) No 1346/2000 of 29 May 2000 on insolvency proceedings." *Official Journal of the European Communities* 160 (2000): 1–18.

European Union. "Directive 2002/13/EC as Regards the Solvency Margin Requirements for Non-Life Insurance Undertakings." *Official Journal of the European Communities* 77 (2002): 17–22.

European Union. "Directive 2002/83/EC Concerning Life Assurance." *Official Journal of the European Communities* 345 (2002): 1–51.

Farny, D. "The Development of European Private Sector Insurance over the Last 25 Years and the Conclusions That Can Be Drawn for Business Management Theory of Insurance Companies." *Geneva Papers on Risk and Insurance* 24 (1999): 145–162.

Farny, D. "Security of Insurers: The American Risk-Based Capital Model Versus the European Model of Solvability for Property and Casualty Insurers." *Geneva Papers on Risk and Insurance* 22 (1997): 69–75.

Feldblum, S. "NAIC Property/Casualty Insurance Company Risk-Based Capital Requirements." *Proceedings of the Casualty Actuarial Society* LXXXIII (1996): 297–418.

Fenn, P., D. Vencappa, S. Diacon, P. Klumpes, and C. O'Brien. "Market Structure and the Efficiency of European Insurance Companies: A Stochastic Frontier Analysis." *Journal of Banking and Finance* 32 (2008): 86–100.

Financial Services Authority. "Principles-Based Regulation—Focusing on the Outcomes That Matter." 2007. http://www.fsa.gov.uk.

Grace, M., S. Harrington, and R. W. Klein. "Identifying Troubled Life Insurers." *Journal of Insurance Regulation* 16 (1998): 249–290.

Grace, M., S. Harrington, and R. W. Klein. "Risk-Based Capital and Solvency Screening in Property-Liability Insurance." *Journal of Risk and Insurance* 65 (1998): 213–243.

Grace, M. F., and R. W. Klein. "The Effects of an Optional Federal Charter on Competition in the Life Insurance Industry." Center for Risk Management and Insurance Research, Georgia State University, Atlanta, October, 2007.

Grace M. F., R. W. Klein, and R. D. Phillips. "Auto Insurance Reform: Salvation in South Carolina. In *Deregulating Property-Liability Insurance,*" edited by J. D. Cummins, pp. 148–194. Washington, DC: Brookings Institution Press, 2002.

Grace, M. F., R. W. Klein, and R. D. Phillips. "Managing the Cost of Property-Casualty Insurer Insolvencies in the U.S." Center for Risk Management and Insurance Research, Georgia State University, Atlanta, Research Report 02-1, 2002.

Hall, B. J. "Regulatory Free Cash Flow and the High Cost of Insurance Company Failures." *Journal of Risk and Insurance* 67 (2000): 415–438.

Harrington, Scott E. "Capital Adequacy in Insurance and Reinsurance." In *Capital Adequacy Beyond Basel: Banking, Securities and Insurance,* edited by Hal Scott. New York: Oxford University Press, 2004.

Harrington, Scott E. "Effects of Prior Approval Rate Regulation of Auto Insurance." In *Deregulating Property-Liability Insurance: Restoring Competition and Increasing Market Efficiency,* edited by J. David Cummins. Washington, DC: Brookings Institution Press, 2002.

Hussels, S., and D. R. Ward. "The Impact of Deregulation on the German and UK Life Insurance Markets: An Analysis of Efficiency and Productivity between 1991 and 2002." Working paper, Cranfield Research Paper Series (4), 2006.

Hussels, S., D. Ward, and R. Zurbruegg. "Stimulating the Demand for Insurance." *Risk Management and Insurance Review* 8 (2005): 257–278.

James, C. "The Losses Realized in Bank Failures." *Journal of Finance* 46 (1991): 1223–1242.

Kaufmann, G. Prepared testimony of George G. Kaufmann for the U.S. Senate Committee on Banking, Housing and Urban Affairs, September 11, 2001. http://www.senate.gov/~banking/ 01_09hrg/091101/kaufman.htm.

Klein, R. W. "Insurance Regulation in Transition." *Journal of Risk and Insurance* 62 (1995): 363–404.

Klein, R. W. *A Regulator's Introduction to the Insurance Industry,* 2nd ed. Kansas City, MO: National Association of Insurance Commissioners, 2005.

Klein, R. W., R. D. Phillips, and W. Shiu. "The Capital Structure of Firms Subject to Price Regulation: Evidence from the Insurance Industry." *Journal of Financial Services Research* 21 (2002): 79–100.

Klein, R. W., and S. Wang. "Catastrophe Risk Financing in the United States and the European Union: A Comparison of Alternative Regulatory Approaches." Paper presented at the New Forms of Risk Sharing and Risk Engineering: A SCOR-JRI Conference on Insurance, Reinsurance, and Capital Market Transformations, Paris, 2007.

Lee, S., D. Mayers, and C. W. Smith Jr. "Guaranty Funds and Risk-Taking: Evidence from the Insurance Industry." *Journal of Financial Economics* 44 (1997): 3–24.

Mahlberg, B. "Technischer Fortschritt und Produktivitätsveränderungen in der deutschen Versicherungswirtschaft." *Jahrbücher für Nationalökonomik und Statistik* 220 (2000): 565–591.

Munch, P., and D. E. Smallwood. "Theory of Solvency Regulation in the Property and Casualty Insurance Industry." In *Studies in Public Regulation*, edited by Gary Fromm. Cambridge, MA: MIT Press, 1981.

National Association of Insurance Companies. "Principles for the NAIC's Adoption of a Principles-Based Reserving Approach." Kansas City, MO, 2008.

National Association of Insurance Companies. "2007 Property-Casualty Risk-Based Capital Overview and Instructions." Kansas City, MO, 2007.

Organization for Economic Cooperation and Development. *Insurance Solvency Supervision: OECD Country Profiles.* Paris, 2002.

Pottier, S. W. "State Insurance Regulation of Life Insurers: Implications for Economic Efficiency and Financial Strength." Report to the ACLI, University of Georgia, 2007.

Pottier, S., and D. Sommer. "The Effectiveness of Public and Private Sector Summary Risk Measures in Predicting Insurer Insolvencies." *Journal of Financial Services Research* 21 (2002): 101–116.

Rees, R., E. Kessner, P. Klemperer, and C. Matutes. "Regulation and Efficiency in European Insurance Markets." *Economic Policy* 14 (1999): 363–397.

Ruhil, A., and P. Teske. "Institutions, Bureaucratic Decisions, and Policy Outcomes: State Insurance Solvency Regulation." *The Policies Studies Journal* 31 (2003): 353–372.

Ryan, H. S., and C. D. Schellhorn. "Life Insurer Cost Efficiency Before and After Implementation of NAIC Risk-Based Capital Standards." *Journal of Insurance Regulation* 18 (2000): 362–382.

Sironi, A. "Testing for Market Discipline in the European Banking Industry: Evidence from Subordinated Debt Issues." *Journal of Money, Credit, and Banking* 35 (2003): 443–472.

Staking, K. B., and D. F. Babbel. "The Relationship between Capital Structure, Interest Rate Sensitivity, and Market Value in the Property-Liability Insurance Industry." *Journal of Risk and Insurance* 62 (1995): 690.

Steffen, T. "Solvency II and the Work of CEIOPS." *Geneva Papers on Risk and Insurance* 33 (2008): 60–65.

Thomason, T., T. P. Schmidle, and J. F. Burton, Jr. *Workers' Compensation: Benefits, Costs and Safety under Alternative Insurance Arrangements*. Kalamazoo, MI: W.E. Upjohn Institute for Employment Research, 2001.

Toppe Shortridge, R., and M. Myring. "Defining Principles-Based Accounting Standards," *The CPA Journal* 74 (2004): 34–37.

U.S. Department of the Treasury. *Blueprint for a Modernized Financial Regulatory Structure*. Washington, DC, 2008.

Willenborg, M. "Regulatory Separation as a Mechanism to Curb Capture: A Study of the Decision to Act Against Distressed Insurers." *Journal of Risk and Insurance* 67 (2000): 593–616.

9

Estimating Efficiency Effects of Uniform Regulation in Property and Casualty Insurance

David L. Eckles
Lawrence S. Powell

Introduction

INSURANCE COMPANIES IN the United States are licensed and regulated at the state level. Each state and territory maintains a distinct regulatory system for insurance companies operating in its jurisdiction. Therefore, a single insurance company in the United States may face as many as fifty-five[1] distinct regulators. While the National Association of Insurance Commissioners (NAIC) coordinates efforts to achieve partial uniformity across states, substantial differences in insurance regulation are observed from state to state.

Differences in insurance regulation across states can occur because the underlying law is not the same, or because regulators subjectively apply identical laws differently. Underwriting and rating restrictions are an example of the former cause. Given the wide variation in restrictions across states, an insurance company operating in all states may have to use more than a dozen different rate-making processes to comply with the laws of every state.[2] Differences in regulation due to subjective application include regulators' responses to rate filings and implementation of financial and market conduct examinations.

Insurers, regulators, and consumers largely agree that, all else equal, such differences across states increase the cost of insurance. Costs are manifest in repetitive tasks and the need for multiple strategies to comply with regulation.

Surprisingly, extant literature measuring the cost of non-uniform regulation for insurance consumers is quite thin. In this chapter, we extend the literature on regulatory efficiency to include empirical evidence from the property-casualty insurance industry. Specifically, we estimate the cost of multiple regulatory regimes by measuring the relation between the number of states in which an insurer does business and two proxies for operating cost.

Background

The U.S. Constitution specifies that while commerce within a state shall be regulated by that state, interstate commerce shall face federal regulation. In 1869, the U.S. Supreme Court decided in *Paul v. Virginia* that insurance was not interstate commerce and should be regulated at the state level.[3] However, the Court overturned the *Paul* decision in 1944, ruling in *United States v. South-Eastern Underwriters Association* that the business of insurance constitutes interstate commerce and is therefore subject to federal jurisdiction under the U.S. Constitution.[4] Among other things, the ruling effectively meant that federal antitrust laws would henceforth be applied to the insurance industry.[5]

Fearing that federal antitrust laws would not serve insurance consumers,[6] the 79th Congress enacted Public Law 15, better known as the McCarran-Ferguson Act of 1945 (McCarran).[7] McCarran grants states the authority to regulate the business of insurance in all but a few rare instances.

More than fourteen decades after the Supreme Court ruled in *Paul v. Virginia*, stakeholders remain divided on the efficacy of state versus federal regulation for property-casualty insurers. Arguments favoring state regulation tout differences across states as value-creating public policy, meeting specific needs of each state's citizens. Insurance consumers' needs and fundamental problems differ across states based on demographic factors like income and age as well as applicable perils and hazards. For example, weather-related perils differ substantially across states, leading regulators to seek different remedies for hurricanes, earthquakes, ice storms, or floods. In the same way, insurance regulatory concerns differ across states based on concentrations of demographic groups such as seniors, those in poverty, or high-wealth individuals. A state-level insurance regulation system can address these issues to best suit its constituents.

On the other hand, opponents point to the same differences across states as inefficient business practices, requiring redundant reporting and adding unnecessary complexity to insurer strategies. Because the majority (90%) of property-casualty insurance is written by insurance carriers operating in multiple states, the cost of inefficiency is largely borne by consumers.

We provide information on the implicit tradeoff between local regulation and efficiency by estimating the cost for consumers to weigh against the perceived benefits of state regulation.

Literature Review

Several studies investigate efficiency effects of regulatory stringency; however, we are aware of only three studies examining the efficiency effects of multiple, state-level regulators on insurance companies. All of them focus on the life insurance industry. Grace and Klein study the effect of regulation costs from the perspective of both the government and the individual insurers. They find that regulatory expenses (among other expenses) are positively related to the number of states licensed.[8] Similarly, McShane and Cox find that expense ratios are positively correlated with the number of regulators.[9] However, the authors also show a positive relation between number of regulators and insurer profit, suggesting a benefit of multiple regulators, at least to investors and owners of insurance companies.

Pottier finds that a life insurer's cost-efficiency declines significantly as the number of states in which an insurer is licensed or domiciled increases.[10] Although his paper is focused on life insurance companies, Pottier is most similar to this study in that he uses frontier efficiency methodology to calculate the cost-efficiency of insurers. To our knowledge, similar analysis has not been conducted on property-casualty insurers.

For property-casualty insurers, research on the cost of regulation is limited. Most of the evidence has focused on the degree to which regulation affects the insurance market within particular states. Most recently, Weiss and Choi find that insurer cost-efficiency varies across states with different regulatory regimes.[11] While they do not investigate the relationship between efficiency and number of regulators, they do find evidence that some insurers in rate-regulated states are less cost-efficient than those in competitive states.

Finally, Grace and Scott provide an excellent review of the current optional federal charter proposal, the objectives of insurance regulation, as well as the theoretical arguments both for and against the implementation of a federal charter.[12] In doing so, they develop several of the arguments we measure in this study.

Variables, Data, and Empirical Tests

Our purpose is to estimate the cost imposed on consumers by insurance regulation that is not uniform across states. For this, we require a measure of cost and the number of states regulating each insurer. Optimal results would present an "all else equal" estimate; therefore, we must also control for variables other than regulatory uniformity that could affect insurer efficiency.

We employ two cost measures. The first, *expense ratio*, is an insurer's total expenses divided by written premium. The second cost measure, *inefficiency score*, is a cost inefficiency score.[13] The cost-inefficiency score represents the difference in required inputs for a given level of output. The most efficient firm will have an inefficiency score of zero. Firms that are less efficient will have larger inefficiency scores. We interpret an inefficiency score of 0.6 as denoting a firm that could potentially improve its efficiency such that it reduces expenses by 60% without changing the amount of insurance it produces. We present the calculation methodology for *inefficiency score* in the appendix.

Our independent variable of primary interest is *regulators*, the number of states regulating each insurer. We count only states in which an insurer underwrites insurance. This differs somewhat from the measures used in extant literature. Pottier and McShane, et al. measure the number of regulators with the number of states in which each insurer holds a license to offer insurance.[14] Our data show that insurers are often licensed in states where they do not underwrite insurance. At the limit, a few companies are licensed in all states and territories, but sell insurance in only one state.

We assert that insurers incur significant regulatory costs only in states where they insure risks. An insurer that does not sell insurance in a state is not likely to catch the attention of that state's regulator. The insurer would not need to make rate filings. It would not be examined by regulators for financial or market conduct verification. It would not need to consider that state's regulatory environment in making or implementing strategy. For these reasons, we believe the number of states in which an insurer sells insurance is a superior indicator of the number of regulators with which it must comply. All other things being equal, we expect a negative relation between the number of regulators and the cost of regulation.

In addition to the number of regulators, several other factors could affect an insurer's operating efficiency. These include size, geographic concentration, concentration in lines of insurance, the types of insurance written, organizational form, and regulatory environment.

If insurers realize efficiencies of scale, the marginal cost of producing another unit of output (dollar of coverage) decreases with the amount produced. The law of large numbers demonstrates decreasing costs of capital as the pool of independent insured exposures increases. Therefore, we expect a negative relation between size and *inefficiency score*. We measure size with natural logarithm of total direct premium written. In our model, this variable is labeled *size*.

Insurers could realize economies of scope if the marginal cost of producing insurance decreases with the number of lines of insurance sold. To control for economies of scope, we include in our model a herfindahl index of premium written by line of business. The herfindahl index is a measure of concentration. If an insurer writes all premiums in the same line of insurance, the index will equal one.[15] If the insurer writes equal amounts of premium in each of L lines of business, the index will equal $1/L$.

The literature on economies of scope in the insurance industry presents mixed results. Cummins et al. find that firms diversifying from property and casualty insurance into health insurance (and vice versa) do not add value.[16] However, an earlier Cummins et al. study finds evidence consistent with diversification via acquisition within the property and casualty insurance industry generally created value.[17] Therefore, we have no firm prior on this coefficient estimate. The variable appears in our model as *line-of-business concentration*.

Instead of scope economies, *line-of-business concentration* could also signal increased solvency concerns from lack of diversification or operating efficiency via specialization. Similar competing hypotheses surround concentration of insurance risk in a geographic area. Therefore, we also control for this type of concentration with a herfindahl index of premiums written by state and territory. This variable is labeled *geographic concentration*.

When insurers underwrite risk exposed to catastrophic losses, they require additional capital and perhaps additional underwriting and claims handling resources. Therefore, we expect a positive relation between potentially catastrophic risk and inefficiency. Following Gron and Powell et al.,[18] we measure catastrophic risk with *catastrophe exposure*, the ratio of premiums written for property insurance in eastern coastal states to total premiums written.[19]

Each line of insurance poses different challenges to consumers and regulators, and regulators and consumers in each state may respond differently to these challenges. For example, while Florida, South Carolina, Louisiana, and Texas have each suffered large losses from hurricanes in the last two decades, responses from regulators and legislators have not been uniform. Florida created a state-run insurer, Citizens, to serve as a residual market. The other states created wind pools via cooperation of insurers in the private market. Some lines of business, such as workers compensation insurance, automobile insurance, and homeowners insurance face heavy-handed price regulation in many states, while others, like products liability insurance, are not regulated for price. Types of rate regulation also differ across states for the same coverage. Therefore, we expect to find differences in regulation and operating efficiency across lines of insurance and states. To control for differences across states and lines of insurance, we add a series of variables to our model capturing the percentage of total premium written in each line of business and each state.[20]

Finally, we control for organizational form. Insurers can be chartered in several forms. Stock insurers are owned by shareholders and operate for profit. Mutual insurers and reciprocal exchanges are owned by policyholders and are organized to their benefit. There is a rich literature on the consequences of organizational form.[21]

For our purposes, organizational form matters because mutual insurers and reciprocal exchanges have less access to external capital than do stock insurers and because management incentives could lead to differences in risk-taking and operational efficiency. We control for organizational form with a dummy variable, *mutual*, equal to one if an insurer is organized as a mutual or reciprocal exchange.

Another type of organizational form is an insurer's decision to affiliate with a group of insurers or to stand alone. Group affiliation facilitates cooperation among affiliates to allocate capital and, perhaps, to achieve other ends.[22] We control for group affiliation with a dummy variable, *group*, equal to one if an insurer is affiliated with a group.

Data and Sample

We collect regulatory reporting data from NAIC.[23] The NAIC InfoPro database provides data on insurance companies used in this study.[24] We use data reported at the firm level for property-liability firms for the ten years from 2000 to 2009.

We utilize firm-level data because each firm is required to be licensed in, and therefore face the regulatory cost of, each state in which it operates. A large number of insurance companies are very small and not representative of the industry. Therefore, we further require that firms in our sample have a minimum of $2 million in assets, surplus, and written premium.[25] They must also have positive inputs and outputs for calculating the efficiency score. Finally, each insurer must appear in our sample in at least two years. After these restrictions are enforced, our sample consists of 11,558 insurer-year observations. The fewest number of firms (956) is observed in 2000. The largest number of firms (1,297) is observed in 2007. Summary statistics for our sample are given in Table 9.1.

Our sample is representative of the property-liability insurance industry. The average insurer writes approximately $270 million in premium, although

Table 9.1: Summary Statistics

	Mean	Standard Deviation	Minimum	Maximum
Inefficiency score	0.66	0.16	0	0.992
Expense ratio	0.41	0.12	0.008	0.989
Regulators	1.79	1.54	0	4.043
Size	17.91	1.65	14.51	24.11
Geographic concentration	0.56	0.38	0.032	1
Line-of-business concentration	0.49	0.28	0.047	1
Catastrophe exposure	0.19	0.27	0	1
Mutual	0.23	0.42	0	1
Group	0.72	0.45	0	1

the median insurer writes only \$57.8 million in premium. About 23 percent of firms are organized as mutuals or reciprocals, and about 72 percent of our firms are members of a group. A majority of the insurers, 74 percent, are licensed in multiple jurisdictions, and the average insurer sells insurance in 16 states.

We calculate *inefficiency score* as one minus the efficiency scores of other papers studying similar time frames.[26] The average insurer in our sample has a cost inefficiency score of approximately 66%, suggesting the insurer could potentially reduce costs by 66% with either more efficient production or a re-allocation of resources.

Empirical Model and Estimation

We pool observations from all ten years and estimate the following unbalanced panel regression models to measure the effect of exposure to multiple regulatory systems on the cost of insurance.[27]

$$inefficency\ score_{it} = \alpha + \beta_1 Regulators_{it} + \boldsymbol{\beta'X} + \iota + \tau + \varepsilon_{it} \qquad \text{(Equation 1)}$$

$$expense\ ratio_{it} = \alpha + \beta_1 Regulators_{it} + \boldsymbol{\beta'X} + \iota + \tau + \varepsilon_{it} \qquad \text{(Equation 2)}$$

Where α is an intercept coefficient, β is a vector of coefficients, *regulators* is the number of states in which an insurer sells insurance and X is a vector of control variables including *geographic concentration*, *line-of-business concentration*, *catastrophe exposure*, *size*, *mutual*, and *group*. X also includes eighty-five variables equal to the percentages of an insurer's premium written in each line of business and state. An *F*-test suggests a fixed-effects model is appropriate; thus, ι and τ are firm and year fixed effects, and ε is an error term. Subscripts i and t denote firms and years, respectively. Each variable is defined in Table 9.2.

Results

Table 9.3 reports the results from estimating equation 1 and equation 2. In both models, the coefficient estimate for *regulators* is significant and positive, demonstrating a clear positive relation between the cost of insurance and the number of regulators an insurer must satisfy.

From these coefficients we estimate the cost of non-uniform regulation for insurance consumers as follows. *Regulators* is the natural logarithm of the num-

Table 9.2. Variable Definitions

Variable	Definition
Inefficiency score	Measure of cost described in the appendix.
Expense ratio	Total expenses incurred ÷ total premium written
Regulators	Natural logarithm of the number of states in which an insurer underwrites insurance
Size	Natural logarithm of total direct premium written.
Geographic concentration	Herfindahl index of premium written by state and territory. Calculated as $s = 156 NPWsNPW2$; where $NPWs$ is net premium written in state s.
Line-of-business concentration	Herfindahl index of premium written by line of business. Calculated as $s = 130 NPWlNPW2$; where $NPWl$ is net premium written in insurance line l.
Catastrophe exposure	Premium written for property insurance in eastern coastal states ÷ total premium written
Mutual	Dummy variable = 1 if insurer is organized as a mutual or reciprocal, otherwise = 0
Group	Dummy variable = 1 if insurer is affiliated with a group, otherwise = 0

ber of regulators an insurer faces. If insurance regulation becomes uniform across states, each insurer would effectively face only one regulator. Therefore, the appropriate adjustment to estimate this change is *regulators* − ln(1) = *regulators*. Given the competitive market for insurance,[28] we expect this savings to be passed through to consumers as lower premiums. The potential savings to consumers from achieving uniform regulation is *regulators* times the coefficient estimate multiplied by total expenses.

For example, suppose a company incurs $100 of expenses annually. If the company faces fifty-five regulators today and next year it faces only one regulator, we expect expenses to change as depicted in Figure 9.1.

Table 9.3. Regression model estimates

Variable	Eq. 1 *Expense ratio* Coefficient estimate (Standard error)	Eq. 2 *Inefficiency score* Coefficient estimate (Standard error)
Intercept	1.077***	1.1***
	(0.071)	(0.074)
Regulators	0.011***	0.007**
	(0.003)	(0.003)
Size	−0.034***	−0.016***
	(0.002)	(0.002)
Geographic concentration	−0.007	0.034***
	(0.012)	(0.012)
Line-of-business Concentration	−0.047***	−0.038***
	(0.01)	(0.011)
Catastrophe exposure	0.059***	−0.009
	(0.016)	(0.017)
Mutual	0.048***	0.003
	(0.009)	(0.01)
Group	0.011**	−0.016***
	(0.005)	(0.005)
R-squared	0.83	0.75

Note: ***, and ** denote statistical significance at the 0.01 and 0.05 levels, respectively. Variable definitions appear in Table 9.2. Models are estimated with firm and year fixed effects. Results for state and line-of-business control variables are included in the models, but not shown.

Assume: *Regulators* = 55, Expenses = $100	
Equation 1: *Expense ratio*	Equation 2: *Inefficiency score*
$\beta_1 = 0.011$	$\beta_1 = 0.007$
Change in *regulators* = ln55 − ln1 = 4	Change in *regulators* = ln55 − ln1 = 4
Percent change in expenses = 4 × .011 = .044	Percent change in expenses = 4 × .011 = .028
Change in expense = .044 ∗ $100 = $4.40	Change in expense = .028 ∗ $100 = $2.80

Figure 9.1. Potential annual savings from uniform insurance regulation.

If we apply this calculation to every company in our sample for data year 2009, it forecasts saving to consumers between \$3.19 billion and \$5.27 billion annually. It is not for us to suggest if this price is shockingly high or if it is a superb bargain for consumers. Rather, we propose distribution of this number as a range for policymakers and consumers to consider in this continuing debate, and as a starting point for further research on the cost of fragmented regulatory regimes.

Coefficient estimates for the control variables are generally consistent with expectations or follow patterns explained in the literature, bolstering confidence in our primary results. The coefficient estimate for *size* is significant and positive in both models. This is consistent with insurers realizing scale economies. The estimate of *geographic concentration* is not significant in the *expense ratio* equation, but it is significant and positive in the *inefficiency score* equation, suggesting that the cost of concentration from increased insolvency risk dominates the reduction in required infrastructure costs. It could also be that states concentrating in a small number of regions struggle to reach achieve critical scale economies. In addition, firms specializing in a state or region may do so to solve a critical problem in that market, leading to operations that appear inefficient compared to less problematic lines of business or the same lines in different regions. This is consistent with the market for medical professional liability insurance, where physicians in states and regions have formed their own mutual insurers to mitigate market problems.[29] It is possible to inform these points with further analysis; however, it is beyond the scope of this study.

Line-of-business concentration is significant and negative in both models; suggesting property and casualty insurers benefit more from specialization than from scope economies. However, recall the model includes variables measuring the percentage of total premium written in each line of business. Therefore, it is possible that some lines of business are complementary, while others are not. Nonetheless, consistent with findings of Cummins et al.,[30] it appears that, on balance, these firms do not realize scope economies.

The coefficient estimate for *catastrophe exposure* is significant and positive in the expense ratio model; this is consistent with increased capital costs and infrastructure requirements for firms offering coverage for hurricane damage. This variable is not significant in the *inefficiency score* model.

Coefficient estimates for the *mutual* and *group* variables also are not consistent across the two models. *Mutual* is significant and positive in the *expense ratio* model but not significant in the *inefficiency score* model. Mayers and Smith's managerial discretion hypothesis[31] suggests that mutual insurers and stock insurers will not focus in the same types of insurance and may have different risk preferences.[32] Therefore, the difference in results across the two models suggests mutual insurers could offer coverage that requires greater expenses than that of stock insurers, but the level of expenses is efficient for production of those types of coverage. It is also consistent with increased cost of external capital for mutual firms that cannot issue common equity.

Group is positive and significant in the *expense ratio* model, but negative and significant in the *inefficiency score* model. Increased complexity of the group structure could increase the level of operating expenses, leading to the positive coefficient in the *expense ratio* model. The negative coefficient estimate in the *inefficiency score* model suggests the ability to allocate capital via an internal capital market may add enough value to offset the added expense.[33] Therefore, the group structure may be both more expensive and more efficient.

Again, specific tests could provide more information on these questions. This would be beyond the scope of our interest. For our purposes, it is enough that results for control variables are neither unreasonable nor counterintuitive.

Conclusions

Proponents of state-level insurance regulation contend it brings value to consumers by crafting regulation to the specific needs of each state. Others argue this specificity comes at the cost of efficiency, increasing the cost of insurance.

In this study, we estimate the potential savings for consumers if insurance regulation were uniform across states. We use panel data regression techniques to estimate effects of the number of regulators a firm must satisfy on the cost of providing insurance. Not surprisingly, we find that the number of regulators a company faces is positively related to two comprehensive measures of cost.

Ultimately, our results provide evidence that a single regulatory agency, or substantial uniformity across regulatory regimes, could increase the operating efficiency of insurers to the benefit of consumers. We estimate a range of potential annual cost savings for consumers from uniform regulation between $3.19 billion and $5.27 billion.

We commend the NAIC and the National Coalition of Insurance Legislators (NCOIL) for their efforts to increase regulatory uniformity, but much more work toward this end remains. Regulators and state legislatures must commit to substantial regulatory uniformity, or risk losing their authority to regulate insurance—and potentially their claims to revenue from insurance premium taxes—to a single federal agency.

Appendix: Efficiency Methodology

We utilize Data Envelopment Analysis (DEA) to measure the efficiency of each firm.[34] DEA calculates firm efficiency relative to "best practice" frontiers. The best practice frontiers are composed of the most efficient firms in the industry.

The efficiency methodology used in this chapter is based on input-oriented distance functions.[35] A "best practice" frontier is estimated for each year using the insurers in our sample. Those insurers who comprise the frontier are assigned an efficiency score equal to one. These insurers are considered to be utilizing optimal levels of input for the outputs they are producing. For the remaining insurers, their efficiency score is calculated based on the distance to the frontier. The efficiency score then measures the degree to which the insurer can reduce its inputs (or cost) while maintaining the same level of output. This overutilizing of inputs is thus inefficient.

In order to calculate efficiency scores, we must first estimate the inputs and outputs of the insurers. We use the *modified value-added* approach suggested by Berger and Humphrey.[36] This approach assigns as an output of a financial service firm those activities to which significant operating costs are allocated. Like many efficiency studies in the property-liability insurance industry,[37] we define insurer outputs to encompass the risk pooling/risk bearing function, the real services associated with insured losses, and financial intermediation.

The risk pooling/risk bearing function provided by insurers is arguably the primary function of an insurer. Individual policyholders reduce their idiosyncratic risk by pooling their risk with other policyholders. To allow for a risk pool devoid of significant problems (lack of capital, adverse selection, moral hazard, etc.), insurers devote significant resources to the underwriting of the policyholders, as well as holding significant capital. Insurers also provide a variety of consulting services (loss control, claims processing, risk management, legal, etc.) to policyholders. Insurers also provide financial intermediation services to their policyholders by investing premiums. The returns earned from these investments help reduce the cost of the insurance to both the insurer and insured.

We use five separate output measures to proxy for these services provided by insurers. To estimate the risk pooling and real services output, we use the present value of incurred losses and allocated loss adjustment expenses for four lines of insurance (personal short-tail, commercial short-tail, personal long-tail, and commercial long-tail).[38] The present value of the losses is thought to be a reasonable proxy for the amount of insurance provided, while the loss adjustment expenses proxy for the real services provided. We further consider the value of the firm's invested assets to proxy for the financial intermediation service provided by the insurer.

Insurers are considered to have three main inputs: labor, business services, and financial capital. For labor inputs, we further distinguish between agent labor and administrative labor, resulting in four total inputs for each insurer. Since insurers report the *total* expenses for labor (both agent and administrative) and remaining business services, we must estimate the price of each component. We then divide the total expenditure from each input by the appropriate price to derive the quantity of input used. To obtain input prices, we use the prices reported by the U.S. Bureau of Labor Statistics (USBLS). For agent labor, we use the national average weekly agent labor cost for property-casualty agents, as reported by the USBLS. For administrative labor, we use the national average weekly labor cost for property-casualty insurers, also reported by the USBLS. The USBLS also provides the average weekly business services wage rate for property-casualty insurers, which we use as our price for business services. Finally, we use the total capital of each insurer as their capital input. Capital is considered an input since holding more capital increases the quality of the product offered by the insurer. Of course, capital is considered costly. As such, for each year, we estimate the cost of capital to be the average short-term T-bill rate plus the average market risk premium for property casualty insurers.[39]

References

Banker, Rajiv D. "Maximum Likelihood, Consistency and Data Envelopment Analysis: A Statistical Foundation." *Management Science* 39 (1993): 1265–1273.

Banker, Rajiv D., Hsihui Chang, and William W. Cooper. "A Simulation Study of DEA and Parametric Frontier Models in the Presence of Heteroscedasticity." *European Journal of Operational Research* 153 (2004): 624–640.

Berger, Allen N., J. David Cummins, and Mary A. Weiss. "The Coexistence of Multiple Distribution Systems for Financial Services: The Case of Property-Liability Insurance." *The Journal of Business* 70 (1997): 515–546.

Berger, Allen N., and David B. Humphrey. "Measurement and Efficiency Issues in Commercial Banking." In *Output Measurement in the Service Sector,* edited by Z. Griliches, 245–279. Chicago: University of Chicago Press, 1992.

Cummins, J. David, and Gregory Nini. "Optimal Capital Utilization by Financial Firms: Evidence from the Property-Liability Insurance Industry." *Journal of Financial Services Research* 21 (2002): 15–53.

Cummins, J. David, Sharon Tennyson, and Mary A. Weiss. "Consolidation and Efficiency in the U.S. Life Insurance Industry." Journal of Banking and Finance 23 (Feb 1999): 325–357.

Cummins, J. David, and Mary A Weiss. "Measuring Cost Efficiency in the Property-Liability Insurance Industry." *Journal of Banking and Finance* 17 (1993): 463–481.

Cummins, J. David, Mary A. Weiss, Xiaoying Xie, and Hongmin Zi. "Economies of Scope in Financial Services: A DEA Efficiency Analysis of the U.S. Insurance Industry." *Journal of Banking and Finance* 34 (2010): 1525–1539.

Farrell, Michael J. "The Measurement of Productive Efficiency." *Journal of the Royal Statistical Society* A 120 (1957): 253–281.

Grace, Martin F., and Klein, Robert. 2000. "Efficiency Implications of Alternative Regulatory Structures for Insurance." In *Optional Federal Chartering and Regulation of Insurance Companies,* edited by P. Wallison, 79–131. Washington, DC: American Enterprise Institute, 2000.

Grace, Martin F., and Hal S. Scott. "Optional Federal Chartering of Insurance: Rationale and Design of a Regulatory Structure." Working paper, 2008.

Gron, Anne. "Insurer Demand for Catastrophe Reinsurance." In *The Financing of Catastrophe Risk,* edited by Kenneth A. Froot. Chicago: University of Chicago Press, 1999.

Grosskopf, Shawna. "Statistical Inference and Nonparametric Efficiency: A Selective Survey." *The Journal of Productivity Analysis* 7 (1996): 161–176.

Hoyt, Robert E., and Lawrence S. Powell. "Assessing Financial Performance in Medical Professional Liability Insurance." *Journal of Insurance Regulation* 25 (2006): 3–13.

Joskow, Paul L. "Cartels, Competition, and Regulation in the Property and Liability Insurance Industry." *Bell Journal of Economics and Management Science* Autumn (1973): 375–427.

Kneip, Alois, Byeong U. Park, and Leopold Simar. "A Note on the Convergence of Nonparametric DEA Estimators for Production Efficiency Scores." *Econometric Theory* 14 (1998): 783–793.

Korostelev, Alexander P., Leopold Simar, and Alexandre B. Tsybakov. "Efficient Estimation of Monotone Boundaries." *Annals of Statistics* 23 (1995): 476–489.

Lamm-Tennant, Joan and Laura T. Starks. "Stock versus Mutual Ownership Structures: the Risk Implications." *Journal of Business* 66 (1993): 29–46.

Leverty, J. Tyler, and Martin F. Grace. "The Robustness of Output Measures in Property-Liability Insurance Efficiency Studies." *Journal of Banking and Finance* 34 (2010): 1510–1524.

Mayers, David, and Clifford W. Smith Jr. "Contractual Provisions, Organizational Structure, and Conflict Control in Insurance Markets." *Journal of Business* 54 (1981): 407–434.

Mayers, David, and Clifford W. Smith Jr. "Managerial Discretion, Regulation, and Stock Insurer Ownership Structure." *Journal of Risk and Insurance* 61 (1994): 638–655.

Mayers, David, and Clifford W. Smith Jr. "Ownership Structure across Lines of Property-Casualty Insurance." *Journal of Law and Economics* 3 (1988): 351–378.

Mayers, David, and Clifford W. Smith Jr. "Ownership Structure and Control: The Mutualization of Stock Life Insurance Companies." *Journal of Financial Economics* 16 (1988): 73–98.

McShane, Michael K., and Larry A. Cox. "Benefits of Multi-Jurisdictional Regulation of the Life Insurance Industry: Fact or Fiction?" *Proceedings of the Risk Theory Society*, 2007. http://www.aria.org/rts/proceedings/2007/mcshane.pdf

McShane, Michael K., Larry A. Cox, and Richard J. Butler. "Regulatory Competition and Forbearance: Evidence from the Life Insurance Industry." *Journal of Banking and Finance* 34 (2010): 522–532.

Powell, Lawrence S. "Assault on the McCarran-Ferguson Act and the Politics of Insurance in the Post-Katrina Era." *Journal of Insurance Regulation*, 26 (2008): 3–21.

Powell, Lawrence S., David W. Sommer, and David L. Eckles. "The Role of Internal Capital Markets in Financial Intermediaries: Evidence from Insurance Groups." *Journal of Risk and Insurance* 75(2008): 439–461.

Shephard, Ronald W. *Theory of Cost and Production Functions*. Princeton, NJ: Princeton University Press, 1970.

Weiss, Mary, and Byeongyong Paul Choi. "State Regulation and the Structure, Conduct, Efficiency and Performance of U.S. Auto Insurers." *Journal of Banking and Finance* 32 (2008): 134–156.

10

Performance of Risk Retention Groups

*Drawing Inferences from a Prototype
of Competitive Federalism*

J. Tyler Leverty

Introduction

MORE THAN SIXTY years after the McCarran-Ferguson Act,
the issue of state versus federal regulation of the insurance industry continues
to be debated both within the industry and academia.[1] Under the current state
regulatory system, insurers must obtain a license for each additional state entered or form a separate insurance company domiciled (and licensed) in the state
of entry. Multistate insurers face multiple regulatory bodies and multiple sets of
regulations with which they must comply. The central complaint against state
regulation is the cost and inefficiencies inherent in a multistate system. Because
of these inefficiencies many insurers now advocate the creation of an optional
federal charter (OFC), and OFC legislation has recently been introduced in
Congress.[2] The proposed legislation would allow insurers to seek either a federal or state charter based on the insurer's particular circumstances.[3] Another
alternative to multistate regulation is a form of competitive federalism, "primary
state" chartering,[4] which would allow insurers the option of designating a primary state and operating nationwide subject predominantly to the regulations
of that state.

Studies analyzing the merits of federal versus state regulation rely either
on comparisons to the banking industry or subjective informed opinions. The
novel aspect of this project is that it is an empirical evaluation of single- and
multi-jurisdictional regulation within the current insurance industry. Unlike
standard insurance companies, risk retention groups (RRGs) are subject to
single-entity regulation. The Federal Liability Risk Retention Act of 1986 mandates that all RRGs be domiciled in a particular state, but once licensed, the

RRG can offer products nationwide. The intent of the Act was to remove unnecessary regulation by states in which the RRG is not domiciled, while at the same time acknowledging the states' role in regulating insurance.[5] To qualify, the RRG must be a cooperative insurance entity composed of owners or members of an association connected by similar business practices and encountering similar liability exposures. RRGs are confined to assuming and spreading the common liability exposures of its members (employers liability is excluded).[6] The preemption of state regulation for RRGs provides an innovative setting to analyze the costs of multijurisdictional insurance regulation.[7]

The primary objective of this chapter is to evaluate the costs of the single- and multi- jurisdictional regulatory systems. It uses RRGs as a proxy for single-entity regulation and standard insurers as a proxy for multi-entity regulation. To make fair comparisons, the control group of standard insurance companies is restricted to the set of firms incorporated during the same time period and operating in the same lines of business as RRGs; that is, they must operate exclusively in commercial liability lines. Four issues regarding regulation and its impact on insurance firms are examined: (1) the compliance costs associated with single- and multiple-jurisdictional regulation; (2) whether compliance costs influence a firm's decision to choose single-jurisdictional regulation; (3) the impact of compliance costs on the operational efficiency of firms; and (4) the per unit price differences of insurance provided by firms subject to single- and multiple-jurisdictional regulation.

The results show that when firms operate in only a single state, there is no significant difference in the regulatory compliance costs of RRGs and the control group of standard insurers. However, when firms operate in more than one state, the compliance costs associated with multi-jurisdictional regulation are significantly higher than those for single-jurisdictional regulation. Even though the average RRG conducts business in 8.5 states and the average standard insurer writes business in only 4.8 states, RRGs have significantly lower compliance costs. Additional analysis suggests that duplicative state regulation restrains firms from operating in multiple states. The number of states in which a firm plans to write business plays a significant role in a firm's decision to organize as an RRG subject to single-jurisdictional regulation.

Moving to a single-entity regulatory structure would result in a substantial reduction in regulatory compliance costs. Estimates suggest that the average firm pays an additional 23.7 percent in expenses per year as a result of multi-jurisdictional regulation. A transition from multi-jurisdictional regulation to single-jurisdictional regulation could result in a $1.2 billion per year reduction in total expenses. In addition, firms regulated by a single regulator are more operationally efficient than firms subject to multiple regulators. The study also finds that the lower regulatory compliance costs and higher operational efficiency associated with single-jurisdictional regulation are passed on to policyholders in the form of substantially lower per unit prices for insurance. Overall, there are significant costs associated with multistate regulation.

The remainder of the chapter is organized as follows. First, we describe the data and the firms under investigation. Next, regulatory compliance costs are examined, followed by an analysis of whether regulatory compliance costs influence a firm's organizational structure decision. An investigation of the operational efficiency of firms subject to different regulatory systems is followed by examination of whether the regulatory costs are passed along to policyholders in the form of higher prices. Finally, we discuss the limitations of the study and conclude.

Data

The majority of the data comes from the 1990–2006 National Association of Insurance Commissioners (NAIC) Property-Casualty Annual Statement Database. The NAIC database contains the yearly regulatory filings of about 2,300 insurance companies. In addition to the regulatory annual statements, input price data for the frontier efficiency analysis is obtained from the U.S. Bureau of Labor Statistics. Information on a firm's ownership structure (RRG or standard insurer) is also extracted from the NAIC database. In the early years of the sample, the NAIC did not always code RRGs correctly; therefore, the coding of RRGs is verified using the listing of RRGs in the *Risk Retention Reporter* (various years).

To make meaningful inferences, only insurance companies that are similar to RRGs are included in the sample. RRGs can write commercial liability insurance only for its members. The homogeneity and specialization of RRGs insurance operations should enhance their control and claims management abilities. The major criterion for the comparison group of insurers is that they must also write all of their business in commercial liability lines (i.e., commercial auto liability, other liability, and medical malpractice). To analyze the decision to adopt the RRG organizational structure, the sample is also limited to those insurers and RRGs that commenced business after 1989. There are 173 RRGs (578 RRG-years) and 126 insurers (399 insurer-years) that meet these conditions.

Table 10.1 reports summary statistics stratified by firm type. The average (median) RRG has approximately $8.8 ($8.6) million in total assets. The average (median) insurer is significantly larger, with roughly $10.2 ($9.5) million in assets. In terms of concentration, the average RRG has a line of business (Product) Herfindahl Index of about 0.944.[8] The average insurer has a line of business Herfindahl Index of 0.978. Even though the difference is statistically significant, both types of firms are concentrated in approximately one line of insurance. For the geographic Herfindahl, the index is approximately 0.646 (0.870) for the average (median) RRG and 0.840 (1.00) for the average (median) insurer.[9] Similarly, the average (median) RRG operates in about 8.4 (2.0) states, while the average insurer operates in 4.8 (1.0) states.[10] Standard insurers are significantly less geographically diversified than RRGs.

Regulatory Compliance Costs

This section investigates the costs of complying with regulation. The direct costs of complying with regulators includes expenses associated with submitting applications for licensing; presenting financial and statistical reports; paying for independent audits and regulatory examinations; preparing and submitting rates and forms filings; ensuring internal compliance with state regulations; responding to regulatory inquiries; and paying taxes, fees and assessments.[11] Many of the activities listed above must be performed for every state in which an insurance company conducts business on a licensed basis. In contrast, RRGs have to perform a majority of these activities for only a single state.

Table 10. 2 shows summary statistics of regulatory compliance costs. Licensing fees represent a small proportion of total premiums written and a small component of the direct costs of regulatory compliance. In contrast, the expense ratio represents all the expenses that are incurred by an insurer and thereby all of the regulatory costs of a firm. For firms operating in only one state, average (median) licensing fees as a percentage of net premiums written are 0.78 (0.17) for RRGs and 0.91 (0.18) for standard insurers. The average (median) expense

Table 10.1. Summary Statistics

Variable:	Risk Retention Groups (Single Jurisdictional Regulation)			Standard Insurers (Multiple Jurisdictional)		
	N	Mean	Median	N	Mean	Median
Ln(Assets)	578	15.994 *	15.972 *	399	16.138	16.069
Ln(NPW)	578	14.610	14.776 *	399	14.521	14.479
Product Herfindahl	578	0.944 ***	1.000 ***	399	0.978	1.000
Geographic Herfindahl	578	0.646 ***	0.871 ***	399	0.840	1.000
Number of States	578	8.429 ***	2.000 ***	399	4.827	1.000
Kenney Ratio	578	0.994 *	0.800 ***	399	1.208	0.613
% PW in Medical Malpractice	578	0.570	0.929	399	0.575	0.979
% PW in Other Liability	408	0.074 *	0.000 ***	323	0.052	0.000
% PW in Commercial Auto Liability	568	0.068 ***	0.000 **	365	0.120	0.000
Reinsurance	578	0.316 *	0.219 **	398	0.280	0.159
Assets / Liabilities	578	2.662 ***	1.658 ***	398	3.626	1.897
Liquid Assets / Liabilities	578	2.042 ***	1.287 ***	398	3.220	1.630

Note: Ln(Assets) is natural logarithm of total assets. Ln(NPW) is natural logarithm of net premiums written. Geographic Herfindahl is the Herfindahl index using the direct premiums written in each state. Number of States is the number of states in which the insurer writes greater than $10,000 in premiums. Product Herfindahl is the line-of-business Herfindahl index using net premiums written. Kenney Ratio is the ratio of net premiums written to policyholders surplus. % PW in Medical Malpractice is the percentage of premiums written in medical malpractice insurance. % PW in Other Liability is the percentage of premiums written in other liability. % PW in Commercial Auto Liability is the percentage of premiums written in commercial auto liability. Growth is the one-year change in net premiums written. Reinsurance is the percent of gross premiums written ceded to reinsurers. Assets / Liabilities is the ratio of total assets to total liabilities. Liquid Assets / Liabilities is the ratio of liquid assets to total liabilities. Significant differences in means (medians) are examined using a t-test (Mann-Whitney). ***, **, and * denote significance at the 1, 5, and 10 percent level.

Table 10.2. Regulatory Compliance Costs

Variable:	Risk Retention Groups (Single Jurisdictional Regulation)			Standard Insurers (Multiple Jurisdictional Regulation)		
	N	Mean	Median	N	Mean	Median
Conducting Business in One State[a]						
Licensing Fee Ratio (%)	153	0.78	0.17	161	0.91	0.18
Expense Ratio (%)	184	57.72	47.29	181	63.43	49.85
Conducting Business in More Than One State[a]						
Licensing Fee Ratio (%)	257	1.33	**	0.45	**	112
Expense Ratio (%)	298	56.30 ***	48.45 **	114	75.20	55.08

Note: Licensing Fee Ratio is the ratio of regulatory license fees to net premiums written. Expense Ratio is the ratio of total expenses incurred to total premiums written. Significant differences in means (medians) are examined using a t-test (Mann-Whitney). ***, **, and * denote significance at the 1, 5, and 10 percent level.

[a]An insurer is classified as doing business in a state if it has more than $10,000 in net premiums written.

ratio, total expenses incurred as a percentage of net premiums written, is 57.72 (47.29) for RRGs and 63.43 (49.85) for standard insurers. The differences between single-state RRGs and insurers are not statistically significant. Thus, when both types of firms are subject to single-entity regulation, there is no difference in regulatory compliance costs.

For the subsample of firms that operate in more than one state, the average (median) RRG operates in 13.85 (10.00) and the average standard insurer operates in 9.28 (4.00) states. The difference is significant at the 1 percent (5 percent) level.[12] Even though RRGs operate in significantly more states than standard insurers, regulatory compliance costs are significantly lower for RRGs. The average (median) licensing fee ratio is 1.33 (0.45) percent for RRGs compared to 2.17 (0.65) percent for standard insurers, indicating that the average standard insurer pays $288,680.69 in licensing fees while the average RRG pays $62,346.41. Although regulatory licensing fees represent a small proportion of total premiums written, in real terms, licensing fees can be large ($1,067,337 is the maximum in the sample). Licensing fees are probably much larger for insurers not in my sample.[13] Turning to total expenses, mean (median) expenses as a percentage of net premiums written are 56.30 (48.45) for RRGs and 75.20 (55.08) for insurers. The difference is significant at the 1 percent (5 percent) level.[14] Overall, despite the greater number of states in which they write insurance, RRGs have significantly lower licensing fee ratios and expense ratios. This is notable considering that Grace and Klein find that the number of states in which an insurer is licensed is significantly and positively related to these ratios.[15]

Organizational Form Decision

In this section, I analyze whether duplicative state-based regulation impedes competition. In particular, it examines whether the compliance costs associated with multi-jurisdictional regulation keep standard insurers from operating in as many states as RRGs. To investigate this, I estimate the probability of a commercial liability insurer writing greater than $10,000 in premiums in *more* than one state.[16] Figure 10.1 shows the results over various time horizons. In the first year of operation, RRGs have a 52.3 percent probability of conducting business in more than one state. In contrast, the probability for standard insurers is only 10.7 percent. When firm characteristics, such as firm size (*Ln(Assets)*), leverage (*Kenney Ratio, Assets / Liabilities,* and *Liquid Assets / Liabilities*), reinsurance, and product line diversification, are controlled, the divergence is even greater: 57.1 percent for RRGs and 9.2 percent for standard insurers. These findings suggest that duplicative state regulation restricts standard insurers from competing in more states.

The impediment that state regulation imposes is not restricted to the first year of operation. In the first two years of operation, the probability of writing insurance in more than one state is 55.0 percent for RRGs and 15.4 percent for standard insurers. It is 56.3 percent for RRGs and 21.0 percent for standard insurers in the first three years of operation and 56.3 and 21.0 percent in the first four years. Over the full sample period, the probability of an RRG writing insurance in more than one state is 60.2 percent, while it is only 31.1 percent for standard insurers.[17] The evidence suggests regulatory compliance costs influence a firm's choice of organizational structure: Multistate firms overwhelmingly select single-jurisdictional regulation.

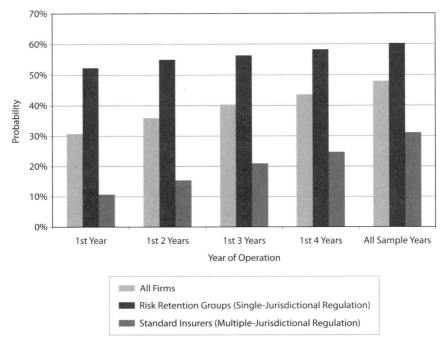

Figure 10.1. Probability of Conducting Business in More than One State.

In addition to the probabilities shown in Figure 10.1, I also estimate firm geographical diversification. Figure 10.2 displays the predicted geographical Herfindahls for each organizational structure. In the first year of operation, standard insurers have a predicted geographical Herfindahl Index of 0.948, indicating that the average insurer writes in only one state. In contrast, the average RRG has a predicted geographical Herfindahl of 0.725, which translates to 1.38 states. Over the sample period, the average insurer has an estimated geographical Herfindahl of .840, while it is 0.646 for the average RRG. These estimates also suggest that multi-jurisdictional regulation impedes insurer's ability to be competitive geographically.

Operational Efficiency

This section investigates whether regulatory compliance costs impact firm efficiency. Like Grace and Klein,[18] I examine the relationship between firm ef-

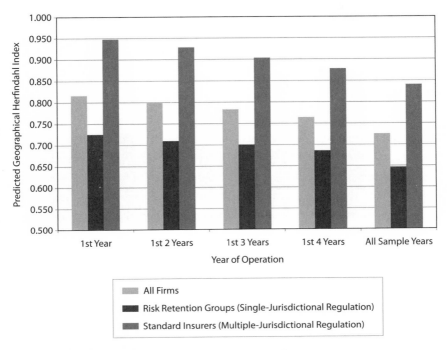

Figure 10.2. Predicted Geographical Herfindahl Index.

ficiency and regulatory compliance costs. If regulation imposes costs on a firm, then it should show up in the expenses of the firm. Higher expenses and lower firm efficiency, all other things held constant, should exist in those environments that are subject to greater regulation. The hypothesis is that standard insurers are less efficient than RRGs.

Grace and Klein also study the relationship between compliance costs and firm performance.[19] They use two indicators of compliance costs: the amount of business written in a restrictive regulatory environment and the number of states/lines in which an insurer conducts business. In contrast, the main indicator of compliance costs in this study is single jurisdictional regulation, that is, an RRG indicator variable. This is arguably a more direct measure of compliance costs since it explicitly acknowledges the difference between complying with one regulator versus complying with many regulators. Moreover, it provides an empirical estimate of the difference between the status quo regulation of insurance and competitive federalism.

As in Grace and Klein, the relationship between an indicator variable of compliance costs and the expense ratio is examined.[20] Expense ratios, however, do not account for the multiproduct nature of the firm, nor do they accurately reflect the economic production function underlying the production of insurance. Moreover, expense ratios do not acknowledge that some expenses may generate positive benefits. Therefore, in addition to the expense ratio, the relationship between compliance costs and measures of frontier efficiency is also investigated. Frontier efficiency measures have theoretical advantages relative to more traditional ratio measures of performance. Derived from micro-economic theory, the methods develop meaningful and reliable measures of performance in a single statistic that controls for differences in input usage and output production in multi-input, multi-output firms.[21]

Efficient production, cost, and revenue frontiers are estimated using data envelopment analysis giving measures of technical, cost, and revenue efficiency for each firm.[22] Technical inefficiency results from firms using excessive resources to produce a given output. Cost-efficiency is the ratio of the minimum required costs to the actual costs used to produce a given level of output. A firm is considered fully efficient if its actual input usage equals optimal input usage for given output quantities and input prices. A firm is inefficient if actual input usage exceeds optimal input usage. Cost-efficiency is composed of allocative efficiency and technical efficiency. Allocative inefficiency results from a firm's use of a suboptimal combination of inputs in producing a given level of output. Revenue efficiency is the ratio of the revenues of a given firm to the revenues of a fully efficient firm with the same input vector and output prices. Estimating both cost and revenue efficiency is important since the objective of the firm is profit maximization. Thus, to be completely efficient, the firm must be both cost-efficient and revenue-efficient.

In accordance with a majority of the recent literature on financial institutions, we adopt a modified version of the value-added approach to identify insurer outputs.[23] Leverty and Grace examine other approaches to measuring insurance output and find that the value-added approach is the most consistent with the economic realities of the insurance market.[24] The value-added approach employs as important outputs all categories that have substantial value added, as judged by operating cost allocations.[25] Operating cost allocations identify three principal services provided by P/L insurers: risk pooling and risk bearing, "real" insurance services, and financial intermediation.[26] The proxy for the quantity of risk pooling and real insurance services is the present value of real losses incurred (PV(L)).[27] The risks and types of services provided differ between the main types of insurance, so lines of insurance with similar characteristics are grouped together: short-tail personal lines, short-tail commercial lines, long-tail personal lines, and long-tail commercial lines.[28] Output prices are measured using the following formula:

$$p_i = [P_i - PV(L_i)] / PV(L_i)$$

where p_i is the price of insurance output i and P_i is the premiums earned for line i, i=1,...,4 for personal short-tail, personal long-tail, commercial short-tail, and commercial long-tail. Premiums implicitly represent the discounting of the loss cash flow stream, thus, using present value of losses preserves consistency by identifying the time value of money in both the premium and loss components of the output price measure.

The value-added approach captures the quantity of intermediation output using average real invested assets of a firm.[29] The price of the intermediation output is measured by the expected rate of return on the insurer's assets.

The inputs of the P/L insurer are classified into five categories: administrative labor, agent labor, business services and materials (including physical capital), financial equity capital, and policyholder-supplied debt capital.[30] Since detailed information for the quantities of labor and materials used by each insurer is not publicly available, the data are imputed from the dollar value of related expenses. The quantity of an input is defined as the current dollar expenditures associated with the particular input from the regulatory annual statement divided by its current price.[31] Efficient frontiers are estimated for each firm in each year of the sample (1990 to 2006). Since the universe of firms determines the production, cost, and revenue frontiers, efficiency is calculated for each of the individual units in the P/L insurance industry, both unaffiliated and affiliated single insurers. The efficiency sample is composed of all P/L insurers reporting to the NAIC.[32] The total number of firm-years is 20,209. The number of insurers in the efficiency analysis varies by year. It is greatest in 2006, with 1,472 insurers and lowest in 2002 with 1,009. On average, the sample consists of about 1,190 insurers per year. Mean (median) technical, cost, and revenue efficiency is 0.652 (0.628), 0.426 (0.415), and 0.396 (0.341), respectively. For the subsample of RRGs and commercial liability specialists that commence business after 1989 mean (median) technical, cost, and revenue efficiency is 0.704 (0.691), 0.426 (0.415), and 0.396 (0.341). Technical and revenue efficiency are significantly greater, and cost efficiency is significantly lower for this subset of firms compared to the full efficiency sample (at the 10 percent level).

To investigate the relationship between firm efficiency and regulatory compliance costs, I estimate the four OLS regressions. The dependent variables are measures of compliance costs and firm efficiency. The first is the ratio of total expenses to premiums. The second, third, and fourth are the natural logarithm of technical, cost, and revenue efficiency. The study design also controls for other factors affecting insurer efficiency, such as firm size, geographical diversification, lines of business, leverage, and reinsurance. The standard errors of the regressions are adjusted for firm and year clustering.[33]

The regression results are shown in Table 10.3.[34] The RRG indicator variable, the proxy for single-jurisdictional regulation, is significantly and negatively related to total expenses, indicating that firms subject to a single regulator have lower expense loads than firms regulated by multiple entities.[35] Holding all other variables at their mean, the regression estimates indicate that the average standard insurer has about $4,129,826 in total expenses, while the average RRG has total expenses of $3,339,957, a reduction of $789,869. Thus, the average firm pays 23.7 percent more in expenses in a year due to multi-jurisdictional regulation. Assuming that the results of my sample were consistent with the property-casualty insurance industry as a whole and that there are 1,500 multistate property-casualty insurers in the United States, a transition from multi-jurisdictional regulation to single-jurisdictional regulation would result in roughly a $1.2 billion per year reduction in total expenses.[36] Grace and Klein (2000) estimate total regulatory compliance costs to be $4.5 billion per year (for both the life and property-casualty insurance industries).[37] Moving to a single-entity regulatory structure could result in a substantial reduction in regulatory compliance costs.

The RRG indicator variable is significantly and positively related to technical, cost, and revenue efficiency. The average firm regulated by multiple entities uses 10.5 percent more resources to produce a given amount of output than if it were regulated by a single entity. In addition to using fewer resources to produce a given amount of output, RRGs are also more inclined to use the correct com-

Table 10.3. Operational Efficiency and Single Jurisdictional Regulation

Dependent Variable:	Expense Ratio	ln (Technical Efficiency)	ln (Cost Efficiency)	ln (Revenue Efficiency)
Variable:	(1)	(2)	(3)	(4)
Intercept	0.762 ***	−1.750 ***	−3.843 ***	−2.281 ***
	(0.224)	(0.28)	(0.499)	(0.599)
RRG	−0.132 **	0.187 ***	0.079 *	0.233 ***
	(0.052)	(0.053)	(0.047)	(0.072)
Ln (Assets)	−0.019	0.066 ***	0.163 ***	0.076 **
	(0.014)	(0.017)	(0.028)	(0.035)
Geographical Herfindahl	0.067	0.139 **	0.107	0.157 **
	(0.084)	(0.061)	(0.076)	(0.077)
% PW in Med. Mal.	−0.019	−0.035	−0.121 **	0.104
	(0.07)	(0.046)	(0.056)	(0.083)
% PW in Comm. Auto Liab.	−0.228 ***	0.195 ***	0.177 ***	0.398 ***
	(0.084)	(0.064)	(0.068)	(0.118)
Kinney Ratio	−0.029 ***	0.028 ***	−0.002	0.052 ***
	(0.011)	(0.004)	(0.008)	(0.01)
Reinsurance	0.454 ***	−0.087	−0.217 ***	−0.195
	(0.096)	(0.072)	(0.081)	(0.124)
Assets / Liabilities	0.035 ***	0.017 ***	−0.002	0.022 **
	(0.008)	(0.006)	(0.005)	(0.01)
Obs	931	395	395	374
R^2	0.210	0.149	0.252	0.144

Note: The table displays the results of OLS regressions. The dependent variable in models 1 thru 4 is the expense ratio, ln(technical efficiency), ln(cost efficiency), and ln(revenue efficiency), respectively. All independent variables are defined in Table 10.1. Standard errors adjusted for firm and year clustering are reported in parentheses below the coefficient. ***, **, and * indicate two-tailed statistical significance at 0.01, 0.05, and 0.10 levels, respectively.

bination of inputs relative to standard insurance companies. The average firm is 2.4 percent more cost-efficient when regulated by a single entity than when it is regulated by multiple entities. Moreover, the average firm regulated by multiple entities is 10.3 percent less revenue-efficient than if it were regulated by a single regulator. Overall, the operational efficiency of insurance companies would be greater under a single-regulator framework than the current state-based regulatory regime.

Benefits to the Policyholder
of Single-Jurisdictional Regulation

This section investigates whether the higher compliance costs associated with multi-jurisdictional regulation lead to a higher per unit price for insurance. Four measures of the per unit price of insurance are used. The first is the inverse loss ratio, total premiums written over total losses incurred. The second is the premium ratio, total premiums written net of expenses and dividends over losses incurred. It accounts for the differences in expenses between the regulatory structures. The third and fourth are variations of the economic premium ratio (EPR) developed by Winter.[38] The EPR is the ratio of the premium revenues to the estimated present value of losses. The EPR has become the standard price measure in the insurance financial literature.[39] Since premiums reflect the discounting of losses in a competitive market, the EPR improves upon the unit price of insurance by also discounting the losses in the denominator of the ratio. *EPR 1* is measured as premiums written over the present value of losses incurred. *EPR 2* uses premiums written net of expenses and dividends in the numerator.[40]

A number of factors can impact the price of insurance, and it is unlikely that standard firm characteristics will be sufficient. Omitted-variables bias may therefore be an issue. If price is driven in part by unobserved attributes particular to each firm, and if those attributes are correlated with observable variables included in the regression, the error term will no longer be uncorrelated with the included explanatory variables, resulting in biased and inconsistent estimates. It is, however, possible to correct for it, if necessary, by including firm-specific fixed effects. The Breusch-Pagan Lagrangean multiplier test indicates that the null hypothesis of no firm-specific effects is soundly rejected (p value < 0.0001). Consequently, allowing for firm-specific effects is a more appropriate specification. Both fixed and random effects models are estimated. Hausman χ^2 test statistics reject the null hypothesis that random effects are appropriate (p value < 0.10). Thus, fixed effects are preferred to random effects.

The results are shown in Table 10.4.[41] Insurance prices are inversely related to firm size (natural logarithm of total assets), reflecting the large firm's enhanced ability to diversify risk. Insurers that hedge a greater extent of their insurance underwriting risk through reinsurance are also associated with lower prices. Prior literature documents insurance prices to be negatively related to insolvency risk.[42] A measure of insurer leverage, Kenney Ratio, the ratio of net premiums written to policyholder surplus, is included in the model to control for insolvency risk. As hypothesized, prices are negatively associated with higher leverage; however, the relationship is only significant for two measures of insurance price: the inverse loss ratio and EPR 1. In unreported regressions, I account for insurer insolvency risk by including a discrete time hazard model estimate of the probability insolvency.[43] In all specifications, insurance prices are significantly negatively related to an insurer's probability of failure. The results for all the other variables are qualitatively unchanged.[44] Turning to the effect of the regulatory environment on the price of insurance, the RRG indicator variable, the proxy for single jurisdictional regulation, is significantly and negatively related to the per unit price of insurance. The estimates indicate that the per unit price of the average standard insurer is 26 to 32 percent greater than that of the average RRG. Figure 10.3 shows the estimated per unit price for the average firm stratified by regulatory environment. Single-body regulation significantly reduces the price of insurance relative to multiple-entity regulation. Thus, the benefits of the lower compliance costs associated with single-entity regulation accrue to policyholders. Conversely, the higher compliance costs associated with multi-jurisdictional regulation lead to higher costs of insurance.

Note: The table displays the results of firm and year fixed effects regressions. The dependent variable is the unit price of insurance. The Inverse Loss Ratio is premiums written over losses incurred. The Premium Ratio is premiums written net of expenses and dividends over losses incurred. EPR is the economic premium ratio (EPR). EPR 1 is total premiums written over present value of losses incurred. EPR 2 is premiums written net of expenses and dividends over present value of losses incurred. Mutual is an indicator variable set equal to one if the standard insurer is a mutual company, and zero otherwise. Reciprocal is an indicator variable set equal to one if the standard insurer is a reciprocal, and zero otherwise. All other variables are defined in Table 10.1. Standard errors adjusted for heteroskedasticity are reported in parentheses below the coefficient.

Table 4: Benefits to the Consumer of Single Jurisdictional Regulation

Dependent Variable:	Inverse Loss Ratio	Premium Ratio	EPR 1	EPR 2
Variable:	(1)	(2)	(3)	(4)
Intercept	5.164 ***	2.826 ***	6.270 ***	3.722 ***
	(1.45)	(0.994)	(1.662)	(1.204)
RRG	−0.736 ***	−0.480 ***	−0.798 **	−0.589 **
	(0.277)	(0.185)	(0.333)	(0.233)
Ln (Assets)	−0.218 ***	−0.072	−0.255 ***	−0.094
	(0.08)	(0.058)	(0.093)	(0.07)
Geographical Herfindahl	0.094	−0.253	0.096	−0.319
	(0.329)	(0.225)	(0.372)	(0.269)
Product Herfindahl	0.685	0.272	0.735	0.254
	(0.49)	(0.417)	(0.564)	(0.488)
Kenney Ratio	−0.052 *	−0.022	−0.062 *	−0.028
	(0.03)	(0.022)	(0.036)	(0.028)
Reinsurance	−0.705 ***	−0.550 ***	−0.819 ***	−0.678 ***
	(0.187)	(0.142)	(0.215)	(0.169)
Assets / Liabilities	0.014	0.017 **	0.017	0.022 **
	(0.012)	(0.008)	(0.014)	(0.009)
Mutual	−0.150	−0.041	−0.163	−0.065
	(0.285)	(0.207)	(0.331)	(0.251)
Reciprocal	0.414	−0.117	0.424	−0.216
	(0.485)	(0.339)	(0.545)	(0.4)
Obs	924	924	924	924

Note: The table displays the results of firm and year fixed effects regressions. The dependent variable is the unit price of insurance. The Inverse Loss Ratio is premiums written over losses incurred. The Premium Ratio is premiums written net of expenses and dividends over losses incurred. EPR is the economic premium ratio (EPR). EPR 1 is total premiums written over present value of losses incurred. EPR 2 is premiums written net of expenses and dividends over present value of losses incurred. Mutual is an indicator variable set equal to one if the standard insurer is a mutual company, and zero otherwise. Reciprocal is an indicator variable set equal to one if the standard insurer is a reciprocal, and zero otherwise. All other variables are defined in Table 1. Standard errors adjusted for heteroskedasticity are reported in parentheses below the coefficient. ***, **, and * indicate two-tailed statistical significance at 0.01, 0.05, and 0.10 levels, respectively.

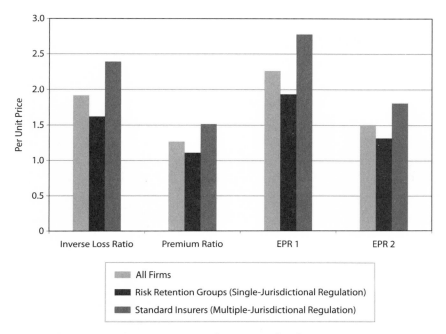

Figure 10.3. Estimated Per Unit Price of Insurance for the Average Firm.

Conclusion

To date, there has not been a great deal of evidence on the cost of duplicative regulation. This chapter attempts to determine the effect of regulation by comparing a set of insurers subject to regulation by a single entity, RRGs, to standard insurance companies subject to regulation by multiple entities. The results show that the number of states in which a firm plans to write business plays a significant role in a firm's decision to organize as a RRG, suggesting that costly duplicative regulation influences a firm's decision-making. In addition, the regulatory compliance costs of single-jurisdictional regulation are significantly lower than multi-jurisdictional regulation. Moreover, the higher compliance costs associated with multi-jurisdictional regulation lead to higher per unit costs of insurance. Overall, this study shows that there are significant benefits associated with moving from a multistate regulatory framework to a single-entity structure.

Estimating the costs and benefits of state regulation of insurers is an important contribution to literature on insurance regulation. The study, however, still has a number of limitations. Throughout the chapter, the advantage of the RRG organizational structure is interpreted to be completely attributable to single-entity regulation. The impact, however, may also be attributable to other advantages inherent in the RRG structure. Policyholder-owned and operated insurers may be better informed than non-policyholder directed insurers.[45] Since RRGs are cooperative insurance entities made up of owners or members of an association connected by similar business practices (e.g., physicians), the lower expense loads, higher operational efficiency, and lower per unit prices of RRGs may be partially attributable to the superior information of RRG managers. In addition, the distribution of insurance in a cooperative may provide a more efficient system than that used by standard insurers. The study also does not address the social desirability of state-based regulation. While it clearly demonstrates some of the tangible costs of duplicative regulation, it does not evaluate potential benefits, such as regulatory competition between the fifty different states or the fact that state regulation can more effectively address local preferences.

References

Aigner, D., C. Lovell, and P. Schmidt. "Formulation and Estimation of Stochastic Frontier Production Function Models. *Journal of Econometrics* 6 (1977): 21–37.

American Council of Life Insurers. "Economic Impact of an Optional Federal Charter on the Life Insurance Industry: A Survey of Leading U.S. Insurance Companies." 2005.

Berger, A. N., and D. B. Humphrey. "Efficiency of Financial Institutions: International Survey and Directions for Future Research." *European Journal of Operational Research* 98 (1997): 175–212.

Berger, A., and D. Humphrey. "Measurement and Efficiency Issues in Commercial Banking." In *Output Measurement in the Services Sector*, edited by Z. Griliches. Chicago: University of Chicago Press, 1992.

Brown, E. F. "The Fatal Flaw of Proposals to Federalize Insurance Regulation." Paper presented at the Searle Center Research Symposium on Insurance Markets and Regulation, 2008.

Butler, H. N., and L. E. Ribstein. "A Single-License Approach to Regulating Insurance." Northwestern Law and Econ Research Paper, 2008.

Cameron, A. C., J. B. Gelbach, and D. L. Miller. "Robust Inference with Multi-Way Clustering." NBER Technical Working Paper No. 327, 2006.

Charnes, A., W. Cooper, and E. Rhodes. "Measuring the Efficiency of Decision Making Units." *European Journal of Operational Research* 2 (1978): 429–444.

Cooke, J. A., and H. D. Skipper. "U.S. Insurance Regulation in a Competitive World Insurance Market: An Evaluation." In *The Future of Insurance Regulation in the United States* edited by M. F. Grace and R. W. Klein. Washington, DC: Brookings Institution Press, 2009.

Cooper, W. W., L. M. Seiford, and K. Tone. *Data Envelopment Analysis.* Norwell, MA: Kluwer Academic Publishers, 2000.

Cummins, J. D., and P. M. Danzon. "Price, Financial Quality, and Capital Flows in Insurance Markets." *Journal of Financial Intermediation* 6 (1997): 3–38.

Cummins, J. D., Y. Lin, and R. D. Phillips. "An Empirical Investigation of the Pricing of Financially Intermediated Risks with Costly External Finance." Working paper, Center for Risk Management & Insurance Research, Georgia State University, 2008.

Cummins, J. David, and Mary Weiss. "Analyzing Firm Performance in the Insurance Industry Using Frontier Efficiency and Productivity Models." In *Handbook of Insurance*, edited by G. Dionne. Boston: Kluwer Academic Publishers, 2001.

Detlefsen, R. "Dual Insurance Chartering: Potential Consequences." In *The Future of Insurance Regulation*, edited by M. F. Grace and R. W. Klein. Washington, DC: Brookings Institution Press, 2009.

Franks, J., S. Schaefer, and M. Staunton. "The Direct and Compliance Costs of Financial Regulation." *Journal of Banking and Finance* (1997), 1547–1572.

Grace, M. F., and R. W. Klein. "The Effects of an Optional Federal Charter on Competition in the Life Insurance Industry." Working paper, Center for Risk Management and Insurance Research, Georgia State University, 2007.

Grace, M. F., and R. W. Klein. "Efficiency Implications of Alternative Regulatory Structures for Insurance." In *Optional Federal Chartering and Regulation of Insurance Companies*, edited by P. Wallison. Washington, DC: American Enterprise Institute, 2000.

Grace, M. F., and R. W. Klein. "Insurance Regulation: The Need for Policy Reform." In *The Future of Insurance Regulation in the United States,* edited by M. F. Grace and R. W. Klein. Washington, DC: Brookings Institution Press.

Grace, M. F., and R. W. Klein. "The Past and Future of Insurance Regulation: The McCarran-Ferguson Act and Beyond." Paper presented at the Searle Center Research Symposium on Insurance Markets and Regulation, 2008.

Grace, M. F., and J. T. Leverty. "Political Cost Incentives for Managing the Property-Liability Insurer Loss Reserve." Working paper, University of Iowa, 2009.

Grace, M. F., J. T. Leverty, and R. D. Phillips. "Value Creation in Enterprise Risk Management." Working paper, Center for Risk Management & Insurance Research, Georgia State University, 2009.

Grace, M. F., and H. S. Scott. "An Optional Federal Charter for Insurance: Rationale and Design." In *The Future of Insurance Regulation in the United States,* edited by M. F. Grace and R. W. Klein. Washington, DC: Brookings Institution Press, 2009.

Harrington, S. E. "Federal Chartering of Insurance Companies: Options and Alternatives for Transforming Insurance Regulation." Networks Financial Institute Policy Brief, 2006.

Klein, R. W. "The Insurance Industry and Its Regulation: An Overview." In *The Future of Insurance Regulation in the United States,* edited by M. F. Grace and R. W. Klein. Washington DC: Brookings Institution Press, 2009.

Laffont, J., and D. Martimort. 1999. Separation of Regulators against Collusive Behavior. *RAND Journal of Economics* 30:232-262.

Lei, Y., and J. T. Schmit. "Influences of Organizational Form on Medical Malpractice Insurer Operations." Working paper, University of Wisconsin-Madison, 2008.

Leverty, J. T., and M. F. Grace. "The Robustness of Output Measures in Property-Liability Insurance Efficiency Studies." *Journal of Banking and Finance* (2009).

Litan, R. E., and P. O'Connor. Consumer Benefits of an Optional Federal Charter: The Case of Auto Insurance." In *The Future of Insurance Regulation in the United States,* edited by M. F. Grace and R. W. Klein. Washington, DC: Brookings Institution Press, 2009.

Phillips, Richard D., J. David Cummins, and Franklin Allen. "Financial Pricing of Insurance in a Multiline Insurance Company." *Journal of Risk and Insurance* 65 (1998): 597–636.

Scott, H. S. "Optional Federal Chartering of Insurance: Design of a Regulatory Structure." Paper presented at the Searle Center Research Symposium on Insurance Markets and Regulation, 2008.

Sommer, D. W. "The Impact of Firm Risk on Property-Liability Insurance Prices." *Journal of Risk and Insurance* 63 (1996): 510–514.

Wallison, P. J. "Convergence in Financial Services Markets: Effects on Insurance Regulation." In *The Future of Insurance Regulation in the United States,* edited by M. F. Grace and R. W. Klein. Washington, DC: Brookings Institution Press, 2009.

Winter, R. "The Dynamics of Competitive Insurance Markets." *Journal of Financial Intermediation* 3 (1994): 379–415.

Zanjani, G. "Pricing and Capital Allocation in Catastrophe Insurance." *Journal of Financial Economics* 65 (2002): 283–305.

Notes

Chapter 1: Introduction

1. Richard A. Derrig and Sharon Tennyson. 2011. "The Impact of Rate Regulation on Claims: Evidence from Massachusetts Automobile Insurance," *Risk Management and Insurance Review* 14(2) Fall 2011: 173-200.
2. A thorough treatment of this motivation is beyond the scope of this project. See Lawrence Powell, "The Assault on the McCarran-Ferguson Act and the Politics of Insurance in the Post-Katrina Era," *Journal of Insurance Regulation,* 2008, for a critical evaluation of the merits of changing current antitrust laws.
3. These interests are voiced by industry groups such as the National Association of Mutual Insurance Companies, the Independent Insurance Agents and Brokers of America, and the Professional Insurance Agents of America.

Chapter 2

The author would like to thank Lars Powell and Alex Tabarrok with helpful comments on an earlier draft. Errors and other inadequacies are my own.

1. *Fortune,* May 3, 2010. Accessed at http://money.cnn.com/magazines/fortune/fortune 500/2010/industries/#1.
2. The teams that play in stadiums named by insurance companies are the Indianapolis Colts, the Green Bay Packers, the Seattle Mariners, the Cincinnati Reds, and the Philadelphia Eagles. Information obtained from http://espn.go.com/sportsbusiness/s/stadium-names.html.
3. 2008 figures. Source: Bureau of Economic Analysis Industry tables: http://www.bea .gov/industry/gpotables/gpo_action.cfm?anon=669581&table_id=26637&format_type=0.
4. See Arnold Kling, "Insulation vs. Insurance," *Cato Unbound,* January 8, 2007, http://www.cato-unbound.org/2007/01/08/arnold-kling/insulation-vs-insurance/.
5. John Cochrane, "Health-Status Insurance: How Markets Can Provide Health Security" (Cato Institute Policy Analysis, February 2009). http://www.cato.org/pub _display.php?pub_id=9986.
6. Alex Tabarrok, "Genetic Testing: An Economic and Contractarian Analysis," *Journal of Health Economics* 13 (March 1994).

7. Michael Rothschild and Joseph Stiglitz, "Equilibrium in Competitive Insurance Markets: An Essay on the Economics of Imperfect Information," *Quarterly Journal of Economics* 90 (November 1976).

8. Mark V. Pauly and Bradley Herring, *Pooling Health Insurance Risks* (American Enterprise Institute, 1999).

9. See, for example, Kerstin Roeder, "Hyperbolic Discounting and the Demand for Long-term Care Insurance" (paper presented at ECHE 2010, Helsinki, Finland, July 7–10, 2010), http://eche2010.abstractbook.org/presentations/162/.

10. David Cutler, "Why Don't Markets Insure Long-term Risk?" (Harvard University, May 1996). http://www.economics.harvard.edu/files/faculty/13_ltc_rev.pdf

11. See "Insurance to Cover firms Against Celebrity 'Disgrace,'" *The Independent* (UK), November 16, 2010, http://www.independent.co.uk/news/people/news/insurance-to-cover-firms-against-celebrity-disgrace-2135001.html.

12. Scott Harrington and Gregory Niehaus, *Risk Management and Insurance,* 2nd ed. (New York: McGraw-Hill/Irwin, 2003), 446.

13. Harrington and Niehaus, 2003. Chapter 20 discusses the capital market frictions. Chapter 21 discusses the tax advantages. See also David Mayers and Clifford W. Smith, Jr., "On the Corporate Demand for Insurance," *Journal of Business* 55 (April, 1982): 181–296.

14. Viviana E. Zelizer, "Home Values and the Market: The Case of Life Insurance and Death in 19th-Century America," *The American Journal of Sociology*, November 1978. http://graphics8.nytimes.com/images/blogs/freakonomics/pdf/ZelizerInsurance Repugnant.pdf (available on JSTOR).

15. See Robert Shiller, *The New Financial Order: Risk in the 21st Century* (Princeton University Press, 2004).

16. See, for example, Testimony before the House Committee on Financial Services, Subcommittee on Oversight and Investigations, August 1, 2001. http://www.brookings.edu/testimony/2001/0801business_litan.aspx.

17. See Stephen B. Pociask, "Consumer Opinions on Insurance Price Regulation" (The American Consumer Institute, June 2007), http://insurancefederationnc.com/elements/media/msg_pdf/insurance20Survey20Study.pdf.

18. See Kirk Hamilton, et al., *Where is the Wealth of Nations? Measuring Capital for the 21st Century.* (Washington, DC: World Bank, 2006).

Chapter 3

1. Scott Harrington, "Effects of Prior Approval Rate Regulation on Auto Insurance," in *Deregulating Property-Liability Insurance: Restoring Competition and Increasing Market Efficiency,* ed. J. David Cummins (Washington: Brookings–AEI Joint Center on Regulation, 2002), http://www.aei-brookings.org/publications/abstract.php?pid=221.

2. Anthony J. Barkume and John W. Ruser, "Deregulating Property-Casualty Insurance Pricing: The Case of Workers' Compensation," *The Journal of Law and Economics* 44 (2001): 37–63.

3. See Suzanne Yelen, "Withdrawal Restrictions in the Automobile Insurance Market," *Yale Law Journal* (102) (1993): 1431–1455. In addition, the combined amount of premiums that left Massachusetts in 1992–1993 was approximately 41 percent of the total market, as noted

in Richard Derrig, "Price Regulation in U.S. Automobile Insurance: A Case Study of Massachusetts Private Passenger Automobile Insurance 1978–1990," *Geneva Papers on Risk and Insurance* 18 (1993): 158–173.

4. State Farm reaches settlement with state, *Orlando Business Journal*, Wednesday, December 16, 2009.

5. Peter A. Kerr, "A Showdown on Workers' Compensation in Maine," *New York Times*, August 9, 1992. http://www.nytimes.com/1992/08/09/us/a-showdown-on-workers-compensation-in-maine.html.

6. Stephen P. D'Arcy, "Insurance Price Deregulation: The Illinois Experience," in *Deregulating Property-Liability Insurance: Restoring Competition and Increasing Market Efficiency*, ed. J. David Cummins (Washington: Brookings–AEI Joint Center on Regulation, 2002). http://www.aei-brookings.org/publications/abstract.php?pid=221.

7. Harrington, "Effects of Prior Approval."

8. (AP 2009).

9. Jeff Harrington and Jennifer Liberto, "State Farm Bails on Us," *St. Petersburg Times*, January 28, 2009, A1.

10. According to the National Association of Insurance Commissioners (2007, 1998), the cumulative profit on homeowners' insurance was negative over the period 1989–2007.

11. Florida HB 1A (2007). It is interesting that the vote for this intervention was very lopsided. In the Florida House it was 116–2 in favor, while it was 40–0 in the Senate. See http://www.myfloridahouse.gov/Sections/Bills/billsdetail.aspx?BillId=34571&BillNumber=&SessionId=56.

12. Florida HB 1171 (2009).

13. (LaModa 2009).

14. Alex Roth, Dan Fitzpatrick, and Paulo Prada. "Florida Braces for Storm's Economic Blow," *Wall Street Journal*, August 19, 2008, http://online.wsj.com/article/SB121910444634651453.html?mod=googlewsj.

15. Quoted in John D. Worrall, "Private Passenger Auto Insurance in New Jersey: A Three-Decade Advertisement for Reform," in *Deregulating Property-Liability Insurance: Restoring Competition and Increasing Market Efficiency*, ed. J. David Cummins. (Washington, DC: Brookings–AEI Joint Center on Regulation, 2002), http://www.aei-brookings.org/publications/abstract.php?pid=221.

16. Marjorie M. Bertie, *Hit Me—I Need the Money: The Politics of Auto Insurance Reform* (San Francisco: ICS Press, 1991).

17. Massachusetts followed New Jersey in most years, and for the three years that New Jersey was not the leader in auto expenditures, Massachusetts had the highest expenditures. Also, two of the three years when New Jersey no longer had the highest expenditures were the last two years of data, suggesting that the market reforms are having some effects. See National Association of Insurance Commissioners, Average Auto Insurance Expenditures (various years).

18. New Jersey Department of Banking and Insurance, "Auto Insurance Reform Continues to Produce Results" (March 1, 2004), http://www.newjersey.gov/dobi/pressreleases/pr040301.htm.

19. New Jersey Department of Banking and Insurance, 2004.

20. New Jersey Department of Banking and Insurance, "More Savings for New Jersey Drivers" (May 18, 2005). http://www.newjersey.gov/dobi/pressreleases/pr050518.htm.

21. New Jersey Department of Banking and Insurance, "New Jersey Welcomes New Auto

Insurance Company" (October 12, 2006). http://www.state.nj.us/dobi/press releases/pro61012.htm.

22. Joseph Treaster, "Where Drivers Are Now Courted." *New York Times,* August 24, 2006. http://query.nytimes.com/gst/fullpage.html?res=9806E5DB133EF937A1575BC0A9609 C8B63.

23. Quoted in Mary Gooderham, "Massachusetts Battles Monster Created by Car Insurance Reform," *Globe and Mail (Toronto),* April 3, 1989.

24. For a history of the Massachusetts automobile insurance laws, see Sharon Tennyson, Mary A. Weiss, and Laureen Regan, "Automobile Insurance Regulation: The Massachusetts Experience," in *Deregulating Property-Liability Insurance: Restoring Competition and Increasing Market Efficiency*, ed. J. David Cummins (Washington: Brookings–AEI Joint Center on Regulation, 2002). http://www.aei-brookings.org/publications/abstract.php?pid=221.

25. Massachusetts Division of Insurance, "Executive Summary: Results of the Survey of the Auto Insurance Market After One Year of Managed Competition" (2009), http://www.mass.gov/?pageID=ocamodulechunk&L=4&L0=Home&L1=Government &L2=Our+Agencies+and+Divisions&L3=Division+of+Insurance&sid=Eoca&b =terminalcontent&f=20090702executivesummary&csid=Eoca.

26. Using data going back to 1980, Tennyson et al., "Automobile Insurance Regulation," show a similar story regarding pricing over time relative to the U.S. market.

27. Tennyson et al. "Automobile Insurance Regulation."

28. Derrig, "Price Regulation."

29. Massachusetts Division of Insurance, "Executive Summary."

30. Office of Consumer Affairs and Regulation. "The Massachusetts Automobile Insurance Study Group" (2007). http://www.mass.gov/Eoca/docs/autoinsurancereport 20070315.pdf.

31. Massachusetts Division of Insurance, "Executive Summary.

32. Quoted in Todd Baurer, "Augusta Georgia: business@ugusta: Auto Insurance Reform at Hand," *Augusta Chronicle,* February 28, 1999. http://chronicle.augusta.com/sto-ries/022899/bus_MPS-4716.000.shtml.Baurer (1999).

33. Martin F. Grace, Robert W. Klein, and Richard D. Phillips, "Auto Insurance Reform: Salvation in South Carolina," in *Deregulating Property-Liability Insurance: Restoring Competition and Increasing Market Efficiency*, ed. J. David Cummins (Washington, DC: Brookings–AEI Joint Center on Regulation, 2002). http://www.aei-brookings.org/publi-cations/abstract.php?pid=221.

34. Scott E. Harrington and S. Travis Pritchett, "Automobile Insurance Reform in South Carolina," *Journal of Insurance Regulation* 8 (1990): 422–445.

35. National Highway Traffic Safety Administration, "Traffic Safety Annual Assessment—Alcohol-Impaired Driving Fatalities," *Traffic Safety Facts: Research Note* (August 2008, DOT HS 811 016). http://www-nrd.nhtsa.dot.gov/Pubs/811016.Pdf.

36. Kerr, "A Showdown."

37. Alan Hunt and Robert W. Klein, "Workers' Compensation Insurance in North America" (Upjohn Institute Technical Report No. 96–010, 1996).

38. The largest workers' compensation provider in 1994 had approximately 64 percent of the market. The next three largest companies had 7 percent, 4 percent, and 3 percent, for a four-firm concentration ratio of nearly 79 percent of the market. See National Association of Insurance Commissioners, AIC Annual Statement State page (1994).

39. Meg Fletcher, "Maine Law Could Prevent Comp System Collapse," *Business Insurance,*

October 26, 1992.

40. "Workers' Comp Still on the Upward Track," *Portland Press Herald*, December 5, 1997. http://global.factiva.com/ha/defa ult.aspx.

Chapter 4

1. P. Danzon and S. E. Harrington, "Workers' Compensation Rate Regulation: How Price Controls Increase Costs," *Journal of Law and Economics* 44 (2001): 1–36. R. A. Derrig and S. L. Tennyson. "The Impact of Rate Regulation on Claims: Evidence from Massachusetts Automobile Insurance" (2008). http://ssrn.com/ abstract=1115377.
2. (EPIC, 2003).
3. Federal Trade Commission, "Credit-Based Insurance Scores: Impacts on Consumers of Automobile Insurance," report to Congress, 2007.
4. W. A. Tillman and G. E. Hobbs, "The Accident-Prone Automobile Driver: A Study of the Psychiatric and Social Background," *The American Journal of Psychiatry* 106 (1949): 321–331.
5. Texas Department of Insurance, "Use of Credit Information by Insurers in Texas," report to the 79th Legislature, 2004.
6. Miller, M. J., and R. A. Smith. "The Relationship of Credit-Based Insurance Scores to Private Passenger Automobile Insurance Loss Propensity" (Actuarial study, EPIC Actuaries, LLC, 2003). http://www.epicactuaries.com. FTC, "Credit-Based Insurance Scores."
7. Miller and Smith. "Relationship of Credit-Based Insurance Scores."
8. TDI (2005).
9. Miller and Smith. "Relationship of Credit-Based Insurance Scores."
10. FTC, "Credit-Based Insurance Scores."
11. FTC, "Credit-Based Insurance Scores."
12. FTC, "Credit-Based Insurance Scores."
13. FTC, "Credit-Based Insurance Scores."
14. FTC, "Credit-Based Insurance Scores."
15. FTC, "Credit-Based Insurance Scores."
16. (ACB, 1992).
17. Insurance Research Council, "A Survey of Public Attitudes on Insurance Fraud, Workers' Compensation, Traffic Violations and Driver Improvement Courses, Financial Stability and Insolvency, and Other Insurance Topics," *Public Attitude Monitor,* October 1991.
18. Insurance Research Council, "A Survey of Public Attitudes."
19. FTC, "Credit-Based Insurance Scores."
20. FTC, "Credit-Based Insurance Scores."
21. NAIC, 2005.

Chapter 5

1. See Swiss Re, "Natural Catastrophes and Man-Made Disasters 2005: High Earthquake Casualties, New Dimension in Windstorm Losses," *Sigma* 2 (2006), www.swissre.com.
2. For a discussion of the criteria of insurability of risks see, for example, Baruch Berliner, *Limits of Insurability of Risks* (Englewood Cliffs, NJ: Prentice Hall, 1982); or John R. Coomber, "Natural and Large Catastrophes—Changing Risk Characteristics and Challenges for the Insurance Industry," *The Geneva Papers* 31 (2006): 88–95.

3. For similar research, see Martin F. Grace and Robert W. Klein. "Overview of Catastrophe Insurance Markets in the U.S." (working paper, 1998); Martin F. Grace and Robert W. Klein, "Overview of Recent Developments in Residential & Commercial Property Insurance" (Final Report, Prepared for the National Association of REALTORS°, 2003). Martin F. Grace, Robert W. Klein, and Zhiyong Liu, "Increased Hurricane Risk and Insurance Market Responses," *Journal of Insurance Regulation* 24 (2005): 3–32. Our focus differs and we evaluate trends over a much longer period.

4. For a detailed description of the conduct and performance of the Florida insurance market with a special focus on prices, availability of coverage, policy terms, and profitability, see Robert W. Klein and Paul R. Kleindorfer, "The Supply of Catastrophe Insurance Under Regulatory Constraints" (working paper 99–25, The Wharton School of Pennsylvania, 1999); Martin F. Grace, Martin F. and Robert W. Klein. "After the Storms: Property Insurance Markets in Florida" (working paper, Center for Risk Management & Insurance Research, Georgia State University, 2006); and Martin F. Grace and Robert W. Klein, "Hurricane Risk and Property Insurance Markets" (working paper, Center for Risk Management & Insurance Research, Georgia State University, 2007). The analyses document the restructuring of the market, the rising price and tighter availability of insurance, and the substantial losses suffered by insurers, which have adversely affected the supply of coverage.

5. Patricia H. Born and W. Kip Viscusi. "The Catastrophic Effects of Natural Disasters on Insurance Markets," *Journal of Risk and Uncertainty* 33 (2006): 55–72.

6. For a detailed description of these regulatory aspects see, for example, Wharton (2008), chapter 2, Harrington / Niehaus (2003), chapter 6, Klein (1995), Klein (2000) and Klein (2007). For an overview of various theories of regulation see Klein (1995). The principles of and reasons for insurance regulation are also explained in Feldhaus / Klein (1997), Grace / Klein (1999) and Wharton (2008).

7. Howard Kunreuther and Erwann O. Michel-Kerjan. "Managing Large-Scale Risks in a New Era of Catastrophes," *Journal of Reinsurance* 15 (2008): 35.

8. For a discussion of the problems and incentive conflicts linked with residual market solutions and insurance guaranty funds see, for example, Scott E. Harrington and Gregory R. Niehaus. *Risk Management and Insurance,* 2nd ed. (New York: McGraw Hill, 2003). 297f.; Oliver Wyman Mercer, "Study of Homeowner, Commercial Property, Liability, and Marine Insurance" (Prepared for the Government of Newfoundland and Labrador, 2004), 39 ff., and Kunreuther and Michel-Kerjan, "Managing Large-Scale Risks," 48 ff.

9. Martin F. Grace and Robert W. Klein, "The Past and Future of Insurance Regulation: The McCarran-Ferguson Act and Beyond" (Unpublished manuscript, Searle Center Research Symposium on Insurance Markets and Regulation, April 14, 2008), 36. That is also the reason why we use the kind of rate regulation as proxy for the intensity of regulation in a certain state in our regression approach.

10. See, for example, William R. Feldhaus and Robert W. Klein, "The Regulation of Commercial Insurance: Initial Evaluation and Recommendations" (working paper, Center for Risk Management and Insurance Research, Georgia State University, 1997).

11. Grace and Klein, "The Past and Future," 36.

12. Scott E. Harrington and Patricia Danzon. "Workers' Compensation Rate Regulation: How Price Controls Increase Costs," *Journal of Law & Economics* 44(2001): 1–36.

13. See Harrington and Niehaus, *Risk Management and Insurance,* 98, 503, 523. Also see www.commercialinsurancefacts.org. For further contributions on regulation of prop-

erty insurance markets in relation to catastrophic risks see Robert W. Klein, "Managing Catastrophe Risk: Problems and Policy Alternatives" (working paper, presented at "Rethinking Insurance Regulation 1998," Competitive Enterprise Institute, Washington, DC, 1998); Robert W. Klein, "Catastrophe Risk and the Regulation of Property Insurance: A Comparative Analysis of Five States" (working paper, Center for Risk Management & Insurance Research, Georgia State University, 2007); Kunreuther and Michel-Kerjan, "Managing Large-Scale Risks," Chapter 2. These studies comment on regulatory issues (regulation of prices, underwriting and policy terms, etc.) with a special focus on catastrophe-prone states (Florida, Texas, California, New York).

14. George E. Rejda, *Principles of Risk Management and Insurance*, 10th ed. (Boston: Pearson/Addison Wesley, 2008), 157.

15. For a description of the typical distribution channels in commercial lines, see Feldhaus and Klein, "Regulation of Commercial Insurance," 30 ff.

16. See Harrington and Niehaus, *Risk Management and Insurance*, 504, 522 f. Also see www.commercialinsurancefacts.org.

17. There are eight different forms of homeowners' policies offering different coverage possibilities for the insureds' various coverage needs. The most common HO-3-policy comprises building and content coverage, with a liability component covering all perils except for the ones that are specially named ("all risk" policy). For details see Harrington and Niehaus, *Risk Management and Insurance,* Chapter 14, and Rejda, *Principles of Risk Management,* Chapters 20 and 21.

18. There are several different lines of business offering coverage for commercial property risks. In our analysis, we include commercial multiple peril, fire, and allied lines. Commercial multiple peril policies are—similar to homeowners contracts—building and content policies for commercial clients, including a liability component as well as some further arbitrary coverage extensions like business interruption insurance. Fire insurance covers property losses caused by fire and lightning. Allied lines refer to coverages that are usually purchased with fire insurance, such as coverage for windstorm, hail, and vandalism. Indirect losses can also be covered, including the loss of business income and extra expenses. While commercial multiple peril policies are usually bought by small and medium-size businesses, fire-policies are purchased by companies of all sizes. Especially big industrial clients usually insure their property risks by fire and allied policies leading to a heterogeneous risk structure in these insurance portfolios. For details see Feldhaus and Klein, "Regulation of Commercial Insurance," 38 ff.; Harrington and Niehaus, *Risk Management and Insurance*, Chapter 23; and Rejda, *Principles of Risk Management,* Chapter 25.

19. The underlying data for Figures 5.7 and 5.8 are adjusted for inflation. We note that surplus is calculated at the firm level, and is not exclusively allocated to the insurer's property business.

20. Our analysis of premium changes is limited to assessing changes in the total volume of business, as we are not able to evaluate the separate effects on prices or quantities.

21. This approach differs somewhat from Born and Viscusi, "The Catastrophic Effects," which used the average catastrophic events over the sample period as the measure of expected catastrophes for each state. We use a four-year rolling window to allow for trends in the number of events over time. Of course, there is much potential for discussion on how to model the variable *unexpected catastrophes,* and there are certainly several other reason-

able ways to do that. We also tried several alternative definitions, for example, a dummy variable that equals one if the actual number of catastrophic events is larger than two times the standard deviation of the number of events per state over the time period. The results (not shown) confirm the robustness of our findings, as the direction of influence is generally unchanged. We chose our approach as we wanted to make sure to capture trends of changes in the number of catastrophes over the observation period.

22. Since our focus is on firm-state units, we do not at this time account for the fact that the total number of unexpected events for firms with multistate operations ranges from −46 to 107.

23. This can also be interpreted as a measure of the insurer's diversification efforts.

24. We do not include variables pertaining to the organizational form as we run the regressions with firm fixed effects. For a review of the effect of organizational form on insurers' performance, see Patricia H. Born, William Gentry, W. Kip Viscusi, and Richard Zeckhauser, "Organizational Form and Insurance Company Performance: Stocks vs. Mutuals," in *The Economics of Property-Casualty Insurance,* ed. David F. Bradford (Chicago: The University of Chicago Press, 1998), 167–192.

25. We lose several years of data due to the inclusion of the lagged covariates.

26. The effect of a contemporaneous (time t) unexpected catastrophe on insurers is determined via a combination of the coefficients of the following variables: *Unexpected Catastrophic Events$_t$, UnexpCat$_t$*(Insurer writes Commercial lines only)* and *UnexpCat$_t$*Strict Rate Regulation$_t$.*

27. The effect of reducing losses two years after an unexpected catastrophe might result either from a reduced quantity of insurance written or the exit of the firm from the state insurance market altogether. But this result is not statistically significant.

28. This was, for example, the case in Florida following the latest years' major hurricanes, when startup insurers saw the opportunity of doing business in certain areas.

29. According to the Florida Office of Insurance Regulation, since early 2006, when the legislature made affordable, competitive-priced insurance a priority, 31 new insurers have entered the Florida market.

30. For the discussion of an optional federal charter/regulation system with a summary of the arguments for and against state regulation compared with federal regulation see, for example, Grace and Klein, "Efficiency Implications"; Harrington and Niehaus, *Risk Management and Insurance,* 104 ff.; and Grace and Klein, "The Past and Future."

31. Feldhaus and Klein, "Regulation of Commercial Insurance," 8.

32. For a comparison of the U.S. regulatory regime with the European approach and a discussion on reformation needs, including some remarks on how these issues are addressed in Europe (Solvency II), see Robert W. Klein and Shaun Wang. "Catastrophe Risk Financing in the U.S. and the EU: A Comparative Analysis of Alternative Regulatory Approaches" (working paper presented at the SCOR-JRI Conference on Insurance, Reinsurance and Capital Market Transformations, 2007). For further reform proposals see Grace and Klein, "The Past and Future."

33. Moreover, the adverse selection problem resulting from average premiums can be reduced. See Howard C. Kunreuther, "Guiding Principles for Mitigating and Insuring Losses from Natural Disasters," *Risk Management Review* (2006): 2; Howard C. Kunreuther and Mark Pauly, "Rules Rather Than Discretion: Lessons From Hurricane Katrina," *Journal of Risk and Uncertainty* 33 (2006): 101–116.

Chapter 6

Previously published in a different form by the Competitive Enterprise Institute, August 2007.

1. Kenneth J. Meier, "The Politics of Insurance Regulation," *The Journal of Risk and Insurance* 58 (December 1991): 700.
2. See, for example, Rutherford H. Platt, *Land Use and Society: Geography, Law, and Public Policy* (Washington, DC: Island Press, 2004), 4–5.
3. As the chances of a disaster hitting approach 100 percent, the premiums necessary become equal to the cost of the property insured. While it's still possible to market insurance policies in this situation, the insurance policies do not serve to transfer any risk.
4. Peter M. Lencis, *Insurance Regulation in the United States: An Overview for Business and Government* (Santa Barbara, CA: Greenwood Press, 2004), 19–25.
5. 49 USC 15 1.
6. Gilbert Fowler White, *Human Adjustment to Floods: A Geographical Approach to the Flood Problem in the United States* (Chicago: University of Chicago, Department of Geography, 1942/1945), 11–12.
7. In 1803, Congress passed the first U.S. disaster relief bill, primarily a system of tax supports and tariff relief for Portsmouth, New Hampshire, following a disastrous fire there. "Bills and Resolutions, House of Representatives, 9th Congress, 2nd Session, Read the first and second time, and committed to a committee of the whole House, to-morrow. A Bill, For the relief of the sufferers by fire, in the tow of Portsmouth, New Hampshire." http://memory.loc.gov/cgi-bin/query/D?hlaw:1:./temp/~ammem_aL2o.
8. John M. Barry, *Rising Tide* (New York: Simon and Schuster, 1998).
9. White, *Human Adjustment,* 1942, 1.
10. Author's calculations based on data in A. Willis Robertson et al., "Insurance and Other Programs for Financial Assistance to Flood Victims: A report from the Secretary of HUD as required by the Southeast Hurricane Disaster Relief Act of 1965" (Washington, DC: U.S. Government Printing Office, 1966), 3.
11. See, for example, Edward Overman, "Flood Peril and the Federal Flood Insurance Act of 1956," *The Annals of the American Academy of Political and Social Science* 309 (1957): 98–106.
12. 15 USC 20.
13. White, *Human Adjustment,* 1942, 201.
14. White, *Human Adjustment,* 1942, 201.
15. A. M. Best and Company, *Best's Directory of Insurers and Underwriters, 1953.*
16. National Oceanic and Atmospheric Administration, "Hurricane History, 2007," http://www.nhc.noaa.gov/HAW2/english/history.shtml.
17. Harry Truman, "119—Special Message to the Congress Transmitting Proposed Legislation on a National System of flood Disaster Insurance" (May 5, 1952), http://www.presidency.ucsb.edu/ws/index.php?pid=14105.
18. On the hurricane season, see Jerry D. Jarrell et al., "The Deadliest, Costliest, and Most Intense Hurricanes from 1900 to 2000" (National Oceanic and Atmospheric Administration, 2001). http://www.aoml.noaa.gov/hrd/Landsea/deadly/index.html.
19. Dwight D. Eisenhower, "Annual Message to Congress on the State of the Union" (January 10, 1957), http://www.presidency.ucsb.edu/ws/index.php?pid=11029.
20. PL 566 (1955).

21. In theory, here is how it worked: The flood program would set a premium identical to the one a private company would charge for the same risk. The homeowner would pay 60 percent of that amount, the homeowners' state would pay 20 percent, and the federal government would pay 20 percent. The legislation did not provide guidance as to how this premium might be set.

22. The information about the proposed regulations is drawn from: David Grossman, "Flood Insurance: Can a Feasible Program Be Created?" *Land Economics* 34 (November 1958): 352–357.

23. Most existing private risk-transfer mechanisms, according to White, *Human Adjustment* (1942), 21, would not have insured these structures at all.

24. Overman, "Flood Peril."

25. American Insurance Institute, "Studies of Floods and Flood Damage, 1952–1955" (New York, 1956).

26. Overman, "Flood Peril," 105.

27. Gilbert White, "Choice of Adjustment to Floods" (University of Chicago, Department of Geography, Research Paper No. 93, 1964), 78. (White, it should be noted, did the actual research two years before the publication date.)

28. For a history of the TVA flood program, see James M. Wright, "The Nation's Responses to Flood Disasters: A Historical Account" (Association of State Floodplain Managers, 2000), 16–21, http://www.floods.org/PDF/hist_fpm.pdf.

29. Wright, "The Nation's Responses to Flood Disasters," 18.

30. The TVA, of course, faced no market forces to make sure it got these estimates right. Given the extreme difficulty of making them—even today—it is likely that initial estimates would not have been very good.

31. Wright, *The Nation's Responses*, 19.

32. U. S. Senate. "A Program for Reducing the National Flood Damage Potential: Memorandum of the Chairman to Members of the Committee on Public Works" (U.S. Senate, 86th Cong., 1st Sess., 31 Aug. 1959).

33. American Institute for Research et al., "A Chronology of Major Events Affecting the National Flood Insurance Program" (Federal Emergency Management Agency, 2002), 8.

34. American Institute for Research et al., "A Chronology of Major Events," 27.

35. The first in the series is *Floods of the Kansas River, Topeka, Kansas, in 1935 and 1951: U.S. Geological Survey Hydrologic Investigations* (Washington, DC: Government Printing Office, 1959), Atlas HA-14.

36. More research is needed to determine the exact shape of the TVA's influence on the USGS process for developing maps.

37. Greg Brouwer, "The Creeping Storm," *Civil Engineering* 73 (June 2003). http://www.pubs.asce.org/ceonline/ceonline03/0603ce.html.

38. 79 Stat. 1301 (1965).

39. Lyndon Johnson, "605—Statement by the President Upon Signing the Southeast Hurricane Disaster Relief Act of 1965" (November 8, 1965).

40. Task Force on Federal Flood Control Policy. *A Unified National Program for Managing Flood Losses* (Washington, DC: U.S. Government Printing Office, August 10, 1966).

41. Task Force, *A Unified National Program for Managing Flood Losses*, 1–2.

42. Task Force, *A Unified National Program for Managing Flood Losses*, 14.

43. Task Force, *A Unified National Program for Managing Flood Losses*, 38–39.

44. Task Force, *A Unified National Program for Managing Flood Losses*, 39.

45. Task Force, *A Unified National Program for Managing Flood Losses*, 39.

46. As noted above, more research is needed on the nature of state regulatory climates.

47. White, "Choice of Adjustment," 78.

48. U.S. Congress, *Insurance and Other Programs for Assistance to Flood Victims: A report from the Secretary of Housing and Urban Development as required by the Southeast Hurricane Disaster Relief Act of 1965*. (Washington, DC: U.S. Government Printing Office, 1966), 89th Congress, Second Session.

49. U.S. Congress, *Insurance and Other Programs for Assistance to Flood Victims*, 128.

50. H.R. 11197, 1967, PL-90 448 codified in Title XII of the Housing and Urban Development Act. Note that nearly all significant hearings on the program took place during 1967, and both chambers passed the great bulk of the program. Despite agreement in principle, several differences between the House and Senate bills held up establishment of the program for a year.

51. Rutherford Platt, *Land Use and Society*, 391.

52. Separate Small Business Administration programs provide low-interest loans to small businesses damaged by flood.

53. Today, private companies create the FIRMs under contract with the National Flood Insurance Program. The process seems reasonably immune from political pressure because the contracts for writing the FIRMs get assigned by means of random selection, and even the FEMA administrator cannot overturn FIRMS. Joseph Albaugh, in fact, tried to do so during early 2001 and found himself rebuffed and publicly embarrassed for doing so.

54. Michael Grunwald, "For S.C. Project, a Torrent of Pressure; Developer Wins Reprieve From FEMA on $4 Billion Project in Columbia Flood Plain," *The Washington Post*, July 13, 2001.

55. As Overman, "Flood Peril," discusses, many states would have had a difficult time participating in a program that so blatantly provided grants to purely private homeowners.

56. It's interesting to note that no environmental groups appear to have testified for or against the program.

57. U.S. Congress, Committee on Banking and Insurance, "Hearings Before the Subcommittee on Banking and Insurance on H.R. 11197" (Ninetieth Congress, First Session), 166.

58. U.S. Congress, Committee on Banking and Insurance, "Hearings Before the Subcommittee on Banking and Insurance on H.R. 11197, 74.

59. American Institute for Research, "A Chronology," 14

60. American Institute for Research, "A Chronology," 15.

61. American Institute for Research, "A Chronology," 16.

62. American Institute for Research, "A Chronology," 18.

63. It did, however, continue to deny participation in some particular programs—such as Small Business Administration loans—to flood insurance-eligible individuals who did not purchase. Even this requirement, however, has been obeyed only in the breach.

64. Clifford Winston, *Government Failure Versus Market Failure: Microeconomics Policy Research and Government Performance* (Washington: AEI-Brookings Joint Center for Regulatory Studies, 2006), 4.

65. Meier, *Politics of Insurance Regulation*.

66. As Gilbert White observed, lenders' lack of information about flooding also made it hard to include it in their calculations.

Chapter 7

1. U.S. Department of the Treasury, *Blueprint for a Modernized Financial Regulatory Structure* (Washington, DC, 2008).
2. For more detailed reviews of the history of state insurance regulation, see J. Day, *Economic Regulation of the Insurance Industry* (Washington, DC: U.S. Department of Transportation, 1970); J. S. Hanson, R. E. Dineen, and M. B. Johnson, *Monitoring Competition: A Means of Regulating the Property and Liability Insurance Business* (Milwaukee, WI: NAIC, 1974); C. C. Lilly, "A History of Insurance Regulation in the United States," *CPCU Annals* 29 (1976): 99–115; K. J. Meier, *The Political Economy of Regulation: The Case of Insurance* (Albany: SUNY Press, 1988).
3. Hanson, Dineen, and Johnson, *Monitoring Competition*.
4. Meier, *The Political Economy*.
5. Meier, *The Political Economy*.
6. This destructive competition was likely due to several factors. These factors could include the lack of good actuarial methods, poor financial management practices, and the general immaturity of the industry and its management. Over time, the industry has matured in terms of its methods and management. In the industry's infancy, regulators allowed the cartels to set prices so as to keep the companies healthy while at the same time limiting insurers' ability to overprice customers. Today there is no need for this type of system, but regulatory oversight of insurers' financial condition is still warranted.
7. R. W. Klein, "Insurance Regulation in Transition," *Journal of Risk and Insurance* 62 (1995): 263–404.
8. R. W. Klein, *A Regulator's Introduction to the Insurance Industry,* 2nd ed. (Kansas City, MO: National Association of Insurance Commissioners, 2005).
9. *U.S. v. South-Eastern Underwriters.* 322 U.S. 533 (1944).
10. McCarran-Ferguson Act. 15 U.S. Code §§ 1011–1015.
11. It should be noted that advocates of federal regulation have argued that recent events further demonstrate the need for federal oversight of insurance. On the other side, advocates of state regulation make the opposite case. Insurance companies, with a few exceptions, did not engage in the types of transactions that have stressed other financial institutions, and the performance of federal financial regulators has been questioned.
12. Trade associations representing large insurers, reinsurers, and brokers strongly support an OFC. These organizations include the American Insurance Association, the American Council of Life Insurance, the Reinsurance Association of America, and the Council of Insurance Agents and Brokers. They are joined by other organizations with a stake in federal insurance regulation, such as the American Bankers Association.
13. S. W. Pottier, "State Insurance Regulation of Life Insurers: Implications for Economic Efficiency and Financial Strength" (report to the ACLI, University of Georgia, 2007); M. F. Grace and R. W. Klein, "Efficiency Implications of Alternative Regulatory Structures for Insurance," in *Optional Federal Chartering and Regulation of Insurance Companies,* ed. Peter Wallison (Washington, DC: American Enterprise Institute, 2000); M. F. Grace and R. W. Klein, "The Effects of an Optional Federal Charter on Competition in the Life Insurance Industry" (SSRN, working paper series. 2007), http://papers.ssrn.com/sol3/papers.cfm?abstract_id=1027135; L. Regan, *The Optional Federal Charter: Implications for Life Insurance Producers* (Washington, DC: American Council of Life Insurers, 2007).
14. For property-casualty insurance, among the states, the mean percentage of premiums

written by nondomestic insurers was 78.9 percent in 2006. For life-health insurance, the mean percentage of premiums written by nondomestic insurers was 92.3 percent.

15. Industry organizations that oppose an OFC include the Property Casualty Insurance Association of America, the National Association of Mutual Insurance Companies, the Independent Insurance Agents and Brokers of America, and the National Association of Professional Insurance Agents.

16. It should be noted that large companies account for most of the insurance sold in the United States. Many small and regional companies might choose to remain state regulated, but they account for less than 25 percent of the total amount of insurance written; M. F. Grace and R. W. Klein, "The Past and Future of Insurance Regulation: The McCarran-Ferguson Act and Beyond" (working paper, Georgia State University, 2008).

17. This view is reflected in the Treasury blueprint, which envisions a phased approach to increasing the federal role in insurance regulation.

18. F. Keating, "Letter to Secretary of the U.S. Treasury" (2008). http://insurancenewsnet .com/article.asp?a=top_pc&q=0&id=98423.

19. Klein, "Insurance Regulation."

20. Klein, *A Regulator's Introduction.*

21. Klein, *A Regulator's Introduction,* discusses the initiatives in greater detail.

22. "Form A" refers to the statement that must be filed with regulators when an insurance company is acquired or there is a change in its control and ownership.

23. See Klein, "Insurance Regulation," and Klein, *A Regulator's Introduction*, for more detailed reviews of state insurance regulation.

24. In practice, the federal government has left the principal regulatory functions for insurance to the states. Congress, from time to time, has threatened greater federal involvement, and that causes the states to change behavior consistent with congressional objectives. The most recent case of this occurred in the late 1980s and early 1990s when Congressman John Dingell held hearings on the failure of state solvency regulation. The states made significant changes to their approach as a direct result of congressional threats to intervene.

25. P. Munch and D. E. Smallwood, "Theory of Solvency Regulation in the Property and Casualty Insurance Industry," in *Studies in Public Regulation*, ed. Gary Fromm (Cambridge, MA: MIT Press, 1981).

26. Life insurers are required to perform some stress testing of their policy reserves. The NAIC is also advancing a principles-based approach to determining the reserve requirements of life insurance companies.

27. M. F. Grace, R. W. Klein, and R. D. Phillips, "Managing the Cost of Property-Casualty Insurer Insolvencies" (report to the National Association of Insurance Commissioners, 2002). Empirical evidence of this problem is also provided by M. Willenborg, "Regulatory Separation as a Mechanism to Curb Capture: A Study of the Decision to Act Against Distressed Insurers," *Journal of Risk and Insurance* 67 (2000): 593–616; and B. J. Hall, "Regulatory Free Cash Flow and the High Cost of Insurance Company Failures," *Journal of Risk and Insurance* 67 (2000): 415–438.

28. J. Barrese and J. M. Nelson, "Some Consequences of Insurer Insolvencies," *Journal of Insurance Regulation* 13 (1994): 3–18. There are some similarities as well as differences between the protections provided by insurance guaranty associations and those provided by the Federal Deposit Insurance Corporation (FDIC) for bank depositors. Klein, *A Regulator's Introduction,* provides a more detailed discussion of insolvency guaranty associations.

29. Regulating insurance markets and insurers' market conduct, arguably, is a much more extensive task than doing the same for banks. This may be partly due to the nature of insurance transactions but also may be influenced by political factors, given the high salience of certain insurance issues (for example, the cost and availability of auto and home insurance).

30. Some states tend to allow market forces to determine rates in these markets while other states seek to assert some control over pricing. Regulatory pricing constraints can become particularly severe in some jurisdictions (such as homeowners insurance in Florida).

31. M. F. Grace and R. W. Klein. "Insurance Regulation: The Need for Policy Reform" (paper presented at The Future of Insurance Regulation Conference, Washington, DC, 2008); R. W. Klein and S. Wang, "Catastrophe Risk Financing in the United States and the European Union: A Comparison of Alternative Regulatory Approaches" (paper presented at the New Forms of Risk Sharing and Risk Engineering: A SCOR-JRI Conference on Insurance, Reinsurance, and Capital Market Transformations, Paris, 2007).

32. In June 2006, Rep. Ginny Brown-Waite introduced part of the SMART Act as H.R. 5637, 109th Cong. 2d Sess., June 19, 2006 (NIA, § 2).

33. U.S. House of Representatives, 1990.

34. See Harrington (2006) for a comparative review of different options and proposals for federalizing insurance regulation.

35. S. E. Harrington, "Federal Chartering of Insurance Companies: Options and Alternatives for Transforming Insurance Regulation" (Networks Financial Institute Policy Brief 2006-PB-02: March 2006).

36. Harrington, "Federal Chartering of Insurance Companies."

37. National Insurance Act of 2007. SB 40. 109th Congress.

38. A number of papers have examined the pros and cons of an OFC, including H. Scott, "Optional Federal Chartering of Insurance: Design of a Regulatory Structure" (paper presented at the Searle Center Research Symposium on Insurance Markets and Regulation, Chicago, 2008); E. F. Brown, "The Fatal Flaw of Proposals to Federalize Insurance Regulation" (paper presented at the Searle Center Research Symposium on Insurance Markets and Regulation, Chicago, 2008); M. F. Grace and H. Scott, "Optional Federal Chartering of Insurance: Rationale and Design of a Regulatory Structure" (paper presented at the "The Future of Insurance Regulation Conference, Washington, DC, 2008); and R. Detlefsen, "Potential Consequences of Dual Insurance Chartering" (paper presented at The Future of Insurance Regulation Conference. Washington, DC, 2008).

39. Note that states also do not regulate life insurance prices per se. The states only regulate prices indirectly in their review and approval of life policy forms, which includes consideration of the relationship between the premiums that would be charged and the benefits that would be paid.

40. We presume that, under this arrangement, the state guaranty association would function essentially as it does under the current state system. Obligations for an insolvent insurer's claims in a given state would be covered by that state's guaranty association. Assessments to cover the guaranty association's claim payments would be allocated to insurers in the state according to the amount of insurance premiums they write in the state.

41. This is more pertinent to non-life insurance than life insurers. Life insurers do not use statistical agents to compile industry data on the amount of benefits they pay, although this information is reported in the public financial statements they file with regulators and others. Life insurers use mortality tables, which the NAIC publishes as a reference to assist

them in pricing life insurance policies and annuities.

42. Arguably, this problem exists, even if the two responsibilities are housed in different agencies within the same government. The Federal Deposit Insurance Corporation (FDIC) has sought to counter this problem by setting its own minimum standards for federally insured banks that are regulated at the federal or state level.

43. Grace and Klein, "The Past and Future."

44. Detlefsen, "Potential Consequences." Brown, "The Fatal Flaw," also identifies flaws in the OFC proposal.

45. In reality, companies would find regulation hopping to be quite expensive. For example, a company undertakes conversion from a state-licensed company to a federal company. A great deal of information concerning marketing practices, contract terms, and other compliance activities must now be set up to comply with federal regulations. Returning to state regulation would require setting up to comply with every state regulatory requirement for each state where the company writes. For a national company this would be costly.

46. U.S. Department of the Treasury, *Blueprint.*

47. A number of commentators have suggested that AIG's failure was the result of state regulation; these include J. Sununu, T. Johnson, M. Bean, and E. Royce, "Insurance Companies Need a Federal Regulator," *Wall Street Journal,* September 23, 2008, http://online.wsj.com/article/SB122212967854565511.html?mod=article-outset-box.

48. Some have argued that it was, in fact, caused by the lack of appropriate federal supervision; among these is R. Rusboldt, "AIG Failure Doesn't Justify Federal Charter for Insurers" (Letter to the Editor). *The Hill,* 2008, http://thehill.com/letters/aig-failure-doesnt-justify-federal-charter-for-insurers-2008-09-25.html. Either way, the recent financial market problems will be part of the discussion.

49. Harrington, "Federal Chartering"; H. N. Butler and L. E. Ribstein. "A Single-License Approach to Regulating Insurance" (Northwestern Law and Econ Research Paper No. 08–10, 2008).

50. Under current federal law, a risk retention group (RRG) can form in one state and operate in any other state without being subject to extra-state regulation. Initially, the states resisted this system, and problems were encountered with RRG insolvencies. However, some of these problems appear to have been resolved, and the relationships between RRG domiciliary states and other states have improved.

51. Grace and Klein, "The Effects."

Chapter 8

1. R. W. Klein, *A Regulator's Introduction to the Insurance Industry,* 2nd ed. (Kansas City, MO: National Association of Insurance Commissioners, 2005) provides a detailed description of U.S. insurance regulation.

2. An insurance company must apply for a license in each jurisdiction in which it writes business. Only surplus lines or non-admitted insurers may sell insurance for certain designated lines or risks (determined by each state commissioner) without a license.

3. While large segments of the industry have been pushing for an optional federal charter (OFC), it is strongly opposed by the states and other industry segments (for example, state and regional insurers and local agents) that wield considerable political power. The U.S. Department of the Treasury under the previous Bush administration supported an OFC and included it in its blueprint for revamping financial institutions' regulation (U.S.

Department of the Treasury, *Blueprint for a Modernized Financial Regulatory Structure*, Washington, DC, 2008).

4. Regulations governing insurers' investments provide a good example. Two NAIC model laws reflect different approaches, and the states have adopted one of these or developed their own specific rules.

5. National Association of Insurance Companies, "Principles for the NAIC's Adoption of a Principles-Based Reserving Approach" (Kansas City, MO, 2008).

6. The states' fixed minimum capital and surplus requirements range from $500,000 to $6 million, depending on the state and the lines that an insurer writes. The median fixed capital requirement is in the area of $2 million. Klein, *A Regulator's Introduction*.

7. For more detailed descriptions of the RBC formula, see S. Feldblum, "NAIC Property/ Casualty Insurance Company Risk-Based Capital Requirements," *Proceedings of the Casualty Actuarial Society* LXXXIII (1996): 297–418; and National Association of Insurance Companies, "2007 Property-Casualty Risk-Based Capital Overview and Instructions" (Kansas City, MO, 2007).

8. R. P. Butsic, "Report on Covariance Method for Property-Casualty Risk-Based Capital," *Casualty Actuarial Society Forum* summer (1993): 173–202.

9. An insurer's TAC is equal to its reported surplus with some minor modifications; for example, additional reserves required by regulators are added to an insurer's surplus in calculating its TAC.

10. The NAIC developed a model law to be adopted by the states that implements the RBC standards. All states have adopted the model law so the same rules have been established in each state.

11. In statistical language, this might be labeled a Type 1 Error. Conversely, a situation where the RBC formula would not require a financially weak insurer to increase its capital to an adequate level would constitute a Type 2 Error. R. W. Klein and S. Wang, "Catastrophe Risk Financing in the United States and the European Union: A Comparison of Alternative Regulatory Approaches" (paper presented at the New Forms of Risk Sharing and Risk Engineering: A SCOR-JRI Conference on Insurance, Reinsurance, and Capital Market Transformations, Paris, 2007) demonstrate that only a small fraction of insurers fall below the company-action level RBC requirement and that rating agency capital-adequacy tests are considerably more stringent than U.S. regulatory standards.

12. American Academy of Actuaries, "An Update to P/C Risk-Based Capital Underwriting Factors" (September 2007 Report to the National Association of Insurance Commissioners P/C Risk-Based Capital Working Group, Washington, DC).

13. J. D. Cummins, S. E. Harrington, and R. W. Klein, "Insolvency Experience, Risk-Based Capital, and Prompt Corrective Action in Property-Liability Insurance," *Journal of Banking and Finance* 19 (1995): 511–527.

14. Based on the current formula, an insurer's RBC requirement increases proportionately with the amount of its premiums, assets, and loss reserves. However, arguably, according to the law of large numbers, an insurer's risk does not increase proportionately with its size. With a size adjustment, a small insurer would have a higher *relative* RBC requirement than a large insurer, all other things equal.

15. For example, Feldblum, "NAIC Requirements," suggests that better factors could be applied to the credit risk associated with reinsurance recoverables based on credit or claims-paying-ability ratings for reinsurers.

16. Conference of Insurance Supervisory Services of the Member States of the European

Union, "Prudential Supervision of Insurance Undertakings" (report prepared under the Chairmanship of Paul Sharma, Head of the Prudential Risks Department of the UK's Financial Services Authority, 2002).

17. Regulatory activities in the U.S. insurance system are not easily classified using the three-pillar framework. Many quantitative elements of U.S. regulation are beyond capital standards that we discuss in this section. When it is discussed in an international context, the second pillar is more closely associated with qualitative aspects of the supervisory review, which includes an evaluation of an insurer's strategies, processes, and reporting procedures, the risks it is or may be exposed to, and its management of those risks. U.S. regulators may consider some of these elements when evaluating an insurer's risk management, but their approach tends to be more quantitative and rules-based than the approach envisioned in Solvency II.

18. J. D. Cummins, "Reinsurance for Natural and Man-Made Catastrophes in the United States: Current State of the Market and Regulatory Reforms," *Risk Management and Insurance Review* 10 (2007): 179–220.

19. In the United States, regulators require insurers to adhere to the NAIC's Statutory Accounting Principles (SAP), which differ somewhat from Generally Accepted Accounting Principles (GAAP). SAP accounting is intended to measure an insurer's liquidation value, while GAAP is intended to measure the value of a company as a going concern. Within the last decade, the NAIC has sought to standardize and document SAP through a series of more than a hundred issue papers that address various aspects of SAP rules.

20. These reports include insurers' RBC calculations, actuarial opinions of reserve adequacy, CPA-audited financial statements, and management opinions. Most but not all of these reports are available for public access.

21. State laws generally authorize regulators to review all books and records of a company at any time.

22. The terms *bench* or *desk audit* refer to an in-house review of an insurers' financial reports performed within the offices of the insurance regulator. This is contrasted with an on-site examination or audit of an insurer that is performed at the insurer's offices and involves a review of its books and records.

23. The NAIC's analysis activities are focused on larger insurers that write business in a significant number of states.

24. A list of FAST scoring system ratios is published in Klein, *A Regulator's Introduction*. However, the parameters used in developing an insurer's score remain confidential. The FAST scoring system is subject to more frequent modifications than the IRIS ratios.

25. NAIC analysis is confined to "nationally significant" companies, which are defined as companies that write business in seventeen or more states and have gross premiums (direct plus assumed) written in excess of $50 million for life-health companies and $30 million for property-casualty insurers.

26. Examiners have been encouraged to go beyond simply verifying the accuracy of an insurer's financial reports and perform additional analysis to assess an insurer's financial risk.

27. One exception to this is mandatory stress testing by life insurers to demonstrate the adequacy of their policy reserves.

28. M. F. Grace, R. W. Klein, and R. D. Phillips, "Managing the Cost of Property-Casualty Insurer Insolvencies in the U.S." (Center for Risk Management and Insurance Research, Georgia State University, Atlanta, Research Report 02-1, 2002).

29. R. W. Klein, "Insurance Regulation in Transition," *Journal of Risk and Insurance* 62 (1995): 363–404, argues that this allows domiciliary states to impose negative externalities on non-domiciliary states. This problem motivates the multilayered monitoring and regulatory system described earlier.

30. The maximum limit for property-casualty claims is typically $300,000, but some states have higher limits up to $500,000. Many states have also enacted provisions that exclude guaranty-association coverage for claimants with a net worth exceeding a certain amount, for example, $50 million.

31. Workers' compensation is an exception—all workers' compensation claims are covered by GAs, and there is no limit on the amount of coverage for each claim. This policy is intended to protect the claims of injured workers.

32. J. Barrese and J. Nelson, "Some Consequences of Insurer Insolvencies," *Journal of Insurance Regulation* 13 (1994): 3–18.

33. J. D. Cummins, "Risk Based Premiums for Insurance Guaranty Funds," *Journal of Finance* 43 (1988): 823–839; S. Lee, D. Mayers, and C. W. Smith, Jr., "Guaranty Funds and Risk-Taking: Evidence from the Insurance Industry," *Journal of Financial Economics* 44 (1997): 3–24.

34. Epermanis, K., and S. Harrington, "Market Discipline in Property/Casualty Insurance: Evidence from Premium Growth Surrounding Changes in Financial Strength Ratings," *Journal of Money, Credit, and Banking* 38 (2006): 1515–1544.

35. State rating laws and policies vary. In some states, regulators seek to constrain overall rate levels and rate structures (for example, differences in rates between low- and high-risk insureds). In other states, regulators tend to allow the market to set rates and do not seek to constrain the prices that insurers' charge.

36. For example, regulators may prohibit the use of criteria such as the value of a home in underwriting homeowners insurance. Some states are also placing limitations on the use of credit scores in underwriting and pricing personal-lines insurance.

37. The states rely heavily on consumer complaints and market conduct examinations of insurers to police insurers' market practices.

38. Thirty-three states belong to the Interstate Insurance Product Regulation Commission for the review and approval of life insurance products according to a common set of standards. States may elect to opt out of a particular standard but agree to accept all products approved by the commission.

39. In current OFC proposals, federally chartered insurers would not be subject to price regulation. Other aspects of market regulation are not specified. However, there is no guarantee that federal regulators would ultimately refrain from some of the market regulation that insurers and economist criticize.

40. Grace et al., "Managing the Cost." B. J. Hall, "Regulatory Free Cash Flow and the High Cost of Insurance Company Failures," *Journal of Risk and Insurance* 67 (2000): 415–438, estimated this cost to be $1.22 for each $1 of pre-insolvency assets, using a shorter time period, 1986–1994. These costs are substantially higher than those for U.S. bank insolvencies, with estimates ranging between $0.20 and $0.30 per $1 of pre-insolvency assets; C. James, "The Losses Realized in Bank Failures," *Journal of Finance* 46 (1991): 1223–1242; Kaufmann, G. Prepared testimony of George G. Kaufmann for the U.S. Senate Committee on Banking, Housing and Urban Affairs, September 11, 2001. http://www.senate.gov/-banking/ 01_09hrg/091101/kaufman.htm.

41. M. Willenborg, "Regulatory Separation as a Mechanism to Curb Capture: A Study of

the Decision to Act Against Distressed Insurers," *Journal of Risk and Insurance* 67 (2000): 593–616. See also D. H. Downs and D. W. Sommer, "Monitoring, Ownership and Risk-Taking: The Impact of Guaranty Funds," *Journal of Risk and Insurance* 66 (1999): 477–497; Hall, "Regulatory Free Cash Flow."

42. Grace et al., "Managing the Cost."

43. A. Ruhil and P. Teske, "Institutions, Bureaucratic Decisions, and Policy Outcomes: State Insurance Solvency Regulation," *The Policies Studies Journal* 31 (2003): 353–372. find some evidence that investing greater regulator resources—for example, conducting more financial examinations—reduces the number of insolvencies.

44. Scott E. Harrington, "Capital Adequacy in Insurance and Reinsurance," in *Capital Adequacy Beyond Basel: Banking, Securities and Insurance,* ed. Hal Scott (New York: Oxford University Press, 2004); Epermanis and Harrington, "Market Discipline."

45. Cummins et al.,"Insolvency Experience."

46. Cummins et al.,"Insolvency Experience."

47. M. Grace, S. Harrington, and R. W. Klein, "Risk-Based Capital and Solvency Screening in Property-Liability Insurance," *Journal of Risk and Insurance* 65 (1998): 213–243.

48. In calibrating models to predict insolvencies, modelers have to balance the ratio of Type 1 errors to Type 2 errors. Models can be calibrated to predict more insolvencies (that is, reduce Type 1 errors), but this raises the number of Type 2 errors. Ultimately, a maximum acceptable level of Type 1 errors has to be established for any model that might be used for regulatory purposes. More accurate models should offer better Type 1/Type 2 error tradeoffs to choose from.

49. M. Grace, S. Harrington, and R. W. Klein, "Identifying Troubled Life Insurers," *Journal of Insurance Regulation* 16 (1998): 249–290.

50. J. D. Cummins, M. Grace, and R. D. Phillips, "Regulatory Solvency Prediction in Property-Liability Insurance: Risk-Based Capital, Audit Ratios, and Cash Flow Simulation," *Journal of Risk and Insurance* 66 (1999): 417–458; S. Pottier and D. Sommer, "The Effectiveness of Public and Private Sector Summary Risk Measures in Predicting Insurer Insolvencies," *Journal of Financial Services Research* 21 (2002): 101–116.

51. Cummins et al., "Regulatory Solvency."

52. J. D. Cummins, ed., *Deregulating Property-Liability Insurance: Restoring Competition and Increasing Market Efficiency* (Washington, DC: Brookings Institution Press, 2002) offers a number of state-specific studies. Scott E. Harrington, "Effects of Prior Approval Rate Regulation of Auto Insurance," in *Deregulating Property-Liability Insurance: Restoring Competition and Increasing Market Efficiency,* ed. J. David Cummins (Washington, DC: Brookings Institution Press, 2002) summarizes and updates previous research on the effect of auto insurance rate regulation. Studies of price regulation in workers' compensation insurance have produced similar findings: A. Barkume and J. W. Ruser, "Deregulating Property-Casualty Insurance: The Case of Workers' Compensation," *Journal of Law and Economics* 44 (2001): 37–63; P. M. Danzon and S. E. Harrington, "Workers' Compensation Rate Regulation: How Price Controls Increase Costs," *Journal of Law and Economics* 44 (2001): 1–36; T. Thomason, T. P. Schmidle, and J. F. Burton, Jr., *Workers' Compensation: Benefits, Costs and Safety under Alternative Insurance Arrangements* (Kalamazoo, MI: W.E. Upjohn Institute for Employment Research, 2001).

53. R. A. Derrig and S. L. Tennyson, "The Impact of Rate Regulation on Claims: Evidence from Massachusetts Automobile Insurance" (2008), http://ssrn.com/abstract=1115377.

54. Danzon and Harrington, "Workers' Compensation."

55. R. W. Klein, R. D. Phillips, and W. Shiu, "The Capital Structure of Firms Subject to Price Regulation: Evidence from the Insurance Industry," *Journal of Financial Services Research* 21 (2002): 79–100.

56. M. F. Grace, R. W. Klein, and R. D. Phillips, "Auto Insurance Reform: Salvation in South Carolina. In *Deregulating Property-Liability Insurance,"* ed. J. D. Cummins, pp. 148–194 (Washington, DC: Brookings Institution Press, 2002) analyzed the turnaround in South Carolina.

57. H. S. Ryan and C. D. Schellhorn, "Life Insurer Cost Efficiency Before and After Implementation of NAIC Risk-Based Capital Standards," *Journal of Insurance Regulation* 18 (2000): 362–382.

58. S. W. Pottier, "State Insurance Regulation of Life Insurers: Implications for Economic Efficiency and Financial Strength" (report to the ACLI, University of Georgia, 2007).

59. M. F. Grace and R. W. Klein, "The Effects of an Optional Federal Charter on Competition in the Life Insurance Industry" (Center for Risk Management and Insurance Research, Georgia State University, Atlanta, October, 2007).

60. For a discussion of the situation before 1994, see D. Farny, "The Development of European Private Sector Insurance over the Last 25 Years and the Conclusions That Can Be Drawn for Business Management Theory of Insurance Companies," *Geneva Papers on Risk and Insurance* 24 (1999): 145–162; R. Rees, E. Kessner, P. Klemperer, and C. Matutes, "Regulation and Efficiency in European Insurance Markets," *Economic Policy* 14 (1999): 363–397.

61. S. Hussels, D. Ward, and R. Zurbruegg, "Stimulating the Demand for Insurance," *Risk Management and Insurance Review* 8 (2005): 257–278.

62. EU Directive 2002/13/EC for non-life insurers; EU Directive 2002/83/EC for life insurers; see European Union, "Directive 2002/13/EC as Regards the Solvency Margin Requirements for Non-Life Insurance Undertakings," *Official Journal of the European Communities* 77 (2002): 17–22; European Union. "Directive 2002/83/EC Concerning Life Assurance," *Official Journal of the European Communities* 345 (2002): 1–51.

63. D. Farny, "Security of Insurers: The American Risk-Based Capital Model Versus the European Model of Solvability for Property and Casualty Insurers," *Geneva Papers on Risk and Insurance* 22 (1997): 69–75.

64. European Commission (EC), "Directive of the European Parliament and the Council on the Taking-Up and Pursuit of the Business of Insurance and Reinsurance—Solvency II, COM: 361" (Brussels, 2007).

65. Steffen, T., "Solvency II and the Work of CEIOPS," *Geneva Papers on Risk and Insurance* 33 (2008): 60–65.

66. Basel Committee on Banking Supervision, "The New Basel Capital Accord" (Bank for International Settlements, 2001), http://www.bis.org.

67. CEIOPS, "Draft Advice to the European Commission in the Framework of the Solvency II Project on Pillar I Issues—Further Advice" (Consultation paper 20, 2006), http://www.ceiops.org.

68. European Commission, "Directive of the European Parliament," 118.

69. Financial Services Authority, "Principles-Based Regulation—Focusing on the Outcomes That Matter" (2007), http://www.fsa.gov.uk.

70. European Commission, "Frequently Asked Questions" (MEMO/07/286). (Brussels, 2007), 9.

71. R. Esson and P. Cooke, "Accounting and Solvency Convergence—Dream or Reality?" *Geneva Papers on Risk and Insurance* 32 (2007): 332–344; D. Duverne and J. Le Douit,

"IFRS for Insurance: CFO Forum Proposals," *Geneva Papers on Risk and Insurance* 32 (2007): 62–74.

72. European Commission, "Directive of the European Parliament," 105 and 323

73. European Commission, "Directive of the European Parliament," 324.

74. European Commission, "Directive of the European Parliament," 107.

75. European Commission, "Frequently Asked Questions," 5.

76. For a related discussion in accounting, see R. Toppe Shortridge, R., and M. Myring, "Defining Principles-Based Accounting Standards," *The CPA Journal* 74 (8): 34–37.

77. For more details on the pros and cons of principle-based regulation, see J. Black, M. Hopper, and C. Band, "Defining Principles-Based Accounting Standards," *Law and Financial Markets Review* 1(2007): 191–206.

78. Conference, "Prudential Supervision."

79. S. Ashby, S. P. Sharma, and W. McDonnell, "Lessons about Risk: Analyzing the Causal Chain of Insurance Company Failure," *Journal of Insurance Research and Practice* 18 (2003): 4–15.

80. S. Ashby, et al., "Lessons about Risk."

81. European Commission, "Directive of the European Parliament," 7.

82. Referred to as the "own risk and solvency assessment," see European Commission, "Directive of the European Parliament," 9.

83. European Commission, "Directive of the European Parliament," 69.

84. A good overview of the variation across EU guaranty mechanisms can be found in Organization for Economic Cooperation and Development. *Insurance Solvency Supervision: OECD Country Profiles* (Paris, 2002), 50–53.

85. G. Dionne, "Commitment and Automobile Insurance Regulation in France, Quebec and Japan" (working paper, HEC Montreal, 2001).

86. J. Basedow and T. Fock, *Europäisches Versicherungsvertragsrecht I.* (Tübingen: Mohr Siebeck, 2003).

87. Rees et al., "Regulation and Efficiency," 373.

88. Council Regulation (EC) no. 1346/2000, Article 9; see European Union, "Council Regulation (EC) No 1346/2000 of 29 May 2000 on insolvency proceedings," *Official Journal of the European Communities* 160 (2000): 1–18.

89. German Insurance Supervision Act, Article 78; see xBaFin, *German Insurance Supervision Act (Versicherungsaufsichtsgesetz)*, 2009, http://www.bafin.de.

90. See M. Eling and M. Luhnen, "Frontier Efficiency Methodologies to Measure Performance in the Insurance Industry: Overview and New Empirical Evidence" (working paper, University of St. Gallen, 2008).

91. Rees et al., "Regulation and Efficiency."

92. B. Mahlberg, "Technischer Fortschritt und Produktivitätsveränderungen in der deutschen Versicherungswirtschaft. " *Jahrbücher für Nationalökonomik und Statistik* 220 (2000): 565–591.

93. S. R. Diacon, K. Starkey, and C. O'Brien. "Size and Efficiency in European Long-Term Insurance Companies: An International Comparison," *Geneva Papers on Risk and Insurance* 27 (2002): 444–466.

94. K. C. Ennsfellner, D. Lewis, and R. I. Anderson, "Production Efficiency in the Austrian Insurance Industry: A Bayesian Examination," *Journal of Risk and Insurance* 71 (2004): 135–159.

95. J. D. Cummins and M. Rubio-Misas, "Deregulation, Consolidation, and Efficiency:

Evidence from the Spanish Insurance Industry," *Journal of Money, Credit, and Banking* 38 (2006): 323–355.

96. S. Hussels and D. R. Ward, "The Impact of Deregulation on the German and UK Life Insurance Markets: An Analysis of Efficiency and Productivity between 1991 and 2002" (working paper, Cranfield Research Paper Series (4), 2006).

97. Fenn, P., D. Vencappa, S. Diacon, P. Klumpes, and C. O'Brien, "Market Structure and the Efficiency of European Insurance Companies: A Stochastic Frontier Analysis," *Journal of Banking and Finance* 32 (2008): 86–100.

98. Dionne, "Commitment and Automobile Insurance."

99. Similar results were obtained by A. Chiappori and B. Salanié, "Testing for Asymmetric Information in Insurance Markets," *The Journal of Political Economy* 108 (2000): 56–78; and Dionne, "Commitment and Automobile Insurance."

100. European Commission, "Directive of the European Parliament," 10.

101. M. Eling and J. T. Schmit, "Market Discipline in the European Insurance Industry: The Case of Germany" (working paper, University of St. Gallen/University of Wisconsin-Madison, 2008); see Epermanis and Harrington, "Market Discipline," for an analysis of the U.S. market; for other fields, see A. Sironi, "Testing for Market Discipline in the European Banking Industry: Evidence from Subordinated Debt Issues," *Journal of Money, Credit, and Banking* 35 (2003): 443–472; I. Distinguin, I., P. Rous, and A. Tarazi. "Market Discipline and the Use of Stock Market Data to Predict Bank Financial Distress," *Journal of Financial Services Research* 30 (2006): 151–176.

102. P. Munch and D. E. Smallwood, "Theory of Solvency Regulation in the Property and Casualty Insurance Industry," in *Studies in Public Regulation*, ed. Gary Fromm (Cambridge, MA: MIT Press, 1981).

103. K. B. Staking and D. F. Babbel, "The Relationship between Capital Structure, Interest Rate Sensitivity, and Market Value in the Property-Liability Insurance Industry," *Journal of Risk and Insurance* 62 (1995): 690.

104. Klein, "Insurance Regulation."

105. M. Eling, M., H. Schmeiser, and J. T. Schmit, "The Solvency II Process: Overview and Critical Analysis," *Risk Management and Insurance Review* 10 (2007): 69–85.

106. Cummins and Rubio-Misas, "Deregulation, Consolidation."

107. Proposed OFC legislation would explicitly preclude price regulation. However, the legislation is essentially silent on other aspects of market regulation. Any legislation that is enacted could contain more provisions on other elements of market regulation and/or this could be left to the discretion of federal regulatory officials. Either way, the scope and nature of market regulation under an OFC is uncertain although its advocates are hoping for less restrictive policies.

108. M. Eling and T. Parnitzke, "Dynamic Financial Analysis: Conception, Classification, and Implementation," *Risk Management and Insurance Review* 10 (2007): 33–50.

109. Farny, "Security of Insurers."

110. M. Eling, N. Gatzert, and H. Schmeiser, "The Swiss Solvency Test and Its Market Implications," *Geneva Papers on Risk and Insurance* 33 (2008): 418–439.

111. Financial Services Authority, "Principles-Based Regulation."

112. Eling et al., "The Solvency II Process."

Chapter 9

1. Fifty states, four territories and the District of Columbia.
2. Such differences are described in the *NAIC Compendium of State Laws on Insurance Topics.*
3. *Paul v. Virginia*, 75 U.S. 168 (1868).
4. *United States v. South-Eastern Underwriters Association*, 322 U.S. 533, 64S.Ct. 1162, 88 L.Ed. 1440 (1944) rehearing denied 323 U.S. 811, 65 S.Ct. 26, 89 L.Ed. 646 (1944); Constitution of the United States, Article 1, Sec. 8.
5. The Sherman Act prohibits restraint of trade and monopolistic practices. The Clayton Act prohibits anticompetitive practices; the Robinson-Patman Act (an amendment to the Clayton Act) prohibits price discrimination among customers who compete against each other. The Federal Trade Commission Act prohibits unfair methods of competition and deceptive practices.
6. Lawrence S. Powell, "Assault on the McCarran-Ferguson Act and the Politics of Insurance in the Post-Katrina Era," *Journal of Insurance Regulation*, 26 (2008): 3–21.
7. McCarran-Ferguson Act, 59 Stat. 33,34 (1945), U.S.C.A. §1012 (1958).
8. Martin F. Grace and Robert Klein, "Efficiency Implications of Alternative Regulatory Structures for Insurance," in *Optional Federal Chartering and Regulation of Insurance Companies,* ed. P. Wallison (Washington, DC: American Enterprise Institute, 2000), 79–131.
9. Michael K. McShane and Larry A. Cox, "Benefits of Multi-Jurisdictional Regulation of the Life Insurance Industry: Fact or Fiction?" *Proceedings of the Risk Theory Society*, 2007. http://www.aria.org/rts/proceedings/2007/mcshane.pdf.
10. Steven Pottier, "Life insurer efficiency and state regulation: evidence of optimal firm behavior" *Journal of Regulatory Economics* (2011) 39:169–193.
11. Mary Weiss and Byeongyong Paul Choi, "State Regulation and the Structure, Conduct, Efficiency and Performance of U.S. Auto Insurers," *Journal of Banking and Finance* 32 (2008): 134–156.
12. Martin F. Grace and Hal S. Scott, "Optional Federal Chartering of Insurance: Rationale and Design of a Regulatory Structure" (working paper, 2008).
13. The literature often presents frontier efficiency scores. We substitute (1-efficiency) as inefficiency to give the inefficiency score and the expense ratio the same expected sign.
14. Pottier (2010); Michael K. McShane, Larry A. Cox, and Richard J. Butler, "Regulatory Competition and Forbearance: Evidence from the Life Insurance Industry," *Journal of Banking and Finance* 34 (2010): 522–532.
15. This herfindahl index is calculated as $s = 130NPWlNPW2$; where $NPWl$ is net premium written in insurance line l.
16. J. David Cummins, Mary A. Weiss, Xiaoying Xie, and Hongmin Zi, "Economies of Scope in Financial Services: A DEA Efficiency Analysis of the U.S. Insurance Industry," *Journal of Banking and Finance* 34 (2010): 1525–1539.
17. J. David Cummins, Sharon Tennyson, and Mary A. Weiss, "Consolidation and Efficiency in the U.S. Life Insurance Industry." *Journal of Banking and Finance* 23 (February 1999): 325–357.
18. Anne Gron, "Insurer Demand for Catastrophe Reinsurance," in *The Financing of Catastrophe Risk*, ed. Kenneth A. Froot (Chicago: University of Chicago Press, 1999); Lawrence S. Powell, David W. Sommer, and David L. Eckles, "The Role of Internal Capital Markets in Financial Intermediaries: Evidence from Insurance Groups," *Journal of Risk and Insurance* 75(2008): 439–461.

19. These include Alabama, Connecticut, Delaware, District of Columbia, Florida, Georgia, Louisiana, Maine, Massachusetts, Maryland, New Hampshire, New Jersey, New York, North Carolina, South Carolina, Texas, and Virginia.

20. One state (Alabama) and one line of business (fire insurance) are omitted from the model to avoid a singular matrix.

21. For example, Joan Lamm-Tennant and Laura T. Starks, "Stock versus Mutual Ownership Structures: the Risk Implications," *Journal of Business* 66 (1993): 29–46; David Mayers and Clifford W. Smith Jr., "Contractual Provisions, Organizational Structure, and Conflict Control in Insurance Markets," *Journal of Business* 54 (1981): 407–434; David Mayers and Clifford W. Smith Jr., "Ownership Structure and Control: The Mutualization of Stock Life Insurance Companies," *Journal of Financial Economics* 16 (1988): 73–98; David Mayers and Clifford W. Smith Jr., "Ownership Structure across Lines of Property-Casualty Insurance," *Journal of Law and Economics* 3 (1988): 351–378; David Mayers and Clifford W. Smith Jr., "Managerial Discretion, Regulation, and Stock Insurer Ownership Structure," *Journal of Risk and Insurance* 61 (1994): 638–655.

22. Powell et al., "Role of Internal Capital."

23. NAIC InfoPro data are used with permission of the NAIC. The NAIC does not endorse any analysis or conclusions based upon the use of its data.

24. Data from the U.S. Bureau of Labor Statistics and several other sources are also used to calculate inefficiency scores as described in the appendix.

25. We choose $2 million as the cutoff because smaller insurers are not required to file several types of regulatory reports including risk-based capital. Increasing the cutoff to $25 million does not change our results significantly.

26. For example, J. Tyler Leverty and Martin F. Grace, "The Robustness of Output Measures in Property-Liability Insurance Efficiency Studies," *Journal of Banking and Finance* 34 (2010): 1510–1524; Cummins et al., "Economies of Scope."

27. Creating a balanced panel reduces our sample by 6,658 firm-year observations that underwrite 38 percent of total premium. However, our results and conclusions do not change substantively.

28. Powell, "Assault on McCarran"; Paul L. Joskow, "Cartels, Competition, and Regulation in the Property and Liability Insurance Industry," *Bell Journal of Economics and Management Science* Autumn (1973): 375–427.

29. Robert E. Hoyt and Lawrence S. Powell, "Assessing Financial Performance in Medical Professional Liability Insurancem" *Journal of Insurance Regulation* 25 (2006): 3–13.

30. Cummins et al., "Economies of Scope."

31. Mayers and Smith, "Contractual Provisions." The managerial discretion hypothesis recognizes that equity holders of stock insurers have better mechanisms for controlling management than do policyholders in mutual firms. Therefore, mutual insurers should specialize in types of insurance requiring less managerial discretion.

32. Lamm-Tennant and Starks, "Stock versus Mutual."

33. Powell et al., "Role of Internal Capital."

34. There exists a considerable literature detailing the pros and cons of using DEA versus econometric-based efficiency models. Neither estimator is perfect, but DEA estimators have been shown to have desirable properties and require fewer assumptions. In addition, the DEA methodology has been widely adopted in the insurance literature. For a discussion of the benefits of DEA, Rajiv D. Banker, "Maximum Likelihood, Consistency and Data Envelopment Analysis: A Statistical Foundation," *Management Science* 39 (1993):

1265–1273; Alexander P. Korostelev, Leopold Simar, and Alexandre B. Tsybakov, "Efficient Estimation of Monotone Boundaries," *Annals of Statistics* 23 (1995): 476–489; Alois Kneip, Byeong U. Park, and Leopold Simar, "A Note on the Convergence of Nonparametric DEA Estimators for Production Efficiency Scores," *Econometric Theory* 14 (1998): 783–793; Shawna Grosskopf, "Statistical Inference and Nonparametric Efficiency: A Selective Survey," *The Journal of Productivity Analysis* 7 (1996): 161–176; Rajiv D. Banker, Hsihui Chang, and William W. Cooper, "A Simulation Study of DEA and Parametric Frontier Models in the Presence of Heteroscedasticity," *European Journal of Operational Research* 153 (2004): 624–640.

35. Michael J. Farrell, "The Measurement of Productive Efficiency," *Journal of the Royal Statistical Society* A 120 (1957): 253–281; Ronald W. Shephard, *Theory of Cost and Production Functions* (Princeton, NJ: Princeton University Press, 1970).

36. Allen N. Berger and David B. Humphrey, "Measurement and Efficiency Issues in Commercial Banking," in *Output Measurement in the Service Sector,* ed. Z. Griliches (Chicago: University of Chicago Press, 1992), 245–279.

37. J. David Cummins and Mary A Weiss, "Measuring Cost Efficiency in the Property-Liability Insurance Industry," *Journal of Banking and Finance* 17 (1993): 463–481; Allen N. Berger, J. David Cummins, and Mary A. Weiss, "The Coexistence of Multiple Distribution Systems for Financial Services: The Case of Property-Liability Insurance," *The Journal of Business* 70 (1997): 515–546; J. David Cummins and Gregory Nini, "Optimal Capital Utilization by Financial Firms: Evidence from the Property-Liability Insurance Industry," *Journal of Financial Services Research* 21 (2002): 15–53; Leverty and Grace, "Robustness of Output."

38. The distinctions we make between personal and commercial short and long tail lines are consistent with other efficiency studies in the property-liability industry (Cummins and Weiss, "Measuring Cost Efficiency"; Berger, Cummins, and Weiss, "Coexistence of Multiple Systems"; Cummins and Nini, "Optimal Capital Utilization"; Leverty and Grace. "Robustness of Output."

39. The short-term T-bill rates are from the St. Louis Federal Reserve Bank and the average market risk premium is provided by Ibbotson Associates.

Chapter 10

1. In the last two years, there has been a large amount of academic research on the regulation of insurance (e.g., S. E. Harrington, "Federal Chartering of Insurance Companies: Options and Alternatives for Transforming Insurance Regulation" (Networks Financial Institute Policy Brief, 2006); M. F. Grace and R. W. Klein, "The Effects of an Optional Federal Charter on Competition in the Life Insurance Industry" (working paper, Center for Risk Management and Insurance Research, Georgia State University, 2007); E. F. Brown, "The Fatal Flaw of Proposals to Federalize Insurance Regulation" (paper presented at the Searle Center Research Symposium on Insurance Markets and Regulation, 2008); H. N. Butler and L. E. Ribstein, "A Single-License Approach to Regulating Insurance" (Northwestern Law and Econ Research Paper, 2008); M. F. Grace and R. W. Klein, "The Past and Future of Insurance Regulation: The McCarran-Ferguson Act and Beyond" (paper presented at the Searle Center Research Symposium on Insurance Markets and Regulation, 2008); H. S. Scott, "Optional Federal Chartering of Insurance: Design of a Regulatory Structure" (paper presented at the Searle Center Research Symposium on

Insurance Markets and Regulation, 2008); J. A. Cooke and H. D. Skipper, "U.S. Insurance Regulation in a Competitive World Insurance Market: An Evaluation," in *The Future of Insurance Regulation in the United States,* ed. M. F. Grace and R. W. Klein (Washington, DC: Brookings Institution Press, 2009); R. Detlefsen, "Dual Insurance Chartering: Potential Consequences," in *The Future of Insurance Regulation,* ed. M. F. Grace and R. W. Klein (Washington, DC: Brookings Institution Press, 2009); M. F. Grace & and H. S. Scott, "An Optional Federal Charter for Insurance: Rationale and Design." In *The Future of Insurance Regulation in the United States,* ed. M. F. Grace and R. W. Klein (Washington, DC: Brookings Institution Press, 2009); M. F. Grace and R. W. Klein, "Insurance Regulation: The Need for Policy Reform," in *The Future of Insurance Regulation in the United States,* ed. M. F. Grace and R. W. Klein (Washington, DC: Brookings Institution Press); R. W. Klein, "The Insurance Industry and Its Regulation: An Overview," in *The Future of Insurance Regulation in the United States,* ed. M. F. Grace and R. W. Klein (Washington DC: Brookings Institution Press, 2009); R. E. Litan and P. O'Connor, "Consumer Benefits of an Optional Federal Charter: The Case of Auto Insurance," in *The Future of Insurance Regulation in the United States,* edited by M. F. Grace and R. W. Klein (Washington, DC: Brookings Institution Press, 2009); P. J. Wallison, "Convergence in Financial Services Markets: Effects on Insurance Regulation," in *The Future of Insurance Regulation in the United States,* edited by M. F. Grace and R. W. Klein (Washington, DC: Brookings Institution Press, 2009).

2. J. Franks, S. Schaefer, and M. Staunton, "The Direct and Compliance Costs of Financial Regulation." *Journal of Banking and Finance* (1997), 1547–1572, find that the direct costs of regulation in the U.S. life insurance industry are significantly greater than in the United Kingdom and France. They attribute the additional costs to state-based regulation.

3. American Council of Life Insurers "Economic Impact of an Optional Federal Charter on the Life Insurance Industry: A Survey of Leading U.S. Insurance Companies," 2005.

4. Harrington, "Federal Chartering."

5. In May 2007, Senators John Sununu and Tim Johnson introduced the National Insurance Act of 2007 (S.40). In July 2007, Representatives Bean and Royce introduced a companion bill in the House (H.R. 3200).

6. There are a few exceptions. For example, non-chartering states can require an RRG to pay premium taxes. Another difference between standard insurers and RRGs is that the policyholders of an RRG are not permitted to gain access to state insurance insolvency guaranty associations in the event of insolvency.

7. In July 2008, the U.S. House Financial Services Subcommittee on Capital Markets, Insurance and Government Sponsored Enterprises marked up a bill to expand RRGs from commercial liability insurance into property coverage ("Increasing Insurance Coverage Options for Consumers Act of 2008"—HR 5792).

8. The Product Herfindahl Index is a measure of the distribution of the total premium revenues by line of business. A lower value of this index implies greater diversification across lines of business.

9. The Geographical Herfindahl Index is a measure of the distribution of the total premium revenues by state. A higher value of this index implies higher geographical concentration.

10. A firm is recorded as operating in a state if it writes more than $10,000 in premium.

11. Grace, M. F., and R. W. Klein, "Efficiency Implications of Alternative Regulatory Structures for Insurance," in *Optional Federal Chartering and Regulation of Insurance Companies,* ed. P. Wallison (Washington, DC: American Enterprise Institute, 2000).

12. Standard insurance companies may face seasoning requirements preventing them from entering new states for three to five years following their formation. (Many states allow exceptions if management is adequately seasoned). Even though these restrictions are evidence of the additional cost of complying with state-based regulation, I investigate whether there are significant differences in the number of states firms operate in three and five years after formation. After three years, the average (median) RRG does business in 16.8 (14.5) states, while the average standard insurer operates in only 9.9 (5.0) states. The differences are statistically significant at the 1 percent level. After five years, the average (median) RRG also conducts business in significantly ($p < 0.01$) more states than the standard insurer—19.4 (18) states compared to 10.0 (5.0). Thus, even after accounting for a direct regulatory burden placed upon standard insurers, RRGs still operate in more states than firms subject to multi-entity regulation.

13. Over the same time period (1990 to 2006), the average U.S. insurer has total assets of $465,154,544 while the average insurer in my sample has total assets of only $21,181,487. Thus, the average insurer in my sample is less than one-twentieth the size of the average U.S. insurer.

14. The expense ratio is generally high for firms in the sample because they are young insurers (the median firm has been operating for three years). Under Statutory Accounting Principles all expenses are charged when incurred.

15. Grace and Klein, "Efficiency Implications."

16. Other thresholds ($50,000 and $100,000) are also evaluated. The results are similar to those presented. The implicit assumption of this test is that all insurance companies want to expand into new states. This, however, is not always the case as some companies choose to specialize in a single state.

17. I also investigate whether seasoning requirements placed upon standard insurers account for the difference in estimated probabilities (see note 9). To do this, I lag standard insurers by three years to account for the fact that these firms may not be permitted to enter a new state for this amount of time. The estimated probability of operating in more than one state with this sample is 61.2 percent for RRGs and 48.2 percent for standard insurers. This evidence suggests that seasoning requirements may be one factor in a firm's choice of organizational structure, but other regulatory compliance costs are also influencing the decision.

18. Grace and Klein, "Efficiency Implications."

19. Grace and Klein, "Efficiency Implications."

20. Grace and Klein, "Efficiency Implications."

21. D. Aigner, C. Lovell, and P. Schmidt, "Formulation and Estimation of Stochastic Frontier Production Function Models, *Journal of Econometrics* 6 (1977): 21–37; A. Charnes, A., W. Cooper, and E. Rhodes, "Measuring the Efficiency of Decision Making Units," *European Journal of Operational Research* 2 (1978): 429–444.

22. For parsimony, data envelopment analysis is not discussed in detail. A description is provided in W. W. Cooper, L. M. Seiford, and K. Tone, *Data Envelopment Analysis* (Norwell, MA: Kluwer Academic Publishers, 2000). The methodology has also been outlined in insurance studies (for example, J. David Cummins and Mary Weiss, "Analyzing Firm Performance in the Insurance Industry Using Frontier Efficiency and Productivity Models," in *Handbook of Insurance*, ed. G. Dionne (Boston: Kluwer Academic Publishers, 2001).

23. A. N. Berger and D. B. Humphrey. "Efficiency of Financial Institutions: International Survey and Directions for Future Research," *European Journal of Operational Research* 98 (1997): 175–212; Cummins and Weiss, "Analyzing Firm Performance."

24. Leverty, J. T., and M. F. Grace, "The Robustness of Output Measures in Property-Liability Insurance Efficiency Studies," *Journal of Banking and Finance* (2009).

25. Berger, A., and D. Humphrey, "Measurement and Efficiency Issues in Commercial Banking," in *Output Measurement in the Services Sector*, ed. Z. Griliches (Chicago: University of Chicago Press, 1992).

26. Cummins and Weiss, "Analyzing Firm Performance."

27. Berger, P., E. Ofek, D. Yermack, 1997, Managerial entrenchment and capital structure decisions, *The Journal of Finance*, Vol. 52: 1411-1438.; and Cummins and Weiss, "Analyzing Firm Performance."

28. The business definitions are described in Richard D. Phillips, J. David Cummins, and Franklin Allen, "Financial Pricing of Insurance in a Multiline Insurance Company," *Journal of Risk and Insurance* 65 (1998): 597–636..

29. For example, Cummins and Weiss, "Analyzing Firm Performance."

30. See Cummins and Weiss, "Analyzing Firm Performance," for a comprehensive explanation of the inputs used in the value-added approach.

31. The price of administrative labor is calculated from the U.S. Department of Labor data on average weekly wage rate for Standard Industrial Classification (SIC 6331), P/L insurer. The price of agent labor is the average weekly wage rate for insurance agents (SIC 6411) and the price of business service and materials is the average weekly wage rate for business services (SIC 7300). The price of financial equity capital is based on the insurers A.M. Best Company financial rating. Similar to J.David Cummins, Sharon Tennyson, Mary A. Weiss, 1999. "Consolidation and efficiency in the US life insurance industry," Volume 23, Issues 2–4, Pages 325–357 (February 1999), the cost of capital is equal to 12 percent for firms rated in the "A" range, 15 percent for firms in the "B" range, and 18 percent for insurers below the "B" range. The cost of policyholder supplied debt capital is the average corporate credit spread of similarly rated firms; M. F. Grace, J. T. Leverty, and R. D. Phillips, "Value Creation in Enterprise Risk Management" (working paper, Center for Risk Management & Insurance Research, Georgia State University, 2009).

32. Because the NAIC database is compiled for regulatory purposes, it contains firms that are not viable operating entities either because they are under regulatory supervision or encountering other financial difficulties. Consequently, firms that are not actively participating in the insurance market are eliminated from the efficiency sample, such as firms with zero or negative equity capital, total premiums, assets, or total insurance output as well as firms with negative or zero labor input.

33. A. C. Cameron, J. B. Gelbach, and D. L. Miller, "Robust Inference with Multi-Way Clustering" (NBER Technical Working Paper No. 327, 2006). The regressions were also performed with state and year fixed effects. The results of these specifications are qualitatively similar to those reported. F-tests on the year (and state) fixed effects never reject the null hypothesis that year (state) fixed effects are zero.

34. To determine whether multicollinearity is an issue, I examine the variance inflation factors (VIF) of the independent variables in these regressions. The mean VIF is around 1.19, and no individual VIF is greater than 1.4; therefore, multicollinearity does not appear to be an issue (a VIF close to ten is a common threshold at which multicollinearity is considered a problem).

35. In unreported regressions, the natural logarithm of the number of states in which a firm is doing business is substituted for the geographical Herfindahl Index. It is positively and significantly related to total expenses. As in Grace and Klein, "Efficiency Implications,"

the data show that an increase in the number of regulatory jurisdictions is associated with higher total expenses.

36. This is most likely a lower bound on the total costs of duplicative regulation as the firms in my sample are smaller than those found in industry as a whole (see footnote 10).

37. Grace and Klein, "Efficiency Implications."

38. R. Winter, "The Dynamics of Competitive Insurance Markets," *Journal of Financial Intermediation* 3 (1994): 379–415.

39. For example, J. D. Cummins and P. M. Danzon, "Price, Financial Quality, and Capital Flows in Insurance Markets," *Journal of Financial Intermediation* 6 (1997): 3–38; and Phillips, Cummins, and Allen, "Financial Pricing."

40. For details on the construction of the EPR, readers are referred to Phillips, Cummins, and Allen, "Financial Pricing"; and J. D. Cummins, Y. Lin, and R. D. Phillips, "An Empirical Investigation of the Pricing of Financially Intermediated Risks with Costly External Finance" (working paper, Center for Risk Management & Insurance Research, Georgia State University, 2008).

41. The dependent variables are winsorized at the fifth and ninety-fifth percentiles to reduce the effect of outliers. The regressions were also performed with state fixed effects. The results of these specifications are qualitatively similar to those reported. F-tests on the state fixed effects never reject the null hypothesis that state fixed effects are zero. Moreover, no individual state effect is statistically significant. To determine whether multicollinearity is an issue, I examine the variance inflation factors (VIF) of the independent variables in these regressions. The mean VIF is around 1.10 and no individual VIF is greater than 1.14; therefore, multicollinearity does not appear to be an issue.

42. For example, D. W. Sommer, "The Impact of Firm Risk on Property-Liability Insurance Prices," *Journal of Risk and Insurance* 63 (1996): 510–514; Cummins and Danzon, "Price, Financial Quality"; Phillips, Cummins, and Allen, "Financial Pricing"; Cummins, Lin, and Phillips, "An Empirical Investigation"; and G. Zanjani, "Pricing and Capital Allocation in Catastrophe Insurance," *Journal of Financial Economics* 65 (2002): 283–305.

43. For details, see M. F. Grace and J. T. Leverty, "Political Cost Incentives for Managing the Property- Liability Insurer Loss Reserve" (working paper, University of Iowa, 2009).

44. Including the insurer's estimated probability of failure reduces the sample size from 924 to 441. To test the hypothesis that price is inversely related to firm insolvency risk, I also explored whether higher A.M. Best's ratings result in higher prices. I find a significantly positive relationship between high Best's ratings and insurance prices. Nevertheless, it is difficult to assign much confidence to these estimates as a vast majority of firms in the sample are not rated by A.M. Best (over 80 percent).

45. Y. Lei and J. T. Schmit, "Influences of Organizational Form on Medical Malpractice Insurer Operations" (working paper, University of Wisconsin-Madison, 2008).

Index

AAA (American Automobile Association), 20
adverse selection, 15–16, 67
Aetna, 31
AIG, 45, 48, 151, 282nn7:47–48
Alabama
    catastrophe exposure, 231–32, 291n9:19
    premiums earned (direct, non-domestic), 152
    premiums written (non-domestic life-health), 154
    rate regulation, property lines, 110
Alaska, 110, 152, 154
Albaugh, J., 277n6:53
Allstate, 48
American Bankers Association, 279n7:12
American Council of Life Insurance, 279n7:12
American Insurance Association, 279n7:12
AMEX, 48
antitrust laws
    Clayton Act, 290n9:5
    Federal Trade Commission Act, 290n9:5
    jurisdiction, 228, 290n9:5
    optional federal charter (OFC), 172, 174 (*See also* optional federal charter (OFC))
    overview, 5, 6
    Robinson-Patman Act, 290n9:5
    Sherman Act, 290n9:5
Arizona, 110, 152, 154
Arkansas, 6, 110, 152, 154
Arkansas Insurance Department, 75–76
Army Corps of Engineers, 121, 122, 130, 132, 141
Ashby, S., 207
Associated Credit Bureaus, 76
Australia, 184
Auto Insurance Reform of 2003, 45, 48
automobile insurance
    bonus-malus system (France), 209, 212
    contract law (EU), 210
    cross-subsidization, 26

    government provision of, 21
    insurance scores (*See* credit-based insurance scores (CBIS))
    loss ratios, 33–34
    as mandatory, 33
    Massachusetts case study, 49–53
    moral hazard, 13–15
    price regulation, 29, 197
    residual market, 34–35
    risk alignment, 25, 34–35
    South Carolina price regulation case study, 53–57
    state regulation of, 164, 281n7:30
    subsidies as penalties, 3
availability bias, 17

Baker, R., 169
Bakke, H., 48
Baresse, J., 196
Barkume, A. J., 29–30
Barry, J., 122–23
Basel II, 183, 185, 203, 211–12
basic solvency capital requirement (BSCR), 205–6
Bean, M., 171, 294n10:5
behavioral economics
    availability bias, 17
    diversifiable risk, 17–18, 23
    hyperbolic discounting (present-biased), 17, 22–23
    loss aversion, 16–17
bench (desk) audits, 162, 192, 194, 284n8:22
Berger, A. N., 239
Bernoulli, Jacob, 67
bonus-malus system, 209, 212
Born, P. H., 4, 83
Breusch-Pagan Lagrangean multiplier test, 258
burial insurance, 19–20

295

Bush, Prescott, 126, 127
business failure insurance, 13–14

California, 110, 152, 154
cash-flow testing, 200
catastrophes. *See* property-casualty insurance
CEIOPS (Committee of European Insurance and Occupational Pension Supervisors), 203, 218
Challinor, G. Richard, 137
Choi, B. P., 229
Chubb, 141
Cincinnati Reds, 267n2:2
Citizens Property Insurance Company, 3, 36, 37, 41, 43
classification. *See* credit-based insurance scores (CBIS)
Clayton Act, 290n9:5
Cochrane, John, 12
Colorado, 110, 152, 154
commercial insurance, 4, 18–19. *See also* property-casualty insurance
commercial multiple peril insurance. *See under* property-casualty insurance
Committee of European Insurance and Occupational Pension Supervisors (CEIOPS), 203, 218
Community Reinvestment Act, 174
competitive federalism
    benefits, 7, 245
    efficiency, 253, 256–58
    potential annual savings, 235–39
    single-state system, 175–77, 282n7:50
    uniform regulation, 159, 175–77
Congress
    flood insurance role, 121, 125–26, 128, 132–33, 138, 139, 141, 275n6:7, 277n6:50
    regulatory oversight role, 156, 169, 174, 280n7:24
Connecticut
    catastrophe exposure, 231–32, 291n9:19
    premiums earned (direct, non-domestic), 152
    premiums written (non-domestic life-health), 154
    rate regulation, property lines, 110
consumer advocates, 5, 174
costs
    compliance costs, RRGs, 246–51, 253, 261, 294n10:12, 295nn13–14
    Florida, loss, 38–40
    insurance scores effects, 73–75
    multiple jurisdictional regulation compliance costs, 246, 251–52, 295nn10:16–17

overview, 7
price regulation (*See* price regulation)
single jurisdictional regulation compliance costs, 246, 253, 256–58, 296n10:35, 296n10:36
Council of Insurance Agents and Brokers, 279n7:12
Cox, L. A., 229
credit-based insurance scores (CBIS)
    accuracy, 75–77
    appropriateness of, 75–78
    benefits of, 75–78
    competition, 77–78
    cost effects, 73–75
    credit scores *vs.*, 68
    criteria, 75
    cross-subsidization, 77
    driving ability in, 69
    loss correlations, 69–73
    market effects, 73–75
    multivariate analysis, 71–72
    overview, 3–4, 67–69, 78–79
    predictive accuracy of, 69–73
    residual markets, 73–75, 77
    variables used, 68
Crist, Charlie, 2, 36, 37, 43
crop insurance, 13
cross-subsidization
    automobile insurance, 26
    credit-based insurance scores, 77
    flood insurance, 26, 118
    Florida, 38
    Massachusetts, 50–52
    overview, 25–27
    premiums, 26
    price regulation, 25–26, 33
    South Carolina, 54, 56, 57
Cummins, J. D., 190, 199, 211, 231, 237, 287n8:52
Cutler, D., 17–18, 23

Danzon, P. M., 201
data envelopment analysis (DEA), 239–40, 292n9:34, 293n9:38
Delaware
    catastrophe exposure, 231–32, 291n9:19
    premiums earned (direct, non-domestic), 152
    premiums written (non-domestic life-health), 154
    rate regulation, property lines, 110
Denmark, 210
Department of Insurance Regulation (DOIR), 36
deposit insurance, 14, 21–22

Derrig, R. A., 201
desk (bench) audits, 162, 192, 194, 284n8:22
Diacon, S. R., 211
Dingell, J., 280n7:24
Dionne, G., 212
District of Columbia
    catastrophe exposure, 231–32, 291n9:19
    premiums earned (direct, non-domestic), 152
    premiums written (non-domestic life-health), 154
    rate regulation, property lines, 110
diversifiable risk, 17–18, 23

Eckles, D., 7
economic premium ratio (EPR), 258, 259, 260
economics, 12–16. *See also* behavioral economics
efficiency (regulatory)
    background, 228–29, 290n9:5
    catastrophe exposure, 231–32, 235, 237, 291n9:19
    competitive federalism, 253, 256–58
    cost-efficiency relationships, 229
    data, 233–34, 292n9:23, 292n9:25
    empirical model, estimation, 234–36, 292n9:27
    European Union, 211–12, 217–18
    expense ratio, 229, 230, 234, 235, 237, 238
    frontier efficiency methodology, 229
    geographic concentration, 231, 235, 237
    group variable, 233, 235, 238
    Herfindahl index, 231, 291n9:15
    inefficiency score, 230, 231, 234, 235, 237, 238, 291n9:13, 291n9:15
    insurer inputs, 240
    life insurance, 201, 229
    line-of-business concentration, 231, 235, 237
    literature review, 229
    managerial discretion hypothesis, 238, 292n9:31
    methodology, 239–40, 292n9:34, 293n9:38
    modified value-added approach, 239
    mutual variable, 233, 235, 238
    optional federal charter, 172–73, 229
    organizational form, 232
    output measures, 240
    overview, 227–28, 238–39, 290n9:1
    regulator number/insurer profit relationships, 229
    regulators, 230, 235
    results, 234–38
    risk pooling/risk bearing function, 239–40
    risk retention groups, 252–58, 296nn10:31–35, 297n10:36

    sample, 233–34, 292n9:23, 292n9:25
    scope measures, 231, 291n9:15
    size measures, 230, 235, 237
    summary statistics, 233
    total premium written measures, 232, 291n9:20
    uniform regulation (potential annual savings), 235–39
    United States, 157, 166–67, 201, 217–18
Eisenhower, Dwight D., 125–26
Eling, M., 7
Ennsfellner, K. C., 211
EPIC Actuaries, 72
Esurance, 48
European Union (EU)
    financial services industry, 202, 208–9, 211–12, 216
    France, 209, 212
    Germany, 208, 210, 211
    Italy, 210
    overview, 7
    principles-based systems, 168
    regulation (*See* regulation (European Union))
    reinsurance, 204
    solvency regulation enforcement, 206
    Spain, 211
    Switzerland, 184
Evans Commission, 135, 137
event rarity, 13
Excess Profits Law, 45
expense ratios
    efficiency (regulatory), 229, 230, 234, 235, 237, 238
    risk retention groups, 248–51, 254, 295n10:14

Fannie Mae, 11, 24–25
FAST (Financial Analysis Solvency Tools) system, 193, 200, 285n8:24
Federal Deposit Insurance Corporation (FDIC), 282n7:42
Federal Emergency Management Agency (FEMA), 137, 277n6:53
Federal Flood Indemnity Administration, 126
Federal Flood Insurance Act of 1956, 125–28
Federal Liability Risk Retention Act of 1986, 245–46, 294n10:5
Federal Trade Commission (FTC), 72, 73, 76
Federal Trade Commission Act, 290n9:5
Feldhaus, W. R., 106
Fenn, P., 211
Financial Analysis Solvency Tools (FAST) system, 193, 200, 285n8:24
Financial Analysis Working Group, 193–94

financial derivatives, 10–11
Financial Services Compensation Scheme, 208–9
financial services industry
  convergence in, 148, 151
  European Union, 202, 208–9, 211–12, 216
  motivations, 5
  reform of, 105, 148, 171
  as regulatory precedent, 177
fire & allied insurance. *See under* property-casualty insurance
flight insurance, 17
Flood Hazard Boundary Maps (FHBMs), 138–40, 142
flood insurance
  admitted market insurance, 118
  coverage information, 134
  cross-subsidization, 26, 118
  first mover disadvantage, 123–25
  flood area standard, 129–30
  flood mitigation, 122, 130, 133, 141
  floodplain zoning ordinances, 130, 136
  government provision of, 21, 118, 275n6:7
  insurer solvency, 118–19
  market, federal suppression of, 128, 131–32, 140
  maximum probable flood standard, 129, 277n6:30
  mechanism, ideal, 117–20, 275n6:3
  as moral hazard (Incentive), 115, 122, 131, 142
  overview, 115–16, 140–42
  price regulation, 123
  private industry development of, 122–23, 127, 134
  profitability, 118–19, 122, 124, 275n6:3
  risk-based pricing, 119, 131–32, 134, 135, 138
  risk data collection (mapping), 128–32, 141–42, 277n6:30
  risk distribution, 124
  risk transfer, 116, 129–30, 275n6:3
  state regulation, 123
  wealth redistribution, 119
  See also National Flood Insurance Program
Flood Insurance Act of 1956, 142
Flood Insurance Rate Maps (FIRMs), 136–39, 277n6:53
floodwalls, 122
Florida
  catastrophe exposure, 231–32, 291n9:19
  catastrophic reinsurance, 43
  centivization, 40
  Citizens Property Insurance Company, 36, 37, 41, 43

cross-subsidization, 38
development incentives, 115
Florida Hurricane Catastrophe Fund, 43
homeowners insurance regulation timeline, 36–37
insurer entry into, 274n5:29
insurer withdrawal from, 3, 31, 42–43, 84, 268n3:3
loss costs, 38–40
loss ratios, 41–42
premium pricing, 39–40, 42
premiums earned (direct, non-domestic), 152
premiums written (non-domestic life-health), 154
price flexibility legislation, 43
price regulation, 36–44, 84
property insurance premiums earned, 274n5:28
rate orders, 43
rate regulation, property lines, 110
wind insurance mechanisms, 115
Florida Hurricane Catastrophe Fund, 43
France, 209, 212
Freddie Mac, 11, 24–25

GEICO, 48, 50, 53
General Insurance Reform Act of 2001, 184
Generally Accepted Accounting Principles (GAAP), 284n8:19
Georgia
  catastrophe exposure, 231–32, 291n9:19
  premiums earned (direct, non-domestic), 152
  premiums written (non-domestic life-health), 154
  rate regulation, property lines, 110
Germany, 208, 210, 211
Grace, M. F., 3, 6, 54, 85, 168, 174, 176, 199, 200, 229, 251, 252, 253, 254, 256
Gramm-Leach-Bliley Act of 1999, 151
Green Bay Packers, 267n2:2
Gron, A., 231–32
Grossman, David, 126–27
Guam, 153, 155
guaranty associations, 163–64, 173–74, 195–96, 281n7:40, 282n7:42, 285n8:29–31

Harrington, S. E., 18, 29, 170, 190, 199, 200, 201
Hausman χ² test, 258
Hawaii, 6, 110, 152, 154
health insurance
  diversifiable risk, 17–18
  economics, 11–12, 22
  government provision of, 21, 22

mandatory, 24–26
moral hazard, 13–15
premium mean percentage (nondomestic insurers), 279n7:14
regulatory constraints, 174
risk-based capital (RBC) standards, 189
trends in, 147–50
health-status insurance, 12
Herfindahl index
efficiency (regulatory), 231, 291n9:15
geographic, 248, 249, 252, 253, 257, 260, 294n10:9
product, 248, 249, 260, 294n10:8
Herring, Bradley, 16
homeowner's insurance
definitions, 87–88, 273nn5:17–18
geographical diversification, 96–98, 274n23
insurer performance and conduct analysis, 92–94, 274n5:nn20–24
loss ratios, 92, 94–98, 274 nn5:25– 26
losses incurred, 92, 98–100, 274n5:27
as mandatory, 33
market exit, entry, 92, 103, 274n5:n20
market overview, 88–92, 274n5:19
market structure post-catastrophe, 103–5, 274n5:29
price regulation, 110–13, 197
profitability, 124
regulation of, 82, 85
regulatory constraints, 174
regulatory levels, 86, 93–94, 274nn5: 23–24
restrictive rate regulation, 26, 94, 96, 274nn5:23–24
state regulation of, 164, 281n7:30
study data, 87–88, 273nn5:17–18
unanticipated catastrophes, 85–86, 92–94, 96, 274n5:nn20–24
See also property-casualty insurance
Hoover, Herbert, 121
Housing and Home Finance Administration (HHFA), 127, 128
Humphrey, D. B., 239
Hurricane Andrew, 36, 41, 42, 84
Hurricane Betsy, 132
Hurricane Camille, 138
Hurricane Cat Fund, 36, 37
Hurricane Katrina, 36, 81
Hurricane Rita, 81
Hurricane Wilma, 81, 84
Hussels, S., 211
hyperbolic discounting (present-biased), 17, 22–23

Idaho, 110, 152, 154
Illinois
managed competition, 52
premium tax rates, 6
premiums earned (direct, non-domestic), 152
premiums written (non-domestic life-health), 154
price regulation, 32–33
rate regulation, property lines, 111
residual market, 52
incentives
business purchase of insurance, 18–19
development, 115
flood insurance as, 115, 122, 131, 142
moral hazards and, 13–15, 21–22
risk subsidization, 34–35
social purpose achievement, 24–25
See also moral hazard
income redistribution, 22, 26
Independent Insurance Agents and Brokers of America, 279n7:15
Indiana, 111, 152, 154
Indianapolis Colts, 267n2:2
inequality insurance, 20–21
InfoPro database, 233, 292n9:23
information restriction, 3. *See also* credit-based insurance scores (CBIS)
insurance
adverse selection, 15–16, 67
behavioral economics, 16–18
business purchase of, 18–19
credibility, 13
cross-subsidization, 25–27, 33, 38, 50–52, 54, 56, 77, 118
definitions, 10–11
future trends, 26–27
government provision of, 21–23, 34–35 (*See also* flood insurance)
importance, measures of, 9–12
moral hazard, 13–15, 21
motivations, 5–6, 13–14, 25
nonexistent markets (social insurance), 20–21
probabilities, 10
profits, losses for, 3
risk transfer, pooling, subdivision, 9–10, 22, 25–26, 67
seasoning requirements, 294n10:12, 295n10:17
sociology of, 19–20
stadium naming rights, 9, 267n2:2
insurance commissioners, 160
Insurance Consumer Protection Act, 177
Insurance Regulatory Information System (IRIS), 193

Insurance Research Council, 76
insurance scores. *See* credit-based insurance
    scores (CBIS)
Insurance Services Office (ISO), 38
Interstate Insurance Product Regulation
    Commission, 286n8:38
Iowa, 111, 152, 154
IRIS (Insurance Regulatory Information
    System), 193
Italy, 210

Japan, 184
Johnson, Lyndon B., 133
Johnson, Tim, 171, 294n10:5
Jones, T. Lawrence, 137

Kansas, 111, 152, 154
Kenney Ratio, 249, 251, 257, 259
Kentucky, 111, 152, 154
Klein, R. W., 6, 7, 85, 106, 168, 174, 176, 190, 199,
    200, 201, 229, 251, 252, 253, 256
Klimaszewski-Blettner, Barbara, 4

law of large numbers, 67, 231
Lehrer, Eli, 4
Leverty, J. T., 254
Leverty, Ty, 7
liability
    deposit insurance, 14, 21–22
    Federal Liability Risk Retention Act of 1986,
        245–46, 294n10:5
    financial regulation, 161–64
    guaranty associations, 163–64, 173–74, 195–
        96, 281n7:40, 282n7:42, 285n8:29–31
    overview, 5–6
    risk retention groups, 249, 251, 257, 260
    See also property-casualty insurance; solvency
        regulation
Liberty Mutual, 58
life insurance
    efficiency, 201, 229
    market regulation, 286n8:38
    premium mean percentage (nondomestic
        insurers), 279n7:14
    price regulation, 197, 281n7:39
    reporting requirements, 281n7:41
    risk-based capital (RBC) standards, 189
    sociology of, 19
    solvency regulation, 280n7:26
    surplus participation (Germany), 210
    trends in, 147–48, 150
long-term care insurance, 13, 16–18
loss-absorbing capacity (LAC), 205–6

loss aversion, 16–17
loss ratios
    automobile insurance, 33–34
    Florida, 41–42
    homeowner's insurance, 92, 94–98, 274
        nn5:25– 26
    Maine, 59, 271n3:38
    Massachusetts, 51–52
    New Jersey, 45–47
    price regulation, 33–34
    property-casualty insurance, 92, 94–98, 274
        nn5:25– 26
    risk retention groups, 258, 259
    South Carolina, 54–55
Louisiana
    catastrophe exposure, 231–32, 291n9:19
    development incentives, 115
    premiums earned (direct, non-domestic), 152
    premiums written (non-domestic life-health),
        154
    rate regulation, property lines, 111
    wind insurance mechanisms, 115

Mahlberg, B., 211
Maine
    arbitration, 60–61
    catastrophe exposure, 231–32, 291n9:19
    deregulation, 58, 60–61
    insurer entry into, 58, 60
    insurer withdrawal from, 31, 58, 60,
        268n3:3
    legal fee caps, 58, 60–61
    loss ratios, 59, 271n3:38
    premiums earned (direct, non-domestic), 152
    premiums written (non-domestic life-health),
        154
    price compression, 58, 60
    rate increases, 58, 60
    rate regulation, property lines, 111
    residual market, 58–60
    safety issue, 61
    social pricing, 58
    timeline, 58
    worker's compensation price regulation,
        57–61, 271n3:38
malpractice (medical), 20
managerial discretion hypothesis, 238, 292n9:31
marine insurance, 19
market conduct regulation, 164, 171–72, 186,
    197–98, 280n7:29
Market Transition Facility (MTF), 47
Maryland
    catastrophe exposure, 231–32, 291n9:19

premiums earned (direct, non-domestic), 152
premiums written (non-domestic life-health), 154
rate regulation, property lines, 111
Massachusetts
assigned risk pool, 50
auto insurance case study, 49–53
auto insurance expenditures, 269n3:17
auto insurance reforms, 50, 53
catastrophe exposure, 231–32, 291n9:19
competitive based rates, 49, 50
cross subsidization, 50–52
fraud, 50
insurer withdrawal from, 31, 50, 53, 268n3:3
loss ratios, 51–52
managed competition, 50, 53
mandated rates, 49–51
mandatory health insurance, 25
no-fault insurance, 49, 50
premium pricing, 49, 51–53
premiums earned (direct, non-domestic), 152
premiums written (non-domestic life-health), 154
price regulation, 49–53, 111, 201
rate regulation, property lines, 111
residual market, 52, 53
timeline, 50
maximum probable flood standard, 129, 277n6:30
Mayers, D., 238
McCarran-Ferguson Act of 1945, 5, 6, 123, 151, 228
McShane, M. K., 229, 230
Medicaid, 16, 21, 22
Medicare, 21, 22
Medicare supplement insurance, 156, 169
Meier, Kenneth, 115, 140
Mercury, 45, 48
Michigan, 111, 152, 154
Miller, M. J., 72
Minnesota, 111, 153, 154
Mississippi
development incentives, 115
premiums earned (direct, non-domestic), 153
premiums written (non-domestic life-health), 154
rate regulation, property lines, 111
wind insurance mechanisms, 115
Missouri, 112, 153, 154
modified value-added approach, 239
Montana, 112, 153, 154
moral hazard

audits as control, 15
automobile insurance, 13–15
flood insurance as, 115, 122, 131, 142
health insurance, 13–15
incentives and, 13–15, 21–22
insurance as, 13–15, 21
mortgage insurance, 14
premiums as control, 14–15
property-casualty insurance, 82
See also incentives
mortgage insurance, 11, 14

National Association of Insurance
Commissioners (NAIC)
analysis activities, 284n8:23, 285n8:25
automobile insurance expenditure data, 52
Financial Analysis Working Group, 193–94
functions of, 147, 148, 162, 167, 186, 198, 227
InfoPro database, 233, 292n9:23
insurance scoring data, 74, 77
OFC support by, 156–57
oversight roles, 187, 190–94, 283n8:4, 283n8:10, 284n8:23, 285n8:25
Principles-Based Reserving Working Group, 187
Property-Casualty Annual Statement Database, 87, 247, 296n10:32
reinsurance policy, 191–92
Reinsurance Review Supervision Division, 192
Risk Assessment Working Group, 187
Statutory Accounting Principles (SAP), 284n8:19
National Association of Mutual Insurance
Companies, 279n7:15
National Association of Professional Insurance
Agents, 279n7:15
National Conference of Insurance Legislators
(NCOIL), 6
National Flood Control Act of 1936, 120–21, 141
National Flood Insurance Program (NFIP)
coverage, 136
development of, 4, 120–32, 275n6:7, 276n6:10, 276n6:21, 277n6:30
disaster relief denial, 137, 278n6:n63
enforcement, 137, 278n6:n63
Evans Commission, 135, 137
Federal Emergency Management Agency
(FEMA), 137, 277n6:53
federal relief efforts, 122–23, 132–33, 275n6:7
Flood Hazard Boundary Maps (FHBMs), 138–40, 142

Flood Insurance Rate Maps (FIRMs), 136–39, 277n6:53
floodplain mapping, 137
as government failure, 140–42
opposition to, 137, 278n6:56
overview, 115–16, 140–42
premium rate cuts, 139–40, 142, 278n6:n63
program described, 136–38, 276n6:21, 277nn6:50–53, 278nn6:54–56
reform of, 138–40
risk-based pricing, 138, 139
subsidy structure, 137–38, 276n6:21, 278n6:55
White Commission, 133–35, 138
zoning ordinances, 136, 137
See also flood insurance
National Insurance Act of 2007, 171–72, 294n10:5
Nebraska, 112, 153, 155
Nelson, J., 196
Nevada, 112, 153, 155
New Hampshire
catastrophe exposure, 231–32, 291n9:19
premiums earned (direct, non-domestic), 153
premiums written (non-domestic life-health), 155
rate regulation, property lines, 112
New Jersey
auto insurance expenditures, 47, 269n3:17
Auto Insurance Reform of 2003, 45, 48
catastrophe exposure, 231–32, 291n9:19
Excess Profits Law, 45
insurer withdrawal from, 45, 47–48
loss ratios, 45–47
Market Transition Facility (MTF), 47
no fault insurance, 45
premium reductions, 48
premiums earned (direct, non-domestic), 153
premiums written (non-domestic life-health), 155
price regulation (auto insurance case study), 44–49, 269n3:17
rate regulation, property lines, 112
residual market, 46, 47
tier rating, 45
timeline, 45
New Mexico, 112, 153, 155
New York
catastrophe exposure, 231–32, 291n9:19
premiums earned (direct, non-domestic), 153
premiums written (non-domestic life-health), 155
rate regulation, property lines, 112
Niehaus, G., 18

nonexistent markets (social insurance), 20–21
North Carolina
catastrophe exposure, 231–32, 291n9:19
development incentives, 115
premiums earned (direct, non-domestic), 153
premiums written (non-domestic life-health), 155
rate regulation, property lines, 112
wind insurance mechanisms, 115
North Dakota, 112, 153, 155

Office of Insurance Information, 156–57, 168
Office of the National Insurance (ONI), 171–72, 281n7:39
Ohio, 112, 153, 155
Oklahoma, 112, 153, 155
optional federal charter (OFC)
antitrust provision, 172, 174
benefits, 171–73
efficiency, 172–73, 229
financial regulation, 173
guaranty associations, 173–74, 282n7:42
legal basis, 171–72, 281n7:39
limitations, 173–74
national insurer, agency prerogatives, 172, 281n7:41
opposition, 151, 156, 174–75, 279n7:12, 279nn15–16, 282nn7:47–48, 283n8:3
overview, 145–46, 186, 215, 290n8:107
price regulation, 173, 286n8:39
regulation hopping, 174, 282n7:45
residual market mechanisms, 173
solvency, 173–74, 282n7:42
state prerogatives, 172, 281n7:40
support, 156–57, 245, 279n7:12, 283n8:3
Oregon, 112, 153, 155
Overman, E., 127
Oxley, M., 168

paternalism, 22–23
Paul v. Virginia, 228
Pauly, Mark, 16
Pennsylvania, 113, 153, 155
personal lines insurance, 4. *See also* property-casualty insurance
Philadelphia Eagles, 267n2:2
Phillips, R. D., 199, 201
Platt, Rutherford, 136
POE Financial Group, 40
policymakers
fairness mindset, 29
mandatory insurance, 24–26

motivations, 2, 3, 5, 22
Pottier, S., 201, 229, 230
Powell, Lawrence S., 3–4, 7, 276n6:10
premiums
  adjustments, 48, 84, 85, 92 (*See also* price
    regulation)
  adverse selection and, 15–16, 67
  cross-subsidization, 26
  economic premium ratio (EPR), 258, 259, 260
  as moral hazard control, 14–15
  NFIP rate cuts, 139–40, 142, 278n6:n63
  premiums earned by state, 152–53
  premiums written by state, 154–55
  risk retention groups ratio, 258, 259, 260
  subsidization of, property-casualty insurance,
    106–7
  taxation as portion of, 6
price regulation
  adverse effects of, 2–4, 31–32, 61–62,
    200–201, 287n8:52
  cross-subsidization, 25–26, 33
  economic basis, 214–15
  economic shocks, 30–32
  economics of, 23–26
  EU, 209–10, 215
  homeowner's wind insurance market (FL),
    36–44, 269nn3:10–11
  loss ratios, 33–34
  mandatory insurance, 24–26
  market exits, 31, 268n3:3
  objectives, 24, 84, 167
  optional federal charter, 173, 286n8:39
  overview, 29–32, 61–62
  property insurance (*See* property-casualty
    insurance)
  rate suppression, 26, 29
  social purpose achievement, 24–25
  state level system, 5–6, 167
  state-made rates, 32–33
  worker's compensation, 28–30, 33, 57–61, 197,
    271n3:38, 287n8:52
Principles-Based Reserving Working Group, 187
Progressive, 48, 50, 53, 73–74
Property-Casualty Annual Statement Database,
  87, 247, 296n10:32
property-casualty insurance
  adaptation, 82
  background, 83–86
  commercial lines, 85–86, 89–92, 110–13,
    274n5:19
  commercial multiple peril policies, 273n5:18
  definitions, 87–88, 273nn5:17–18
  deregulation, 86, 106

efficiency (*See* efficiency (regulatory))
  geographical diversification, 96–98, 274n5:23
  guaranty associations, 285n8:30
  history, 146–47, 279n7:6
  homeowner's (*See* homeowner's insurance)
  insurer performance and conduct analysis,
    92–94, 274n5:nn20–24
  loss control, mitigation, 82
  loss ratios, 92, 94–98, 274 nn5:25– 26
  losses incurred, 92, 98–100, 274n5:27
  market exit, entry, 92, 103, 274n5:n20
  market exit restrictions, 84
  market overview, 88–92, 274n5:19
  market structure post-catastrophe, 103–5,
    274n5:29
  moral hazard, 82
  overview, 81–83, 105–7
  personal lines, 85–86, 89–92, 274n5:19
  premium adjustments, 84, 85, 92
  premium mean percentage (nondomestic
    insurers), 279n7:14
  premiums, subsidization of, 106–7
  premiums earned, 92, 99–103, 274n5:28
  price regulation, 84, 85, 92, 110–13, 197
  product standardization, 86
  regulatory chain reactions, 85, 106
  regulatory constraints, 174
  regulatory levels, 86, 93–94, 274nn5:23–24
  regulatory objectives, 83–84
  residual market solutions, 84–85, 106
  restrictive rate regulation, 26, 94, 96,
    274nn5:23–24
  risk-based capital (RBC) standards, 187–89,
    283n8:6
  risk exposure, 85
  risk transfer, 86
  state regulation of, 164, 281n7:30
  study data, 87–88, 273nn5:17–18
  trends in, 147–49
  unanticipated catastrophes, 85–86, 92–94, 96,
    274n5:nn20–24
Property Casualty Insurance Association of
  America, 279n7:15
Property Claims Service (PCS), 87
Protector and Medicator Fund, 208
Public Law 15. *See* McCarran-Ferguson Act of
  1945
Puerto Rico, 153, 155

rate regulation limitations, 4. *See also* price
  regulation
rate suppression, 26, 29
rating agencies, 196–97

receiverships, 195, 199, 210
Rees, R., 211
regulation (European Union)
  basic solvency capital requirement (BSCR), 205–6
  Committee of European Insurance and Occupational Pension Supervisors (CEIOPS), 203, 218
  contract law, 209–10
  country-of-destination principle, 209
  disclosure requirements, 212
  efficiency, 211–12, 217–18
  loss-absorbing capacity (LAC), 205–6
  market entry (insurers), 209–10
  market value determinations, 204–5
  minimum capital requirement, 203–7
  operational risk (OpRisk), 205–6
  overview, 183–85, 202
  price regulation, 209–10, 215
  profit distribution, 209–10
  receivership, 210
  receiverships, 210
  risk-based capital (RBC) standards, 202–7
  risk modules, 205–6
  solvency capital requirement, 203–7
  Solvency I, 183, 202
  Solvency II (See Solvency II)
  supervision, oversight, 207–9, 211–12
  Swiss solvency test, 184
  technical provisions, 205
  Third Generation Insurance Directive, 202
  transparency, market regulation, 214
  trends in, 216–18
regulation (United States)
  accounting perspective paradigm, 186–87, 190, 192, 284n8:19
  agents, 164, 186
  alternatives, 165–66
  bench (desk) audits, 162, 192, 194, 284n8:22
  cost burdens, 157
  efficiency, 157, 166–67, 201, 217–18
  enforcement, 162, 163, 167–68, 189–90, 192, 194–95, 283n8:11, 284n8:21
  federal standards in, 168–71
  federal-state system, 177
  financial (solvency), 161–65, 191–96, 200, 280n7:26 284n8:17, 284nn8:19–23, 285nn8:24–27
  Form A, 158, 280n7:22
  framework (current), 159–61, 166–68, 185–87, 280n7:24, 282n8:2, 283nn3–4, 284n8:17
  guaranty associations, 163–64, 173–74, 195–

  96, 281n7:40, 282n7:42, 285n8:29–31
  history, 146–47, 279n7:6
  market, 164–65, 280n7:29, 281n7:30
  market conduct, 164, 171–72, 186, 197–98, 280n7:29
  market regulation, 196–201, 214, 285nn8:35–37, 286n8:43, 286n8:48, 286nn8:38–40, 287n8:52
  OFC (See optional federal charter (OFC))
  overview, 145–46, 178
  premiums earned (direct, non-domestic), 152–53
  premiums written (non-domestic life-health), 154–55
  price (See price regulation)
  principles-based systems, 168, 184, 187, 207, 217
  producers, 164
  rating agencies, 196–97
  receiverships, 195, 199
  reform initiatives (state-level), 157–59, 280n7:22
  risk-based capital (RBC) standards, 162–63, 184, 186, 187–91, 193, 199–200, 213–14, 280n7:26, 283n8:6, 283nn8:9–11, 284n8:17, 284nn8:14–15
  single-state system, 175–77, 282n7:50
  solvency (See solvency regulation)
  State Modernization and Regulatory Transparency (SMART) Act, 168–71
  state vs. federal debate, 148–57, 279nn7:11–12, 279nn14–16, 280n17
  supervision, oversight, 191–96, 284n8:17, 284nn8:19–23, 285n8:29–31, 285nn8:24–27
  transparency, 196–201, 214, 285nn8:35–37, 286n8:43, 286n8:48, 286nn8:38–40, 287n8:52
  trends in, 147–50, 216–18
  uniform, 159, 175–77
regulatory reform
  market-based, 2–4
  unified system, 5, 159, 175–77
  See also competitive federalism
reinsurance
  European Union, 204
  NAIC policy, 191–92
  POE reinsurers, US, 191–92
  Reinsurance Review Supervision Division (NAIC), 192
  risk retention groups, 249, 251, 257, 259, 260
Reinsurance Association of America, 279n7:12
Reinsurance Review Supervision Division, 192

Rejda, G. E., 86
renters insurance, 141
residual market
  automobile insurance, 34–35
  credit-based insurance scores (CBIS), 73–75,
    77
  Illinois, 52
  Maine, 58–60
  Massachusetts, 52, 53
  New Jersey, 46, 47
  optional federal charter (OFC), 173
  property-casualty insurance, 84–85, 106
  South Carolina, 54–56
retirement savings, 23
Rhode Island, 113, 153, 155
risk aversion
  basic participles, 12–16
  behavioral economics, 16–18
  loss aversion, 16–17
risk-based capital model (RBC)
  European Union, 202–7
  life insurance, 189
  property-casualty insurance, 187–89, 283n8:6
  solvency, 162–63, 184, 186, 199–200, 280n7:26
  United States, 187–91, 193, 199–200,
    213–14, 283n8:6, 283nn8:9–11, 284n8:17,
    284nn8:14–15
risk classification. *See* credit-based insurance
  scores (CBIS)
risk retention groups (RRGs)
  allocative inefficiency, 254
  assets/liabilities ratio, 249, 251, 257, 260
  Breusch-Pagan Lagrangean multiplier test,
    258
  compliance costs, 246–51, 253, 261, 294n10:12,
    295nn13–14
  cost efficiency, 254
  data, sample, 247–48, 261–62
  diversification, 251, 252
  economic premium ratio (EPR), 258, 259, 260
  expense ratios, 248–51, 254, 295n10:14
  frontier efficiency, 254, 255
  Hausman $\chi 2$ test, 258
  Herfindahl Index (geographic), 248, 249, 252,
    253, 257, 260, 294n10:9
  Herfindahl Index (product), 248, 249, 260,
    294n10:8
  insolvency risk, 259, 297n10:44
  inverse loss ratio, 258, 259
  Kenney Ratio, 249, 251, 257, 259
  licensing fees, 248, 250–51, 295n10:13
  limitations, 262, 294n10:6

multicollinearity, 296n10:34, 297n10:41
multiple jurisdictional regulation compliance
  costs, 246, 251–52, 295nn10:16–17
Mutual variable, 260
number of states operating, 248, 249,
  294n10:10, 294n10:12
operational efficiency, 252–58, 296nn10:31–35,
  297n10:36
organizational form decision. 251–52, 261,
  295nn10:16–17
output prices, 255
overview, 7, 245–47, 261–62, 294nn10:5–7
per unit price differences, 246, 256–61,
  297n10:41, 297n10:44
premium ratio, 258, 259, 260
present value of real losses incurred (PV(L)),
  255
Reciprocal variable, 260
regression results, 256–58, 296n10:33,
  296n10:35, 296n10:36
regulation of, 282n7:50
reinsurance, 249, 251, 257, 259, 260
revenue efficiency, 254, 255
RRG indicator variable, 259, 260
seasoning requirements, 294n10:12, 295n10:17
single entity regulatory structure benefits,
  246–47
single jurisdictional regulation compliance costs, 246, 253, 256–58, 296n10:35,
  296n10:36
summary statistics, 248, 249
technical efficiency, 254, 255
variance inflation factors (VIF), 296n10:34,
  297n10:41
risk transfer, pooling, subdivision, 9–10, 22,
  25–26, 67
Robinson-Patman Act, 290n9:5
Rothschild, Michael, 15
Royal Exchange Assurance, 19
Royce, E, 171, 294n10:5
Rubio-Misas, M., 211
Ruser, J. W., 29–30
Ryan, H. S., 201

Schellhorn, C. D., 201
Schmit, Joan, 7
Scott, H. S., 229
seasoning requirements, 294n10:12, 295n10:17
Seattle Mariners, 267n2:2
Sherman Act, 290n9:5
Shiller, Robert, 20–21
Shiu, W., 201

Small Business Administration, 277n6:52, 278n6:n63
SMART (State Modernization and Regulatory Transparency) Act, 168–71
Smith, C. W. Jr., 238
Smith, R. A., 72
social insurance (nonexistent markets), 20–21
Social Security, 21, 22
Solvency I, 183, 202
Solvency II
   basic solvency capital requirement (BSCR), 205–6
   benefits of, 214–17
   disclosure requirements, 212
   guaranty mechanisms, 208–9
   loss-absorbing capacity (LAC), 205–6
   market value determinations, 204–5
   minimum capital requirement, 203–7
   operational risk (OpRisk), 205–6
   overview, 183–85, 202
   risk modules, 205–6
   supervision, oversight, 207–9
solvency margin standard, 184
solvency regulation
   accounting perspective paradigm, 186–87, 190, 192, 284n8:19
   basic solvency capital requirement (BSCR) (EU), 205–6
   bench (desk) audits (US), 162, 192, 194, 284n8:22
   cash-flow testing, 200
   comparison, US vs EU, 212–15, 290n8:107
   disclosure requirements (EU), 212
   enforcement (EU), 206
   enforcement (US), 162, 163, 167–68, 189–90, 192, 194–95, 283n8:11, 284n8:21, 285n8:29–31
   European Union, generally, 202–7
   evolution of, (US), 157, 158
   Financial Analysis Solvency Tools (FAST) system, 193, 200, 285n8:24
   fixed-minimum requirement (US), 187, 283n8:6
   guaranty associations, 163–64, 173–74, 195–96, 281n7:40, 282n7:42, 285n8:29–31
   guaranty mechanisms (EU), 208–9
   insolvency (US), 199, 286n8:40, 286n8:43, 286n8:48
   Insurance Regulatory Information System (IRIS), 193
   loss-absorbing capacity (LAC) (EU), 205–6

market conduct, 164, 171–72, 186, 197–98, 280n7:29
market entry (EU), 209–10
market regulation (US), 196–201, 214, 285nn8:35–37, 286n8:43, 286n8:48, 286nn8:38–40, 287n8:52
market value determinations (EU), 204–5
minimum capital requirement (EU), 203–7
Office of the National Insurance (ONI), 171–72, 281n7:39
operational risk (OpRisk) (EU), 205–6
overview, 183–85, 215–18
price regulation (See price regulation)
principles-based systems, 168, 184, 187, 207, 217
profit distribution (EU), 209–10
rating agencies (US), 196–97
receiverships (EU), 210
receiverships (US), 195, 199
reinsurance (EU), 204
reinsurance (POE reinsurers, US), 191–92
risk-based capital (RBC) standards (EU), 202–7
risk-based capital (RBC) standards (US), 184, 187–91, 193, 199–200, 213–14, 283n8:6, 283nn8:9–11, 284n8:17, 284nn8:14–15
risk modules (EU), 205–6
securitization (EU), 204
solvency capital requirement (EU), 203–7
supervision, oversight (EU), 207–9, 211–12
supervision, oversight (US), 191–96, 284n8:17, 284nn8:19–23, 285n8:29–31, 285nn8:24–27
total balance sheet approach, 185
transparency (US), 196–201, 214, 285nn8:35–37, 286n8:43, 286n8:48, 286nn8:38–40, 287n8:52
transparency, market regulation (EU), 214
trends in, 216–18
United States, generally, 161–64, 185–87, 280n7:24, 280n7:26, 281n7:40, 282n8:2, 283nn3–4, 284n8:17
See also regulation (European Union); regulation (United States)
South Carolina
   auto fatalities, 56
   catastrophe exposure, 231–32, 291n9:19
   cross-subsidization, 54, 56, 57
   development incentives, 115
   insurer entry to, 54–57
   loss ratios, 54–55
   mandating of insurance, 54, 56

market reforms, 54–57
premium pricing, 54
premiums earned (direct, non-domestic), 153
premiums written (non-domestic life-health), 155
price regulation (auto insurance case study), 53–57
rate regulation, property lines, 113
recoupment fee, 54, 56, 57
residual market, 54–56
timeline, 56
wind insurance mechanisms, 115
South Dakota, 113, 153, 155
South-Eastern Underwriters Association, United States v., 149–51, 228
Southeast Hurricane Disaster Relief Act of 1965, 132–33
Spain, 211
State Farm, 31, 36, 43, 45, 48
State Modernization and Regulatory Transparency (SMART) Act, 168–71
Stiglitz, Joseph, 15
Sununu, John, 171, 294n10:5
surplus participation, 210
Swiss Re Sigma, 83, 87–88
Swiss solvency test, 184
Switzerland, 184

Tabarrok, Alex, 12
taxation, 6, 19, 156, 172, 196, 206, 239, 248, 294n10:6, 309
Tennessee, 113, 153, 155
Tennessee Valley Authority (TVA), 129–31 141–142, 277n6:30
Tennyson, S., 51
Tennyson, S. L., 201
Texas
    catastrophe exposure, 231–32, 291n9:19
    premiums earned (direct, non-domestic), 153
    premiums written (non-domestic life-health), 155
    rate regulation, property lines, 113
Texas Department of Insurance, 70–72
Third Generation Insurance Directive, 202
towing insurance, 20
TransUnion, 76
Truman, Harry, 125
21st Century, 48

United Kingdom (UK), 184, 208–9, 211
United States v. South-Eastern Underwriters Association, 149–51, 228
Unitrin, 48
U.S. Geological Survey, 130
USAA, 141
Utah, 113, 153, 155

Vermont, 113, 153, 155
Virgin Islands, 153, 155
Virginia
    catastrophe exposure, 231–32, 291n9:19
    premiums earned (direct, non-domestic), 153
    premiums written (non-domestic life-health), 155
    rate regulation, property lines, 113
Virginia, Paul v., 228
Viscusi, W. K., 83

Wang, S., 168
Ward, D. R., 211
warranties, 11, 16, 17
Washington
    floodplain zoning ordinances, 130
    premiums earned (direct, non-domestic), 153
    premiums written (non-domestic life-health), 155
    rate regulation, property lines, 113
Weiss, M., 229
West Virginia, 113, 153, 155
White, Gilbert F., 120–21, 128, 132, 133, 138
White Commission, 133–35, 138
Willenborg, M., 199
Winter, R., 258
Wisconsin, 113, 153, 155
worker's compensation
    guaranty associations, 285n8:31
    price regulation, 28–30, 33, 57–61, 197, 271n3:38, 287n8:52
    state regulation of, 164, 281n7:30
Wright, James, 129
Wyoming, 113, 153, 155

Zelizer, Viviana, 19

About the Contributors

Editor

LAWRENCE S. POWELL is Research Fellow at The Independent Institute and holds the Whitbeck-Beyer Chair of Insurance and Financial Services at the University of Arkansas, Little Rock. He earned a bachelor's degree in Insurance and Finance from the University of South Carolina and a Ph.D. in Risk Management and Insurance from the University of Georgia. His research focuses on the effects of regulation on insurance markets and appears in leading academic and practitioner journals. Before pursuing an academic career, Powell worked in several aspects of the insurance industry including production and claims. An active consultant to public and private entities, he participates in formation, operation, and evaluation of insurance companies and provides expert services to support legislation and litigation. He belongs to several academic and professional organizations including the American Risk and Insurance Association and the Risk Theory Society.

Contributors

PATRICIA H. BORN is Research Fellow at The Independent Institute, Associate Professor at the College of Business at Florida State University, and a research associate in the Florida Catastrophic Storm Risk Management Center. She received her Ph.D. in economics from Duke University and AB in economics from the University of Michigan. She has held appointments at California State University-Northridge, Shanghai Normal University, the University of Connecticut, NOVA Southeastern University, and DePaul University. She also worked in the Center for Health Care Policy and Research at the American Medical Association.

Dr. Born's research interests include insurer profitability, medical malpractice, managed care finance, tort reform, risk retention groups, and catastrophe modeling. Current research projects focus on property insurance market responses to catastrophic events, and factors affecting state adoption of medical malpractice reforms. She has published in the *Journal of Risk and Uncertainty, Journal of Risk and Insurance, Journal of Regulatory Economics, Risk Management and Insurance Review, Journal of Business and Economic Statistics, Journal of Legal Studies, Brookings Papers on Microeconomic Activity, Benefits Quarterly,* and *Health Affairs.*

Dr. Born served three years on the RIMS Technology Advisory Council, and is a past-president of the Western Risk and Insurance Association. She currently serves on the boards of the American Risk and Insurance Association, the Asia-Pacific Risk and Insurance Association, and the Southern Risk and Insurance Association.

DAVID L. ECKLES received his undergraduate degree in Risk Management and Insurance from the University of Georgia and his M.A. and Ph.D. from the Wharton School at the University of Pennsylvania. He is currently an Associate Professor of Risk Management and Insurance at the University of Georgia, where he also serves as the Graduate Coordinator for the Risk Management and Insurance Ph.D. program. His research interests include insurance company efficiency, insurer reserving practices, and insurer regulation issues. He has published articles in several insurance journals, including the *Journal of Risk and Insurance*, the *Risk Management and Insurance Review*, and the *Journal of Insurance Issues*. He currently serves as an Associate Editor of the *Journal of Insurance Issues*.

MARTIN ELING is Research Fellow at The Independent Institute, profes-sor in insurance, and director of the Institute of Insurance Science at the University of Ulm (Germany). He received his doctoral degree from the University of Munster (Germany) and his habilitation from the University of St. Gallen (Switzerland). In 2008 he was visiting professor at the University of Wisconsin-Madison. His research interests in-clude risk management, asset liability management, and empirical aspects of finance and insurance. He has published articles in leading international journals such as the *Journal of Risk and Insurance*, the *Journal of Banking and Finance*, and *Insurance: Mathematics and Economics*.

MARTIN F. GRACE is currently the Associate Director and Research Associate at the Center for Risk Management and Insurance Research, Georgia State University. He is also an Associate in the Andrew Young School of Policy Studies, Fiscal Policy Center. Dr. Grace's research has been published in various journals in economics and insurance concerning the economics and public policy aspects of regulation and taxation. In particular, Dr. Grace has studied various aspects of the regulation and taxation of the insurance industry. Dr. Grace is a former President of the Risk Theory Society and he is a current associate editor of the Journal of Risk and Insurance. Dr. Grace earned his B.A. in economics and political science from the University of New Hampshire and both a Ph.D. in economics and a J.D. from the University of Florida. In 1998 Dr. Grace was appointed Professor of Legal Studies and Risk Management and Insurance, and in 2002, he was named the James S. Kemper Professor of Risk Management. Over his career Dr. Grace has consulted with the National Association of Insurance Commissioners, various state regulators, and industry associations. He has testified before Congress on the future of insurance regulation as well as before state legislatures on insurance regulation and taxation.

ROBERT W. KLEIN is Research Fellow at The Independent Institute, Director of the Center for Risk Management and Insurance Research, and an Associate Professor of Risk Management and Insurance at Georgia State University in Atlanta. Dr. Klein is a leading expert on insurance regulation and markets with 30 years of experience as a regulator and academic researcher. He has published extensively on various topics in insurance and its regulation, and he also has testified frequently at legislative and regulatory hearings on significant issues affecting insurance consumers and the industry. Prior to joining Georgia State University in September 1996, Dr. Klein was the director of research and chief economist for the National Association of Insurance Commissioners. He also has served as staff economist for the insurance department and state legislature in Michigan. He has a B.A., M.A., and Ph.D. in economics from Michigan State University. Dr. Klein is a Sloan Fellow at the Financial Institutions Center at the Wharton School of Business. He has served on the Board of Directors for the American Risk and Insurance Association and currently serves on the editorial boards for the *Journal of Insurance Regulation and Risk Management* and *Insurance Review.*

BARBARA KLIMASZEWSKI-BLETTNER is a research assistant and doctoral candidate at the Munich School of Management's Institute for Risk and Insurance Management at Ludwig-Maximilians-Universitaet (LMU) Munich, Germany. She holds a Diploma in business administration as well as a Master in Business Research from LMU. Barbara received the Ottmar Bühler Award 2007 for excellent student achievements in business management as well as the Mark Dorfman Doctoral Student Award 2008 at the Western Risk and Insurance Association annual meeting. Her research interests lie in the area of catastrophe risk management, the major field of her Ph.D. thesis. In 2010, she conducted research at the Risk Management and Decision Processes Center at the Wharton School, University of Pennsylvania, Philadelphia.

ARNOLD KLING received his Ph.D. in economics from the Massachusetts Institute of Technology in 1980. He was an economist on the staff of the Board of Governors of the Federal Reserve System from 1980-1986. He was a senior economist at Freddie Mac from 1986-1994. In 1994, he started Homefair.com, one of the first commercial sites on the World Wide Web. (Homefair was sold in 1999 to Homestore.com.) Kling is an adjunct scholar with the Cato Institute and a member of the Financial Markets Working Group at the Mercatus Center at George Mason University. He teaches statistics and economics at the Berman Hebrew Academy in Rockville, Maryland. Kling is the author of five books: *Unchecked and Unbalanced: How the Discrepancy between Knowledge and Power Caused the Financial Crisis and Threatens Democracy, Invisible Wealth: The Hidden Story of How Markets Work* (with Nick Schulz), *Crisis of Abundance: Rethinking How We Pay for Health Care, Learning Economics,* and *Under the Radar: Starting Your Internet Business without Venture Capital.* His website at arnoldkling.

com has been cited by *The New York Times* and in the *Journal of Economic Perspectives* as being entertaining and educational on the subjects of economics and technology.

ELI LEHRER is Research Fellow at The Independent Institute and President of the R Street Institute. Lehrer worked as speechwriter to United States Senate Majority Leader Bill Frist (R.-Tenn.).

He has previously worked as Senior Fellow at the Competitive Enterprise Institute, a manager in the Unisys Corporation's Homeland Security Practice, Senior Editor of *The American Enterprise* magazine, and as a Fellow for the Heritage Foundation. He has spoken at Yale and George Washington Universities. He holds a B.A. (Cum Laude) from Cornell University and a M.A. (with honors) from The Johns Hopkins University where his Master's thesis focused on the Federal Emergency Management Agency and flood insurance.

His work has appeared in the *New York Times, Washington Post, USA Today, Washington Times, Weekly Standard, National Review, The Public Interest, Salon.com*, and dozens of other publications. Lehrer lives in Oak Hill, Virginia with his wife Kari and son Andrew.

J. TYLER LEVERTY is Associate Professor of Finance and the TRISTAR Risk Management Research Fellow at the University of Iowa. His research on the economics and public policy aspects of insurance markets has appeared in the *Journal of Accounting Research*, the *Journal of Risk and Insurance*, the *Journal of Money, Credit, and Banking*, the *Journal of Law, Economics and Organization*, and the *Journal of Banking and Finance*, among others. Leverty earned his B.A. in history and economics from the University of Washington and his Ph.D. in Risk Management and Insurance from Georgia State University. He currently serves on the editorial board for the *Journal of Insurance Regulation*.

JOAN T. SCHMIT is Research Fellow at The Independent Institute and holds the American Family Insurance Chair in Risk Management and Insurance at the University of Wisconsin, Madison, where she has been on the faculty since 1988. Currently, she is the senior associate dean of the Wisconsin School of business, following a period as chair of the Actuarial Science, Risk Management and Insurance Department in the School of Business, one of the oldest such programs in the nation. She also serves as an affiliate faculty member at the University of St. Gallen in Switzerland. Dr. Schmit has published extensively in insurance and legal journals. Her area of expertise is the interaction of law and economics, primarily focused on the effects of tort law. Recently, she has expanded her research into the enterprise risk management field, including projects sponsored by the Casualty Actuarial Society and Society of Actuaries, as well as a variety of other papers on the topic. Professor Schmit has enjoyed being an academic moderator for the International Insurance Society since 1997.

Independent Studies in Political Economy

THE ACADEMY IN CRISIS | *Ed. by John W. Sommer*

AGAINST LEVIATHAN | *Robert Higgs*

ALIENATION AND THE SOVIET ECONOMY | *Paul Craig Roberts*

AMERICAN HEALTH CARE | *Ed. by Roger D. Feldman*

ANARCHY AND THE LAW | *Ed. by Edward P. Stringham*

AQUANOMICS | *Ed. by B. Delworth Gardner & Randy T. Simmons*

ANTITRUST AND MONOPOLY | *D. T. Armentano*

AQUANOMICS | *Ed. by B. Delworth Gardner and Randy T. Simmons*

ARMS, POLITICS, AND THE ECONOMY | *Ed. by Robert Higgs*

BEYOND POLITICS | *Randy T. Simmons*

BOOM AND BUST BANKING | *Ed. by David Beckworth*

CAN TEACHERS OWN THEIR OWN SCHOOLS? | *Richard K. Vedder*

THE CAPITALIST REVOLUTION IN LATIN AMERICA | *Paul Craig Roberts & Karen Araujo*

THE CHALLENGE OF LIBERTY | *Ed. by Robert Higgs & Carl P. Close*

CHANGING THE GUARD | *Ed. by Alexander Tabarrok*

THE CHE GUEVARA MYTH AND THE FUTURE OF LIBERTY | *Alvaro Vargas Llosa*

THE CIVILIAN AND THE MILITARY | *Arthur A. Ekirch, Jr.*

CUTTING GREEN TAPE | *Ed. by Richard L. Stroup & Roger E. Meiners*

THE DECLINE OF AMERICAN LIBERALISM | *Arthur A. Ekirch, Jr.*

DELUSIONS OF POWER | *Robert Higgs*

DEPRESSION, WAR, AND COLD WAR | *Robert Higgs*

THE DIVERSITY MYTH | *David O. Sacks & Peter A. Thiel*

DRUG WAR CRIMES | *Jeffrey A. Miron*

ELECTRIC CHOICES | *Ed. by Andrew N. Kleit*

THE EMPIRE HAS NO CLOTHES | *Ivan Eland*

ENTREPRENEURIAL ECONOMICS | *Ed. by Alexander Tabarrok*

THE ENTERPRISE OF LAW | *Bruce L. Benson*

FAULTY TOWERS | *Ryan C. Amacher & Roger E. Meiners*

FINANCING FAILURE | *Vern McKinley*

FIRE & SMOKE | *Michael I. Krauss*

THE FOUNDERS' SECOND AMENDMENT | *Stephen P. Halbrook*

FREEDOM, FEMINISM, AND THE STATE | *Ed. by Wendy McElroy*

GOOD MONEY | *George Selgin*

HAZARDOUS TO OUR HEALTH? | *Ed. by Robert Higgs*

HOT TALK, COLD SCIENCE | *S. Fred Singer*

HOUSING AMERICA | *Ed. by Randall G. Holcombe & Benjamin Powell*

JUDGE AND JURY | *Eric Helland & Alexander Tabarrok*

LESSONS FROM THE POOR | *Ed. by Alvaro Vargas Llosa*

LIBERTY FOR LATIN AMERICA | *Alvaro Vargas Llosa*

LIBERTY FOR WOMEN | *Ed. by Wendy McElroy*

LIVING ECONOMICS | *Peter J. Boettke*

MAKING POOR NATIONS RICH | *Ed. by Benjamin Powell*

MARKET FAILURE OR SUCCESS | *Ed. by Tyler Cowen & Eric Crampton*

MONEY AND THE NATION STATE | *Ed. by Kevin Dowd & Richard H. Timberlake, Jr.*

NEITHER LIBERTY NOR SAFETY | *Robert Higgs*

THE NEW HOLY WARS | *Robert H. Nelson*

NO WAR FOR OIL | *Ivan Eland*

OPPOSING THE CRUSADER STATE | *Ed. by Robert Higgs & Carl P. Close*

OUT OF WORK | *Richard K. Vedder & Lowell E. Gallaway*

PARTITIONING FOR PEACE | *Ivan Eland*

PLOWSHARES AND PORK BARRELS | *E. C. Pasour, Jr. & Randal R. Rucker*

A POVERTY OF REASON | *Wilfred Beckerman*

PRICELESS | *John C. Goodman*

PRIVATE RIGHTS & PUBLIC ILLUSIONS | *Tibor R. Machan*

PROPERTY RIGHTS | *Ed. by Bruce L. Benson*

THE PURSUIT OF JUSTICE | *Ed. by Edward J. López*

RACE & LIBERTY IN AMERICA | *Ed. by Jonathan Bean*

RECARVING RUSHMORE | *Ivan Eland*

RECLAIMING THE AMERICAN REVOLUTION | *William J. Watkins, Jr.*

REGULATION AND THE REAGAN ERA | *Ed. by Roger E. Meiners & Bruce Yandle*

RESTORING FREE SPEECH AND LIBERTY ON CAMPUS | *Donald A. Downs*

RESURGENCE OF THE WARFARE STATE | *Robert Higgs*

RE-THINKING GREEN | *Ed. by Robert Higgs & Carl P. Close*

RISKY BUSINESS | *Ed. by Lawrence S. Powell*

SCHOOL CHOICES | *John Merrifield*

SECURING CIVIL RIGHTS | *Stephen P. Halbrook*

STRANGE BREW | *Douglas Glen Whitman*

STREET SMART | *Ed. by Gabriel Roth*

TAXING CHOICE | *Ed. by William F. Shughart, II*

TAXING ENERGY | *Robert Deacon, Stephen DeCanio, H. E. Frech, III, & M. Bruce Johnson*

THAT EVERY MAN BE ARMED | *Stephen P. Halbrook*

TO SERVE AND PROTECT | *Bruce L. Benson*

TWILIGHT WAR | *Mike Moore*

VIETNAM RISING | *William Ratliff*

THE VOLUNTARY CITY | *Ed. by David T. Beito, Peter Gordon, & Alexander Tabarrok*

WINNERS, LOSERS & MICROSOFT | *Stan J. Liebowitz & Stephen E. Margolis*

WRITING OFF IDEAS | *Randall G. Holcombe*